A Concise History of Mexico

The second edition of this accessible guide to Mexico brings the story up to date with an examination of the presidency of Vicente Fox who came to power in the elections of 2000. Additional illustrations highlight Mexico's development during this period. The book also includes a new section on the country's cultural development from the founding of the country in 1821 to the present day. This section reinforces the importance of Mexico's long and disparate history in the forging of the modern nation. This theme is central to the narrative, which charts Mexico's history from the pre-Columbian era, through the European incursion and the colonisation of the country under the Spanish, to the collapse of New Spain in the nineteenth century and the founding of the Republic. In combination with an integrated account of Mexico's political, social, economic and cultural history, the book tackles major themes including the relationship between constitutionalism and personal power, the debate over federalism and centralism, and the role of the Catholic Church in a secular state. The author's first-hand knowledge of the country which he has been visiting for most of his life, and his appreciation of its complex and vibrant past, come through on every page. This book will be bought by students, travellers and all those interested in modern-day America.

BRIAN R. HAMNETT is a Research Professor in History at the University of Essex. He has researched and travelled widely in the Iberian peninsula and Latin America, and has written extensively on Mexico. His recent publications deal with the late Spanish colonial period, the struggles for Independence, and nineteenth-century Mexican history.

CAMBRIDGE CONCISE HISTORIES

This is a series of illustrated 'concise histories' of selected individual countries, intended both as university and college textbooks and as historical introductions for general readers, travellers and members of the business community.

For a list of titles in the series, see end of book.

A Concise History of Mexico

SECOND EDITION

BRIAN R. HAMNETT
University of Essex

CAMBRIDGE
UNIVERSITY PRESS

CAMBRIDGE UNIVERSITY PRESS

Cambridge, New York, Melbourne, Madrid, Cape Town, Singapore, São Paulo

Cambridge University Press
The Edinburgh Building, Cambridge CB2 2RU, UK

Published in the United States of America by Cambridge University Press, New York

www.cambridge.org
Information on this title: www.cambridge.org/9780521618021

First edition published 1999
Reprinted three times
Second edition 2006

Printed in the United Kingdom at the University Press, Cambridge

Typeface Monotype Sabon 10/13 pt   *System* QuarkXPress™   [SE]

A catalogue record for this publication is available from the British Library

ISBN-13 978-0-521-85284-5 hardback
ISBN-10 0-521-85284-6 hardback

ISBN-13 978-0-521-61802-1 paperback
ISBN-10 0-521-61802-9 paperback

Dionisio alegaba que él no era antiyanqui . . . por más que no hubíese niño nacido en México que no supiera que los gringos, en el siglo XIX, nos despojaron de la mitad de nuestro territorio, California, Utah Nevada, Colorado, Arizona, Nuevo México y Texas. La generosidad de México, acostumbraba decir Dionisio, es que no guardaba rencor por ese terrible despojo, aunque sí memoria. En cambio, los gringos ni se acordaban de esa guerra, ni sabían que era injusta. Dionisio los llamaba 'Estados Unidos de Amnesia' . . . El hecho es que si los gringos nos chingaron en 1848 con su 'destino manifesto', ahora México les daría una sopa de su propio chocolate, reconquistándolos con mexicanísimas baterís lingüísticas, raciales y culinarias.

Dionisio maintained that he wasn't anti-Yank . . . even though everyone born in Mexico knew that the Gringos in the nineteenth century had stripped Mexico of half its national territory – California, Utah, Nevada, Colorado, Arizona, New Mexico and Texas. Mexico's natural generosity, Dionisio was accustomed to say, meant that she bore no grudges: however, that didn't mean she'd forgotten. The Gringos, though, didn't even remember they'd fought the war, let alone that it had been unjustified. For that reason, Dionisio would call their country the 'United States of Amnesia' . . . The fact is that, if the Gringos fucked us up in 1848 with their 'Manifest Destiny', now Mexico would give them a taste of their own medicine, reconquering the lost territories by the most Mexican of methods – the Spanish language, racial identity, and the national cuisine.

Carlos Fuentes, *La frontera cristalina* (Mexico 1995)

CONTENTS

ILLUSTRATIONS

MAPS

CHRONOLOGY

2250–1400 BC	Farming villages in Gulf Coast zone of Tabasco
1500–950 BC	Early Formative 'Olmec' Period
1200–300 BC	Flourishing of 'Olmec' culture
1400–850 BC	Tierras Largas and San José Mogote cultures in Valley of Oaxaca
500–100 BC	Late Pre-Classic Period in Valley of Mexico
300–100 BC	Cuicuilco, largest centre in Valley of Mexico
AD 100–600	Maximum development of Monte Albán in central Oaxaca
AD 300–900	Classic Period in Valley of Mexico (Teotihuacan, 150 BC–c. AD 700); Valley of Oaxaca; Lowland Maya: 320–790 Yaxchilán (Chiapas), 615–721 Palenque (Chiapas) at peak, 850–925 Uxmal (C. Yucatán) at peak; El Tajín (Veracruz), AD 100–1100
AD 500–800	La Quemada (S. Zacatecas) at peak
AD 600–900	Mixtec cultures in western Oaxaca
750–950	'Time of Troubles' in central Mexico
800–1170	Toltec Period
950–1250	Toltec-Maya Period at Chichén Itzá (N. Yucatán)
1250–1450	Mayapan Confederation (N. Yucatán)
1160–1522	Mixtec Kingdoms of western and southern Oaxaca; later Zapotec cultures
1250–1400	Military rivalries in central Mexico
1418–1515	Key position of Texcoco
1428–1519	Aztec imperial expansion: 1428, Triple Alliance of Tenochtitlán, Tlatelolco, and Tlacopan

1847–8	14 September 1847 – 12 June 1848, US forces occupy Mexico City
1848	February, Treaty of Guadalupe Hidalgo: Mexico loses Upper California and New Mexico to the USA
1854	March, Revolution of Ayutla, which brings down Santa Anna in August 1855
1855–76	Liberal Reform era
1857	February, Second Federal Constitution
1857	July, Reform Laws
1858–61	January 1858 – January 1861, Civil War of the Reform
1858–72	Benito Juárez, President
1861–62	December 1861 – April 1862, Tripartite Intervention by Great Britain, Spain and France
1861	April–February 1867, French Intervention
1863–67	Second Mexican Empire: April 1864, arrival of Maximilian and Carlota
1867	19 June, Execution of Maximilian and Conservative Generals Miramón and Mejía at Querétaro
1867–76	Restored Republic
1876–77	Rebellion of Tuxtepec and accession of General Porfirio Díaz to power
1880	Mexican railroad system linked to US through El Paso (Texas)
1884–1911	Personal rule of Díaz – seven re-elections
1889–91	Manuel Payno, *Los bandidos de Río Frío*
1893–1911	Limantour, Finance Minister
1897	José María Velasco (1840–1912) paints 'The Pico de Orizaba'
1903	Federico Gamboa, *Santa*
1906–12	*Ateneo de la Juventud*
1907	Recession
1910–25	Mexico a major oil producer
1910–11	First phase of the Mexican Revolution overthrows Díaz and secures election of Francisco I. Madero
1913	February, Assassination of Madero and Vice-President, Pino Suárez

1913–16	Second phase of the Mexican Revolution: success of Carranza and Obregón; defeat and marginalisation of Villa and Zapata
1915	Mariano Azuela, *Los de abajo* (*The Underdogs*).
1917	Third Federal Constitution (continuously in force to date)
1920s–1940s	Main period of mural-painting in public buildings by Diego Rivera (1886–1957), José Clemente Orozco (1883–1949), and David Alfaro Siqueiros (1896–1974)
1924–34	Supremacy (*Maximato*) of Calles
1925	José Vasconcelos, *La raza cósmica* (*The Cosmic Race*)
1926–29	Cristero Rebellion
1929	Electoral defeat of Vasconcelos
1929	Martín Luis Guzmán, *La sombra del caudillo* (*The Chieftain's Shadow*)
1929–33	Impact of the Great Depression
1934–40	Lázaro Cárdenas, President
1938	18 March, Nationalization of the petroleum industry
1940s to late 1960s	Economic expansion: Mexican predominantly urban
1946	Prior official parties, PNR (1929–38) and PRM (1938–46), transformed into PRI, which holds power until 2000
1947	Agustín Yáñez, *Al filo del agua* (*The Brink of the Storm*)
1950	Octavo Paz, *El laberinto de la soledad* (*The Labyrinth of Solitude*)
1953	Juan Rulfo, *El llano en llamas* (*The Plain in Flames*)
1955	Juan Rulfo, *Pedro Páramo*
1958	Carlos Fuentes, *La región más transparente* (*The Clearest Region*)
1962	Carlos Fuentes, *La muerte de Artemio Cruz* (*The Death of Artemio Cruz*)
1968	Repression of the protest movements in Mexico City on the eve of the Olympic Games
1970s–90s	Economic difficulties, despite oil boom of 1977–81
1975	Carlos Fuentes, *Terra Nostra* (*Our Land*)
1982	Beginning of long debt crisis

1987	Fernando del Paso, *Noticias del Imperio* (*News from the Empire*)
1991	Death of painter, Rufino Tamayo (b.1899)
1993	February, re-establishment of diplomatic relations between Mexico and the Holy See, ruptured in 1867. Five papal visits by John Paul II, 1979–2002
1994	1 January, North American Free Trade Area comes into effect. Chiapas uprising by neo-Zapatistas
2000	July, electoral defeat of the PRI and victory of opposition candidate, Vicente Fox
2006	July, Presidential Election

PREFACE TO THE SECOND EDITION

In the years since the publication of the first edition, Mexican studies have continued to expand, as the additions to the bibliography clearly demonstrate. Mexico entered a new phase in its history, when in the presidential elections of July 2000, the electorate voted the *Partido Revolucionario Institucional* (PRI) out of power. Mexicans asked themselves in 2000 whether their country had finally become a working democracy, in which opposition parties gained national power and the institutions of federalism functioned effectively. High expectations of a reforming presidency gradually petered out in the subsequent years amid charges of empty rhetoric, unfulfilled promises and political confusion. I have included a brief analysis of the Fox Presidency of 2000–06 in a new Chapter 8. Since I am a historian and not a 'political scientist', I make no predictions about either forthcoming election results or future developments in the country.

This second edition retains the structure, periodisation and themes of the first. However, I have amended certain sections, particularly in Chapter 2, in the light of further reading, and corrected a factual error in Chapter 4, which should never have appeared in the first place. At the same time, I have removed several comments on the events of the later 1990s in Chapter 7, which seemed to be important at the time but which now do not. In retrospect, the first edition seemed to lean too far in the direction of economic and political analysis. I have sought to correct the balance by including discussion in a new Chapter 9 on key aspects of Mexican cultural life, particularly literature and cinema. Both of these have had considerable impact in the international community. This chapter also responds to comment received in conversation that Mexico first struck the attention through its contemporary literature and cinema.

Mexican newspapers can be read on the Internet. 'Latin American Newsletters: Latin American Regional Report – Mexico and NAFTA', published in London monthly, provides detailed information to English-language readers.

I am particularly grateful to Professor Valerie Fraser, Department of Art History and Theory, University of Essex, and Curator of the University of Essex Collection of Latin American Art, for assistance in selecting three images from the collection as fresh illustrations for this edition. Similarly, I must thank Dr Roderick McCrorie, Department of Mathematics, University of Essex, for the use of his Private Collection of Mexican Lithographs. I received considerable help in the technology of picture transmission from Belinda Waterman, Secretary in the Department of History.

PREFACE TO THE FIRST EDITION

Research on Mexico is an exciting and fast-developing topic. Perspectives are repeatedly changing. Mexico, with a population around 95 million, forms part of the North American sub-continent. Since the early sixteenth century, it has been part of the Atlantic world that resulted from European expansion. Before that time, Mexico was also part of a pre-Columbian world unknown to Europeans. For that reason, the country has a complex multi-ethnic and multi-cultural pattern that continues to have an impact on contemporary events. Nevertheless, anyone interested in Mexico quickly discovers that there are few things for the beginner to read. At the same time, those who perhaps might have returned from their first visit to the country will frequently look in vain for a book which enables them to analyse what they have seen with any thematic coherence.

I first went to Mexico as a research student in January 1966. A great deal of my own history has been lived there since that time, and the country itself has in some respects changed beyond recognition. Yet, at the same time, particularly in the provinces and the villages, and in general attitudes and assumptions, a great deal of the traditional outlook, for better or for worse, still persists.

Approaching Mexican history as I initially did from the geographical perspectives of the centre and south, the core zones of Mesoamerican civilisation, I was always conscious of the deeply rooted inheritance of the indigenous American past. My consciousness of the importance of the pre-Columbian era has grown over the years, particularly since the region I originally studied was Oaxaca, the centre of Zapotec and

Mixtec cultures and still a state with an indigenous majority. My specialisation then was the late colonial era. When I first arrived in Mexico I came by sea from Cádiz after a long period of study in the Archive of the Indies in Seville. I sailed on a 6,000-ton Spanish ship which took two and a half weeks to reach Veracruz by way of Venezuela, Puerto Rico, and the Dominican Republic. After the turbulent January winds across the Gulf of Mexico, I certainly did not feel like a Conquistador when I first arrived on Mexican soil. Nevertheless, I had come to Mexico to study the colonial era, and bold decisions had to be made as to how to go about it. In the cities and towns of the central core of Mexico from Zacatecas (where the north begins) to Oaxaca in the south, the richness of a colonial culture transforming from European to American can be immediately appreciated. Cities such as Puebla, Tlaxcala, Querétaro, Guanajuato, Morelia (then Valladolid), San Luis Potosí, Zacatecas and the capital itself all exhibit an architectural and artistic wealth comparable to European cities of the period. My experience as a 'Mexicanist' began that way. However, many other tendencies have emerged since then, the most recent being deepening interest in the north. Readers will find the north and the 'far north' (currently described in the USA as the 'American Southwest') abundantly present in the following pages.

This book adopts a number of significant positions. It does not start in 1821 with the independence of Mexico from the Spanish Empire. It does not assume that in historical perspective Mexico should be defined as the truncated political entity of the period after 1836–53, when the United States acquired half of Mexico's claimed territory. The approach is thematic as well as chronological, allusive perhaps rather than all-inclusive. The book opens with a look at Mexico today and a few suggestions about how it came to be that way. After this, we shall then go back to the pre-Columbian era for the real historical beginning, and continue forwards from there through a combination of themes and chronology. The periodisation I have adopted corresponds more to contemporary reinterpretations of Mexican history than to traditional approaches.

In attempting a revised periodisation, I still found I had to compromise significantly. I had originally hoped to bridge the traditional historiographical divisions at Independence (1810–21) and the Revolution (1910–40) by a more radical periodisation: 'Destabilisation and Fragmentation, 1770–1867'; 'Reconstruction, 1867–1940'; and

'The Monopoly Party, 1940–2000'. However, I still found that the dividing lines at 1810 and 1910 could not and should not be avoided. At the same time, I have compromised by placing these more traditional turning points within the context of my original broader sweeps. It seemed to me also that the collapse of the French Intervention and with it Maximilian's Second Empire in 1867 represented a major turning point in the nineteenth century. This signified the end of European attempts to recover control in Mexico and assured the survival of the sovereign state which had emerged from the War with the United States (1846–48). Similarly, 1940 and 1970 emerged as subsequent points of arrival and departure. The former initiated the period of consolidation of revolutionary changes and provided a symbolic starting point for three decades of economic expansion and political stability; the latter opened the way for descent into three decades of political division and economic dislocation. These lines of demarcation are, of course, subject to criticism and revision. I hope that the question of periodisation will occupy part of the ongoing historical debate concerning the interpretation of Mexican (and Latin American) history.

Colleagues and friends in Mexico and elsewhere have contributed to this book, sometimes without realising it. Many rewarding conversations helped to give it shape. Dr Josefina Zoraída Vázquez (El Colegio de México) has been a continuous source of encouragement and support in many of my recent projects, and always a stimulating critic and discussant. Professor Brian Connaughton (UAM – Iztapalapa) has also been a great help in probing the problems and issues of late-colonial and nineteenth-century Mexican history, not only as a result of seminars at the UAM, but also in regular, three-hour breakfasts in Mexico City, which have ranged across the dynamics of Mexican culture. Dr Bernardo García Martínez (El Colegio de México), author of an alternative concise history of Mexico, pressed home to me the dynamics of the north in a memorable conversation in a Galician restaurant in Mexico City in March 1996, and thereby contributed decisively to my shift in perspective. Professor Paul Vanderwood (San Diego State University), who has been a source of ideas and a good critic over two decades, gave me his hospitality in San Diego at a crucial stage of rethinking and writing early in January 1998. The libraries of the Instituto José María Luis Mora and the Centro de Estudios de Historia de México (CONDUMEX) provided agreeable places of study.

Students and colleagues at the State University of New York at Stony Brook, Strathclyde University, and Essex University helped refine the ideas and interpretations offered here. I am particularly grateful to Xavier Guzmán Urbiola and Carlos Silva Cázares, in Mexico City, for their help in selecting the illustrations and maps which form a significant part of this work.

I

Mexico in perspective

Mexico may be part of the 'New World' (in the European nomenclature), but in reality much of the territory included within the present-day Republic formed part of a very old world unknown to Europeans before the end of the fifteenth century. This pre-Columbian past needs to be appreciated when attempting to explain both colonial and contemporary Mexico. We need to examine the way a distinct Mexican civilisation has expressed itself through time. The chronological and thematic sweep explains the structure and approach. The main purpose is to lay out the principal themes and issues. The detail may be found in many specific works. Contemporary Mexico has both an ostensibly stable political system and a capacity for grass-roots mobilisation, centrifugal tendencies, varied beliefs and distinctive local practices.

Modern territorial boundaries distort the cultural unities of the pre-Columbian world. The geographical dimension of Maya civilisation, for instance, included areas that would in colonial times become the southeastern territories of the Viceroyalty of New Spain (namely Yucatán) and the core territories of the Kingdom of Guatemala. Although sites like Palenque, Bonampak, and Yaxchilán are located in Chiapas, and Uxmal and Chichén Itzá in Yucatán, both states part of the Mexican Republic, Classic Period Maya sites such as Tikal, Uaxactún, and Copán are in the Republics of Guatemala and Honduras, respectively. Today, knowledge of Maya civilisation is disseminated in Mesoamerica from the capital city museums of contemporary states, even though these cities, particularly Mexico City, played no part at all in its original flourishing. In that sense, the Maya inheritance has been appropriated by the national states

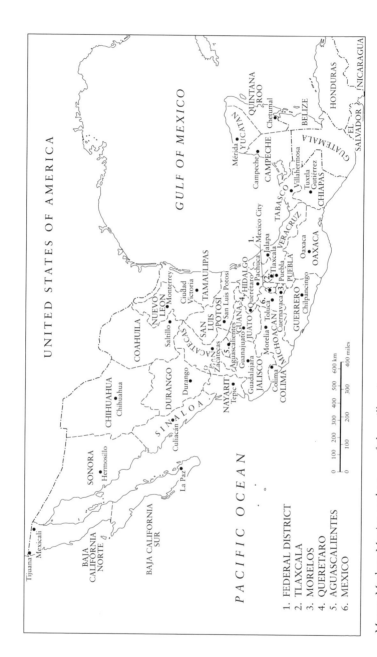

Map 1 Modern Mexico at the turn of the millennium.

to reinforce their historical identity and legitimacy. As in many other instances, the once-vanished Maya world has been brought back to life in order to serve a contemporary political purpose.

Two central processes have been at work since the collapse of the pre-Columbian world: the creation of a Spanish colonial viceroyalty out of the existing indigenous political and ethnic units, and the development of a modern Mexican nation-state out of the former viceroyalty. One can see immediately that in both processes discontinuities and continuities existed side by side. The discontinuities and radical differences between contemporary Mexico and the pre-Columbian and colonial eras make it imperative that we do not write history backwards from the perspective of the present day.

Geography and environment help to explain economic and political developments in Mexico through the historical perspective. Ethnic and linguistic diversity combined with regional and local disparities have shaped Mexican society and have defined its distinctive culture. A number of obvious contrasts come to mind immediately: the modernity, dynamism, and openness of the north, the cultural and ethnic mixtures of the core zone from Zacatecas and San Luis Potosí to Oaxaca, and the Maya world of Yucatán and Chiapas. Federalism, first adopted in 1824, was intended to reflect this diversity and give institutional life to the changing relationships between region and centre and between the regions themselves. For much of the twentieth century, however, federalism remained a dead letter.

NATIONALISM AND TERRITORY

The makers of Independence saw their country as the successor state not only to the Spanish colonial Viceroyalty of New Spain but also to the Aztec Empire originally established in 1325 in Tenochtitlán at the centre of Lake Texcoco. For Mexican nationalists of the nineteenth and twentieth centuries, the Aztec inheritance became fundamental to any comprehension of nationhood. It distinguished Mexico from other Hispanic-American societies, as well as from the United States. At the same time, the argument that Mexico existed as a nation before the Spanish Conquest in 1521 not only undermined the legitimacy of Spanish rule but also provided a platform of resistance to the French Intervention of 1862–67. Liberal President Benito Juárez (1806–72), though born a

Zapotec from the southern state of Oaxaca, identified himself with Cuauhtémoc, the last Aztec Emperor, who had resisted Hernán Cortés until put to death by him. The victorious Liberals of the Reform era (1855–76) portrayed the execution of the Archduke Maximilian of Habsburg, who had presided over the Second Mexican Empire (1864–67), as the revindication of the fallen Aztec Empire, the reaffirmation of independence, and the means of solidifying republican institutions. As a Habsburg, Maximilian was the descendant of Charles V, in whose name Cortés had overthrown the Aztec Empire.

The Revolution of 1910–40 reaffirmed the symbolism of Mexican republican nationalism, which has formed an essential aspect of the ideology of the monopoly ruling party since its first constitution as the Partido Nacional Revolucionario (PNR) in 1929. The Aztec myth has been carried beyond its original territorial base to encompass the entire Republic. Neo-Aztecism, which first emerged in the eighteenth century, has formed part of the ideology of the contemporary state. In fact, Octavio Paz (1914–98), awarded the Nobel Prize for Literature in 1990, has argued that the Aztec pyramid was the paradigm for the monopoly-party state, which characterised much of twentieth-century Mexican history.

Modern Mexico, however, is not and never was coterminous with the looser political units ruled at the time of Cortés's arrival by Moctezuma II and his predecessors. Effectively, the northern limits of the Aztec state hardly reached present-day San Juan del Río, about two hours' drive north of Mexico City. This line did not, however, signify the northern limits of settled culture, since the Tarascan territory of Michoacán and the princedoms in the territory of present-day central Jalisco existed beyond Aztec control. Furthermore, the sites of La Quemada and Altavista, in the present-day State of Zacatecas, provide evidence of sedentary cultures in Tuitlán in the heart of territory later under nomad control.

When the Spanish Conquerors established their capital on the ruins of Tenochtitlán, they could hardly have imagined that within a few decades Hispanic rule would push further northwards into hitherto unsubdued territories. Similarly, they could not have anticipated the tenacity of the resistance they would encounter throughout the rest of the century. The Spaniards founded several specifically Hispanic cities within the settled Indian heartlands in the aftermath of the Conquest.

Puebla de los Angeles (1531) and Guadalajara (1542) were the principal examples. These cities became centres of expansion for Hispanic culture among the surviving indigenous population. Contemporary Mexico, however, also developed from the original, sixteenth-century thrust northwards, with Guadalajara itself in a forward position in the centre-west.

The Viceroyalty of New Spain, established in 1535, was a Spanish political entity superimposed upon pre-existing indigenous states and subdued peoples. Until its collapse in 1821, it remained subordinate to the metropolitan government in Spain. The discovery of rich silver deposits in the north-centre and north required military expansion well beyond the Río Lerma and the prompt consolidation of Hispanic rule. In such a way, the push to the north became a dynamic element in New Spain's history from early in the colonial experience. The north ensured that New Spain would be much more than the agglomeration of distinct indigenous polities under Hispanic rule.

The Mexican north and far north (the latter refers to territory beyond the Río Bravo or Rio Grande now in the United States) remained only loosely connected to the political centre in Mexico City. A series of administrative units generally under a military commander attempted to define Spanish control. Though called Kingdoms – such as Nueva Galicia (capital: Guadalajara), Nueva Vizcaya (Durango), and Nuevo León (Monterrey) – they formed part of the Viceroyalty until the organisation of the Commandancy General of the Interior Provinces in 1776. The uncertainties of the northern frontier and Mexico City's reluctance to contribute effective financing to resolve the military problem with the unpacified Indian groups continually frustrated territorial consolidation. New Spain bequeathed this ongoing problem to the Mexican sovereign state after 1821. As we shall see in chapter five, decades of deteriorating government finance in the late colonial period left independent Mexico with a debt problem. External loans and trade recession compounded this problem. Internal political divisions undermined any attempt to apply a consistent policy with regard to the far northern territories. When the crisis over Texas secession broke in 1835, Mexico was in no position to assert its sovereignty successfully in the face of resistance from Anglo-Saxon settlers.

Mexico became independent of metropolitan Spain in 1821 not as a republic but as the Mexican Empire, a monarchy which extended at least nominally from Panama in the south to Oregon in the north. Its capital, Mexico City, remained the largest city of the Americas and probably the most architecturally distinguished at that time. The Mexican silver peso or dollar remained one of the world's major denominations: the US dollar was based on the peso and the two currencies retained parity until the mid-nineteenth century. The Chinese Empire, perennially short of silver, used the peso as its principal medium of exchange until the turn of the century. In 1821, it did not seem inevitable that the Mexican Empire would lose a large part of its territory and after 1848 be surpassed and increasingly dwarfed by the United States of America.

Defeat in the War with the United States (1846–48) at a time of internal division meant that an international border was drawn through what had formerly been claimed as part of Hispanic North America. After 1846, Mexicans in territories that fell under US occupation frequently became second-class citizens in what had been their own country: pushed off their lands or confined to 'barrios', they faced discrimination in a variety of ways. Out of that experience sprang the Chicano movement from the 1960s which expressed itself in both culture and politics. While beset by its own historic ambiguities, the Chicano movement sought to reassert the authenticity and dignity of the Mexican experience (and its connection to Mexico) within the United States. At the same time, Mexican (and other Latin American) migrations into US cities altered their character and ultimately their political life. Chicago, the second largest Polish city in the world, acquired in recent decades a significant Mexican character as well, far beyond the traditional territories of the Hispanic orbit.

LIVING WITH THE USA

Mexico and the United States were products of the same historical epoch, the Age of Enlightenment and Revolution over the period from 1776 to 1826. Both became sovereign states as a result of revolutionary movements which overthrew European colonial regimes. Why are they so different and why has their relationship taken the course that it has? In Mexico, the Enlightenment, the Atlantic Revolutions, and nineteenth-century Liberalism encountered the inheritance of the Spanish Conquest, Hispanic absolutism, and the Counter-Reformation, all powerful counter-influences. None of them was disposed towards government by consultation and consent. Although both Mexico and the United States adopted federalism, the comparative study of how this functioned remains in its infancy. The question of why federalism broke down in Mexico in 1835–36, only a decade and a half after Independence, still generates controversy.

For Mexico, the unavoidable relationship with the United States has been the predominant element in external policy since the Texas War of 1836. For Mexicans, the Treaty of Guadalupe Hidalgo (1848), which confirmed the loss of the far north, continues to be a significant event. It confirmed the shift in the balance of power within the North American continent in favour of the United States. By contrast, the United States' perspectives are not those of Latin Americans in general, nor of Mexicans in particular. For the United States, the rest of the American continent is largely a sideshow at best and a nuisance factor at worst. As a twentieth-century world power, the principal focus of United States foreign policy was always Western and Central Europe, on the one hand, and the North Pacific Basin (Japan and China), on the other hand. Mediterranean, Middle Eastern, and South-East Asian affairs formed a necessary but secondary sphere. This is not to deny the significance of sporadic US attention to Caribbean or Latin American issues, but to affirm, nevertheless, its tertiary nature. This is not the place to debate whether these policy priorities have been the correct ones, given the American location of the United States. They do help to explain, though, why United States–Mexican relations – two countries which share the longest common border in Latin America – have remained so fraught with misunderstanding throughout the period from 1836 to the present.

From the vantage point of the United States, Mexico appears to be underdeveloped, potentially unstable, and even conceivably a security risk. The primacy of negative sentiments remains a striking feature of US perceptions of Mexico, which has not diminished but may even have increased during the 1990s through media attention to drug trafficking, human-rights abuses, and widespread corruption. Failure to eradicate these problems makes Mexico seem culpable across a wide span of US opinion. Mexican perceptions of the United States frequently tend to be equally, if not more, negative. The loss of the far north is the starting point, re-examined in full detail in a series of conferences in Mexico

City and in regional capitals during the course of 1997–98, the 150th anniversary of the defeat. 'What went wrong?' was the question asked. In the United States, the anniversary, still overshadowed by the impact of its own Civil War (1861–65), passed with scarcely a murmur.

Any discussion in Mexico of the projected McLane-Ocampo Treaty of 1859 for US transit rights across Mexican territory reopens the rival nationalisms inherited from mid-nineteenth-century Liberals and Conservatives. Two landings of US forces in Veracruz, in 1847 and 1914, are usually commemorated in Mexico with nationalist excoriation of US treachery and violations of national sovereignty. Deep suspicion, frequently justified, characterised much of US–Mexican relations during the course of the twentieth century, right through to the establishment of the North American Free Trade Agreement in 1992. Yet, political and economic developments during the 1980s and 1990s emphasised all the more the interdependence of the two countries with a common border of 3,000 km. Even so, the significance of NAFTA still remains unclear, especially in view of the uneven development of the three participating states and their differing perceptions of the free trade treaty's purpose. Since the treaty involved major concessions by the Mexican state to US private capital, intense warnings followed in Mexico concerning the dire social consequences. These forebodings seemed to be given reality with the outbreak of the Chiapas rebellion in January 1994, which threw the focus once again on long-standing indigenous grievances.

The NAFTA resulted from a Mexican initiative, to which the US government responded. Mexican motives were political as well as economic, and reflected internal circumstances as well as external goals. In that sense, the Mexican government was drawing the United States deeper into Mexican affairs, while at the same time expecting gains for Mexico in the US market. Any analysis of the relationship between the two countries needs to recognise not only US misinterpretations of Mexican conditions and misunderstanding of the language and local susceptibilities, but also the Mexican capacity for manipulation. How to 'handle the Americans' forms an essential part of Mexican foreign relations.

Fundamentally, the Mexican–US relationship involves disparities of wealth and power. These disparities are the crux of the issue. Mexico and the United States, despite parallels and similarities, operate in different worlds. Their international context and terms of reference are wide apart. Perhaps worst of all, the two countries are not really seriously thinking about one another. Mexico's obsession is with itself. Few Mexican newspapers or journals have any broad and profound coverage of international affairs, still less any informed analysis of US developments, except perhaps where the behaviour of the New York stock market is concerned. Enrique Krauze's comment that Mexico is symbolically an island is very much to the point. There are remarkably few Institutes of US Studies in Mexico and few historians specialise in US history. The Centro de Investigaciones sobre América del Norte, based at the UNAM in Mexico City, which also deals with Canada as its name implies, is a notable exception.

Although Mexico and the United States have still not managed to work out a satisfactory relationship after two centuries, not everything in this North American 'special relationship' has been a disaster. US Presidents usually meet more often with their Mexican counterparts than with any other Heads of State; there are annual meetings of US and Mexican Governors of border states. For the US President a certain international proportion is inevitably involved. In November 1997, for instance, President Ernesto Zedillo's visit to the White House followed in the wake of that of the Chinese President, Jiang Zemin (who subsequently visited Mexico). The two visits highlighted the dimensional difference between China and Mexico in terms of their ranking in US foreign policy considerations. Furthermore, the three decades of Mexican economic difficulties since 1970 cost the country a great deal in terms of its position on the US scale of world importance. Issues such as the border and drug trafficking were inevitably discussed between Zedillo and President Bill Clinton.

Mexico, unlike the United States, is neither a world power nor a significant military force. Mexican self-contemplation – looking into the mirror – effectively removes the country from any possibility of exercising influence in world affairs. While Mexico certainly has a strong and resilient culture, it shares with most of Latin America an inability to project itself in any significant capacity onto the world political stage. In that sense, Latin America represents a missing factor, a huge area in terms of territory and population, but without an influence on the course of events. Given the relationship to the USA, the image of Mexico is frequently one projected to the rest of the world through the medium of the United States. Accordingly, the image is rarely a favourable one.

THE BORDER

The Mexican presence 'north of the border' helps to explain further the uneasy relationship between Mexico and the United States. The border issue, as it is seen inside the United States, continues to be an unresolved problem between the two countries. Even so, the border remains more political than cultural, in the sense that the 'American South-West' has never entirely superseded the Mexican far north. Quite the reverse, the growing Mexican impact in former territories such as Texas, Arizona, and California is evident to anyone who lives or travels there. A slow, persistent recovery of 'Mex-America' has been taking place beneath the political superimpositions of 1848. Some might even portray this as a 'Reconquista'. For generations, families in northern Mexico have had relations across the 'border', and transit for one purpose or another has been constant. For many Mexican families in the border zone (regardless of which side) it is simply a formality that has to be passed through whenever meetings take place. Carlos Fuentes (b.1928) in *La frontera cristalina* (Mexico 1996) directly portrayed this experience in ten short stories that form a type of novel. Recent border novels by the US author Cormac McCarthy, such as *All the Pretty Horses* (New York 1992), gave a distinct Texan perspective to the frontier experience.

The border itself, in spite of the ongoing argument over illegal immigrants, is more a crossroads than a frontier. The string of twin cities – Calexico–Mexicali, Nogales (Arizona)–Nogales (Sonora), Douglas–Agua Prieta, El Paso–Ciudad Juárez, Eagle Pass–Piedras Negras, Laredo (Texas)–Nuevo Laredo (Tamaulipas), McAllen–Reynosa, Brownsville–Matamoros – gives an idea of the dimensions involved. Life in Monterrey (Nuevo León) is not radically different from life in San Antonio (Texas), and certainly a good deal more similar to it than to prevailing cultures in central Mexico. Even so, there are some striking distinctions on and beyond the frontier. San Diego, California, fourteen miles from the Mexican border, remains a characteristically US city oriented more towards the rest of the USA than southwards to Mexico, despite the large Mexican presence in the vicinity and in spite of the rhetoric of urban cooperation with Tijuana.

Immigration studies, strong in assessing European entry into the USA, Argentina, Uruguay, or Brazil, frequently overlook Latin American migration into the United States. Although many such immigrants may aspire to US citizenship and the benefits of US material life, Latin American culture is strong enough to resist absorption into prevailing English-language culture and most such immigrants would not wish to forfeit their distinct identities. Accordingly, the late twentieth-century reinforcement of the already existing Latin American historical presence within US-controlled territory has raised the question of cultural and linguistic integration. Along with the Mexican 'border question' is the issue of the status of the Spanish language within the United States in relation to the (at present) unique official status of the English language. This latter issue goes well beyond the question of the Mexican border, since it involves at least the Cuban, Puerto Rican, and Central American presence in the United States as well. Mexicans, in view of their own cultural inheritance and the contiguity of the Mexican Republic, have proved to be the strongest group of 'unmeltables' within the United States.

Earlier migration resulted from Porfirian land policies and conditions during the Revolution in the 1910s. Much mid-century cross-border migration derived from the US bracero programme of 1942–64, which introduced the concept of the 'wet-back' to California and Texas popular culture. Failed agricultural reform policies in the aftermath of the Revolution led to the recreation of 'branches' of Mexican villages within the US cities themselves. Re-planted communities from Jalisco, Michoacán or Oaxaca, for instance, resemble the transplanted dissenter communities of seventeenth-century Essex and Suffolk which contributed so much to the establishment of New England, though they are rarely viewed through US eyes in the same perspective. In January 1998, Jalisco was reputed to be the Mexican state with the largest number of migrants: 1.5 million people originating from there lived in the United States, particularly in California, Chicago, and Washington DC. Migrants sent around US$800 million back into the Jalisco economy.

The US Immigration Reform and Control Act of 1986, which was considered in Mexico to be a response to Mexican Government independence on Central American issues, seemed to ignore the dependence of significant sectors of the US economy on Mexican labour. The first Clinton Administration, which took office in 1993, began another attempt in the following year to stem Mexican immigration by increasing the number of patrols and constructing more barriers, but four years later no one could tell whether it had been a success or not.

Plate 1 Visit to the border barriers at Tijuana by Secretary of
Foreign Relations, Rosario Green, 9 December 1998. During the
visit, the Secretary commented that the international border
between the United States and Mexico appeared to be between
two hostile countries. She stated that Mexico had so far failed to
persuade the United States of a humanitarian policy, instead of
the current situation in which potential migrants put their lives
at risk in attempting night-crossings. The Secretary inspected the
metal barrier constructed by the US authorities from the El
Mirador Hill across the Tijuana beach and 50 m out into the sea
to prevent Mexicans swimming into US territory. The Mexican
press drew attention to the construction of a highway on the US
side designed to strengthen Border Patrol responses to
clandestine immigration. According to the Mexican Migrant
Defence Coalition in San Diego, California, 141
'indocumentados' had died mainly from hypothermia and
drowning in attempts to beat the US Border Patrol, which itself
shot dead two potential migrants in the Tijuana area in
September 1998.

    Rosario Green, author of a work published in 1976 examining
Mexico's external debt from 1940 to 1973, is a former Senator
and deputy Foreign Minister, and was Ambassador in the Federal
Republic of Germany in 1989.

Funding for frontier control increased from US$374 million to US$631 million between 1994 and 1997. Operation Hard-Line has been in force along the US southern border since 1995.

In the 'border question', the USA sees itself at its most vulnerable. A society formed of immigrants from other continents has been in the process of trying to seal the border with one of its two North American neighbours, though significantly not with the other. The incongruity of that situation – the attempted creation of a North American Berlin Wall when the European original had already collapsed – has had repercussions at many levels. It flies in the face of North American history as an immigrant society; it exposes yet again US failure to understand even the most basic facts about Mexico.

Immigration has become a political issue between the parties in US elections, with the result that short-term party advantage is allowed to prejudice US–Mexican relations. The topic is rarely accorded rational treatment, least of all in the US media. The US government invests huge sums in border restrictions, but, instead, dialogue at the border-state level on both sides of the frontier might prove to be a better way to resolve the issue. Mexican and US perspectives on the immigration issue differ radically at national level: Mexico sees immigration to the US (regardless of whether it is legal or illegal) as a necessary social and economic release; the US sees illegal immigration as a threat to living standards and a violation of national sovereignty. Both US and Mexican nationalism have repeatedly thrown obstacles in the way of any amicable resolution of the question. The widely differing living standards between the two societies remain at the heart of the problem.

DRUG TRAFFICKING

A prevailing issue between Mexico (and other Latin American countries) and the USA continues to be drug trafficking. The penetration of several Latin American countries' governmental, judicial and security systems by *narcotraficantes* has caused consternation among commentators. Even so, the prime explanation for the problem lies not in Latin America but in the United States. In early November 1997, a US Government Report stated that Americans spent an estimated US$57,300 million on the purchase of illegal drugs during 1995. Of this sum, US$38,000 million was spent on cocaine alone and a further

US$9,600 million on heroin. The same report stated that three-quarters of world cocaine production was destined for the United States. These figures help to put the Latin American situation into perspective. Early in 1998, the Director of the FBI argued before the Senate Intelligence Committee that the activities of Mexican drug cartels presented the principal criminal threat to the United States. The Director of the Central Intelligence Agency held a similar view, arguing that divisions within the Mafia had enabled Mexican cartels to gain control of the international drug trade. The FBI identified seven large Mexican organisations which controlled distribution, and singled out the Tijuana cartel as the most dangerous, its alleged leader on its 'most-wanted' list. The controversial US Government policy of publicly categorising drug-risk sources led to strong opposition by its Mexican counterpart.

A joint US–Mexican anti-narcotics strategy has usually proved difficult to implement. Nevertheless, the US Drug Enforcement Agency (DEA) operates inside Mexico in cooperation with the security services but the problem of supply in response to demand continues unabated and affects relations between the two countries. A newspaper report in December 1998 suggested at least 400 clandestine landing strips used in the drug trade in secluded parts of Baja California alone. Remote locations in Mexico have become areas of Marijuana cultivation, or provide air-strips for Colombian cartels to land cocaine destined for the US market by way of Mexican channels. In the Lacandonian Forest in Chiapas, such landing strips promote this clandestine trade, which accounts for around 60 per cent of the cocaine bound for the USA. US budget proposals for the fiscal year 1999 included the relatively small sum of US$13 million towards anti-drug trafficking measures inside Mexico. The package put before the US Congress on 2 February 1998 earmarked a total of US$17,000 million for anti-narcotics operations out of a total Federal budget of US$173,000 million.

Perhaps the most serious problem which surfaced in Mexico during the 1980s and 1990s was the extent of the penetration of the political processes, armed forces, and security services by the drug cartels. The most notorious case involved a range of dubious activities by Raúl Salinas de Gortari, brother of ex-President Carlos Salinas de Gortari (1988–94). Salinas was arrested on 28 February 1995 for alleged involvement in the assassination of the ex-President of the governing Partido Revolucionario Institucional (PRI), José Francisco Ruiz Massieu, in late

September 1994, and was confined to the Federal maximum security prison at Almoloya. The Swiss Government, late in 1997, revealed suspected 'money-laundering' by Salinas of over US$100 million, embargoed since 1995, allegedly acquired through drug trafficking. From exile in Ireland, Carlos Salinas, in November 1998 denied all knowledge of his elder brother's dealings. General Jesús Gutiérrez Rebollo, head of anti-drug-traffic operations, was arrested on 18 February 1997, for allegedly protecting one of the principal cartels. Gutiérrez, who was convicted of hoarding heavy-calibre weapons, had apparently collaborated in eliminating rival barons. He was sentenced in March 1998 to thirteen years in prison.

Newspapers regularly carry reports of suspected drug involvements by political figures such as state governors. On 23 January 1998, for instance, the Office of the Federal Prosecutor (Procuraduría General de la República) ordered the arrest of Flavio Romero de Velasco, Governor of Jalisco from 1977 to 1983 and three times federal deputy for Chapala, on the grounds that he had maintained contact, while in office and thereafter, with identified *narcotraficantes*. Romero governed at a time when 'Operación Condor' pushed the *narcos* out of the state of Sinaloa, where they had been entrenched, with the result that they became established in Jalisco. Although considered by some a possible President of the PRI in 1995, the party's National Executive Committee expelled him after his arrest and confinement in Almoloya, in order to ensure a cleaner public image. Romero's alleged contacts were Rigoberto Gaxiola Medina and Jorge Alberto Abrego Reyna (alias Gabriel Pineda Castro), wanted for fraud. The former was believed to have transferred money from the Cayman Islands to Mexico and used front accounts for money-laundering. At the Mexican Government's request, the US DEA arrested Reyna in Phoenix, Arizona, late in January 1998, while attempting to withdraw one million dollars from a hotel bank. The PGR was also investigating the relationship of the Governor of Quintana Roo, Mario Villanueva Madrid, to the Ciudad Juárez cartel, allegedly operating in that state and receiving cocaine from Colombia.

The presence in Mexico in early April 1998 of Barry McCaffrey, the US 'anti-drug tsar', as the press called him, was expected to produce a further joint initiative in the campaign of both governments to clip the power of the *narcotraficantes*. This problem, which came to the forefront

Plate 2 Federal maximum security Prison at Almoloya de Juárez (State of Mexico), near Toluca. Ex-President Carlos Salinas de Gortari's brother, Raúl Salinas, was confined in the Almoloya prison from 1995 until cleared of the murder charge in 2005, although the charge of illicit enrichment so far remains. Also held there is Mario Aburto, apparently the assassin of PRI presidential candidate Luis Donaldo Colosio, in Tijuana in March 1994.

after the 1970s, is one of the gravest faced by present-day Mexico. The recrudescence of the 'Indian question', linked to broader social and economic problems, presents a further, seemingly insoluble issue.

INDIGENOUS MEXICO

The pre-Columbian world, which we shall shortly examine, presented the European invaders of the early sixteenth century with the problem of understanding American societies of which they had no previous conception. Although the 'Indian' world changed radically under the impact of conquest, colonisation, and legislation, the Indian presence in contemporary Mexico remains real and pervading. No one reading newspapers or watching television news in the 1990s could escape the conclusion that contemporary Mexico faced an 'indigenous problem'. Although it is difficult to calculate with any accuracy the extent of the population component described as 'Indian', some estimates opt for a figure of around 10 million and argue that its annual rate of growth exceeds the national average of 2 per cent. Since the term 'Indian' in contemporary Mexico (particularly in urban areas) refers more to social position than to ethnic character, the basis of such calculations remains uncertain. Primary use of an indigenous language – there are estimated to be fifty-six linguistic groups – is frequently a criterion of inclusion. In Chiapas, for instance, the population described as 'Indian' represents about one million out of a total state population of 3.5 million. Of this million, around one-third speak no Spanish.

The Indian question in present-day Mexico is an urban as well as a rural phenomenon. Internal migration during past decades has been motivated by adverse conditions on the land – soil erosion, inadequate water-supply, failed land-reform policies, lack of credit, landlord abuses, domination by local bosses or *caciques* and their armed men. This has compounded problems of overpopulation in the metropolitan areas, most especially in Mexico City, with their large areas of shanty towns and inadequate sanitation.

The contemporary ferment in the state of Oaxaca, the complex pre-colonial history of which we shall look at in the next chapter, provides a major example of indigenous mobilisation. Although the state capital frequently presents a deceptive façade of colonial-era tranquillity, both the city and the countryside have been seedbeds of constant ferment

over issues such as control of land and water, domination of local communities by armed bosses sometimes connected to the state and
national political processes, labour conditions and unofficial unionisation, and the autonomy of municipal institutions. Frequent large-scale
mobilisation by rural school-teachers and by local peasant groups has
kept Oaxaca politics simmering for the past decades. The struggle for
political supremacy within indigenous towns and villages has similarly
provided a constant source of agitation. The violent conflicts in the
southern Isthmus zone of Juchitán and Tehuantepec since the late 1960s
clearly demonstrate the intensity of these issues. Many parallel conflicts
have surfaced in other areas and at other times, lately in the states of
Guerrero, Puebla, Tlaxcala, and Veracruz. During the early 1970s the
Mexican army put down an insurrection in Guerrero, led by Lucio
Cabañas, which attempted to connect district-level issues to wider
political ideologies in an embracing military organisation. That model
has provided an example for the entry of the EZLN ('Zapatista Army
of National Liberation') into the Chiapas indigenous question after
1983. The guerrilla band originated from the 'Fuerzas de Liberación
Nacional' (FLN), founded in Monterrey in August 1969, in the aftermath of government repression of the Mexico City student protests in
the previous year.

The following chapters refer to a range of factors altering the demographic and cultural balance within Mexico since the early sixteenth
century to the disadvantage of the indigenous population. These factors
raise the question: if the Indian population collapsed so drastically in the
aftermath of the Spanish Conquest, then why is there an Indian problem
in contemporary Mexico? A number of answers rapidly spring to mind:
Spanish colonial policy never intended to eliminate the indigenous
population but to offer protection in the disastrous aftermath of conquest; colonial law reconstituted and safeguarded (where practicable)
Indian community institutions, including landownership; weak nineteenth-century governments largely failed to transform Indian peasants
into individual smallholders; the neo-indigenist tradition in the Mexican
Revolution pressed for re-establishment of community landownership
and the provision of credit for peasant farmers. Above all, there is the
factor of Indian population recovery from the late seventeenth century
onwards. To that should be added another factor, only recently explored
in the historical literature: the reconstitution of indigenous community

Plate 3 Local market in Tlacolula, Valley of Oaxaca. 'Indian'
Mexico has always been characterised by networks of markets,
some specialising in local produce such as the textiles of
Teotitlan del Valle, the glazed green pottery of Atzompa, or the
black pottery of San Bartolo Coyotepec, all three villages in the
Valley of Oaxaca. The market of Tlacolula, one of the main
valley towns, existed during the colonial period and was
probably of pre-Columbian origin. It was an important market
for the sierra villages as well. Periodic markets are usually known
by the Náhuatl term, *tianguis*, while fixed markets take the
Spanish term, *mercado*. Urban markets, covered and uncovered,
proliferate, not least in Mexico City.

identity under the impact of political changes imposed at provincial
and national levels from the late eighteenth century. It has been argued
that this became more pronounced in response to the mid-nineteenth-
century Liberal Reform movement.

One major issue has recently surfaced in discussion of the contemporary indigenous question: political autonomy for indigenous areas.
This position explicitly rejects the nineteenth-century Liberal and early
twentieth-century revolutionary constitutional tradition. For that
reason, it became a highly contentious issue in the 1990s. The demand
for the formation of autonomous territories within the context of the
nation-state radically contradicts that tradition. Liberal state-building

sought to eliminate the corporative inheritance of the Spanish colonial era and thereby construct a homogeneous Mexican nation.

The Constitutions of 1824, 1857, and 1917 saw in the guarantee of individual liberties and the establishment of a federal system the best legal protection for the 'citizens' of a modern republic. In the autumn of 1997, by contrast, a spokesman for the Otomí Indian communities of the state of Querétaro complained that the 1917 Constitution, product of large-scale popular mobilisation during the Revolution, made no provision for indigenous communities as such.

The 1917 Constitution, in part heir to the nineteenth-century Liberal tradition but in other respects a response to social pressures on the land and from urban workers, assumed the existence of a Mexican nation rather than a series of distinct ethno-linguistic communities each striving to safeguard its identity. The controversy in 1992 over the quincentenary of Christopher Columbus's 'discovery' of the Americas involved the issue of European subordination of indigenous cultures. The continuation of this process led to rejection by indigenous groups of what, in the negative terminology of the late 1990s, is described as 'occidentalisation'.

Contemporary indigenous groups repeatedly refer to mid-nineteenth-century legislation as a failure. Their critique of the Reform movement rests on the argument that Liberal attempts to transform Indian-community peasants into smallholders resulted in land loss and deepening social deprivation. The focus of criticism has turned towards 'neo-Liberalism', a political economy implemented at government level in Mexico since the mid-1980s, though particularly during the Salinas presidency. Salinas's revision in 1992 of article 27 of the 1917 Constitution sought to reduce on economic grounds the communitarian element in the reconstituted agrarian units which arose largely from revolutionary legislation during the 1930s. Indigenous mobilisation during the 1990s did not arise, however, uniquely from hostility towards the consequences, real or imagined, of 'neo-liberalism'. Long-term and short-term trends within the economy as a whole – at national and global levels – had far-reaching social and political repercussions. The coffee recession in the Chiapas production sector, for instance, blocked opportunities for migrant labour from the predominantly indigenous areas of the central sierra at a time of rising population and deepening social tensions.

The Indian question, which Mexico shares, though in very different ways, with Guatemala, Ecuador, Peru, and Bolivia, differentiates the country from societies such as Argentina, or Venezuela, in which the indigenous presence has been either eradicated or marginalised. A recrudescence of Indian political demands can be seen from Canada to Chile, not least in the United States and Mexico. The indigenous presence distinguishes Mexico and the Indo-American cultures from Europe: they are not simply European societies transported to another continent, but complex mixtures (and conflicts) of many cultures of remote historical origins.

In contrast to the United States and Argentina, Mexico was never a country of large-scale immigration. That in itself helps to explain the continuing impact of the pre-Columbian world and the strong Indian presence in the nineteenth and twentieth centuries. Mexico, it is correct to say, has received immigrants, but more as manual workers like the Chinese of the late Díaz era, or as specific groups such as the Spanish Republican exiles of the late 1930s. None of this, however, altered either the structure of the population or the prevailing culture.

2

The pre-Columbian era

Migrating hunters in pursuit of animals during the Ice Age may have crossed the land bridge from Asia, now the Bering Straits, into the American continent some 12,000 years ago. Controversy still surrounds both provenance and dating, although this seems to be the preferred explanation for the populating of the Americas. At the end of the Ice Age, the land was less able to sustain large, foraging population groups. With the extinction of the hunted mastodons around 8000 BC, hunters needed to find a new balance between nutritional needs and their environment's food potential. For several thousand years, however, foraging and farming coexisted, before maize cultivation became the basis of the economy. The domestication of plants required regular rainfall or proximity to fresh water. Similarly, the need for tools led to the development of trade routes, especially between highland sources of obsidian, the principal cutting agent, and the tropical lowlands with their diversity of foodstuffs.

Agriculture possibly developed in Mesoamerica between 5500 BC and 3500, considerably later than in Syria and Mesopotamia, where cultivation of wheat began around 9000 BC and 8000 BC respectively, and in the Indus Valley, where barley cultivation began around 7000 BC. In the central Mexican Basin, pre-ceramic society, a mixture of sedentary and semi-sedentary peoples, existed possibly around 4000 BC, taking nourishment from the plant and animal life around the extensive lakeshore of the Valley of Mexico. At an altitude of 2,200 m, the temperate climate and abundant water on this *altiplano* created by volcanic activity would provide the basis for settled life. So far, however, the earliest known permanent villages of farmers cultivating maize dates from BC 2250 to 1400 in tropical Tabasco on the southern Gulf coast. Small villages with varied diet and using obsidian, a black, volcanic glass, and basalt tools grew up on the river levees. San Lorenzo (1500–1350 BC) was the principal centre.

The core of the Olmec culture lay in the area of the Papaloapan, Coatzacoalcos, and Tonalá Rivers. In the Early Formative Period (1500–900 BC), urban areas with many specialised buildings and a social stratification emerged out of a previously egalitarian farming society. The sculptures had a ritual and symbolic significance, which arose immediately from local agricultural and artisan society. Although naturalistic rather than abstract, they frequently portrayed a spiritual state rather than a specific physical condition, and were executed by skilled craftsmen, evidently spiritually prepared for the task, in highly polished jade, jadeite, or serpentine. Archaeologists have so far identified the seventeen permanent settlements of the Tierras Largas complex, northeast of Monte Albán, in the Valley of Oaxaca during the period 1400–1150 BC, and the San José Mogote area (1150–850 BC) on the River Atoyac in the north-eastern part of the Valley in the Etla district, as the earliest population centres on that region. Both of these centres have yielded large ceramic finds. San José, the focus of a network of eighteen to twenty villages, showed evidence of a more stratified society and inter-regional commerce. Olmec symbols appeared in the decorative use of the fire-serpent and the were-jaguar.

In the period, 900–500 BC, population in the central highlands increased rapidly with the result that larger and more numerous villages appeared, despite the continued decline of the lake level in the Valley of Mexico. Elites began to emerge and the number of local chiefdoms grew, making alliances necessary. At the same time, exchange networks expanded. In the Late Pre-Classic Period (500–100 BC), urban centres arose as the population concentrated around central villages, which had public buildings, including pyramids. More land was cleared from forest and irrigation used more extensively in order to make farming more productive. Favourable agricultural conditions on the southern lakeshore accounted for the rise of Cuicuilco, which became the largest centre by 300 BC, covering some 400 ha and sustaining a population around 20,000. This centre had a 27-m high circular and stone-faced pyramid of 80 m diameter. Large irrigations canals and eleven other pyramids have been discovered beneath the lava deposited in the volcanic activity, which destroyed the site around 100 BC. Cuicuilco may possibly have been Mesoamerica's first city state, although others, such as Tlapacoya and Cholula, also existed at that time in central Mexico.

During the Classic Period (AD 300–900) a great cultural flowering took place throughout Mesoamerica – in the Valley of Oaxaca, at Teotihuacan, in the lowland Maya districts, and on the Gulf coast, notably at El Tajín in Veracruz, which was occupied from AD 100–1100. Commercial networks continued to expand, linking the highland areas to the lowlands and coasts, both from western Mexico through the central valleys to the Gulf coast and southwards along the Papaloapan River to the Petén jungles, highland Guatemala, and the Pacific coastal areas from Chiapas to El Salvador.

THE OLMECS

There is an ongoing debate concerning whether Olmec culture, which flourished between 1200 BC and 300 BC in the Gulf lowlands, represented the base from which later cultures developed in different geographical directions, or whether it was simply a culture parallel to others which flourished contemporaneously. Although the Olmecs never apparently formed a great empire, their political organisation and religious system, long-distance commerce, astronomy, and calendar reached sophisticated levels. Their linguistic group was probably Mixe-Zoque, which was related to the Maya languages. Although Olmec influences may be found across central and southern Mesoamerica, no evidence exists for any political control beyond the Gulf base area. Olmec culture flourished from different sites for a period of some six hundred years from c. 1200 BC, a chronology established by radiocarbon tests in the mid-1950s. The Olmecs appear to have been the first to construct large-scale ceremonial sites. Their name is a misnomer, based on the later Aztec name for the southern Gulf zone – Olman (the land of rubber) – and first applied to them in 1927. Having vanished for over two millennia, evidence of Olmec culture slowly began to re-emerge from the swamps and forests into which it had sunk. In 1862, the first gigantic Olmec head was uncovered in the Veracruz district of San Andrés Tuxtla. Axes and jade figures followed at later dates. Then, in 1925, Frans Blom and Oliver La Fage made further decisive discoveries

Plate 4 Olmec sculpture in the Jalapa Museum of Anthropology, Veracruz (author's photo). Discovered in 1945 at the San Lorenzo site in the southern Veracruz district of Texistepec, south-west of Minatitlán, this and other basalt heads date from 1200–1000 BC. San Lorenzo, an artificial mound with a gigantic platform, was one of the oldest Olmec sites.

in the Laguna de Catemaco, a crater lake near the volcano of Pajapan. The heads were carved from basalt boulders flung from erupting volcanoes: a fiery birth from the centre of the earth. Transporting these immense boulders by land and river from the Tuxtla Mountains and then transforming them into ritual shapes demonstrated the power the Olmecs derived from their relationship to supernatural sources.

Shaman-kings, emerging from the elite, interpreted the cosmos, creation, and the cycle of human life. Since the ceremonial sites required the organisation of a large labour force, a state organisation became necessary, and took the form of chiefdoms exercising control over limited territories. The focal points were the San Lorenzo and La Venta sites, which flourished from 1200–900 BC and 900–600 BC, respectively. Michael D. Coe worked on the former site in 1964–67: San Lorenzo consisted of an artificial mound about 1200 m long with many monuments on it raised above the swamps. The site was the nexus of a series of small villages and shrines beyond its circumference. Alfonso Caso and Ignacio Bernal (Director of the National Institute of Anthropology and History [INAH] from 1968 to 1971) worked on Olmec sites during much of the 1960s; Bernal suggested linguistic links with the early Zapotec culture of the Valley of Oaxaca. In chronological terms, Tres Zapotes was the last significant Olmec site, though it was researched in 1938–39, before San Lorenzo and La Venta.

The Olmec belief system pointed to a cosmos in which all elements and creatures were infused with a spiritual power. This energy gave the universe its momentum. Olmec art formed an expression of this power. Humans sought the means of gaining access to spiritual power through discipline, fasting, meditation, and mutilation in the form of blood-letting. They sought access, for instance, to animal spirits, such as the power of the jaguar, in order to transcend human consciousness, often by means of hallucinogenic drugs, such as ritual snuff powders. Shamans were sometimes portrayed in the sculpture in the process of taking on the jaguar spirit. This transformation process explains the widespread use of masks, often carved from jade, which combined jaguar and human features, and conveyed a state of spiritual ecstacy. Contorted facial expressions portrayed the strain of passing from one reality into another. The jaguar held especial significance as the creature which lived in the jungle, swam, and hunted both by day and by night, thereby encompassing land, water, and air, and light and darkness at the same time. The American eagle was the jaguar of the sky. The pyramid of La Venta, a symbol of Pajapan, reached into the sky, and thereby gained access to the heavens. The earth and sky were linked by special deities, which combined aspects of both. Olmec sculpture portrayed a flying jaguar, with a human passenger, or winged jaguars bearing the earth on their backs. In the jungle trees was the poisonous snake, the fer-de-lance, which had a crested brow: since it struck from above rather than from below, it combined the properties of the earth and the sky, and became symbolised as the serpent of the skies, the forerunner of the Plumed Serpent of Teotihuacan, with the attributes of rain and wind.

Virtually all Mesoamerican cultures attached great religious signi-ficance to a ritual ball-game with specially laid-out courts at the monumental sites. From at least Olmec times, human sacrifice, which accompanied the ball-game ritual, was possibly associated with the rain god and a component of rain-making, whether in the form of supernatural beings devouring humans or as shamans impersonating sacred beings through ritual trance. Rain-making was also associated with the carrying of feather bundles or live vipers, symbolising the serpent of the skies.

Since 1985 discoveries concerning the Olmecs have multiplied. Even so, basic questions posed by anthropologists remain largely unanswered: when did Gulf cultures adopt subsistence agriculture? How did population growth influence social diversification? What was the relation of smaller to larger centres? What influenced chronology and location? How did control of resources affect status? What was the nature of religion and how did style reflect this? What relations did the Olmecs have with other Mesoamerican peoples? Were they unique? Why did their civilisation collapse? The Olmecs provided a significant legacy for subsequent Mesoamerican cultures: the belief that meditation, austerities, and sacrifice could enable the attainment of a superior spiritual state; that contact could be made with the reality beyond the human and physical world; that ceremonial sites reflected supernatural sanction for earthly cultures; that humanity not only existed in conjunction with cosmic powers and deities, but also shared identities with them; and their development of a religious complexity founded on rain and agricultural fertility. The Maya Chac, Zapotec Cocijo, and Toltec Tlaloc seem all to have been derived from an Olmec rain god.

The economic basis for Olmec civilisation lay in the extreme fertility of the Gulf basin rivers zone, which yielded two annual maize crops and provided not only animal life but fish as well. Available food supply from this land base sustained a large population. Much of the subsequent reputation of the Olmecs among Mesoamerican peoples may have derived from their agricultural success. The broad influence of the Olmec culture suggests the possibility of a shared cosmology, symbolism, artistic style, and rituals across Mesoamerica, allowing for differences of region and language, throughout the period 900–500 BC.

MONTE ALBÁN AND THE ZAPOTEC CULTURES OF OAXACA

The Monte Albán culture dominated Oaxaca for a thousand years from its first phase (or Monte Albán Ia) in 500–400 BC. The immediate antecedent was the Rosario phase (700–500 BC) in the Huitzo district, from which Monte Albán I pottery, art, architecture, and masonry emerged.

Growth of population and the strain on resources may have required a more concentrated labour force with greater social direction, in order to guarantee the food supply. In such a way, an economic and political reordering beyond the level of the peasant household addressed a basic need at a specific historical period. The concentration of landownership in the valley would have explained an increasing social differentiation and the emergence of a ruling elite with an agrarian base. By 400–200 BC, Monte Albán had passed through its key period in state development, and between 200 BC and AD 100 (Monte Albán II) clear evidence of statehood had emerged. This, then, had proved to be a slow process, covering some three hundred years, after which it reached its maximum development between AD 100 and 600. Already in Monte Albán II, writing in double-columned hieroglyphics testified to the existence of a Zapotec state before the foundation of Teotihuacán in central Mexico or the Classic Maya city of Tikal. An urban centre for several hundred years before its 'Classic' Period (Monte Albán IIIa and IIIb), in those centuries the Zapotec state reached the height of its power in terms of construction, religious expression, social stratification, and rulership. The total population possibly reached between 15,000 and 30,000 inhabitants, supported by the valley agricultural system and receipt of tribute.

The site of Monte Albán, a fortified position at the top of a 400-m mountain overlooking the three sectors of the Valley of Oaxaca, consisted of a concentration of temples with stairways situated around a rectangular square, where public ritual took place. The Zapotec rulers usually passed through a year of religious instruction before taking office. Dead rulers became intermediaries between the living and supernatural forces at work in the universe. At Monte Albán, a graded hierarchy of residences corresponded to their occupants' status. The professional ruling caste and upper tier of the city, some 2–4 per cent of its inhabitants, lived in stone or adobe palaces. They married within their caste or with nobilities from other regions. The Monte Albán tombs were for rulers and members of the nobility, and contained extraordinary funeral urns crafted in the form of living human faces, though sometimes wearing ritual masks. Ancestor worship, it appears, formed a major part of Zapotec religious expression.

The ball-game also assumed great significance in Zapotec culture. Some forty ball-courts have been located in the Valley of Oaxaca, though

Plate 5 Zapotec pyramid (labelled L Alfonso Caso) at Monte Albán, Valley of Oaxaca (author's photo). The site contains several pyramids constructed around the central plaza under the auspices of local rulers, and a northern platform 'acropolis'. Their characteristic form probably dates from the prime period, Monte Albán IIIa and IIIb (AD 350–700). Population at the site itself possibly reached a peak of 24,000 in Period IIIb; the Valley of Oaxaca population exceeded 100,000 distributed through 1,075 known communities, of which the largest number were in the Tlacolula subvalley. Tombs at the Monte Albán site, of which the most remarkable is tomb 104, contain wall-paintings, and funeral urns, shaped with distinctive human characteristics, placed in niches.

most are unexcavated and undated. Those that have been excavated appear to have been constructed in Monte Albán II. They continued to be built thereafter, as the Monte Albán IV ball-court at Dainzú in the Tlacolula Valley, dating from 900–1000, shows. Players wore protective masks, knee-guards, and gloves, and the balls were made of latex. The significance of the game still remains unclear. It seems to have been officially sanctioned, perhaps as a type of political ritual designed to determine implicitly with divine sanction the outcome of disputes between communities. Such disputes may well have been over land or water usage.

The traditional view used to be that the Olmecs stimulated Monte Albán I and that Teotihuacan influenced Monte Albán III. Since the time of Bernal's first workings at Monte Albán during the early 1940s, the view has changed to one which from the 1970s and 1980s has emphasised the autochthonous nature of the development of Zapotec civilisation. Monte Albán differed from Teotihuacan in that it was not a commercial centre, since in Oaxaca the craftsmen who sustained the urban complex and inter-market trades lived in the villages of the valley floor. The city itself expanded well beyond its earlier walls during the Classic period. The maximum territorial extent of Monte Alban's power was in Period II between 100 BC and AD 100. At this time there were four outlying zones, which acted as nuclei for defence and expansion, as well as cultural influence: on the Ejutla River and in the Valley of Miahuatlán, both directly on the route southwards to the Pacific Ocean, in Nejapa on the way to the lagoons of Tehuantepec, and in the Cañada of Cuicatlán, a tropical valley at 500–700 m above sea level, which produced cotton and fruits usually by means of irrigation. This latter zone had a vital strategic significance for Monte Albán, since it controlled access from the Valley of Tehuacán into Oaxaca, that is from the routes leading directly from the Valley of Mexico. For that reason, the Zapotecs constructed a powerful fortress at Quiotepec overlooking the edge of the Cañada and the Tehuacán Valley. In effect, Quiotepec marked the northernmost expansion of the Monte Albán state. It appears that the rulers of the Zapotec state were attempting to control the passage across Oaxaca from the principal access routes from the Valley of Mexico to the Pacific Ocean and the Isthmus of Tehuantepec.

After 500, however, the growth of provincial centres which were founded led to the slackening of Monte Albán's authority and increasing autonomy. Nevertheless, Joyce Marcus and Kent Flannery describe the period 350–700, which corresponds to Monte Albán IIIa (to 550) and IIIb as 'the Golden Age of Zapotec civilisation'.

THE MAYAS

Apart from a few works by Franciscan friars, knowledge of Maya civilisation largely disappeared after the Spanish Conquest. However, the publication of descriptions of the ruined cities by John Lloyd Stephens in 1839–42, which were illustrated by the engravings of Frederick Catherwood, awakened a new interest. Together they travelled through the rainforests of Chiapas and the Guatemalan Petén and across the Yucatán savannah. Their findings stimulated awareness of Maya culture in a period already fascinated by the rediscovery of Ancient Egypt, where written records dated back to 3000 BC. Jean-François Champollion's decipherment of the Egyptian hieroglyphs in 1822 by means of the parallel scripts on the Rosetta Stone, pointed to the importance of a similar interpretation of the Maya writing. Stephens and Catherwood had drawn attention to the upright stone slabs or stelae, found at the centre of the sites or at the stairways, on which were carved glyphs. However, at the time no one knew whether the sites were ceremonial centres or urban conglomerations, or whether the glyphs represented religious ideas. The first attempt at glyph transcription began during the years 1864 to 1882, though evidently the key to understanding Mayan writing had been lost.

Although the Minoan script known as Linear B was deciphered during the 1950s, Maya glyphs remained the subject of considerable dispute in the following decade, when it was argued that they recorded the history of Mayan cities. This realisation made it possible to reconstruct the dynastic history of the rulers of Tikal from 292 until 869. The breakthrough in the decipherment of written language came after 1973, when it was realised that the glyphs represented a spoken language with a fixed word order, which made possible the identification of verbs and nouns, syntax and sound. In this way, Maya inscriptions, which had mystified scholars for so long, became texts revealing the history of the ruling groups in particular states. A lost history was recovered from the stone, clay, jade, bone, or shell on which it had been recorded. The rediscovery of the language further emphasised the cultural coherence of the Maya world over a period of a thousand years.

During the Pre-Classic period (1500 BC to AD 200), the Maya peoples developed agriculture and built villages. The swamp beds and river banks of the lowland forests provided fertile material for high-yield products, such as maize, cacao, and cotton. The Hondo, Usumacinta, and Grijalva Rivers provided access to the sea by canoe. Farming settlements existed at Tikal, which would become the great Classical-era site in the Petén, by AD 600, its principal temples constructed between AD 300 and 800. A greater social stratification took place during the

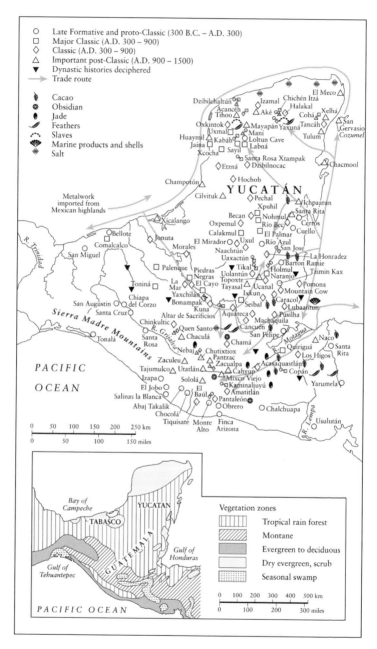

○   Late Formative and proto-Classic (300 B.C. – A.D. 300)
□   Major Classic (A.D. 300 – 900)
◇   Classic (A.D. 300 – 900)
△   Important post-Classic (A.D. 900 – 1500)
▼   Dynastic histories deciphered
⟶   Trade route

Cacao
Obsidian
Jade
Feathers
Slaves
Marine products and shells
Salt

YUCATÁN

Metalwork
imported from
Mexican highlands

R. Trinidad

Sierra Madre Mountains

PACIFIC

OCEAN

Bay of
Campeche   **YUCATAN**

TABASCO

Gulf of
Tehuantepec   Gulf of
Honduras

GUATEMALA

PACIFIC OCEAN

Vegetation zones

Tropical rain forest
Montane
Evergreen to deciduous
Dry evergreen, scrub
Seasonal swamp

0   100 200 300 400 500 km

0   100   200   300 miles

Map 2 Location of Maya Sites and Trade Routes.

Middle Pre-Classic period of 900–300 BC, when Olmec influences were at their height. In due course, the traditional extended family, village, shaman, and patriarch supported the emergence of kingship, an institution which had earlier cultural precedents in Mesoamerica. The sharper division of wealth sustained a kingly office and a nobiliar caste, related to the king in varying degrees of intimacy. The king, who in religious terms symbolised the Tree of Life, contained the power required for communion with the other reality of the gods and supra-human entities.

The Classic Maya period covered the years 250 to 900, subdivided into three categories: Early, 250–600; Late, 600–800; Terminal, 800–900. Since no manuscripts survived from that era, the stelae became the principal historical sources. The deciphered date of the earliest stelae was AD 199. From at least early Classical times, a thriving network of long-distance trade connected the Maya lowlands with the Guatemalan highlands and south-eastern Mexico. Central Mexican cults and architectural styles appeared in Maya cities, such as the cult of Tlaloc, for instance, in Tikal. The Maya and central Mexican calendars had remarkable similarities.

Yaxchilán (on the Chiapas bank of the Usumacinta River) and Uxmal (below Yucatán's Puuc hills) both flourished in the eighth and ninth centuries. Yaxchilán flourished through the period 320 to 790, according to the stone-carved hieroglyphic texts recording the history of its lords, but declined over the years 790–810. Uxmal reached its peak period between 850 and 925, only to be abandoned shortly thereafter. This centre contained large buildings with expertly crafted decorations. The Puuc sites represented an extension of Late Classic styles of the period 700–900. The recorded dynastic history of Palenque, located in the Chiapas rainforest, began in 431. The city reached its maximum influence under Pacal the Great (615–683), Chan-Bahlum II (684–702), and Kan-Xul who reigned sometime between 702 and 721, but the power of the Palenque kings finally petered out by the end of the eighth century. Written history and pyramid and temple construction, asserted dynastic legitimacy in the deep reaches of Maya history and cosmology. The tablets on which Chan-Bahlum wrote his detailed discussion of kingship came to light again in 1841, when Stephens and Catherwood published their *Incidents of Travel in Central America, Chiapas, and Yucatán*, though they were unable to decipher the glyphs they encountered.

Plate 6 Maya pyramid at Uxmal (author's photo). Uxmal,
founded at the end of the tenth century in the Puuc hills of
Yucatán, south of Mérida, consists of six principal groups
of buildings, of which the great pyramid is the highest
construction. Names have been given to several buildings – the
Governor's Palace, the House of Turtles, and so on. The Uxmal
style is distinct from that of Chichén Itzá and lacks its central
Mexican features. The site reached its peak period between
AD 850 and 925.

Pacal's tomb was not discovered inside the Temple of Inscriptions until 1949.

As in the case of the Olmecs, the rituals of the Maya were designed to harness the sacred energies. Blood-letting stood at the centre of these religious rites. Along with limited human sacrifice, it accompanied the dying and burial of kings. In this way, the shaman-king, whether by small drops of blood or by greater flows from the tongue or penis, gained a vision into the other reality of the sacred energies beyond the material and human universe, and sought communion with the divinities and ancestors. Razor-sharp blades of obsidian cut clean wounds for these ritual purposes.

Exaltation of dynastic kingship, combined with ritual propitiation of the gods, did not save the Maya from the collapse of urban life and high civilisation after the eighth century. From Palenque to Copán, as kingship collapsed, the great monuments were abandoned in favour of a reversion to peasant life on forest strips. By 910, no more temple-pyramids appear to have been constructed in the southern lowlands. The failure of the city-states ruled by dynasties of kings led to the general abandonment of literacy by the political elite as the principal means of understanding the cosmos. Maya civilisation, however, did not come to an end, but rekindled in the north on the plains of Yucatán from the ninth century onwards.

TEOTIHUACAN

The predominant historical influence in central Mexico was Teotihuacan, an urban and religious centre which at its height contained a population of over 100,000 inhabitants, sustained by the Valley of Mexico's agricultural system. Teotihuacan, which flourished for eight centuries from c. 150 BC to between AD 650 and AD 750, greatly influenced the subsequent Nahua civilisations of the Toltecs and Aztecs. The site, about 50 km to the east of Mexico City, covered some 2,000 ha. Only a small area has so far been excavated. Some twenty pyramids are now believed to have existed. Teotihuacan was a functioning city and not, as previously supposed, simply a ceremonial site. The so-called Pyramids of the Sun and Moon and the Temple of Quetzalcóatl were linked by a long causeway running north to south. By c. 500, Teotihuacan had become the metropolitan and religious centre of

Mesoamerica, the model for the more modest Toltec capital, Tollán (Tula, 65 km north of Mexico City), and subsequently the Aztec Tenochtitlán. Unlike Monte Albán, Teotihuacan was constructed on a grid plan. Most of the city's inhabitants lived in some 2,000 compounds divided into a multiplicity of apartments. Workshops demonstrate the commercial nature of the settlement, alongside its religious purpose.

The name, Teotihuacan, was an Aztec attribution meaning Place of the Gods. We do not, in fact, know the original name of the city, its chronological history or the names of its rulers, or even the language spoken there. Nahuatl seems only to have been spoken in the city after 500. No written texts or glyphs associated with them, as there were in the case of the Mayas or Zapotecs, have so far appeared. In fact, the only writing encountered to date has been in the so-called Oaxaca barrio for resident Zapotec diplomats or merchants. As a result, we have little knowledge of the type of government which functioned in Teotihuacan. There does not seem to have been an official dynastic cult as there was among the Mayas, which has suggested to some archaeologists that the city might have been ruled by an oligarchy.

Teotihuacan was the first major state in central Mexico. From the first century AD, population (up to 90,000) concentrated in the city rather than the surrounding countryside. For most of the Teotihuacan era, no other great population concentration existed in the Valley of Mexico. The city exercised tight control over the Mexican Basin and probably held sway over contiguous territories outside the Valley. It had direct contact with the Gulf lowlands, but probably did not exercise either political control or a commercial monopoly over them. So far we lack sufficient evidence to explain the population concentration in the city, though the reason may be the impetus of a great religious myth. At Teotihuacan, a major religious theme was water and the life associated with it. When excavated in 1917–20, the Citadel revealed a pyramid of the feathered serpent, which Manuel Gamio, then Director of Anthropology, identified as Quetzalcóatl, and the Rain God, Tlaloc, alternating in six tiers at either side of the pyramid steps. The cult of the feathered serpent effectively originated in Teotihuacan, where the symbols of the god proliferated in stone and in murals.

The cult of Quetzalcóatl (Plumed Serpent), the most pervading cult in Mesoamerica, may have arisen from the notion of a deity associated

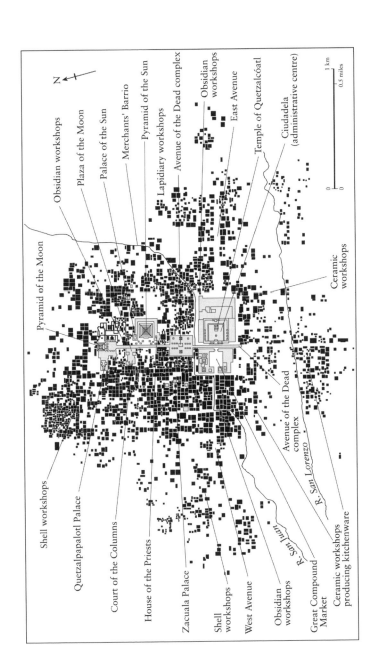

Map 3 Plan of the city of Teotihuacán.
The sixth largest city in the world in 500 AD, Teotihuacán covered a considerably larger area than Monte Albán and dominated Mesoamerica. Built on a grid-iron pattern, the city covered 20 km².

with the cultivation of maize, the staple crop. When the seed was planted in the darkness of earth, the struggle between the lords of darkness and the celestial twins began. The growth of the plant forced the lords of darkness to recognise the annual cycle and return it to the light of day. In this sense, earth became a fertile womb, and creation triumphed over death. The maize god, portrayed in the Maya city of Copán as a beautiful youth, provided food for the human race. A clear interrelationship existed between cosmology and the mythical world, on the one hand, and the natural world and human experience in society, on the other hand. Out of this confluence Quetzalcóatl emerged.

The Plumed Serpent represented the union of heavenly and earthly powers, the symbol of fertility and regeneration, the duality of spirit and matter. In mythological terms, Quetzalcóatl had been miraculously conceived during the Age of the Fourth Sun (the fourth cosmic age) by Chimalman without sexual contact with any male. According to one version, she had swallowed a precious stone and thereby conceived a son.

After considerable material prosperity and peace, when the city was at the height of its influence, an internal crisis seems to have brought its downfall. The explanation still remains unclear. The system of government and political leadership may have broken down and the state-supported ritual been under attack. At some stage, the principal temples, formerly topped with elaborate decoration, and many houses in the central area were destroyed by fire. In the early eighth century, Teotihuacan ceased to be a major urban unit. Its abandonment left decaying, wind-swept ruins for the following twelve hundred years. One modern visitor to the site, then in process of reclamation, was D.H. Lawrence, who had arrived in Mexico for the first time in March 1923. Lawrence considered Teotihuacan to be a more impressive site than the ruins of Ancient Rome or Pompeii, and wrote in his novel, *The Plumed Serpent* (1926), that Quetzalcóatl was more alive than the Hispanic churches in Mexico. Gamio, who had brought to life this vanished universe, became the model for Don Ramón in the novel, the revolutionary leader who wants to replace Christianity with a rebirth of the ancient religion and thereby bring Quetzalcóatl back into ordinary people's lives.

THE NORTH

Sedentary life began in Durango around 500 BC, in response to population growth. By around AD 500, the Chachihuites culture had developed around the site of Alta Vista in the centre-south of the present-day state. By AD 200–300, the north-central zone of the present-day Republic, from the Bajío as far as Durango, Zacatecas, and San Luis Potosí, was already inhabited by sedentary groups linked to the cultures further south. From the sixth to the ninth centuries, the Chalchihuites culture flourished in the Valleys of San Antonio and Colorado in western Zacatecas. Irrigation and an extended commerce accounted for the long duration of these sites. Hundreds of Precolumbian mining sites have been discovered across this region dating from AD 500 to 900. These discoveries suggest the mining was not a colonial innovation but a significant element in economic life there. A broad commercial network developed, which linked the cultures in Durango and Zacatecas, at mid-point to areas as far north as New Mexico and southwards to the Valley of Mexico, and accounted for their importance as trade emporia. Teotihuacan exercised an enormous influence on them. Turquoise, serpentine and copper, in demand in the great city, came from New Mexico by way of this route. Local mines provided further commodities. In such a way the pre-Columbian Turquoise and Copper Roads through the north anticipated the future Silver Road of the Spanish colonial era.

The Chalchihuites culture reached its climax at La Quemada in southern Zacatecas from AD 500–800, when construction of the civil and religious buildings took place on a commanding hill top at the edge of a series of hills. The Hall of Columns, the Pyramid and the Ball Game Court all dated from this period of maximum influence. Adams and Macleod point to the development of copper metallurgy in western and north-western Mexico around AD 800, which suggests that technological advances continued. By 1200–1300, these regions were producing alloys with tin and silver.

The collapse of Teotihuacan in the mid-eighth century may have cut this zone off from the centre and left it exposed to the nomadic tribes generically known as the Chichimecas. The rise of the Toltec culture at Tollán (Tula) during the tenth century pointed to a partial reoccupation

Plate 7   La Quemada in profile, from the approach road
(author's photograph, August 1999).

of these areas, until its collapse in the twelfth century. After the twelfth
century, Chichimecas of different sorts dominated the territory north
of the Río Lerma, which not even the Aztecs managed to penetrate.

THE TIME OF TROUBLES, 750–950

During the eighth century, the main political units which had taken centuries to construct declined, collapsed or were overthrown. Monte Albán
declined during the period of instability from AD 600–900 throughout
Mesoamerica. Although its public buildings fell into ruin, the city itself
was never abandoned. The explanation for this decline may lie in the
competition for resources between the city and the villages of the valley
floor. Rapid population growth in the valley would have led to land disputes and possibly to conflict with the city's requirements. Food shortages in the frequent dry years, when the expected rainfall failed, would
have pressed heavily on the administrative institutions of the city.
Furthermore, the decline of Teotihuacan around AD 700–750 removed a
rival centre of power, against which the Zapotecs had sought to preserve
their independence and identity. Population no longer required such

concentration in the Valley of Oaxaca. Authority became dispersed through a number of smaller centres in the subsequent period.

In central Mexico, itinerant armed bands roved the countryside. A number of lesser, more peripheral states rose in significance, such as El Tajín (Veracruz), Cacaxtla (Tlaxcala), and Xochicalco in the present-day state of Morelos. Xochicalco flourished between 600 and 900 as a wartime state situated in a strong, defensible position, although it would ultimately be brought down by violence. The prominence of the cult of the Plumed Serpent was evident there at its principal pyramid, and there was also a ball-court.

The explanations for the collapse of the great Classic Maya centres of the southern lowlands during the ninth century continue to be disputed. A combination of factors probably accounted for the abandonment of the urban centres. Military rivalries and internal conflicts between kings and nobles may provide the main cause. During the same period, repeated fighting between rival city-states worsened the impact of population growth on delicate and complex agricultural systems. Outside pressures and internal conflict would have undermined the effectiveness of central government, necessary for the coordination of effort in the struggle with the forest environment. The collapse of Teotihuacan may also have affected conditions in the Maya lands by loosening control over border territories between the principal cultural zones. Semi-civilised groups such as the Maya-speaking Chontal in the southern Gulf zone of present-day Tabasco established control of the trade routes in this period.

THE TOLTECS

Tula was located in an environment harsher than that of Teotihuacan and neither very prosperous nor extensive in its area of control. Migration from northern areas of Mexico probably accounted for the increase of population in this area even before the decline of Teotihuacan and the arrival of Nahua speakers. During the Toltec period (800–1170), trade with the north-west continued at least in the first centuries. The Quetzalcóatl myth became elaborated in political terms and formed part of the power struggle within the city of Tollán. In the history of Tollán, Quetzalcóatl became confused with the human figure, Ce Acatl Topiltzin, either the founder of the city or its last ruler (or both), to whom the name Quetzalcóatl was given. In the former version, Ce Acatl, said to have been born in Tepoztlán (Morelos) around 940, arrived in Tollán in 968, but was expelled in 987. The father of the human Quetzalcóatl was a semi-god, the Cloud-Serpent, Mixcóatl, who had first established Toltec power. The twinning of man and god became a characteristic feature of Toltec and Aztec religion and politics. Tollán adopted the myths of Teotihuacan as part of its own legitimisation, and the Quetzalcóatl cult reached its peak. The internal political struggle, which might have involved the challenge by the secular warrior caste to proponents of priestly rule, resulted in the overthrow of the cult of Quetzalcóatl, interpreted metaphorically as the flight of the god into exile.

The victory went to the warrior caste, symbolised in the triumph of the Lord of Life and Death, Tezcatlipoca, its patron. The predominance of Tezcatlipoca led to the prevalence of human sacrifice in Mesoamerican religion, which rose to a climax during the Aztec period. According to the myth, Tezcatlipoca was the source of Quetzalcóatl's destruction: he had brought him the goddess of prostitution, Xochiquetzal, with whom he had intercourse, thereby subjecting himself to the punishment of death by fire. The god's heart, however, rose through the flames and ascended into the heavens to become the morning star or the planet Venus. Quetzalcóatl, however, remained a creator, and before his rising into the heavens, he had first to descend into hell. This he did in the company of his double or twin, the dog, Xólotl, in order to obtain from the Lord of the Underworld the bones of those who had died during the fourth cosmic age. With these, he would create the new race of mankind for the Age of the Fifth Sun, which in historical terms corresponded to the age of the Nahua peoples. Quetzalcóatl, then, was the Mesoamerican deity most associated with humanity and, from the Nahua perspective, with human history. Enrique Florescano argues that the various divine forms associated with the god merged in the century 900–1000, as one personality. During the Toltec period, the maize god became transformed into Quetzalcóatl.

The Chichimecas destroyed Tollán, dangerously exposed to the nomad frontier, around 1170. The myths of Quetzalcóatl and Tezcatlipoca were the means through which this historical event was subsequently interpreted. The struggle between the gods symbolised the conflict between Topiltzin and his enemy, Huemac, both of whom were identified with the gods themselves. The struggle also took place in the other great cities of the epoch, Culhuacan and Cholula. The expulsion of Quetzalcóatl from Tollán led, according to historical tradition, to the merging of Toltec and Maya influences in the civilisation of Chichén Itzá, where the cult flourished anew. Cholula had been specifically founded by Quetzalcóatl, and the greatest of its temples was dedicated to him in his attribute as Ehécatl, the Lord of the Winds.

THE POST-CLASSIC MAYA

The so-called Toltec-Maya phase (c. 950–1250) at Chichén Itzá followed the collapse of the Classic cultures of Uxmal, Palenque, Bonampak, Tikal, and Copán and led to a period of Yucatecan predominance in Mesoamerica during the eleventh century for the first time. The precise nature of the relationship with central Mexico, particularly Tula, remains unclear. It now seems that Tula may have been dependent on Chichén Itzá, rather than the reverse. The cult of Quetzalcóatl, known in Chichén Itzá as Kukulcan, was celebrated at the highest pyramid, where the setting sun at the equinox cast its shadow across the body of a serpent aligned with the northern steps and joined the sculpted heads at their base.

The topographical context of savannah Yucatán radically differed from the forest cultures of earlier periods, and made for greater religious and commercial contact with outside cultures. No cultural frontier existed between the forest Maya and the new states which arose in the savannah zones. In Yucatán, water came from underground wells, known as *cenotes*, into which sacrificial virgins would be thrown at times of difficulty in order to propitiate the gods. Differing historical circumstances complemented geographical conditions. The tenth-century cultures of the Yucatán savannah were the product of the time of troubles. The political failures of the earlier cultures encouraged renewed attempts to define the basis of social organisation and rulership. The predominance of Chichén Itzá, which was clearly not simply a city-state like those of the Classic period but the core of an imperial system, rested on a structure of alliances, which anticipated the Aztec style of expansion during the fifteenth century. The city initially arose from the era of troubles, though its chronology is still imprecise, since the rulers, in contrast to their predecessors in the forest sites, did not use

Plate 8 Maya-Toltec pyramid at Chichén Itzá.
The Spaniards called this pyramid 'El Castillo'. It was the
Temple of Kukulcan (Quetzalcóatl) located in the ceremonial
precinct. Chichén Itzá, south-east of Mérida, was a Late Classic
site with strong Toltec influences in styles and religious practice,
though originally founded by the Itzá in the early sixth century.
It was reoccupied in 987. Maya-Toltec influences are also evident
in the so-called Temple of the Warriors. A skull platform
(*tzompantil*) stood next to the ball-court. The city flourished
into the thirteenth century but finally collapsed in 1441.

stelae and hieroglyphs to record their history. Partly for this reason we
do not know how long it took the rulers of Chichén Itzá to establish
their supremacy over northern Yucatán, let alone elsewhere. The
Temple of the Warriors, which may have commemorated their victory,
appears to have been constructed between AD 850 and 950.

Vase-paintings and frescoes portrayed battle scenes, court life, and
rituals in several of the Maya cities. Successful warfare, flourishing
commerce, and a sophisticated nobility characterised the new imperial
city. The nobles seem to have shared greater authority with their kings
than in the forest Maya states. The origin and identity of these ruling
groups, however, remain largely unexplained.

A type of confederacy, dominated by the Cocom family, appears to
have ruled the last of the great Maya states of the Post-Classic period,

Mayapan, in the period 1250–1450. This city copied the architectural structures of Chichén Itzá, but was walled for defence like Tulum, the eastern coastal city. Although a series of small states, soon to face an Aztec threat from the west, characterised the peninsula during the fourteenth and fifteenth centuries, Maya culture still remained a unity.

THE ZAPOTECS AND MIXTECS OF THE POST-CLASSIC ERA

Lesser centres emerged in Oaxaca after the decline of Monte Albán, such as Lambityeco, situated 2 km west of present-day Tlacolula in the eastern sector of the valley, during the phase known as Monte Albán IV (700–1000). Other sites, such as Zaachila, Mitla, and Cuilapan, arose in the period between 600 and 900. The earliest settlement at Mitla, situated at the edge of a river, had been around BC 1200, and expanded rapidly until the Monte Albán II period around the first century AD. Mitla, a nucleated urban centre with important religious and civic buildings and a suburban residential area, was supported by a surrounding agricultural hinterland. Like Yagul, Mitla rose to prominence in the Monte Albán V era (1000–1500). Most of these smaller towns grew from earlier sites, which even antedated Monte Albán and were already ceremonial sites during the Monte Albán II and IIa periods. They flourished, however, as the great mountain urban centre declined. Temples were constructed on pyramid mounds, and a ruling caste, concerned to establish marriage networks, took up residence in stone buildings.

At the same time, other centres emerged across the mountainous west of Oaxaca, in the Mixteca Alta. There were generally smaller chieftainships known as *cacicazgos*. Like the valley sites, they had long antecedents. They were small states ruled by a local nobility, with inherited land titles which often directly controlled agricultural labour. The Mixteca was a region of high-altitude valleys with a cooler climate than the Valley of Oaxaca. Although there had been nothing in the Mixteca comparable in size or cultural development to San José Mogote, still less Monte Albán, Yucuita in the Valley of Nochixtlán became the principal urban centre surrounded by many lesser settlements. Contemporaneous with Monte Albán in the Classic period, Yucuñudahui, in the same valley, also represented a large, stratified centre with public buildings for religious and civic functions, dependent on an integrated rural hinterland. The Mixteca lay across the route between the Valleys of Mexico and Oaxaca, and for that reason Mixtec culture felt the influence of both the Toltecs and the Zapotecs, while retaining its own characteristic features and languages. The Mixtec chieftainships were sustained by effective mobilisation of agricultural manpower in terraced maize farming as well as in warfare.

During the period of dislocation, urban centres arose in the Mixteca Baja, a series of semi-tropical valleys at 1000–2000 m above sea level on the Puebla–Oaxaca border, between 600 and 900. Mixtec centres re-emerged after the fall of Tula with a more developed style from the 1160s. Mixtec kings, furthermore, reinforced their legitimacy by reference to Toltec descent. In this they anticipated later Aztec practice in the Valley of Mexico. The first Mixtec rulership established possibly modelled on Tula was the state of Tilantongo in the Mixteca Alta from 1030. A warlike mountain people, the Mixtecs expanded towards the Pacific Coast. The ruler of Tilantongo took advantage of the existence of a Mixtec colony in that area to establish a further state at Tututepec, subordinating the Chatinos and the southern Zapotecs living between Miahuatlán and the coast. This became the focus of Mixtec dominance of the western coastal zone of Oaxaca, known as the Mixteca de la Costa, until the Spanish conquest in 1522 destroyed it with a mixture of trickery and brutality. On the death of the last Mixtec ruler of Tututepec, Hernán Cortés bestowed the lordship on his second-in-command, Pedro de Alvarado.

The wealthy Kingdom of Yanhuitlán arose in the Post-Classic era on the basis of subject peasant communities in the Nochixtlán Valley. On the eve of the Spanish conquest, it was the largest of the Nochixtlán cacicazgos, and controlled up to twenty-five other settlements including Yucuita which had been the Classic era centre. Mixtec lords gave protection to peasant-workers who paid tribute to them, laboured or acted as soldiers. The Mixtec *caciques* consolidated their position through marriage alliances, including with the Valley of Oaxaca Zapotecs. This process gradually introduced a Mixtec element into the Valley, including a colony in the Cuilapan district. By about 1280, Cuilapan appears to have had Mixtec-speakers among its local population, reinforced by further immigrants in the later fifteenth and early sixteenth centuries.

The principal political centre in the Valley of Oaxaca in the Monte Albán V era was the Kingdom of Zaachila. Available evidence suggests that the ruling dynasty began in the late fourteenth or early fifteenth century, the first ruler dying in 1415. Under the fourth ruler, Cosijoeza (1487–1529), the Zaachila Zapotecs expanded their commerce and political authority into the Isthmus, with the result that Tehuantepec became a second Zapotec capital. Pushing the Huaves on to the narrow coastal strips around the Tehuantepec lagoons, the Zapotecs gained control of the salt deposits of the Isthmus, already a valuable commodity in their regional trade. Cosijoeza's son, Cosijopii (b. 1502), became the ruler of Tehuantepec at the age of sixteen until his death in 1563, although subordinated to Spanish hegemony after 1521 and Christianised in 1527.

CENTRAL MEXICO

Even before the fall of Tollán, large groups of population moved into the Valley of Mexico from the north, possibly as a result of climate change, and formed multi-ethnic communities there. These laid the basis for a new city-state system there: by the end of the thirteenth century some fifty small urban units, semi-autonomous and with their own religious centres, occupied defined territories in the valley. They remained intact throughout the period of Aztec (or, more correctly, Mexica) hegemony and survived the Spanish Conquest into the colonial era. Each of these states derived their legitimacy from the claim of Toltec descent.

During the century after 1250 military rivalry among the city states intensified, although the tribal state system still remained fragile. The Mexica continued to be just a minor group until around 1400, dependent on more powerful states.

Accelerated urbanisation within the Valley of Mexico required a complex agricultural system to sustain its population, especially since none of the principal cities was self-sufficient. Irrigation and terraced, mountainside agriculture intensified production. Marshes at the lake edge were drained to form 'floating gardens' (*chinampas*) for extra food cultivation. No wheeled vehicles had been developed and there were no draught animals in Mesoamerica. Accordingly, the rising population of central Mexico faced enormous ecological and technological obstacles to the increase in food supply. The *chinampas* formed part (but only part) of the solution. Fertilised by lake-bed mud, they provided year-round crops. At the height of Tenochtitlán's power around 1500, they covered an estimated 9,000 hectares, even allowing for pools and canals. Since the *chinampas* required a constant water level, dikes, aqueducts, and canals were built, particularly from the second quarter of the fifteenth century, for regulation and to separate fresh from saline waters. Tenochtitlán's location differentiated the nature of the city from any other established in Mesoamerica, especially since the absence of an immediate agricultural hinterland required subordination of surrounding cities and their rural perimeters.

By the late fifteenth century, at least a dozen such cities had populations of over 10,000, with that of the Aztec capital, Tenochtitlán, passing 150,000 inhabitants at that time. Other cities, such as Texcoco, ruled by the poet-kings, Nezahualcóyotl (1418–72) and Nezahualpilli (1472–1515), stood along the lake shore. Texcoco played a central role in helping the Spanish to bring down Tenochtitlán in 1520–21. If we could successfully piece together the fifteenth-century political history of Mesoamerica, we would understand more clearly how the Spanish conquest was possible. The shifting alliances and rivalries between indigenous states would provide the focus.

THE AZTECS

Most Valley states adopted the form of rule by a *tlatoani* or principal noble figure. The Aztecs adopted this system from the 1370s, though only after 1426 did it fall under the control of one dynasty. Divine right and hereditary rule provided the political means for the imperial expansion of the period from 1428 to 1519. The Aztec rulers legitimised their position by identifying with the Toltecs, whose successors they claimed to be through intermarriage with the dynasty of Culhuacan.

According to Aztec tradition, Xólotl, this time as the evening star, guided these Nahua people from their ancestral home in Aztlán on their journey into the promised land of central Mexico. The Aztecs effectively replaced Quetzalcóatl with Huitzilopochtli, the God of War, whose specific disciples they were. In this way, they departed significantly from the tradition of Tollán, which they expropriated as their own, although they retained Tlaloc in the Teotihuacán tradition. The Aztecs imposed Huitzilopochtli among the creator gods wherever their supremacy was recognised.

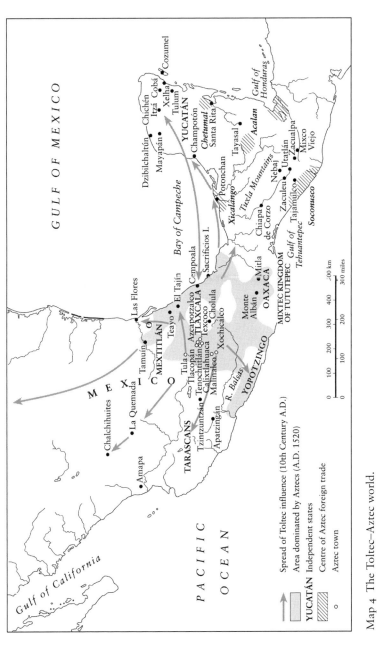

Map 4 The Toltec–Aztec world.

An educated elite of 'nobles' (*pipiltin*) stood at the apex of Aztec society: they performed the function of guardians of knowledge and historical tradition. The *pipiltin* were educated in a special nobles school in the oral and pictorial tradition of glyph writing on agave paper, skin, or canvas. Among the Aztecs and other Mesoamerican peoples the oral tradition remained a powerful means of transmitting knowledge. A professional group of merchants (*pochtecas*), some of them trading well beyond the frontiers of Aztec-subordinated territory, formed a highly significant part of the Tenochtitlán hegemony. Merchants of lesser but allied states, such as Texcoco, were not permitted to trade beyond the limits of the empire.

Tenochtitlán, founded in 1325, arose from an island in the western part of Lake Texcoco, the largest of a five-lake system in the Valley of Mexico. The two northern lakes were in the driest part of the valley, while the two southern lakes, Xochimilco and Chalco, lay in the most fertile agricultural zones. Three long causeways, dating from the reign of Itzcóatl (1427–40), linked the city to the mainland at Tepeyac in the north, Tlacopan (Tacuba) in the west, and Iztapalapa and Coyoacán in the south. Since evaporation exceeded precipitation, the lakes were gradually shrinking. As a result, the northern lakes became inaccessible by canoe during the dry season from October to May. Tenochtitlán, with an estimated peak population of 200,000 inhabitants, considerably larger than Seville at that time, constantly depended on effective transportation, by canoe or by foot. The system of professional porterage by carriers known as *tlamemes*, a hereditary group probably from among the landless, had diminished effectiveness, due to the human limitations of weight and distance. The lakes, location, however, gave Tenochtitlán the advantage of being able to transfer to canoe transportation at the lakesides. Important urban concentrations arose or relocated to the edge of the lakes as part of this system of supply. Canoes proved to be forty times more effective than individual humans with respect not to their speed but to the amount that could be carried.

Aztec political practice relied on dominant influence rather than territorial control. It was an hegemonic rather than a territorial empire, and as such experienced repeated revolts from subordinated states attempting to repudiate their tribute obligations. The Aztecs had no costly, standing army, with the result that their 'empire' did not depend on political centralisation but on the subordination of a series of client states under their local *tlatoani*, which maintained Aztec supremacy within their own spheres. The Aztec empire generally left in place existing political structures, allowing the army to concentrate on priority expansion. Warfare, in any case, followed the agricultural cycle, that is, it took place after the harvest in October and before the rainy season began at the end of May. The authorities in Tenochtitlán received tribute from all client states. Failure to pay tribute would become a pretext for war. In such a way, the Aztecs were able to dominate extensive spheres of territory across central and southern Mesoamerica.

Aztec campaigns within the Valley of Mexico began in the last quarter of the fourteenth century, with incursions into present-day Puebla and Morelos. During the first half of the fifteenth century, Aztec penetration reached Tula to the north, Tulancingo in the northeast, and into present-day Guerrero to the south-west. Under Itzcóatl, the Aztecs first became a military power. Moctezuma I (1440–69) made the Aztec presence felt in Puebla, on the Gulf Coast, and in northern Oaxaca. Axayácatl (1469–81) pushed it westwards and north-eastwards to Tuxpan on the Gulf Coast.

Early Aztec power rested on the Triple Alliance of Tenochtitlán, Tlatelolco, and Tlacopan, formed in 1428, a league of tribute-receiving cities which dominated the Valley of Mexico and the territory beyond. Subordinated territories were required to cover the cost of transporting tribute commodities to Tenochtitlán. If a town resisted subordination, the rate of tribute would be doubled. The two basic components of Tenochtitlán's authority were receipt of tribute and the introduction of Aztec gods into the local pantheon. Tribute, in effect, supplemented the intricate market system inherited from Mesoamerica's long past. Aztec expansion followed the trade routes, and, in turn, the *pochtecas* followed the soldiers. It represented the pursuit of economic sustenance by political and military means. Expansion through the agricultural zones led to the economic subordination of less powerful city-states within the Valley of Mexico, which were reduced from manufacturing centres for their own rural hinterlands to primary suppliers for the great metropolis. Craft skills, furthermore, were increasingly centralised in Tenochtitlán, in part because of the greater input of raw materials from the *pochtecas*' long-distance trades. Tenochtitlán became the dominant manufacturing and distribution centre.

Plate 9 Diego Rivera's mural, *La gran Tenochtitlan* (1945).
Rivera (1886–1957), and other muralists of his generation such as José Clemente Orozco (1883–1949) and David Alfaro Siqueiros (1896–1974), aligned with the revolutionary left and rejected the colonial era and capitalism. They projected a radical, Mexican nationalism, and reshaped history accordingly. Rivera, in particular, asserted a continuity between Aztec culture and post-revolutionary Mexico. This section forms part of a series of large murals covering the stairways of the National Palace in Mexico City. Rivera also portrayed the Conquest in a mural in the Palace de Cortés in Cuernavaca (Morelos).

Political considerations complemented Aztec economic expansion. Essentially, the tactic was to avoid outright war through intimidation or low-intensity conflict. Logistics inhibited full-scale mobilisation on a regular basis. Instead, the Aztecs preferred demonstrations of power, designed to induce voluntary submission. In such a way, they asserted their supremacy. In cases where this failed or when subordinated states rebelled, the Aztecs launched 'flower wars', designed to keep rivals on the defensive, as a warning. From the mid-fifteenth century, these wars appear to have involved the taking of large numbers of warrior-captives for sacrifice to the principal gods of Tenochtitlán. The interpretation of these wars is still disputed. However, the later Aztec state developed an increasing preoccupation with human sacrifice on a large scale as a means of propitiating the gods upon whose goodwill the agricultural cycle depended. What this implied in political terms remains unclear, but it does suggest a deepening consciousness of the precarious basis of the empire on the part of its rulers and, perhaps, at the same time an appreciation that the material base of the whole structure remained subject to unpredictable meteorological fluctuations. Mesoamerican cosmology, inherited by the Aztecs, was designed to ward off disasters brought upon human beings from extra-terrestrial sources.

The weak link in the Aztec system continued to be the unpacified powers, particularly Tlaxcala, which had allied with Huejotzingo and Cholula, and the Tarascan kingdom of Michoacán to the north-west of the central valleys. The latter held out under the Cazonci kings from the late fifteenth century through the first two decades of the sixteenth. The authorities in Tenochtitlán kept garrison troops on the exposed frontiers and in areas of uncertain loyalty, such as the Valley of Oaxaca. Although some colonists did reside in subordinated areas, the Aztec kings never undermined local rulers if they remained loyal. A series of buffer states was maintained on the imperial peripheries, which paid tribute in arms and military service.

The Aztecs never fully controlled Oaxaca, in spite of many campaigns into the region and the consequent imposition of tribute. The process of subordination from the Valley of Mexico would be completed by the Spanish conquerors after 1520. The principal Aztec aim was control of the direct route from the Valley of Mexico through the Mixteca and Valley of Oaxaca to the Isthmus and thence to Soconusco, one of the main cacao-producing zones. Moctezuma I campaigned across central Puebla, into Veracruz, and thence the Mixteca, taking the Mixtec stronghold of Coixtlahuaca in 1478. Ahuitzotl (1486–1502) pushed towards the Valley of Oaxaca and thence to the Isthmus in 1496–98. The rise of Aztec power, and its terrible implications, led to a series of extemporary alliances between Mixtec and Zapotec rulers designed to keep the Mexica out altogether or at least to mitigate their impact. At first the alliance between Zaachila and the Mixtec chieftains kept the Aztecs out of the valley, obliging them to use the Pacific coastal route to Soconusco. Zapotec watchtowers in the Cañada of Cuicatlán surveyed the movements of both the Aztecs and the Mixtecs. Mixtec garrisons in Huitzo and near Cuilapan reinforced the position of Zaachila, while at the same time posing a potential threat to it. The alliance managed to push back the first Aztec thrust at Huitzo in 1486 but the Zapotecs, unable to keep them out definitively, reached a uni-lateral accord with them to allow military passage across the Valley. Near the centre of the valley, the Aztecs established a settlement at Huaxyacac, which in the Spanish colonial period would form the base for the Hispanic town of Antequera de Oaxaca.

In 1495, the Zapotec–Mixtec alliance was renewed to counter a further major threat from the Valley of Mexico. This renewed Aztec attempt to control the routes to the Isthmus resulted in their failure after a long siege to take the Zapotec fortress of Guiengola, situated 1000 m above the Tehuantepec River. Guiengola, however, was more than just a fortress: it possibly originated as a religious and administrative centre in the Post-Classic era with two pyramids and eighty other structures in imitation of Monte Albán, and was always associated with the royal dynasty of Zaachila. Again, however, the Zapotecs reached a compro-mise with the Aztecs in accordance with which Cosijoeza married Ahuitzotl's daughter in 1496, associating the two rulerships in a mar-riage alliance. Aztec southern expansion and imposition of tributary status continued, nevertheless, under Moctezuma II (1502–20). The Aztec presence in Oaxaca resulted in the appearance of Nahua settle-ments and place-names alongside those of the Zapotecs, Mixtecs, and other ethnic groups in the region. On the eve of the Spanish incursion, then, Oaxaca represented a complex multi-ethnicity of peoples at dif-ferent stages of development.

Alliances within Meso-America made the Spanish conquest possible. It could not have been achieved without them. Rival American states sought to take advantage of the presence of the small, well-armed band of Castilian fighting men in pursuit of their own traditional objectives. In this way, the alliance system constructed by the rulers of Tenochtitlán was subverted and ultimately disintegrated, leaving the Aztec metropolis politically and materially isolated. Smallpox, brought by the Europeans, had already struck the city for the first time in 1520, even before the establishment of colonial rule. The Spanish brought with them the three gifts of medieval Europe: the cultural traditions of their age, the Christian religion, and epidemic disease. All three would have a drastic effect on the Americans. The Europeans justified their intervention on the grounds of superior morality and civilisation. They focussed on the Aztec abuse of the traditionally limited religious practice of human sacrifice as their principal justification for destroying the cosmological system developed in Mesoamerica over thousands of years. Spanish atrocities, however, were striking. Hernán Cortés's massacre in Cholula in the autumn of 1519 left an estimated 3,000 dead, and Pedro de Alvarado's massacre of worshippers in Tenochtitlán in the summer of 1520 initiated full-scale warfare between the Aztecs and the invaders. In the fifteenth and sixteenth centuries, Mesoamerica experienced two catastrophes from which it took centuries to recover (if it ever did): the hegemony of the Aztecs and the European incursion.

The Aztecs of the present day

The Aztec attempt to concentrate power and wealth in Tenochtitlán through a network of subordination foreshadowed the centralisation of authority in its successor city by the Spanish viceroys. In many respects, the focus on Mexico City during the colonial era had more far-reaching consequences than in the less technologically advanced Aztec era. Although certain continuities ran through the Aztec and colonial periods, their political cultures remained widely different. Even so, Octavio Paz in *El laberinto de la soledad* (The Labyrinth of Solitude), (Mexico 1950) and *Posdata* (1970) argued for a continuity between the Aztec *tlatoani*, the Spanish colonial viceroy, and the modern Mexican President – in effect, the successor of Moctezuma. The pyramid structure of power characterised the authoritarianism of all three systems. The pre-Columbian cultures mythologised the human predicament and the structures of religious and political power. For Paz, modern Mexican political culture has mythologised the Presidency and the monopoly party, the PRI, in a similar manner. For that reason, he concluded that Mexican emancipation, begun with the War of Independence in 1810, has remained incomplete. In the judgement of Paz, Mexico, instead of concluding that the overthrow of Spanish colonial rule completed the process of emancipation, should finish the process altogether by emancipating itself from the Aztecs, whose power he considered to be a usurpation. This view contradicted the basic tenet of twentieth-century Mexican nationalism, that the modern republic is the successor state to the Aztec Empire.

The rejection of the Hispanic tradition led to the glorification of the Aztecs by the dominant party in the aftermath of the Mexican Revolution of 1910. Reaffirming the centralism of previous systems (in spite of the ostensibly federal nature of the Constitution of 1917), the Mexico City-based regime increasingly portrayed the Aztecs as the culmination of the pre-Columbian experience. The Aztec Empire became in this way the forerunner and anticipation of the contemporary Mexican state. This perspective has received its maximum expression in the National Museum of Anthropology and History, the state-financed collection of antiquities operated under the auspices of the INAH, established in 1939 at the end of a period of intense radical nationalism. The National Museum incorporates exhibits from all the pre-Columbian cultures, which are organised in a chronological order that reaches its apogee with Tenochtitlán. Paz has described the building not as a museum but as a mirror. With the subsequent excavation of the Aztec Great Temple, after the demolition of colonial buildings located on the north-east corner of the central square between the National Palace (constructed on the site of Moctezuma's Palace) and the Cathedral, the world of Tenochtitlán began once more to rise up from the earth and assume a fresh life under the auspices of the PRI-dominated state.

The National Museum, so magnificent in its contemporary form and location that it could be described as a wonder of the modern world, has a history of its own. Early colonial fascination with the pre-Columbian cultures led ultimately to American assertion of the authenticity of the historical experience of the continent in opposition to European ignorance and deprecation. From the later eighteenth century, defence, if not propagation, of the idea of the pre-Columbian epoch as the 'Ancient

History' of the Americas, on a par with Egypt, Mesopotamia, and the Aegean, became associated with American patriotism. A 'neo-Aztecism' filtered through the Mexican Enlightenment into the ideology of the Independence movement. In 1813, for instance, Mexican separatists named their new country the 'Republic of Anáhuac', the Aztec name for their core territory. Independence in 1821 brought the name 'The Mexican Empire' for the new state, even though the Mexica had controlled only a section of the vast territory and faced rebellions from those they subordinated and opposition from those who remained free of them. In 1825, the Mexican government legislated for the establishment of a National Museum within which pre-Columbian antiquities could be assembled for exhibit. In such a way, the creators of the new Mexican nation began the appropriation of the pre-Hispanic past as part of their process of 'forging the nation', in both senses of the term.

3

The European incursion, 1519–1620

Aztec hegemony in central and southern Mexico during the fifteenth century had already accustomed the population to subordination, assimilation, and strategies of survival. The modern dominance of the central valley originated in the pre-Columbian era. Indian opponents of the Aztecs allied with the Spanish conquerors, in order to bring down Tenochtitlán. For a time, they made use of the fortuitous arrival of the strangers in the internal power struggle within Mesoamerica. In such a way, they believed they could restore a world freed of Aztec domination. Spanish objectives and methods, however, ensured that the real beneficiaries of the destruction of Tenochtitlán were not the Indians themselves, and that the post-Conquest era would not be one of revindication but one of deepening servitude. The Spaniards intended to put themselves into the position held by the Aztec elite and rule their conquered territory in a substantially similar manner, though on a different religious basis. They could not themselves foresee the dramatic impact of the Conquest over the subsequent decades.

The Spanish who arrived in Mesoamerica had passed through two previous conquests beforehand, those of the Muslim Kingdom of Granada and the Caribbean islands, both from 1492. Although scarcely knowing what they would find on the American mainland, they arrived with a set of assumptions about conquered territories of different religions. They came at an epoch of proven Castilian military prowess demonstrated in the Italian campaigns of the 'Gran Capitán' Gonzalo Fernández de Córdoba against the French during the 1490s and 1500s. At the same time, Castile and Aragon, its associated eastern kingdom, were deeply involved in the power struggles of the Mediterranean and western-European orbit. The Italian involvement ensured the mingling of Renaissance intellectual and artistic influences with the Mozarabic inheritance of Iberia. From 1516, these would be complemented by Flemish influences, as a result of the Habsburg dynastic connection.

THE IMPACT OF THE FALL OF TENOCHTITLÁN

The destruction of Aztec hegemony resulted from a series of intensely fought campaigns involving the use of Spanish artillery and naval power. The details are well known from the *ex post facto* narrative of Bernal Díaz del Castillo (1495–c. 1583), the title of whose work, *The True History of the Conquest of New Spain* (written in Guatemala by 1568 but first published in 1632), should immediately arouse the reader's suspicions, especially since the author began it when he was seventy years old. Recent studies by Ross Hassig and Hugh Thomas have emphasised the complex political and military situation into which the Extremaduran Hernán Cortés (1485–1547) inserted his rough Spanish band of some 600 men. Cortés, who had arrived in Hispaniola in 1504, succeeded in establishing a position on mainland America after the failure of two previous Spanish attempts in 1517 and 1518. Cortés took advantage of political rivalries within the Mesoamerican world. The American political groupings, once they had recovered from the shock of the initial encounter, equally intended to exploit the presence of a well-armed band of foreigners in order to advance their own causes. The appearance of a non-American alien group within central Mexico suddenly exposed the precarious nature of Tenochtitlán's hegemony and invited opposition to rally against it. The Spanish presence tilted the political balance against Tenochtitlán for the first time since the late fourteenth century.

Cortés represented more the turn of the century *condottiere* than the royal servant. He behaved more as an independent actor on a newly encountered political stage. By style he might well have been an exponent of the exercise of power and the methods of rulership outlined in Niccolò Machiavelli's *The Prince* (1513). Even so, Cortés did not establish an independent, conquered territory under his own personal rule, but remained loyal to the Habsburg Emperor Charles V, who was also King of Spain (1516–56) and its associated European territories. Cortés's

Plate 10 Hernán Cortés and La Malinche (detail).
This formed part of the *Lienzo de Tlaxcala*, painted on linen or coarse cotton cloth, around 1550. Like codices or painted, folded manuscripts, the *lienzos* recorded events in images and delineated boundaries. The codices dated perhaps from around 500 BC at Monte Albán and from 300 AD in the Maya area. Only three pre-Hispanic codices have survived. The detail above is from one of three originals of the *Lienzo de Tlaxcala* supposedly sent with a Tlaxcalan deputation to the Emperor Charles V around 1550. None of these originals is known to have survived. In the *lienzo*, Tlaxcala emphasised its usefulness to Cortés in the destruction of Tenochtitlán's power.

enemies in Spain portrayed him as an ambitious and untrustworthy adventurer and sought to ruin him. The Five Letters written by Cortés to Charles V sought to explain his position and prove his loyalty. In 1528–30, he travelled in person to Spain and was received at court in Toledo by the Emperor, who, nevertheless, appointed him Marqués del Valle de Oaxaca rather than Governor of New Spain. Cortés finally returned to Spain in 1540, five years after the successful establishment of the viceregal office in Mexico City, the former Tenochtitlán. He died in misery and poverty, ruined by litigation, in 1547.

Plate 11 Titian's *Portrait of the Emperor Charles V* (1548).
Titian (1488/90–1576) painted this seated portrait (now in
the Bayerische Staatsgemäldesammlung, Munich) of an
exhausted and disillusioned monarch on a visit to
Augsburg. This is a more realistic image than the 'Portrait
of Charles V on Horseback', painted in the same year (now
in the Prado Museum, Madrid). Titian first met the
emperor in Parma in 1529 and then in Bologna in 1533, and
again in Augsburg in 1550. Titian's portrait of 'Philip II in
Armour' (1551) is also in the Prado.

Cortés was particularly fortunate in securing the assistance of the captive Indian woman, Malintzin, who spoke Náhuatl, the language of the Aztec Empire. Malintzin, known to the Spanish at the time as Doña Marina, became the symbolic Mexican figure of 'La Malinche', who, guilty by association, handed over the Indian world to the European conquerors. She played a crucial part in Cortés's dealings with Moctezuma. From this name comes the discredited action, 'malinchismo', which signifies the betrayal of Mexican integrity and values to foreigners. 'Malinchismo' (or 'entreguismo' [handing-over]) arouses intense opposition, and 'La Malinche' represents one of the fundamental symbols in Mexican popular culture.

Cortés's strategic advantage was to have arrived in Tenochtitlán at a time of political weakness within the governing regime. At the same time, rival and subordinated powers were seething with resentment at Aztec rule and searching for an opportunity to hit back. Although the city's hegemony had ostensibly reached its peak, Moctezuma's tactical errors provided the opportunity for a swift strike against the authority of the head of the Aztec state. The reduction of Tenochtitlán still required huge effort, since Aztec methods of warfare presented the Spanish with great difficulties. In the first place, the 7-m wide causeways linking the city to the lake shores could be cut for defensive purposes. This and their narrowness neutralised the Spanish advantage of horse-borne warfare; the Aztecs demonstrated great skill in archery; their stone-pointed spear blades cut better than Spanish steel; darts flung from throwers could penetrate armour and kill; stones from slings also inflicted damage on the Spaniards. As a result of sustained resistance, although undermined by the early impact of European diseases, the Spanish and their allies had to conquer the Aztec capital street by street.

It seems probable that the Spanish destruction of Tenochtitlán occurred at a time when the population of the Valley of Mexico had already reached the limit of the capacity of the land to sustain it. With a higher population density than in metropolitan Spain, the Valley possibly contained around 1.5 million inhabitants out of a total estimated population of 25 million for the entire zone between San Luis Potosí and the Isthmus of Tehuantepec. Pre-Hispanic cultures had exploited the land intensively, usually with some method of irrigation, in order to maximise cereal production. This delicate ecological system was overthrown at the Conquest, since Hispanic culture was in large part based on livestock raising, an occupation entirely unknown in pre-Columbian America. The Spanish had not come to Mexico for the humanitarian purpose of sustaining the cereal system of a completely alien population, but in general terms to reproduce in Mesoamerica the pattern of life they were accustomed to in Castile. From their perspective, the indigenous population would fulfil a subordinate role in this process, as the physical instruments of sustaining Hispanic dominance.

Although the fall of Tenochtitlán was a swift and definitive occurrence, this did not imply that the Spanish domination of Mesoamerica (still less its northern extremities) would be a rapid process. Indian cooperation in the destruction of Aztec power ensured that Cortés and his band would have to take allied interests into consideration as well. The manner in which Indian states had brought the Spanish into their own political conflicts meant that the latter would have to learn to survive in a vast territory that remained overwhelmingly native American in character. Mesoamerica did not become automatically Hispanic in the immediate aftermath of the collapse of Moctezuma II's empire. Indigenous population decline ultimately assisted the process of Hispanisation, but the Europeans still remained a minority.

The Spaniards had initially expected to replace the Aztec ruling class and administer their Mesoamerican territories in much the same way. Given their small numbers, they could hardly impose a completely different order on the indigenous population. Early Hispanic colonialism, then, consisted of little more than piecemeal measures designed to accustom the American inhabitants to an alien ruling caste and accommodate the conquerors and first settlers to the new environment. The unsuspected consequence of the European incursion was the American population catastrophe. Sherburne Cook and Woodrow Borah estimated in 1971 that a 95 per cent fall in population took place, leaving an indigenous population of around 1.2 million by the 1620s. Although the first of the great sixteenth-century epidemics struck in 1520–21 before the Spanish and their Indian allies had taken Tenochtitlán, the indigenous population began its rapid decline first during the epidemic of 1545–48, since by 1548 the level had fallen to 6.3 million, and again in 1576–81. Between 1568 and 1591, the population fell from 2.64 million to 1.37 million. Accordingly, the original Spanish intentions disintegrated. The magnitude of this population collapse still needs to be digested, whatever are the preferred figures. There have been few parallels in the history of humanity. By the end of the six-teenth century, new realities, derived from both the colonial system and the territorial advance of Hispanic power northwards well beyond the frontiers of the Aztec empire, fundamentally altered the nature of Mesoamerica.

THE IMPOSITION OF CHRISTIANITY

The Spanish intention was that the Catholic religion would become the exclusive religion of the newly acquired dominions. Spanish Catholicism had passed through a thorough reform during the reign of Isabella (1479–1504), which reaffirmed medieval doctrines but tight-ened up discipline and practice. State authority, reinforced through the newly introduced Holy Office of the Inquisition after 1480, comple-mented the power of the Church. A strengthened episcopate, closely tied to the crown, took the leadership of the reformed Church along with the mendicant orders.

In New Spain, Indian responses to the appearance of Christianity dif-fered widely and according to generation. The Franciscan friars began their work in the mid-1520s, and it was continued by the first Bishop of Mexico, Fray Juan de Zumárraga, during the 1530s. Among the first twelve – the 'apostles', as they were called – was Fray Toribio de Motolinía, who took part in the foundation of the Hispanic city of Puebla de los Angeles in 1531 adjacent to Cholula, the once great city and holy place of Quetzalcóatl. Motolinía founded the convent of Atlixco just south of the city, and became guardian of the Tlaxcala convent. He learned Náhuatl, and sought to disseminate knowledge of the pre-Columbian peoples through his *Historia de los indios de la Nueva España*, published in 1541.

The historical interpretation of the impact of Christianity upon the American population has varied greatly over the past decades since the publication of Robert Ricard's *La conquête spirituelle du Mexique* in 1933. The emphasis has shifted from the friars themselves and the notion of a conquering Church to a subtle process of acculturation. The American population adjusted to those aspects of Christianity which accorded with their own vision of the cosmos and they accommodated to the political reality of the superimposition of a new religious power backed by the authority of the colonial state. For the incoming Christian clergy, the indigenous religions, clearly different from the Islam they had encountered in Granada and North Africa, represented 'paganism'. At the same time, they did constitute in the eyes of the friars a form of authentic religious experience, which had been captured by demonic powers. The process of evangelisation did not result in a full-scale onslaught on indigenous belief but in an attempt to shift this into Christian directions. The Hispanic cults of the saints and the many and varied forms of the Virgin Mary, the product of an even earlier grafting-on of 'pagan' cults in Europe and a conscious reaction to the exclusive monotheism of Islam, lent themselves to early adaptation to existing indigenous devotions. This, however, meant more than just a changing of the names, since by incorporation into the world of Roman Catholicism, indigenous America became gradually subsumed into a universal, religious power, the focus of which lay far away from the American world and had emerged from a completely different historical tradition.

Serge Gruzinski's *La conquête de l'imaginaire* (1988) portrayed the slow adaptation to Christianity as a process of 'occidentalisation'. Through the gradual supersession of the oral and pictorial tradition of the indigenous cultures and the adoption of Roman script, the incorporation of the American world into the culture of western Europe was given effect. For several decades the continuation of the pictographic tradition alongside the Hispanic literary culture made possible the communication of American religious beliefs and history to Europeans struggling with their own incomprehension. At the same time, European friars and scholars introduced the concepts of the late Renaissance into the American world. In such a way, the European inheritance of Ancient Greece and Rome entered the Americas, portrayed as the 'New World', along with the Christianity that had supplanted them in the 'Old World'. The Europeans rejected indigenous cyclical concepts of time and replaced them with the idea of history as a linear process.

The surviving American population learned not only to adapt to the new spiritual order but also to take it over when it suited their own purpose. Christian terms of reference became transformed in Indian hands and turned against the brutality and usurpation of the Conquerors. In this they received support from the religious orders, who were engaged in the contradictory enterprise of undermining the foundations of indigenous religious belief while at the same time seeking to protect Indians from physical and material abuse by their own compatriots. Accordingly, the deep ambiguities of Spanish colonialism – exploitation versus evangelisation – appeared in the very first years. Local Indian communities beyond the immediate reach of Christian authorities concealed and preserved what they could of their own inheritance, in order to keep faith with the ancestors and maintain the symbols which had always given meaning to the universe.

The conversion of small numbers produced factions allied to Spanish rule, a situation which divided Indian communities and complicated responses to the imposition of colonial rule. The objective of Christian conversion was to strengthen alternative sources of legitimacy to the traditional authority of the *tlatoani*, who presided over the basic American social organisation, the *altepetl*. Charles Gibson, writing in 1952, pointed to the strong resistance in Tlaxcala to an early introduction of Christianity. Outside central Mexico, resistance to Christianity was sometimes violent. The Oaxaca sierra continued to resist into the 1550s, the Otomís north of the Valley of Mexico until the late 1560s, and parts of Michoacán into the 1580s.

The Maya, who had been the first to encounter the Europeans on their coasts in 1517, struggled in the decades from the 1520s to the 1560s to understand what had happened and how to respond. As in the case of other American groups with long cultural and religious traditions, they sought to preserve what they could of their traditional way of life. Frequent antagonism with the Spanish interlopers culminated in the Maya resistance movement of 1546–47. Failure to expel the *dzules* (white intruders), however, resulted in a further attempt at evangelisation by the friars. The Franciscans conducted in 1562 over a six-month period a series of detailed investigations of Maya religious practice, and were shocked to discover the extent to which traditional beliefs had been preserved. Accordingly, under the leadership of Fray Diego de Landa, who had arrived in New Spain in the late 1540s, they set out to make a terrible example of those they identified as back-sliders without regard to proper legal formalities. Large numbers of people were subjected to torture and as many of the Maya sacred books as could be found were burned to the great affliction of those who witnessed the scene. The burning of the Maya manuscripts symbolised in the minds of the friars the destruction of the demons worshipped in secret by the Yucatecan communities. For the Maya, it represented the destruction of their own identity and of the perception of the cosmos which had taken centuries to elaborate.

The Christianisation of New Spain proved to be an incomplete process. Residual pre-Columbian beliefs and practices survived within the new religion and coloured its expression. Although a keen proponent of the preservation of indigenous cultural traditions, the Franciscan Fray Bernardino de Sahagún suspected that the emerging cult of the Virgin of Guadalupe, which originated with the vision at Tepeyac in 1531, represented a post-Conquest adaptation of the Aztec cult of Tonantzin, the moon goddess, who on occasions doubled with Coatlicue, the mother goddess who had given birth to Huitzilopochtli, conceived without prior intercourse. Sahagún's *Historia general de las cosas de la Nueva España*, written between 1558 and 1569, attempted to provide his fellow friars with an encyclopedia of knowledge concerning the indigenous cultures, which he had come to admire. Considerable attention was given to the cult of Quetzalcóatl. Sahagún, however, stressed the mortality of the god and his historic role in the city of Tula. In such a way, he sought to avoid any inference that Quetzalcóatl might have represented an earlier Christian evangelisation of America, in the form perhaps of the Apostle Thomas.

A series of three ecclesiastical councils met during the course of the sixteenth century to give shape to the newly established Church in New Spain. In 1565, the Second Mexican Ecclesiastical Council met to discuss how to give effect to the decisions of the Council of Trent (1546–63). Catholic Christianity, redefined and reasserted at the Counter-Reformation, was a synthesis which required total assent from its believers. Its main thrust was not on individual belief or conscience but on collective observation of clerically ordained precepts and practices. This combination of authoritarianism and collectivism became transferred to the Indies during the course of the sixteenth century. On principle, Catholicism remained absolutely exclusive of any other religious belief: in practice, it enabled incorporation of whatever did not conflict outright with it. Providing the authority of the teaching Church was upheld on principle, many variants appeared in practice. Accordingly, when the Church sought to remove Aztec religious practice, it encouraged, on the other hand, the communal expression of religion by indigenous communities. As a result, indigenous life gradually became expressed in Christianised terms, whether in the festivals celebrated or the name of the village or town itself. If anything, the impact of

Christianity remained ambivalent – entrenched but superficial, permitting but not permitting, both at the same time.

One centrally important Indian institution encapsulated popular resistance to official Christian impositions and the determination to conserve traditional practices: this was the religious confraternity (*cofradía*) in the Indian villages. These lay-brotherhoods existed at the Hispanic level as well, but there they functioned within an officially sanctioned context and on the Spanish model. Indian confraternities, however, frequently expressed a disguised resistance to Hispanic religious norms. Their emergence, considerably after the impact of the Conquest had been felt, reflected yet another indigenous strategy of survival at the base levels of colonial society. The Indian confraternity emerged at a time of moral crisis for the indigenous population, confronted as it was by the appalling spectre of population collapse and the constant threat of Hispanic encroachment and subversion. This religious defence sought to consolidate what had been left of Indian beliefs and weld them into a form sufficiently coherent to recreate local identity within the changed circumstances of the later sixteenth century. Significantly, the Indian confraternity was not usually under the control of parish priests. Furthermore, the appropriate indigenous language, rather than Spanish, was the usual medium of business. As they developed during the seventeenth century, these corporations bolstered the identity of the vulnerable indigenous community.

The early evangelisation of New Spain remained the work of the regular orders, principally the Franciscans, Dominicans, and Augustinians. By 1560, these three orders controlled some 160 houses for their members, who totalled just over 800. The first members of the Society of Jesus, founded by St Ignatius Loyola, arrived in New Spain during the autumn of 1572. In the following year, the principal Jesuit institution in Mexico City, the College of SS Peter and Paul, was founded. The Holy Office of the Inquisition had been established in New Spain in the previous year, though it exercised no jurisdiction over Indians. The arrival of the Inquisition a half a century after the Conquest did not imply any laxity beforehand, since the full faculties of inquisition had been exercised by the bishops themselves. The Inquisition henceforth controlled the printed word, not just in Spanish but in the indigenous languages as well. The numbers of Catholic clergy continued to grow: from 1,500 in 1580 to 3,000 by 1650.

However, their attention was drawn increasingly away from the Indians through internal struggles between the regular and secular clergy, within and between the religious orders, and between the clergy and the laity.

Indian institutions and Spanish encomenderos

The Indian nobility in Mexico, as in Peru, had sought to benefit from the overthrow of the imperial hierarchy. The *caciques*, as the Spanish called them, specifically received royal protection from 1557, providing they were Christians. They became preferred instruments of colonial control, although in New Spain their influence diminished as their internal base of power collapsed with Indian population decline. In contrast to Peru, the indigenous nobility did not survive as a political group into the eighteenth century. The *tlatoani* tradition of the Aztec world became transposed onto whoever exercised effective power in the locality and could act as the protector of a vulnerable populace in relation to higher authorities.

The private-enterprise nature of the Conquest meant that the conquerors' interests preceded definition of those of the Spanish state. In the first instance, a working compromise operated between the two in accordance with which the private interests exercised authority over the conquered population until the crown was able to establish organs of its own. Under this compromise, the *encomienda* system was transposed from the Spanish Caribbean islands to New Spain after 1521. Each *encomendero* or specifically commissioned individual received in trust groups of Indians, and undertook to Christianise them in return for their labour services and tribute payments. No land transfer was legally involved. The *encomendero* did not own the Indians as his property, and only the crown remained their 'lord'. This system was imposed by the Conquerors above the existing Indian nobility's structure of dependency. They regarded the *encomiendas* as their just rewards of conquest. In effect, the conquerors gained a large, unpaid labour force which considerably assisted their process of capital accumulation.

When the crown tried to prohibit *encomiendas* in 1523, Cortés objected, arguing disingenuously that they liberated the Indians from subjection to their native rulers. The crown soon faced the problem of *encomendero* desire to become a hereditary nobility in the new Spanish territory. Even so, it managed to secure jurisdiction over Tenochtitlán in 1526, prohibited *encomiendas* of more than 300 Indians in 1528, and finally in 1529 ejected Cortés from the Valley of Mexico, offering him instead the distant 'Marquesado del Valle' in Oaxaca with a few other scattered locations.

The *encomenderos* remained a powerful challenge to royal supremacy throughout the 1530s. Around thirty *encomiendas* remained in the Valley of Mexico, controlling some 180,000 tributaries. The *encomenderos* were strong enough to block the implementation of the New Laws of 1542–43, which tried to restrict the *encomiendas* to one lifetime and to prevent royal officials from holding them. However, the principle was established in the 1550s that the crown determined the tribute quotas. The central issues by then were inheritance of the *encomiendas* and the nature of Indian labour in the colony, especially after the opening of the silver mines in the previous decade. *Encomendero* power, already weakened by population losses and royal policies, was definitively broken by the crushing of the settlers' conspiracy of 1566 and crown assumption of the richest *encomienda* in the Valley of Mexico at Cuautitlán.

The struggle for control of the labour force and the moral campaign to ensure fair treatment of the conquered population illustrated the strengths and weaknesses of the early modern Spanish state. Royal authority had been steadily increasing since the formation of the second *audiencia* in 1529 and the establishment of the viceroyalty in 1535. The *audiencia* was a typically Castilian institution which had arisen as the principal expression of royal judicial authority during the High Middle Ages. Isabella had used the *audiencias* of Castile to curb the autonomous power of the nobility. The viceregal office was a typically Aragonese institution, which acted as the substitute of the king in the outlying territories of the medieval Aragonese-Catalan Empire in the Mediterranean. In the Indies, beginning with New Spain, it was put, however, to a specifically Castilian purpose: the enforcement of royal authority and the closer integration of the royal dominions. In reality, the Viceroy of New Spain became a power in his own right, with a court, to which the principal figures of the day would gravitate, and with an immense range of patronage. New Spain's first viceroy, Antonio de Mendoza (1535–50), came from one of the most distinguished noble families of Castile with a long tradition of military and diplomatic service. The *audiencia*, accordingly, was designed in part to limit the viceroy's actions and to call him to account when necessary. In such a way, a distant royal authority sought to maintain its position by pitting the governing bodies against one another. Both the *audiencia* and viceroy remained directly responsible to the Council of the Indies in Spain. The *audiencia*, as the principal court of law in the Indies, acted as the intermediary between local magistrates and the Council of the Indies, the high court of appeal. By contrast to the peninsular *audiencias*, those of America also exercised executive and legislative faculties, and acted as the viceroy's consultative committee when required to do so. The *audiencia* could also exercise the supreme office as the *audiencia gobernadora*, if a viceroy died in office or before a replacement had been appointed.

Between the 1530s and the 1550s the establishment of town and district officials (*corregidores* and *alcaldes mayores*), who exercised royal judicial and administrative authority, progressively increased alongside the pattern of privately controlled *encomiendas*. The crown had used the *corregidores* in Castile as a means of ensuring a controlling position in the towns, traditionally royal allies in the perennial conflicts with the territorial nobility. In the Indies, these officials increasingly tended to curb the original political autonomy of the municipal councils. Imperial Spain's financial difficulties ensured that the crown needed to control direct access to revenue. This situation helps to explain why the metropolitan government remained determined to prevent municipal councils in America from claiming the privilege of either forming representative bodies such as the Cortes of the Spanish kingdoms or sending representatives to the Castilian Cortes.

By the 1570s, there were 15 *corregimientos* in the Valley of Mexico alone, and a combined total of some 155 *corregidores* and *alcaldes mayores* in New Spain as a whole. An example of these political processes at work may be seen in the Mixteca, for instance. Cortés divided the Mixteca, which had submitted without a struggle on receipt of the news of the fall of Tenochtitlán, into some twenty *encomiendas* in 1524. Although the number of Mixtec *cacicazgos* was only around twelve on the eve of the Conquest, they roughly corresponded to them. Even so the crown began the process of constraining the *encomiendas* after 1531 by establishing the *corregimiento* of Teposcolula and in 1550 the *alcaldía mayor* of Yanhuitlán, still a district of major political and economic importance. This process of establishing royal officials at the district level also had the effect of reducing the local importance of the Indian nobility. After the collapse of the two Mixteca rebellions of 1528–31 and 1548, the viceregal government consolidated Hispanic authority and the *caciques* increasingly adopted Spanish ways, including the Catholic religion. As elsewhere in New Spain, the decisive factor proved to be population decline. The population of the Mixteca Alta fell from 350,000 to 35,000 between 1520 and 1620, and did not begin to recover until after 1675.

Hispanic presence and Indian survival

Demographic collapse undermined the possibility of sustained and widespread resistance to the Europeans in the zones most affected. However, once they had recovered from the immediate shock of the European incursion, Indian cultures in what had become New Spain demonstrated a remarkable survival capacity. Acculturation led to Indian litigation through the colonial courts. The Spanish established their centres of power right in the midst of Indian population concentrations, as in the cases of the Valleys of Mexico, Puebla, and Oaxaca. Mexico City, unlike the new Spanish foundation of Lima in Peru, rose from the ruins of Tenochtitlán, in contrast to the Inca capital, Cuzco, which became a provincial capital retaining much of its Indian character. In this respect Mexico has been a living city since its foundation in the early fourteenth century. For the fourteen years between the fall of Tenochtitlán and the arrival of the first viceroy, it became virtually a conquerors' city-state, incorporating a large Indian populace, loosely subordinate to the universal monarchy of Emperor Charles V.

Charles Gibson examined the adaptation of the people of Tlaxcala, allies of Cortés, to the phenomenon of Hispanic domination. Tlaxcala had been defeated, though it had not been conquered in the same way that Tenochtitlán had. Nevertheless Spanish colonial rule presented a completely new situation for the Tlaxcaltecans. Ultimately, a compromise would be worked out between the colonial authorities, who found their aspirations limited by realities, and the Tlaxcaltecans, who learned how to survive within the new structures. The Spanish had no unified vision of how their New Spain was to be organised, and the divisions between administrators, religious orders, *encomenderos*, and landowners provided openings for Indian exploitation. In Tlaxcala, as elsewhere, the contradictions within Spanish colonial practice were much in evidence. The first task of integrating Tlaxcalan society into the Hispanic world had been performed by the first Franciscans, who sought to protect the population from the disasters which had befallen the inhabitants of the Caribbean islands after the 1490s. Their objective, supported by the metropolitan and viceregal authorities, was the peaceful christianisation of the Tlaxcalans and their instruction in the Roman script and Hispanic literary techniques. Local Indians, however, had first to digest the implications of these innovations for their own culture, which had evolved over the previous centuries. They accepted what they could reconcile with it, as in the case of municipal institutions, or what promoted their own interests as a people. By and large, the Indian economy in the 1530s and 1540s continued to operate with considerable freedom in Tlaxcala, which did not become a principal area of Hispanic settlement. Indian social structure initially also remained intact. By the end of the sixteenth century, however, Tlaxcala's deepening colonial situation had become evident, emphasised all the more by Indian population decline. The viceregal authorities removed the province's autonomy and Spanish landowners or workshop operators exerted pressure on labour. The local nobility lost control of the workforce.

Gibson published in 1964 a much larger study of the impact of Hispanic rule on the Nahua peoples of the Valley of Mexico, which showed the complexity of Indian responses to the Spanish presence. The Valley had a higher population density than anywhere in Spain. The Spanish presence upset the equilibrium of resources, a situation which accelerated population changes already set in motion through the impact of European diseases. The basic factor was the depletion of agricultural land in the decades after the Conquest. Spanish colonialism developed in the Valley of Mexico in a radically deteriorating environment. Ultimately, the specific local circumstances determined the shape of inter-ethnic relations as the sixteenth century moved forward. Spanish pressure on an Indian society weakened by population loss concentrated on land, labour, and tribute-payment.

Castilian models of municipal organisation were introduced to the American world. The principal focus of indigenous life became the colonial *pueblo*, a term that conveys considerably more than the English 'village'. The Spaniards adopted this term as the translation of the

Náhuatl, *altepetl*, which signified a small lordship with subordinate settlements under its jurisdiction. In this way, the pre-Columbian *altepetl*
combined political institutions, presided over either by a hereditary lord
(*cacique*) or by a body of elders known as *principales*, with territorial
extent. The colonial pueblo, however, was not the simple continuation
of the *altepetl*, but a new and distinct institution on the European
model, designed for the congregation of dispersed indigenous settlements into a political unit for the purpose of evangelisation, government, and taxation. Colonial law recognised the pueblo as a corporate
landowner and colonial practice used it as the basis of tribute receipt.
In this way, the pueblo authorities, their positions guaranteed, were
closely bound into the colonial structure. Possession of land and the
establishment of Indian municipal institutions with which the Hispanic
population was forbidden to interfere provided the pueblo with the
means of subsistence and internal autonomy. Accordingly, the pre-
Columbian association of land, religion, and ethnic identity became
transposed onto the pueblo, known in colonial legal terms as the
república de indios. The Castilians sought to understand Indian structures of authority and territorial divisions in European terms, which did
not have accurate parallels. Accordingly, population centres under the
fifty or so indigenous nobles of the pre-Conquest Valley became head-
towns of districts or *cabeceras*, while lesser units were subordinated to
them as *sujetos*. The *cabecera–sujeto* relationship remained a constant,
though changing, feature of the colonial era.

During the course of the colonial era, Hispanic practices and modes
of thought gradually permeated Nahua culture. Initially, very few
Indians gave up their native speech. Wills, public documents, and confraternity ledgers continued to be written in Náhuatl by professional
native scribes throughout the colonial period. The Hispanic courts, furthermore, frequently employed interpreters in cases involving Indians.
Similar practices occurred with regard to civil, religious, and hacienda
authorities. James Lockhart published in 1992 an innovative study of
what Nahua linguistic changes revealed concerning the degree of
Hispanic penetration of the indigenous mind. In the Valley of Mexico,
Nahua adaptation to Hispanic literary techniques in the generation
after the Conquest led to the appearance of texts, particularly in the
period 1545–65, which provided an entry into the subject. Lockhart
found that in the early post-Conquest period from 1519 to the

mid-1540s, very little cultural readjustment took place, the result of minimal routine contact. Only small changes, such as the addition of Christian names at baptism, took place. However, significant linguistic changes took place during the following century with the adoption of Spanish nouns and the influence of Spanish semantics. Náhuatl pronunciation and syntax, however, remained unaffected, although the language was written in Roman script for the first time. Lockhart attributed these changes to contact through intermediaries and interpreters. From the mid-seventeenth century onwards, however, the incorporation of Spanish verbs, idioms, syntax, and sounds into Náhuatl spread rapidly through large-scale individual contact. This investigation demonstrated how indigenous frameworks of reference survived for more than a century after the initial Conquest, while at the same time the Nahua peoples adopted from the Spanish what they saw as useful for their own survival.

After the violence of the Conquest and the abuses perpetrated by the conquerors and *encomenderos*, the Spanish Church and Crown became deeply sensitive concerning the moral basis of Hispanic rule in the Americas. Las Casas's polemical attacks on these abuses led to the great debate in Valladolid (Spain) in 1550–51. In 1550, the Crown established the office of Indian General Procurator *(Procurador General de Indios)* within the *Audiencia*, in order to guarantee a proper hearing for Indian complaints against enslavement and coercive labour. Throughout his reign Philip II sought to maintain a high standard of administration throughout the empire, but the pressures of European warfare and the strain on the Spanish financial system made this difficult to achieve. Reports of corruption within the administration in New Spain led the king to appoint Archbishop Pedro Moya de Contreras, who was also Inquisitor General, as official Visitor General of the viceroyalty with full powers. Moya, who acted as interim viceroy in 1583–85, began a campaign to remove unreliable officials.

HISPANIC LAND ACQUISITION

The colonial courts generally defended the rights of peasant communities to at least subsistence landholdings and minimal local autonomy. Viceroy Luis de Velasco the Younger (1590–95) established the High Court of Indian Justice *(Juzgado General de los Indios)* in 1592. The relationship of Crown, colonial courts, and Indian communities formed a nexus which provided some amount of protection for Indian pueblos and their properties. The crown was able, at least in theory, to balance defence of Indian property rights and labour freedom against the interests of Hispanic landed-proprietors, and thereby limit elite power. The Spanish colonial state upheld its authority by asserting a mediating role between peasant communities and Hispanic land-owners. Accordingly, the two types of landownership and, often, ways of life, coexisted, sometimes uneasily, through the colonial era and into the nineteenth century.

Indian communities closed ranks in opposition to Spanish land usurpations, which threatened their economic viability and their cultural identity. The hacienda, an Hispanic private property and frequently diversified unit of production, became the predominant Spanish focus in the countryside by the end of the century. The term did not denote size. Indians from communities could work on hacienda lands as private individuals (*gañanes*) without becoming resident workers (*peones*) or losing their corporate identity. This practice had already appeared by the 1580s. It was symptomatic of the competition for labour between the Indian community and the private estate at a time of declining population. By the late colonial period, there were some 160 haciendas in the Valley of Mexico, though varying in size and importance.

Population decline accelerated Spanish acquisition of land. The emphasis of royal policy during the early seventeenth century moved away from defence of the Indian population and its right to landownership towards the legal recognition of Spanish private estates. The demographic collapse also undermined the material position of the Church, which received a 10 per cent tithe on agricultural production. This was the Church's principal revenue, although the Crown, as Royal Patron of the American Church by papal commission, took a portion of the tithe. The decade 1575–85, became the critical period in the aftermath of heavy Indian mortality in the epidemic of 1575. Even though Indians were exempt from the tithe on their own produce, their labour on Hispanic lands produced the wealth which was taxed by Church and state. From 1550 to 1574, tithe revenues in the dioceses of Mexico, Michoacán, and Guadalajara had doubled or trebled, but fell sharply thereafter. A considerable decline in agricultural wealth took place, especially in those three areas, from the mid-1570s.

The Spanish state in 1577 instructed the Viceroy of New Spain to gather information through the medium of the district official concerning all important aspects of his territory. Between 1578 and 1582 a series of reports known as *Relaciones* was drawn up, of which 168 remain, giving details of 415 pueblos. They revealed the Indian perception of the break with traditional customs caused by the Conquest and the despair at the extent of population loss. Indian respondents blamed the burdens of imposed labour and mine work, forced resettlement, poor diet, and the absence of the guidance given by the old gods. As in Peru, they associated the imposition of Christianity with the proliferation of human deaths. Traditional practices, though bereft of the priestly superstructure of pre-Columbian days, continued at the local level in Indian daily life, kept alive by travelling faith-healers (*curanderos*) who passed through a clandestine network largely unseen by the colonial authorities.

Territorial advance and repulse

The general absence of settled American communities across the north meant that northern society would be more fluid and more mobile than the Indian core zones of the centre and south. The north-centre and north was the Chichimeca frontier, the vast area controlled by free-ranging Indians whom the Aztecs had never pacified. This task fell to the Spanish. Viceroy Mendoza took an army of 500 Spaniards and 50,000 Indian allies into the present-day Guadalajara zone to crush opposition to the northward advance. The fiercely fought Mixton War (1541–42), in which Alvarado met his end, opened the northern frontier of New Spain. Its immediate consequence was the discovery of silver at Zacatecas and the foundation of the Hispanic city there in 1546. This new industrial centre became the starting point of the Royal Silver Highway across the Bajío, the north-central plateau, to Mexico City. Settlements and military posts known as *presidios* grew up along this route. The entire Zacatecas area, however, remained a war zone, since the highway continued to be subject to attack from the Zacateco Indians. For that reason the Spanish and their Indian allies from the central zones, began a concerted campaign to pacify the unsubdued Indians from 1560 to 1585, known as the War of the Chichimecas. By 1591, Velasco the Younger had established control over the silver zones northwards from Zacatecas. Long after the fall of Tenochtitlán, then, the struggle for the subjugation of the north was still being fought by the Spanish. In effect, the conquest of New Spain, portrayed from a centre zone perspective as a lightning phenomenon of the years 1519–21, took, in fact, a further seventy years.

From July 1540 until April 1542, an advance expedition under Francisco Vázquez de Coronado moved up the Río Grande Valley into what is now New Mexico. The Spanish did not encounter legendary cities but the hundred or so settlements of the Pueblo Indians, organised in ten loose groupings linguistically distinct and situated for the most part on the margins of the river's flood plain. They represented population concentrations in contrast to the itinerant peoples of the surrounding areas. The Pueblo Indians dressed in cotton clothing, cultivated maize and other basic crops, lived in solid, terraced dwellings, and produced ceramics. It appears that at the time of contact with the Spanish, they were experiencing a cultural flourishing through the period 1300–1600. The Spanish presence was not initially welcomed, due to the pressure on local food supplies, and considerable conflict ensued. The Spanish did not reappear until 1581–82, the first of five other expeditions which finished with the establishment of Spanish rule in 1598.

In the meantime, the Spanish attempted to consolidate their position in the north-east by the foundation of Monterrey in 1596. In effect, this represented the end of a process which had begun with the conquest of the Bajío during the 1540s. The subsequent development of the north, which had experienced a completely different history to that of the sedentary cultures of the pre-Hispanic centre and south, showed the emergence of two distinct New Spains. The traditional zones of the centre-south, upon which Hispanic culture was grafted, contrasted significantly with the 'new' territories of the north, in which the Hispanic implant would ultimately become the defining experience. Even so, the Spanish brought with them to the north colonies of Indians from the central zone for resettlement, such as the Tlaxcaltecans who became early settlers in Coahuila.

The Spanish never completed the conquest of the north and far north, in spite of the large territorial expanse claimed there by the crown. Effective Indian resistance held the Spanish advance or managed to reverse it with significant loss of life, influence, and territory. The geo-politics of the Hispanic frontier was a complicated and long-term process, which has still not been fully understood. Ultimately, inability to extend effective Spanish power throughout those vast regions, the habitat of Indian groups themselves under pressure, helped to explain the loss of the far north in the mid-nineteenth century. In many respects, the missing link in the historical interpretation of the northern territories has been the absence of written records on the part of the major player in the game, the so-called 'barbarian Indians'.

4

New Spain, 1620–1770: Spanish colonialism and American society

The Americas became part of the Atlantic world from the sixteenth century. Each territory had a specific relationship to its metropolis and to the world market. The importance of Spain's two principal colonial territories, New Spain and Peru, lay in their role as principal world producers of silver. This commodity was in short supply in early modern Europe, though demand was great, especially as the main medium of exchange in the Asiatic trade. For nearly four hundred years, until the collapse of world silver prices from the 1870s, Mexico, which surpassed Peru in capacity after the 1690s, placed large quantities of silver on the world market.

Spain's international position, however, deteriorated significantly after the 1640s. In many respects, the American territories were left to their own devices. Substantial colonial revenues remained within the American territories, allocated to the internal budget and to defence needs. In economic terms, the empire moved away from the Spanish metropolis during the course of the seventeenth century, especially after the 1620s, when the transatlantic trade declined. In spite of strong efforts to tap American resources, Spain's European position worsened. This situation, however, did not lead to increased political independence on the part of the American territories, since the political centre of the empire still remained in Spain and the incentive to separate was absent at that time.

SPAIN AND THE EMPIRE: MERCHANTS, FINANCIERS, AND MARKETS

Historians, especially those viewing Ibero-America from Europeanist perspectives, have focussed on the issue of how America fared during the European recession of the mid-seventeenth century. New Spain's economy appeared to be affected only after 1635–40, primarily for internal reasons, when it contracted until a gradual revival during the 1660s and a pulling out from recession after 1675. Spanish historians have identified the low point of Castile's fortunes in the period from the 1650s to the 1690s. Although Pierre Chaunu placed prime focus on the patterns of the Atlantic trade, later scholars have thrown light on the growth and behaviour of the internal market within the American territories, while internal routes of communication and distribution centres operated to supply colonial demand.

The picture emerges of a seventeenth-century New Spain with a rather ambiguous social structure, in which several leading figures, particularly the wholesalers, originated from lower social backgrounds. New Spain became a society in which the decisive element was not so much the landowner as such (who, of course, remained socially predominant) but the merchant-financier with accumulated capital, earned as a monopoly importer in the Atlantic trade, at his disposal. Traditional and modern practices coexisted among the merchant-financiers. Matrimony and personal ties continued to be the principal means of solidifying business interests. Nephews, other relatives, 'compadres', and friends formed broad networks of interest over a wide geographical area from the capital cities into the countryside and through the span of economic activities. They did not generally purchase landed estates themselves. Such large-scale activities required a close working arrangement with the colonial state.

The Consulado of Mexico, established in 1592, expressed mercantile power in New Spain. Throughout the following two centuries, this corporation, which also formed a court for the adjudication of commercial disputes, dominated New Spain's economic life. The relationship between its members, overwhelmingly peninsular merchants from the Basque provinces and Santander, and the *audiencia* and viceregal government remained intimate. The Consulado, the *audiencia* and the ecclesiastical hierarchy represented the bulwarks of Spanish colonialism. They enabled the colonial system to function during the long period of metropolitan weakness between the 1640s and the 1760s, although modified considerably in relation to Mexican realities. Based in Mexico City alongside the viceregal government and court, these institutions expressed the predominance of the capital within the political territory of New Spain. They provided in their different ways the linkages which held that vast (and expanding) territory together. During the seventeenth century the Crown continually pressed the Consulado for loans and donations towards the cost of maintaining Spain's European position. The ability of the Consulado to resist such pressures further demonstrated the weakness of the imperial state. In the absence of an effective fiscal bureaucracy, the Crown leased Mexico City's sales-tax collection to the Consulado as a tax-farm for a specific period throughout the latter part of the seventeenth and first part of the eighteenth centuries. This process of tax-farming continued throughout the period from 1602 until 1753.

The contraction of Spanish power emphasised the growing importance of the internal market and the inter-colonial trades. Unlike Brazil or Peru, Mexico spanned both the Atlantic and the Pacific worlds. In effect, the Philippines were colonised and evangelised from Mexico rather than directly from Spain itself. From the late 1560s until 1813, the annual Manila Galleon took Mexican silver from the fledgling port of Acapulco across the Pacific to Manila, entrepot of the China trade, in exchange for Chinese silks and porcelain brought from Canton. The metropolitan government sought to restrict cargoes and frequency on the grounds that the Asiatic trade diverted silver from the principal route which was to Europe. At the same time, the Crown in a series of laws issued from the 1590s to the 1630s tried to restrict, and then in 1631 and 1634 prohibit, trade between New Spain and Peru, with the particular intention of preventing Peruvian silver from passing into the Manila trade. Although not always possible to bring into full effect, the metropolitan objective continued to be that the overseas dependencies should trade directly with Spain (where permitted to do so) rather than with each other, and, still less, with the colonies of rival European states. The end result of the prohibition was that Mexico City merchants lost control of the Pacific trade, which fell under the control of contrabandists operating from the smaller ports of Guatemala and Nicaragua.

Practical commercial relations sometimes overcame policy restrictions. The principal case in point was the Mexico–Venezuela trade, which flourished in the century from the 1620s to the 1720s. The cacao trade passed through Maracaibo to Veracruz, superseding the previous route up the Pacific coast from Guayaquil after the legal restrictions of the 1630s. Venezuelan planters were able to exchange cacao, in great demand at the time as the principal popular drink before the development of coffee, for Mexican silver, and thereby broaden their own capacity to import manufactures, mostly from foreign sources. Such practices conflicted with the strict interpretation of the principles of empire. The metropolitan government, however, was too weak to stop them. The device it eventually adopted in 1728 was the chartered, monopoly company. The aim of the Caracas Company, controlled by Basque merchants from Guipúzcoa, was to divert the cacao trade away from New Spain and reorient it directly to the peninsula.

The mining sector

Although the mining industry continued to prosper during the 1620s and viceregal government revenue reached peak levels, an overall downturn had already begun in the long term. A depression set in during the period from 1630 to 1660. Even so, regional variations appeared within that pattern. The principal zone of production continued to be Zacatecas, which was passing through its peak period between 1615 and 1635, while Parral (Chihuahua), opened in 1631, reached its peak during the 1630s. The state of the mines rather than shortage of manpower explained the problems faced in the Zacatecas zone. Furthermore, New Spain's proportion of the transatlantic trade declined after the 1620s in relation to Peru's share, but Spain's Atlantic trade was in overall decline. Demand for Spanish products diminished as New Spain produced more at home. In the same period, the cost of defence rose within the Americas and the Philippines in view of the threat from the Dutch, French, and English, and the general insecurity of the seas. As a result, the viceregal administration retained an increasing proportion of silver revenue within New Spain itself. Contraband export of coined silver – New Spain's way of bypassing the colonial monopoly and gaining direct access to the international market – accounted for a significant share of Atlantic commerce. In 1660, the colonial authorities estimated that untaxed silver accounted for one-third more than registered shipments.

New Spain's rapid adaptation to the adverse conditions presented by heavy indigenous population loss accounted for the decline in demand for Spanish produce. By the 1620s, the Indian population had fallen as low as 1.2 million. The Hispanic hacienda superseded the Indian communities as principal food suppliers, and a variety of labour systems were adopted to compensate for the fall in population. By the mid-seventeenth century, the mining sector had already transferred to predominantly free, salaried labour rather than labour drafts from the villages, or indebted workers. Earlier use of negro slavery did not have lasting significance in New Spain. Zacatecas, located considerably north of the main centres of indigenous settlement, owed its predominance to its ability to adapt to the new conditions in terms of capital and labour. The overall significance of silver ensured that the prosperity of the Zacatecas zone of production influenced the viceregal economy as a whole.

Recovery began late in the seventeenth century. Mexican mining production rose some 30 per cent between 1671–80 and 1691–1700. One of the key zones of recovery was Sombrerete, north of the city of Zacatecas. By the 1960s, total production reached 50,751,914 pesos, slightly below the 1611–20 level of 53,646,127 pesos. New Spain became the world's chief supplier of silver by overtaking Peruvian production at the end of the seventeenth century. Between 1695–99 and 1805–9, the distance between these two major world producers increased. In New Spain, silver production grew at the rate of 1.7 per cent p.a. (or fivefold) in that broad period, when population grew at the rate of 0.5 per cent p.a. Mintage of coin increased from 19.6 million pesos in 1695–99 to 122 million pesos in 1805–9. The gold boom in the south-eastern Brazilian province of Minas Gerais from the 1690s combined with existing supplies from New Granada and West Africa to provide an abundance of gold on the world market until the mid-1720s. As a result, the price of silver rose.

There has been much discussion concerning both the periodisation of the recovery of silver and the impact of the mining sector on the rest of the economy. The real value of mining output grew more rapidly during the first half of the eighteenth century than in the second half, the period usually associated with the 'Bourbon reforms'. New Spain's highest production rate was in the period between 1695–99 and

1720–24, at 3.2 per cent p.a., with production averaging 10 million pesos annually during the early 1720s. A period of stagnation followed, but between 1740–44 and 1745–49 the growth rate reached 4.1 per cent p.a., with annual production averaging up to 12 million pesos in the late 1740s. Two decades of fluctuation came next, after which renewed high rates continued until the mid-1790s. Production reached 16–20 million pesos during the 1770s and 1780s. An abrupt decline accompanied the subsistence crisis of 1785–86. During the decade of international warfare and continuing inflation at home, the rate of production collapsed to 0.1 per cent between 1795–99 and 1805–09.

Further discoveries of silver deposits, for instance in 1701 in the province of Chihuahua, took the frontier further northwards. Since a total of 60 million pesos was produced between 1703 and 1737, one-quarter of the viceroyalty's total output, Chihuahua played a major role in the economic growth of New Spain during the first half of the eighteenth century. Part of the explanation may have been the paradoxical behaviour of the Zacatecas zone, which between 1725 and 1765 was the only major centre contracting or stagnating. In Chihuahua, the Santa Eulalia mine provided the focus of expansion, with the town of San Felipe el Real de Chihuahua founded in 1718 in response. Silver, as on all other occasions, attracted population northwards from elsewhere within New Spain. Cheryl Martin has emphasised the fluidity of social relations beyond the central zones of New Spain: 'the social history of colonial Mexico was everywhere marked by the constant negotiation of social boundaries', though especially so in the north.

Mine-operators rarely confined their investments solely to that costly and volatile activity, but spread their interests across a range of activities that included agriculture, finance, and industry. They were closely connected to merchant financial backers, who acted not only as guarantors, but also as creditors and investors. This relationship was logical in view of the merchants' predominant role as importers of European commodities. Effectively, they controlled the market price of imports in New Spain and paid for them largely with silver from the mines. The impact of the mining sector on the economy as a whole stemmed from its demand for inputs from the immediate locality and region and, through its output, the circulating medium used for commodity purchase, whether from the domestic or the international economy.

Provincial economies and commercial networks

A broad range of textiles was produced in New Spain, in spite of the ostensible colonial situation. Metropolitan Spain's industries, in decline from the 1590s at the latest, could not supply demand in the colonies. At the same time, foreign products passed through the Seville and Cádiz trades along with Spanish goods, which increasingly catered to a restricted, luxury market. Local production in the American territories responded to home demand. Handicraft and domestic production predominated, though they were concentrated in specific areas, notably Puebla-Tlaxcala, the Bajío, Michoacán, the Guadalajara district, Oaxaca both in the city and in specific villages in the valley and the sierra (such as Villa Alta), and in and around Mexico City. Heavy woollens tended to be produced in workshops known as *obrajes* – there were thirty-five in Puebla in 1604.

The Spanish colonisers added woollens to the indigenous tradition of cotton-textile production. At the same time, mercantile capital enabled immigrant Spanish artisans and indigenous weavers to expand production in response largely to urban demand among the Hispanic and mixed components of the population. Indian communities continued to weave their own clothing, several villages specialising in the production of particular types or styles of textile and trading them through the local market networks. The highland Oaxaca village of Villa Alta became one of the principal suppliers of cotton cloth, the raw material brought up from the lowland villages of the Gulf hinterland. Textiles from Villa Alta reached as far as the mining zones of the centre-north. Hispanic merchants, acting through the agency of the district administrators, managed to interpose themselves at the three stages of the textile process – raw material production, manufacture, and distribution. Nevertheless, indigenous producers did not entirely lose their autonomy, in spite of increased mercantile and administrative pressures during the eighteenth century.

The principal Spanish innovation was the enclosed woollen-textile workshop known as the *obraje*. This institution grew in response to the emergence of Hispanic cities and mining zones in the centre-north. It first arose from the combination of cheap labour in the *encomienda* with the emerging livestock economy. Cheap labour enabled Hispanic producers to accumulate sufficient capital to maintain these workshops, though the technological level remained basic. Even though they supplied a steady colonial demand, they could not be described as the basis of a modern manufacturing industry. As with mining, few, if any, investors concentrated their interests in manufacturing; on the contrary, their range of activities from landowning to commerce or mine-investment was impressive. In Querétaro, which became the principal *obraje* town during the eighteenth century, operators of workshops also tended to be landowners and city councillors. Several Bajío towns north of Querétaro also operated as textile centres, producing woollens of differing types: San Miguel el Grande and Acámbaro were the two principal areas.

Between the 1680s and 1730s, Puebla lost the earlier market for its agricultural and industrial products in the north-centre to the rising production areas in the Bajío and Guadalajara. As a result, Puebla, which until the late seventeenth century had supplied Zacatecas, was no longer able to exchange its products for silver. The contraction of the regional economy had repercussions throughout the agricultural sector, particularly in the main wheat-producing districts of Atlixco, Huejotzingo, and Cholula. Within the region, however, the Tepeaca district, the principal maize district, continued to expand until the middle of the 1800s. Facing competition from Querétaro's woollen industry, Puebla's broadcloth manufacture declined rapidly. As sheep-raising moved northwards and the Bajío transferred from livestock to cereals, the cost of raw-material supply favoured Querétaro over Puebla. Factors such as this, combined with low-yield agricultural production, influenced Puebla's transfer to cotton manufacture from the 1740s. Producers in the province, furthermore, had easier access to the two principal areas of cotton cultivation on the Gulf and Pacific coasts.

Artisan and domestic cotton manufacture, in which women featured prominently, enabled Puebla to regain access to the Mexico City market and even further north during the mid-eighteenth century. The growth of cotton manufacture in Puebla stimulated raw-material production in the central Veracruz lowlands. Frequently, increased textile production in New Spain responded to adverse conditions in the transatlantic trade. Guy Thomson suggests that the resumption of transatlantic warfare from the 1740s may have encouraged importers mainly based in Veracruz to reinvest in textile manufacture within New Spain. A similar pattern would recur in the early 1780s and more especially after 1795, even though the technological backwardness of New Spain's textile sector was gradually becoming exposed to competition from mechanised production in north-western Europe.

The consolidation of the Hispanic private estate

Between the 1590s and the 1640s the Hispanic private estate consolidated its position across the central zones which had previously been densely populated. Indian population decline, which reached its lowest point between 1620 and 1640, explained in part the transition to the new type of landed proprietorship. Since much Hispanic land acquisition had no legal form, the crown instituted a process of regularisation, known as '*composición*', which provided for the issue of legal titles by the viceregal government in return for payment of a fee. This process reached its climax during the 1640s. In this way, the hacienda consolidated its base in a countryside which a hundred years earlier had been characterised by the predominance of the indigenous peasant community.

Society and economy in New Spain neither consisted of isolated or virtually autonomous pockets nor was dominated by great estates oriented largely inwards. Instead, recent research has argued that market-orientation provided the major factor in economic organisation, even allowing for the continuation of pre-capitalist labour relations on the land or in the textile sector. Both the Hispanic private estate and the indigenous peasant community related as much to towns and cities with slowly expanding populations as to the land itself. In notable instances, local production was similarly oriented towards mining communities, which had a heavy demand for foodstuffs, clothing, and work animals. As we have seen, complex internal trade networks functioned at many levels, providing linkages across broad ranges of territory.

Different forms of labour organisation existed in many haciendas across central New Spain. Permanent labourers, who no longer associated with Indian communities, had their own places of residence on hacienda land and received a weekly maize ration as part of their payment. Spanish colonial law insisted on the free legal status of these workers, and the *audiencia* in test cases regularly upheld their right to take their labour where they chose. A major problem, however, lay not so much in resident-worker indebtedness to employers but in the frequent inability of hard-pressed estates to honour their financial obligations to their workers. A range of temporary workers and seasonal workers from the villages complemented the labour structure on the haciendas.

The hacienda predominated as the principal Hispanic form of landownership from the cereal-producing valleys of Puebla northwards into the Bajío. In the provinces of Puebla and Mexico, which covered the bulk of central Mexican territory, the indigenous community remained strongly present, even growing in resilience as population slowly recovered from the latter part of the seventeenth century. Further south, in the province of Oaxaca, the Indian communities overwhelmingly predominated as the principal owners of land. The hacienda emerged in the Valley of Oaxaca, in the Valley of Ejutla, in the Mixteca Alta, and in the southern Isthmus, but apart from the latter, these tended to be impoverished estates with frequent changes of ownership.

Instability of ownership was one of the most salient characteristics of the Hispanic private estate. The legal cost of inheritance alone explained this. Furthermore, meteorological uncertainties and the high costs of production and marketing kept profits low, except in the case of the fringe of sugar estates located below the central valleys of Mexico and Puebla. On the whole, large incomes were earned in transatlantic commerce or in silver mining rather than in cereal agriculture.

Livestock estates oriented towards urban markets, mining communities, or the woollen textile sector tended to fare better than the cereal estate. This helped to account for the gradual expansion of the hacienda northwards into San Luis Potosí, Durango, and Coahuila, which had never been predominantly areas of indigenous community agriculture. Between the 1730s and the 1800s, the territorial empire of the Marqués de Aguayo, for instance, increased to a dimension that equalled two-thirds the size of Portugal. The Aguayos left their northern estates in the hands of administrators, backed by armed retinues to ward off Indian attack, and lived off the revenues in Mexico City, where they possessed four palatial residences. Their speciality was sheep raising – they had over 200,000 head – for the supply of meat to the capital and wool to the textile workshops. The title had been awarded in 1682, but the land purchases dated from the 1580s. Marriage joined the Aguayo line to the Conde de San Pedro del Álamo title in 1734. The Count's 1.9 million acres of sheep-rearing land had their core in

Durango. The great estates of the north arose during the latter part of the seventeenth century in response to the economic and demographic changes of the central zone. The shift in the Bajío from livestock production to cereal agriculture during the eighteenth century emphasised this relationship all the more. The northern estates and towns tended to become the economic hinterland of the flourishing economy and society of the eighteenth-century Bajío.

INDIAN COMMUNITIES

During this broad period, a formerly Indian society became transformed into a colonial, Hispano-mestizo culture. The most striking feature was territorial advance northwards beyond the limits of pre-Columbian polities. Within New Spain proper, local Indian communities learned to live with the hacienda, often in forms of mutual dependence. Although colonial archives are replete with documents revealing disputes between haciendas and peasant villages over land, labour usage, and water rights, the daily reality tended to reflect cooperation rather than conflict. While colonial legal documents testified to instances of hacienda cattle invading peasant subsistence lands or of hacienda administrators verbally or physically abusing Indian workers, the private estate frequently depended on labour from the villages at times of planting and harvest. Villagers, furthermore, needed extra income to cover the cost of tribute payment to the royal authorities, ecclesiastical dues, and the costs of maintaining their own confraternity cults.

Indian communities participated in the colonial economy both as producers and as consumers. They frequently traded in their own right, in response to fiscal and market pressures. Such pressures intensified local commercial activity and led also to labour migration. In many pueblos, males and females worked as artisans, as well as in the fields. A considerable degree of monetarisation could be seen in the villages, in response to the range of activities pursued. Accordingly, the extent of stratification was probably higher than has been supposed. The supply of credit, voluntary or coerced, came through the *repartimiento* administered by royal district officials acting informally as agents of the merchant-financiers. District officials often tried to impose local commercial monopolies in order to push down purchase prices and raise the cost of supplies. They struggled to bind Indian producers within a framework of credit and debt. These district officials, with their network of dependency, formed less a part of the colonial state than part of the local power structure. Accordingly, it would be wrong to portray them as powerless representatives of a viceregal government. They should be seen primarily in relation to the merchant-financiers who sustained them and to the local population which they sought to dominate. The imperial government found itself caught between moral protection of Indian communities and the economic need to integrate peasant and artisan producers more closely into the wider economy. Indian communities with strong artisan and commercial traditions did not need monopolies imposed by outsiders for the discharge of their produce. Nevertheless, defenders of coercion, recognised by bishops and senior magistrates as an abuse, belittled Indian economic capacity, in order to justify control.

NEW SPAIN'S BAROQUE CULTURE

The style of art and architecture known as the Baroque, which predominated in central and southern Europe from the late sixteenth to the early eighteenth century reached its climax in Spanish and Portuguese America several decades later. In Brazil and New Spain, for instance, important buildings in the Baroque style were still in construction after the mid-eighteenth century. This style had a deep and lasting influence in New Spain. The Baroque attempted a synthesis of opposite conditions and experiences, a balance based on the tension between mortality and immortality, sensuality and asceticism, youth and age. Its predominant religious themes and architectural styles reflected less the influence of the classicism which had inspired the Italian Renaissance than the expressionism of the Hellenistic period. At the same time, the Baroque sentiment and style grew with the Catholic or Counter-Reformation, which reaffirmed and elaborated the traditional doctrines of the Eucharist as a sacrifice, the intermediary role of the priesthood, devotion to the Mother of God, the intercessionary powers of both Mary and the saints, the spiritual value of the religious life, and the efficacy of popular and collective religious devotions and pilgrimages.

Diffusion of belief in such ideologies and symbols made possible the acceptance of official marginalisation or even physical destruction of those caught deviating from them. The rebellion of Portugal, which in

1640 struggled to break out of the union of crowns with Habsburg Spain, threw suspicion on crypto-Jews of Portuguese descent. Jews who refused to convert to Christianity had been expelled from Spain in 1492 and from Portugal in 1537. The union of crowns had led to the arrival of Portuguese New Christians in the Spanish dominions, looking for commercial opportunities. In 1642, 150 individuals were arrested within three or four days, and the Inquisition began a series of trials. Many suspected 'judaisers' were merchants involved in New Spain's principal activities. On 11 April 1649, the viceregal state staged the largest ever *auto da fe* in New Spain, in which twelve of the accused were burned after prior strangulation and one person was burned alive. Most of the remainder who were 'reconciled' were deported to Spain. After a series of denunciations followed by arrests, the Royal Criminal Court sentenced fourteen men from different social and ethnic backgrounds to death by public burning for homosexual activities, in accordance with a law passed by Isabella the Catholic in 1497. The sentences were carried out together on one day, 6 November 1658. From the trials, evidence appeared of widespread and long-term practices, which suggested that Mexico City, like other great cities of the epoch, had an active and varied underworld, the existence of which the authorities only rarely discovered. The attempted round-up included 123 persons, 99 of whom had managed to disappear. The public burnings, not unusual in Christian Europe, were meant to be exemplary demonstrations of the joint power of Church and state over individual actions, the autonomous significance of which did not enter into consideration. Further instances occurred in October 1660, in November 1673 when seven men were burned to death, and in 1687. These unpleasant events revealed the other face of the Catholic monarchy.

After the early construction of late Gothic churches such as those of the Franciscan convent in Huejotzingo (Puebla) or the Dominican convent in Yanhuitlán (Oaxaca), with its vaulted nave, the principal churches and cathedrals in New Spain were Baroque structures, which in central and southern Mexico frequently involved indigenous craftsmen in their external decoration. The polychrome exuberance of the interior of Santa María Tonantzintla (Puebla) and the gold and stucco interiors of the Dominican convent of Oaxaca and the Chapel of the Rosary in Puebla amply illustrated this. Tonantzintla is situated in the vicinity of the pre-Columbian shrine of Cholula. The village itself, named after

Tonantzin, means in Náhuatl 'place of our mother'. By adding Santa María to the name of the village, the Christian evangelists intended that only the Virgin Mary would be the mother in that context. The church is a temple to the cult of the Mother of God, portrayed as the Immaculate Conception. There, as in so many other instances, the focus of Mexican Catholicism on the Virgin is evident from an early date. At the same time, the paradoxes of Mary's humanity but absence of sexuality ('full of grace'), and maternity but virginity, are also clear.

Baroque painting in New Spain absorbed a wide range of European influences, which went beyond the Spanish schools of Seville and Madrid to include Titian and Rubens. Religious themes predominated, but distinct Hispanic American emphases emerged in the choices of Catholic doctrine or devotion. The preoccupation with the Immaculate Conception and the Assumption was a case in point. Early painters such as José Rodríguez Juárez (1617–61) expressed the Catholic triumphalism of the Counter-Reformation. Nicholás Rodríguez Juárez (1667–1734) and his brother Juan (1675–1728) represented the softer influences of the Seville school of Bartolomé Estéban Murillo (1617–82). They formed the core of a painting academy in Mexico City established in 1722, a testament to the rich cultural life of the viceregal capital. José de Ibarra (1685–1756), who originated from Guadalajara, developed his talents in association with the academy.

The formidable output of Cristóbal de Villalpando (c. 1649–1714) brought the New Spanish baroque style to a climax during the 1680s and 1690s. Villalpando, who painted over five decades from the mid-1670s, received the patronage of the great Mexican cathedrals, notably Mexico City and Puebla, the principal religious houses, and the leading families. His subjects reflected the religious preoccupations of his time: the Immaculate Conception and Assumption (of which several were painted), the Trinity, the Eucharist, the Passion (painted for the Mexico City Franciscan convent in 1700–14), and the lives of the Saints (such as the scenes from the life of St Ignatius Loyola painted for the Jesuit Convent at Tepotzotlán, again in 1700–14). 'The Triumph of the Catholic Church', for instance, painted during the 1680s, showed as the two central motifs the crossed keys of St Peter and the elevated monstrance with the consecrated host. Around 1695, Villalpando painted a magnificent and intricately detailed picture of Mexico City's central square, showing not only the cathedral and viceregal palace at the sides

Plate 12 Detail from Cristóbal de Villalpando's painting of
Mexico City's central square. *La Plaza Mayor de México* (1695)
was painted on canvas 1.95 m broad and 1.58 m high. The
painting shows the cathedral on the north side and the viceregal
palace on the east. As well as carriages and horses, there are
1,283 individuals in the picture. Indian women with their daily
wares laid out before them are clearly depicted, while in the

and the two volcanoes in the background, but also the merchants' booths and peasant women's stacks of vegetables and fruit for sale. Carriages and costumes of the time are clearly portrayed.

Juan Correa (1646–1739) was also influenced by the colour and clarity of Rubens and the European Baroque. One of New Spain's principal painters, along with Villalpando, Correa took up similar themes. His 'Scenes from the Life of St. Francis' was painted in 1675–81 for the Convent of San Diego in Aguascalientes, and his 'Scenes from the Life of the Virgin' was painted in 1681 for the Rosary Chapel of the Azcapotzalco convent. Like Villalpando, he also painted for the Mexico City Cathedral sacristy.

After 1750, New Spain's most celebrated painter was the Oaxaca-born Miguel Cabrera (1695–1768), though little is known of his life until 1740, when his paintings received clear recognition in Querétaro. An orphaned son of mulattoes, he subsequently became official painter to the archdiocese of Mexico during the time of Archbishop Manuel Rubio y Salinas (1749–56). His works appeared in the capital, Tepotzotlán (the altar-piece, 1753–57), Querétaro (the altar-piece in the convent of Santa Rosa of Viterbo), and the mining centres of Zacatecas, San Luis Potosí, and Taxco (the altar-piece in the church of Santa Prisca, the church itself a paragon of the Mexican Baroque). Heavily influenced by the Seville school of Murillo, Cabrera covered a wide range of predominantly religious themes and a considerable number of portraits of viceroys and nobles, mainly by commission. In great demand, Cabrera consequently painted against time. He founded and directed a second Academy of Painting in Mexico City in 1753. His

Caption for Plate 12 (*cont.*)

background the volcanoes at the southern edge of the Valley of Mexico can be seen. Villalpando seems to have been the only seventeeth-century painter to have attempted such a panoramic representation. The choice of subject matter may have been influenced by the impact of the riot of 9 June 1692, during which the southern wing of the viceregal palace was set alight and merchants' wooden stalls in the square destroyed. The new mercantile precinct, known as the Parián and built of masonry, was finished in 1703, and the work of renovation on the palace was completed in 1713.

Plate 13 *La Dolorosa* by Cristóbal de Villalpando.
This painting is located in the former Jesuit College of
Tepotzotlán, north of Mexico City. Although Villalpando was
heavily influenced by Pieter Paul Rubens, the direct influence
here is the Seville painter, Francisco de Zurbarán. The pierced
heart of the Virgin, which symbolises the grief experienced at the
crucifixion, was a common motif of the epoch.

contribution to the developing Virgin of Guadalupe tradition could be seen in the publication of his *Maravilla Americana* in 1756.

Early attempts to reform the educational curriculum to keep abreast of contemporary European influences were snuffed out during the 1640s and 1650s by the Inquisition. The central figure was Fray Diego Rodríguez (1596–1668), who took the first Chair in Mathematics and Astronomy at the Royal and Pontifical University in 1637, and sought from that position to introduce the scientific ideas of Galileo and Kepler. For thirty years he argued for the application of science to the transformation of the physical world and for the removal of theology and metaphysics from the study of science. Rodríguez formed the centre of a small circle of discussants that met semi-clandestinely in private homes to discuss the new ideas. The deteriorating political atmosphere of the 1640s, however, brought the suspicions of the Inquisition down upon them and a series of investigations and trials followed into the middle of the 1650s. A rapid hiding of books accompanied the Holy Office's edict imposing close censorship on scientific works in 1647. In July 1655, the Inquisition required all six booksellers in the city to subject their lists to the Holy Office for scrutiny on pain of fine and excommunication.

Colonial society produced two of Mexico's most important intellectual figures: Carlos de Sigüenza y Góngora (1645–1700) and Sor Juana Inés de la Cruz (1651–95). Cabrera painted a posthumous portrait of Sor Juana in 1751. Sigüenza, a Jesuit during the years, 1662–68, was expelled from the Society. He subsequently pursued secular interests, and in 1672 became professor of Astrology and Mathematics at the Royal and Pontifical University until 1694, and used this position to attack the tradition of Aristotelian thought as the impediment to modern scientific methods. Although he never wrote a major scientific or philosophical work, Sigüenza remained highly influential in his time. His championship of the idea of a creole *patria*, which looked back to the Aztec past rather than to Europe as its Antiquity, influenced eighteenth-century thinkers such as the Jesuit Francisco Xavier Clavigero (1731–87). He also promoted the cult of the Virgin of Guadalupe. Sigüenza's writings included a number of narratives, such as 'Primavera Indiana' (1668), 'Paraíso occidental' (1684), and 'Los infortunios de Alonso Ramírez' (1690). He wrote an eye-witness account of the riot of 8 June 1692 in Mexico City, which resulted from government mismanagement of food supplies at a time of escalating prices following heavy rainfall.

Plate 14 Miguel Cabrera (1695–1768), *The Virgin of Guadalupe
with the three Juans*. The three Juans are Juan Diego, to whom
the Virgin revealed herself at Tepeyac in December 1531 and on
four subsequent occasions, the first Bishop of Mexico Fray Juan
de Zumárraga OFM (1468–1548), and St John the Baptist. The
painting, oil on laminated copper, is now in the National Art
Museum.

Plate 15 *Portrait of Sor Juana Inés de la Cruz* (1648–1695) by
Juan de Miranda. The painting, the oldest known of Sor Juana,
is at present located in the Rectory of the National University
(UNAM). There is some discussion as to whether this painting is
the original, dating from between 1680 and 1688, or a copy made
by another painter in 1713. Cabrera painted another famous
portrait of Sor Juana (seated) in 1730 based on that of Miranda.
Both paintings focus clearly on the library in the background. In
2004–05, the Royal Shakespeare Company successfully
performed an English version by Catherine Boyle of Sor Juana's
play, *House of Desires* (1683), the original title of which was a
pun on a title by Pedro Calderón de la Barca.

Sor Juana, influenced by the Spanish poets and dramatists, Lope de
Vega (1562–1635) and Pedro Calderón de la Barca (1600–81), and the
poet Luis de Góngora (1561–1627), became Mexico's principal Baroque
poet. Born on a hacienda in the province of Mexico, she was the illegitimate daughter of a Basque father and a Mexican mother. At a very
early age she showed a brilliance that soon led to her transfer to Mexico
City as a student of Latin. By the time she was fourteen, she joined the
viceregal court of the period of the Marqués de Mancera (1664–73) in
the entourage of the vicereine. Her brilliance attracted the attention of
moral critics in the Church, who pressed her to become a nun. Although
she bowed to this pressure and entered the Order of the Discalced
Carmelites in 1667, the experience ruined her health. She left the
convent and finally professed in the Jeronymite Order two years later.
Although this ended her period at court, she was still able to continue
her studies and publish, accumulating a vast library. Sor Juana's work
was known in the viceregal courts and noble houses of the principal
cities of the Hispanic world and in Madrid as well. Her writings,
although circumscribed by the requirements of not offending against
the Church, have interested the later twentieth century more than
perhaps previous epochs. Octavio Paz was a foremost champion of her
achievement, as his study, *Sor Juana Inés de la Cruz: las trampas de la
fe* (Mexico City 1982), demonstrated. Sor Juana's poetry revealed a
predominantly intellectual content, resembling at times discourses
examining the relationship of the mind to the exterior world. She wrote
love poetry, which balanced the desires of the heart with the sublimity
of the soul. Her most original poem, 'Primero sueño', written possibly
around 1685, was a case in point, though this poem relates to her own
intellectual development under the guise of a soul wandering, though
without a guide, through the hemispheres during sleep. Sor Juana drew
from the hermetic and neo-Platonist traditions of the Renaissance generally through the medium of the German Jesuit, Athanasius Kircher
(1601–81). One-third of her work was for the theatre, writing on both
religious and secular themes. Sor Juana's experience as a writer and
scholar reflected the tensions and limitations of colonial culture.
Although searching for greater knowledge through the sciences and
experimentation, she was unaware of the rapid intellectual developments in Europe beyond the Counter-Reformation world. As a woman,
and especially as a nun, her ecclesiastical superiors regarded her

achievements as an affront to their view of the world. Sor Juana herself, although conversant in theology, made her reputation in the field of secular literature rather than religion. She vigorously defended her pursuit of secular learning and the right of women to education expressed in a celebrated polemical letter in 1691.

The Archbishop of Mexico, Francisco Aguiar y Seijas (d. 1698), a self-flagellating misogynist from Galicia, was determined to ban theatre performances, bullfights and cock-fighting, and to reverse what he perceived to be the laxity of community observance of the conventual rule. Sor Juana, although faced with Aguiar's disapproval, had powerful protectors both in Mexico and in Madrid. Her fortunes changed, however, in 1692–93, as her protective defences collapsed. The Bishop of Puebla turned against her, and her Jesuit confessor, who for decades acted as censor for the Inquisition, urged her to abandon literary and intellectual pursuits for what he considered to be a life of greater sanctity. Under ecclesiastical obedience as a nun, she complied, signed several confessions of her errors, and gave away her library, mathematical and musical instruments in 1693. After inflicting severe punishments on herself, she died in the epidemic of 1695. A witty woman of wide-ranging scholarship, Sor Juana was obliged to submit to the moral pressure of suspicious and disapproving, celibate men. Much still remains unanswered concerning the silencing of Sor Juana by churchmen. Paz sees her as victim of political struggles within the Church combined with the aftermath of the riot of 1692, which the archbishop rather than the viceroy was able to pacify. With strengthened powers and in an atmosphere of religious exaltation, the archbishop was able to extinguish the influence of a figure he regarded as proud and rebellious.

THE CULT OF THE VIRGIN

The central devotion in New Spain was the cult of the Virgin, expressed particularly through the Immaculate Conception, a notion which in turn explained Mary's Assumption into Heaven. Though not proclaimed *ex cathedra* by the Papacy as a doctrine necessary to salvation until 1854, papal recognition of the cult's centrality led in 1760 to the proclamation of the Immaculate Conception as the patroness of Spain and the Indies. The specific devotion to the Virgin of Guadalupe did not

Plate 16 Basilica of the Virgin of Solitude, Oaxaca.
The sanctuary of the Virgen de la Soledad, particularly
venerated in Oaxaca, was originally constructed on the site of a
hermitage in 1582, though the present structure dates from 1682.
The church was consecrated in 1690.

develop widely until later in this period. William Taylor has argued
that in the seventeenth and eighteenth centuries Guadalupe was not
associated, as some historians have argued, with proto-nationalism, but
with miracles, especially at times of drought. By the mid-seventeenth

century, the official Church had clearly taken up the cult of Guadalupe. A secular cleric, Miguel Sánchez, first gave *guadalupanismo* its theological coherence, as a specifically creole cult, in a work published in Spanish in 1648 and in Náhuatl in the following year. In Sánchez's work, the Virgin of the Apocalypse replaced the Aztec eagle poised on the cactus plant. Although Indian attraction to Guadalupe stemmed from the obvious associations with Tonantzin, who could be adored in the guise of the Virgin Mary, this cult originated in Spain and had Hispanic adherents in New Spain from the latter part of the sixteenth century. Successful appeal to the Virgin of Guadalupe to stem the typhus epidemic of 1737 in Mexico City appears to have provided the turning point in the dissemination of the cult. Thereafter, the Guadalupe devotion increased significantly in New Spain, although Tepeyac had become the principal site of pilgrimage from the beginning of the century. The process of mingling and maturing, which took place in the seventeenth century, revealed the definitive legacy of the Baroque era to modern Mexico. The Virgin of Guadalupe became the Queen of Mexico who, unlike the absent and mortal King of Spain, belonged to an ever-present spiritual world. This was the cultural inheritance which the mid-nineteenth-century Liberal Reform movement struggled to combat.

New Spain has been described as *tierra mariana*. Although *guadalupanismo* related initially to central Mexico, many other manifestations of the cult of the Virgin appeared in different localities across Mexico, with basilicas or sanctuaries constructed around them. The Virgin of Solitude in Oaxaca, the Virgin of Ocotlan in Tlaxcala, the Virgin of Zapopan in Guadalajara, the Virgin of the Pueblito in Querétaro were just some of these powerful popular devotions. From the mid-eighteenth century, however, Guadalupan devotion increased, disseminated through the cities north of Mexico City by parish priests trained in the capital. These were the least Indian areas of New Spain.

The extraordinary depth of the cult of the Virgin in both New Spain and its Mexican successor state raises many questions. The parallel with Malintzin has been drawn: two female symbols at opposite poles – or two aspects of the same personality on the lines of the duality of the pre-Columbian gods. Commentators on Mexican collective psychology have pointed to popular surrender to the mother figure epitomised by the Virgin. Mary has become the mother who redeems the 'patria'

handed over to Cortés by Malintzin. Almost any contemporary definition of Mexican identity leads sooner or later to *guadalupanismo*.
The virginity-maternity cults explain in part the contribution of the
era of the Baroque to the cultural formation of modern Mexico.
Guadalupanismo subsequently contributed to the definition of
Mexican nationalism – a powerful protection against threats from the
outside.

THE EXPOSED NORTH AND FAR NORTH

In the north-west, Yaqui resistance delayed the Hispanic advance for
one hundred years after the first Spanish incursion in the 1530s. The
arrival of Jesuit priests in the area in the 1610s led initially to a pacific
compromise with the 30,000 Yaquis and the establishment of more than
50 mission pueblos in the Sonora river valleys. The Jesuits, however,
incurred hostility by their opposition to the Indian shamans who mediated between the living and the departed souls. On the fringes of the
Sierra Madre, the Ópatas became Spanish allies. Thence the Jesuits
began to move into Pima and Papago territories before reaching the
edges of the Apache frontier. The Gran Apachería was a zone stretch-
ing from the Colorado River in Texas in the east to the Gila River in the
west, 750 miles in breadth and 500 miles in depth, the desert core of the
far north. The Apaches were linguistically one nation, though divided
between the Chiricahuas in the west and the Mescaleros, Lipanes, and
other groups in the east. They were surrounded, however, by hostile
nations, such as the Comanches who controlled the buffalo plains, and
the New Mexico Pueblos, whose hatred of the Apaches accounted for
their fortress-type dwelling places. After the Spanish had broken
through the Chichimeca frontier in the 1590s, they then encountered the
Apache frontier.

In the north, Indian responses to the creeping Hispanic presence
were alternately violent and pacific, as differing strategies of survival
were employed. Indian uprisings attempted to restore the balance on
the frontiers in face of land loss and threats to autonomy and cultural
identity by settler, presidio, and mission. For the Hispanic settlers,
peace was necessary, in order to secure Indian labour in the fields and
the mines, but frequently they sought to impose this peace by violent
methods. Settler bands raided into Indian territories in reprisal and

for slaves and livestock. The frontiers moved constantly; conflict became savage on both sides; the ravages of uncompromising warfare conflicted with the values of mission culture. In 1616, the Tepehuanes rose against Hispanic settlers and early Jesuit missions in concert with Indian allies from the Chihuahua zone, including Tarahumara groups. Mission attempts to settle semi-nomadic Indians permanently, when they changed their abode seasonally, threatened both religion and culture. From the 1630s, the Jesuits began to establish missions among the Tarahumara. Their intention was to provide an agricultural base for their missions, which meant Indian cultivation of their lands.

A series of Tarahumara risings in western Chihuahua in 1646, 1650, 1652, 1689, and 1696–97 pushed back Hispanic penetration of the Sierra Madre and destroyed many of the Jesuit missions established there. The Tarahumara were one of those semi-nomadic peoples. They had, however, absorbed a great deal of Hispanic influence in order to strengthen their own resistance. They specialised in ambushes and their fortified defence positions neutralised initial Spanish advantages in firearms and horses. They traded in captured livestock further north-wards. The Tarahumara zone covered some 5,000 square miles between the 26th and the 30th parallels. The final revolt, which led to the destruction of seven missions and spread into Sonora and Sinaloa, left much of this zone free of Hispanic penetration for several decades.

In 1680, a major Pueblo uprising killed some 380 Hispanic settlers and 21 Franciscan missionaries. The rest of the 2,000 settlers and Christianised Indians fled down the Río Grande to the vicinity of El Paso, where the Jesuits had founded a mission in 1659. Conflicts over labour distribution, ill-treatment of Indians, and the behaviour of corrupt officials lay at the roots of the great Pueblo insurrection. Furthermore, the Franciscans had begun an attack on Indian rituals, which continued alongside Catholic practice. In 1661 they had prohibited Indian dances, masks, and prayer feathers, and, in face of great local resentment, destroyed large quantities of masks. Even after the suppression of the uprising, Indian rituals and official Catholicism (highly coloured in any case by local practice) existed in a dual relationship. The Spanish authorities did not attempt a reconquest until 1692.

Throughout the far north and north-west, there had been since the 1680s a clear rejection of the Spanish presence, whether it took the form of landed estate, mine, *presidio*, or mission. The impact of the successful Pueblo uprising, in which *mestizos* also participated, spread into the Tarahumara lands and influenced the uprisings of 1689 and 1696–97. Most Indian uprisings defended threatened religious practices, upheld village autonomy and land usage, and sought alliances beyond the immediate group. These were not tribal rebellions but opposition alliances constructed by Indian leaders themselves. In the Pueblo and Tarahumara cases, these were often men caught between the two societies and with an ambiguous response to the dilemma of their peoples. The latter, frequently confused and divided, were themselves caught between the apparent safety of an authoritarian Jesuit culture and their shamans' promises of imminent redress.

In 1683 the Álamos mines were discovered in Sonora, at a time when the Hispanic population there reached some 1,300 inhabitants. In their last advance, between 1685 and 1700, the Jesuits founded twenty-five missions in the Pimería area, among them San Javier del Bac and San Agustín del Tucson on the Santa Cruz river – towns later transferred to the United States in 1853 as part of the Gadsden Purchase. In 1697, the Jesuits founded the mission of Nuestra Señora de Loreto in Lower California, the first of a number of tenuously held positions in the inhospitable peninsula.

The metropolitan government attempted to consolidate the Spanish position in 1687 by the establishment of a governorship in the northeastern province of Coahuila, with its seat in Monclova, separate from Durango. By the 1690s, however, Hispanic frontier society had begun to buckle under the impact of Indian hostilities. Resistance in the north delayed the settlement of Texas until 1716, in spite of the urgency of a Spanish presence there to contain potential French penetration westwards from Louisiana. In 1718, San Antonio de Bexar was founded. Brigadier Pedro de Rivera's military inspection of twenty-three *presidios* in 1727 resulted in a Royal Regulation in 1729 for the reorganisation of the frontier, but nothing concrete followed. Texas remained the most sparsely settled of Spain's far northern territories.

Early in the eighteenth century, nomad Indian raids worsened across the entire northern area. The Comanches had moved down from the Rocky Mountains and were pushing the Apaches across the Texas plains and into New Mexico. They combined trading at the Taos fair with bloody raids around Pecos and Galisteo. The Apaches themselves posed a repeated threat along the Ópata and Pima frontiers, in spite of the establishment of a *presidio* at Fronteras (Sonora) in 1692. A major Seri rebellion took place in the Sonora coastal zone in 1725–26, and two rebellions in Baja California in the 1730s and 1740s effectively deprived the authorities of control of the peninsula. The situation in Sonora, however, went from bad to worse. In 1740 a large part of the Yaqui nation rose in concert with the Mayos to expel the Hispanic settlers. The rebellion covered the vast area across the Yaqui, Mayo, and Fuerte Rivers almost to the Sinaloa River. Hostility stemmed from goverment attempts to alter land-holding and tribute rates in the mission towns, and Jesuit retention of labour on mission land for heavy duties with no pay. The Yaquis demanded the right to sell their produce freely, carry their own weapons, and go freely to work in the mines. Effectively, the rebellion of 1740–42 destroyed the credibility of the Jesuit mission enterprise in the north-west. A further Seri insurrection took place in 1748, which had Pima and Papago support, and dragged on into the 1750s.

By 1760, there was possibly a total population of 233,600 inhabitants in the Mexican north, of whom fewer than half belonged to Indian nations. 54,000 of these Indians were in Sonora and 47,150 in Nueva Vizcaya. Halfway through the eighteenth century, the situation in the north and far north remained in disarray.

THE POLITICAL PROCESSES

The weakening of Spanish metropolitan power exposed the changing nature of relations between state and society in the Americas. The royal bureaucracy became increasingly subordinate to the interests of colonial elites. The political predominance of local oligarchies during the seventeenth century meant that the key relationship at the top levels of colonial society was between the central bureaucratic organs and the mercantile-financial elite. The viceregal office and the *audiencia* increasingly harmonised with the interests of the resident elite. Viceregal authority could even seem precarious at times, as in 1624 and 1692, when the viceregal palace was attacked during city riots. Political control was temporarily lost through disputes between institutions and personalities at the highest level.

The brief metropolitan attempt to assert predominance during the 1640s led to far-reaching political tensions. At the centre of these conflicts was the Bishop of Puebla, Juan de Palafox y Mendoza (1600–59), protégé of Philip IV's principal minister, the Count-Duke of Olivares (1587–1645). Olivares's policies increased fiscal pressure both in Spain and the Empire and provoked opposition or non-compliance. The Union of Arms, imposed in 1624, was designed to maximise fiscal contributions from all areas of the monarchy towards the maintenance of Spain as an imperial power. The struggle between Spain and the United Provinces of the Netherlands, interrupted in 1598, renewed in 1621, led in the following decades to Dutch attacks on Spanish shipping and the American dominions. The cost of warfare provided a cause of the rebellions of Catalonia and Portugal in 1640, precisely the time Palafox arrived in New Spain. The fall of Olivares in 1643, however, left Palafox vulnerable. He concentrated on Puebla diocesan affairs and made three separate visitations of groups of parishes between 1643 and 1646, in order to discover for himself the condition of religion and the state of the villages. A proponent of the supremacy of the secular clergy over the religious, Palafox secularised a large number of parishes in Puebla, which further exposed the indigenous population to outside influences and facilitated voluntary labour on the lands of nearby haciendas, growing in economic significance at the time. Palafox criticised the regular clergy for monopolising the richest parishes in the diocese, while members of the secular clergy remained without secure positions. His attack on the position of the Jesuits, the predominant religious and cultural influence in seventeenth-century New Spain, ultimately led to his own downfall. The Jesuits had become the wealthiest landowners in the viceroyalty, with properties nominally valued at up to four million pesos. Palafox went so far as to question the very existence of the Society. These conflicts and his attempt to tighten imperial control as Visitor-General of New Spain from 1640 and later as Viceroy in 1642 brought about the most intense conflicts of the century. The resulting destabilisation of New Spain's political system ultimately led to Palafox's recall in 1649.

The Spanish Crown's desperate search for funds explained the extension of sales of office, initiated under Philip II, to positions in the *audiencias*. In such a way, Americans gained access to the senior magistracy and gradually established their hegemony in full contravention of the Laws of the Indies, which were to be codified in 1680–81. At the same time, several prominent Spanish-born magistrates married and owned property within the territory in which they exercised jurisdiction, again contrary to the spirit of the laws. The *audiencia*, originally the bastion of Castilian absolutism, gradually became an organ which expressed the views of the resident interest-groups, whether of Spanish or American provenance. The viceregal court in Mexico City similarly reflected such interests.

As long as the metropolitan government remained weak, Mexico City rather than Madrid dominated New Spain in practice. This is not to imply that Spain had lost control of its overseas territories. The authority of the crown was nowhere significantly challenged; the close relationship between Church and state guaranteed the religious sanction behind royal authority; repeated threats to Spanish American territories from rival powers made the peninsular connection vital. The prevailing reality, however, was that resident Spaniards and Americans were left to themselves as to how they coped with their problems. The Spanish colonial system, modified by American realities, remained the means of legitimising the position of the predominant interest-groups within New Spain. A complex series of linkages and dependencies, which operated in both lay and ecclesiastical contexts, spread downwards from the levels of power and wealth to the poorer reaches of society.

Although these tendencies continued into the 1760s, the metropolitan government slowly began the laborious process of reforming governmental structures and practices both in Spain and in the Empire. This had already started during the 1690s, as Spain emerged from the worst decade of its experience as a power. The establishment of the junior branch of the French Bourbon dynasty on the Spanish throne after the War of the Spanish Succession (1700–15) reinforced the policy of reform. Philip V (1700–46) tentatively sought to establish the French-style Intendant system in the peninsula in 1718 but this centralised administrative structure was not consolidated until after 1739. Metropolitan policy sought to make Spain a more effective colonial authority by a series of administrative and commercial reforms which provided the basis for later measures during the reign of Charles III (1759–88). The first attempts to rationalise the taxation of American trade were made in 1720, and in 1742 licensed ships were authorised to trade to Peru by way of the Atlantic route. The Jalapa trade fairs were established in New Spain in 1727, in an attempt to encourage wider distribution of transatlantic produce.

Within New Spain, the viceregal government initiated a series of measures which would have later significance. In the first place, the royal authorities in 1733 took over the direct administration of the Royal Mint, with the object of centralising the production of gold and silver coinage. This policy began a long process of terminating private and corporate leases of royal functions and revenues. During the 1740s, Viceroy Revillagigedo the Elder (1745–54) called in the lease of the *alcabala* for Mexico City and its immediate zone administered by the Consulado. Revillagigedo's measure illustrated the Bourbon government's intention to regain control of the administration of royal revenues and thereby increase receipts. The clear implication was that state organs within the empire would be expanded in order to make metropolitan authority more effective. The style of government which accompanied these policies announced a change in metropolitan Spain's thinking on the nature and purpose of empire. Although rarely consistent in approach and application, Bourbon policies began to alter the balance of relationships between Spain and the Indies, and within the American dominions themselves.

5

Destabilisation and fragmentation, 1770–1867

During this period a relatively prosperous society organised as the Spanish colonial Viceroyalty of New Spain became transformed into a weak and divided Mexican Republic. How this process took place and what it implied continues to provoke disagreement in the historical literature. Until 1821, New Spain formed part of a wider Spanish imperial entity. The metropolis gave priority to the interests of the Empire as a whole rather than to any specific part of it. Spanish government support for the Mexican mining industry, while it benefited Mexican investors in the short term, was designed to promote not Mexican but imperial interests. The high stakes involved in the mining industry helped to explain both government and investor neglect of the cereal sector, vulnerable at a time of population recovery.

Spain itself also formed part of the imperial system, though by the 1780s and 1790s it became clear that the metropolis did not have sufficient resources to sustain the imperial burden for much longer, in the face of increasing international competition. The disintegration of the Spanish financial system under the pressure of warfare in the 1790s and 1800s increased metropolitan pressure on the Mexican Treasury General. After 1796, Spain effectively depended more and more on Mexican subsidies to sustain its faltering position. The political collapse of Bourbon Spain in 1808 began the process of American reorganisation which finally culminated in the total collapse of the empire in mainland America during the 1820s.

While the process of Independence certainly formed the climactic event of the period, it represented, nevertheless, part of an ongoing

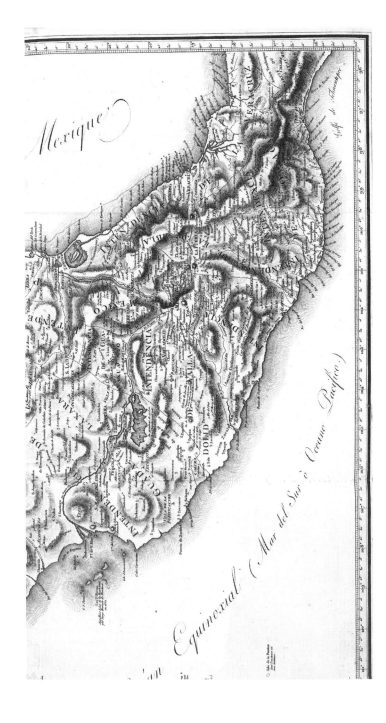

transformation from a European colonial territory to an internally divided sovereign state existing precariously in a threatening outside world. Although Independence undoubtedly represented a break in political terms, much continuity existed between the Bourbon reforms of the years 1760–95, and the Liberal Reform movement which struggled to hold power in the period 1855 to 1867.

In terms of territory claimed, New Spain predominated on the North American sub-continent in the centuries before 1800. By contrast, Mexico between 1836 and 1853 was stripped of half the territory inherited from the colonial viceroyalty by an expansionist United States, and was subjected to the armed intervention of France, then regarded as Europe's principal military power, between 1862 and 1867. Some historians, faced with this reversal of fortunes, have referred to the 'decline of Mexico' during the first three-quarters of the nineteenth century. If we are to speak of decline, then, it should be understood as relative to the rise of the United States as a continental power in the period from 1800 to 1870.

The Viceroyalty of New Spain collapsed as a viable political entity during the period 1795–1821. However, in the period from 1821 to 1867 Mexicans were largely unsuccessful at working out durable alternative structures. The historiography of those years is still struggling with the explanations for that. In this book, 1867 is regarded as a terminal date because it signified the effective end of the foreign threats of dismemberment or domination, and signalled to the outside world the survival of an independent, Mexican sovereign state. Weakened though it was, this state was conscious of its identity and its ability to survive in a

Plate 17 (*opposite*) The Viceroyalty of New Spain (1811). Detail from the 'Carte du Mexique et des pays limitrophes situés au nord et à l'est', the large map attached to the first volume of Alexander von Humboldt's *Essai politique sur le royaume de la Nouvelle Espagne*, 5 vols. (Paris: Chez F. Schoell, Libraire, 1811). This central section shows the Intendancy boundaries established after 1786. The Intendancy of San Luis Potosí (on the full map) includes the provinces of Coahuila, Texas, and Nuevo Santander, the northern boundary of which is clearly shown as the Río Nueces.

dangerous world by virtue of its own inner strengths. The failure of the French Intervention, and the disintegration of the Mexican Second Empire, which it had been designed to promote, demonstrated the country's success in staving off the threat of reimposed subordination to a European metropolis. This success came in the aftermath of the traumatic military defeat by the United States in 1846–48. Internal political struggles, however, continued unabated during both the wars against the United States and the French Intervention. The restoration of the Republic in 1867 did not signify their termination but, on the contrary, their intensification.

PART ONE: THE CLIMAX AND COLLAPSE OF NEW SPAIN, 1770–1821

An expanding economy or distorted development?

Population recovery and economic growth explained the vibrancy and growing wealth of eighteenth-century New Spain. Mexican silver production increased from 12 million pesos by 1762 to 27 million pesos by 1804. In reality, however, the eighteenth-century mining boom was a phenomenon of earlier rather than later decades. The metropolitan government assisted mine-operators by halving the price of mercury and gunpowder between 1776 and 1801, freeing mining and refining equipment from sales tax, and granting tax privileges in the case of high-risk investments. This ostensible expansion and these seemingly enlightened measures were, however, fraught with complications. The growth of the mining sector responded not just to government policies but, more especially, to demand in the international economy. Metropolitan Spain sought to take advantage of the recovery of the Mexican mining industry during the eighteenth century, in order to boost its revenues. As always, its motives were primarily fiscal, rather than any general concern with the balance of the economy. Mexican economic performance was measured in Madrid in terms of its capacity to yield revenue through increased or more efficient taxation. These imperial considerations lay at the heart of the 'Bourbon reforms' and Spanish Enlightened Despotism.

In the 1790s, Mexico City had the largest Mint in the world. Royal revenues rose from 3 million pesos in 1712 to 20 million pesos during the 1790s. Between 1770 and 1820, Mexico exported between 500 million and 600 million pesos by public and private accounts: this represented a substantial proportion of silver output. Consequently, the world's greatest silver producer repeatedly experienced a shortage of circulating medium. This became a major issue by the 1800s. After 1792, currency export finally exceeded registered coined silver. In 1802–5 alone, New Spain exported 96.7 million pesos, the equivalent of all the silver minted since 1799. Most of this was on the public account, which pointed to the depressing impact of the Royal Treasury on the economy as a whole. By the end of the century, the mining industry depended heavily on government support and on diverting resources from elsewhere in the economy.

At the same time, New Spain's agricultural base remained precariously weak in terms of resources allocated to it and because of its continued exposure to abrupt meteorological changes. The contradictions in New Spain's economy and social system ultimately contributed to deepening crisis during the last decades of the century. The imprecise relationship between economic, social, cultural, and political elements in the collapse of Spanish colonial rule in New Spain in the period between 1800 and 1821 accounts for the diverging interpretations of the broader period covered in this chapter.

Social and economic contrasts in late colonial New Spain

A general picture of late colonial New Spain has emerged from recent research which shows a prosperous society increasingly undermined by sharp divisions of wealth and characterised by regional disparities. At the same time, the expansion of Spanish entrepreneurial influence throughout New Spain clashed with traditional popular perceptions of how social relations should be managed. Ethnic tensions and racialist disdain on the part of Spaniards exacerbated these economic and cultural divergencies. Eric Van Young, for instance, has put forward the notion of cities with striking Baroque architecture but beggars on the streets and bandits in the outskirts. At the same time, the educated elite sought to disseminate the ideas of the European Enlightenment, while peasant society defended its traditional way of life. Most historians agree that the economy was heading for crisis by the end of the century. Social tensions resulting in part from deteriorating living standards at a time of static wages and population growth assumed alarming proportions in specific areas of the country.

A small circle of businessmen dominated the principal economic activities of eighteenth-century New Spain. Their personal wealth, often ostentatiously displayed, distinguished them from the other levels of colonial society. Many of the leading entrepreneurial figures were of Spanish peninsular origin, although their principal economic interests and family connections were within New Spain. The Andalusian, Pedro Romero de Terreros, for example, who became Conde de Regla in 1768, made his money in silver mining at Real del Monte, near Pachuca, from 1742. Labour relations at Regla's mines remained notoriously conflictive. His attempts in 1766–67 to reduce labour costs by removing the workers' traditional entitlement to a share of the ore, known as the *partido*, at the end of each shift provoked a major strike. Doris Ladd has described this as the conflict of two value systems. The crown's arbitrator, Francisco de Gamboa, the leading American political figure in the *audiencia* of Mexico and an authority on mining legislation, upheld worker grievances. For his part, the conservatively minded Viceroy Antonio María de Bucareli (1771–79) upheld the *partido*. Although initially obliged to back down, Regla, along with other silver-operators, subsequently renewed his efforts to cut labour costs in the mining industry. In consequence, labour relations in the mining zones remained volatile for the remainder of the colonial period. Regla held municipal office in Querétaro from the 1740s, purchased five appropriated Jesuit haciendas for just over a million pesos in order to supply Mexico City with pulque, and married into the Mexican titled nobility.

Basque immigrants played the principal role in the rehabilitation of the Zacatecas mines during the 1780s and 1790s. Among a handful of mine-operators who predominated in that zone were the Fagoaga brothers. Colonel Francisco Manuel Fagoaga, a native of Mexico City, made his money in the Zacatecas mines, and became Marqués del Apartado in 1771. Resident in Mexico City, the Fagoaga brothers invested large amounts of capital in the 1780s to little avail in the flooded Pabellón mines at Sombrerete. In 1792, they secured temporary relief from the Royal Fifth tax, in order to assist the recovery of production there. Within one year, however, the mine produced a bonanza, which led the viceregal government to question the wisdom of the tax concessions. By reinvesting the proceeds in further enterprises in

Fresnillo and Zacatecas itself, the Fagoagas commanded by 1805 liquid assets of more than three and a half million pesos. Each of the two brothers founded an extensive dynasty which resulted in marriage connections with the Condes de Santiago, Torre de Cosío, and Alacaraz. Francisco Manuel married into the Villaurrutia family in 1772. His wife was the sister of Jacobo and Antonio de Villaurrutia, magistrates respectively of the *audiencias* of Mexico City and Guadalajara. The former played a leading role in the autonomy movement of 1808 in the capital. Francisco Manuel's sons and nephews were to play a significant role during the political changes of the 1810s. The second Marqués, for instance, became a Mexican substitute deputy in the Spanish Cortes in 1813–14 and attended the Madrid Cortes of 1821.

In Coahuila, the Sánchez Navarro family controlled by 1805 a total of 671,438 acres of sheep-raising land across Coahuila. In contrast to the Aguayos, whose entire estate they purchased in 1840, the family administered its properties directly. Their business associate in Mexico City was the Spanish merchant Gabriel de Yermo, a leading member of the Consulado, who placed their produce on the market. Yermo would become the central figure in the peninsular coup d'état of September 1808 designed to abort the drift towards autonomy. By 1815, the estimated value of the Sánchez Navarro's estates reached 1,172,383 pesos.

The display of wealth at the top levels of society contrasted with living conditions for the majority of the population. New Spain's agriculture remained subject to abrupt subsistence crises, which threatened popular livelihood. Meteorological fluctuation and inadequate supply resulted in dearth. The infrastructure failed for the most part to cope with the strain placed on it. Subsistence crises, furthermore, affected the entire economy. Rises in cereal prices in 1713–14, 1749–50, 1785–86, and 1808–9 were passed on to all other foodstuffs. The Guanajuato mining zone, for instance, needed huge quantities of maize to feed the 14,000 mules used in the amalgamation of ore and the refining process. In both 1785–86 and 1808–09, food shortages in the mining districts and in the Bajío in general proved to be far more serious than in the central valleys. The impact of dearth, however, differed from locality to locality, depending on types of soil and efficiency of relief. The Mexican central valleys and the central highlands of Michoacan had access to lower-altitude supplies. Mining zones, however, remained too far away. San Luis Potosí, for instance, was hit disastrously in 1785–86, but rapidly recovered, only to face further shortages in 1788 and 1789. Abundance followed in 1791–92. In 1808–09, drought hit the main cattle zones at a time of escalating maize prices. In San Luis Potosí and Zacatecas, the maize price stood at 40 reales, in contrast to the Mexico City price of 30 reales. The calamities of 1785–86 recurred throughout the Bajío, though the central zone of Guadalajara was less affected in 1809 and 1810 than earlier. The sugar-producing zone of the present-day State of Morelos also escaped the worst impact of food shortages in 1809–10. As in 1785–86, the mining areas felt the severest effects of dearth, especially since in 1809–10 a shortage of mercury exacerbated the problem.

The social and political impact of dearth is open to debate. No automatic connection existed between food shortages and insurrection. The subsistence crisis of 1785–86 was more severe than the crisis of 1808–9, which preceded the outbreak of insurrection in 1810. Yet, no uprising accompanied or followed the former. Dislocation, however, could provide conditions in which insurgency flourished. The overriding difference between the dearths of 1785–86 and 1809–10 was that the latter formed part of a multidimensional crisis. This involved both long- and short-term factors and a crisis at imperial level with the collapse of the Spanish Bourbon monarchy in 1808 and the Peninsular War of 1808–14.

Metropolitan Spain and imperial reorganisation

As long as this imperial superstructure survived, the interests of Mexico itself could not be given priority. On the contrary, Mexican resources and interests were subordinated to imperial strategies. As a result, resources which might have been put towards the defence and settlement of the far north were diverted out of the country into the imperial system as a whole. Furthermore, Spain's financial needs in time of war pressed heavily upon its rich American dependency. These pressures increased from the mid-1760s to the 1810s, a period of deepening contradictions in New Spain's society and economy. The strength of New Spain's silver currency bolstered Imperial Spain's international position, which could not be sustained solely from peninsular resources.

The British threat in the Caribbean and the Philippines in 1761–63 stimulated a renewal of the Bourbon reform measures begun under Philip V earlier in the century. Defence considerations accompanied policies designed to tighten the political and commercial relationship of metropolis and empire. The imperial government in Madrid identified New Spain as one of its perilously exposed dominions. Accordingly, a military mission under Juan de Villalba arrived there in 1764 in an attempt to raise a colonial militia force. Perennially beset by financial difficulties, imperial Spain could not afford to pay for a professional army to be sent to Mexico or raised there, but sought, instead, to rely on the resources of its richest dependency. Madrid, for instance, refused to accept a 1776 proposal for an army of 13,000 regular soldiers at the cost of 1.3 million pesos. Regular troops were normally paid out of general revenues: instead, the metropolitan government intended to charge the municipal councils of New Spain for the cost of raising local militias.

Fiscal preoccupations remained at the heart of late Bourbon colonial policy. New Spain, the richest dependency, increasingly felt the pressure of taxation. The official visitation by José de Gálvez (1720–87) in 1765–71 intensified fiscal pressures. Even so, the *visita* formed part of a broader range of measures. In 1733, for instance, the crown established its monopoly of coinage, and in 1754 abolished the tax-farm for Mexico City and its immediate region, leased to the Consulado of Mexico. Twenty years later, Bucareli completed the process of re-establishing royal control over the collection of the sales tax. Gálvez himself had little interest in Mexican agriculture or industry, since his prime concern was to increase royal revenues and expand the export sector. Both objectives entailed the strengthening and expansion of the viceregal bureaucracy. At the governmental level, Viceroy Revillagegido in 1790 could count on five secretarial departments, in contrast to the two before 1756, with a staff of thirty.

Gálvez's recommendation of 1768 for the establishment of new authorities at the provincial level throughout the empire only took effect in 1786, when he became Minister of the Indies. The Intendant system was originally intended to be a method of tightening imperial unity. Gálvez had recommended the supersession of the viceregal office (and thereby the removal of the Mexican court) in favour of direct control from Madrid through the Intendants. Traditionalist interests in both Madrid and Mexico City managed to subvert such a radical measure. When the Royal Ordinance of Intendants established the system in 1786, the result proved to be a compromise, the viceroy still strong enough to water down those aspects of the reform which conflicted with his position. Gálvez had sought to apply seventeenth-century French administrative principles tempered with late eighteenth-century reform from above. Enlightened Despotism rapidly crumbled in the face of Mexican realities. Although Bucareli had contributed to the delay in establishing the Intendancies through objections on financial grounds and Viceroy Manuel Antonio Flórez (1787–89) opposed them outright, Viceroy Revillagegido the Younger (1789–94) gave the new administrative structure his full support. The main success of the Intendant system lay in the tax-raising capacity of the administrative reorganisation. The principal failure lay at the district level, where the new subdelegate was to have replaced the financial and commercial networks of the *alcaldes mayores* and *corregidores*. Crown inability to pay its new district commissioners a satisfactory salary led to the return of many of the traditional abuses. By 1795, the viceroy had recovered full control over financial administration. Finally, political division in Madrid aborted last attempts to overhaul the Intendant system in 1803.

In the aftermath of Spanish participation in the War of American Independence (1776–83) on the side of the Anglo-American colonists in alliance with France, the metropolitan government took the decision in 1788 to finance a militia force of 11,000 troops supplemented by 6,000 regular soldiers (in peacetime) at the cost of 1.5 million pesos. During the 1790s, however, the viceregal government was divided over how best to respond to the defence issue. Revillagigedo argued that the Mexican Treasury could sustain the cost of a regular army, since its revenues had doubled between 1769 and 1789. A strong proponent of centralised reforms designed to tighten imperial control, Revillagigedo disliked the idea of relying on colonial militiamen as the principal line of defence. By 1792, the cost of regular and provincial militia forces rose to 2.8 million pesos. Viceroy Branciforte (1794–97), by contrast, pushed forward the formation of provincial militias. Imperial considerations, furthermore, placed a heavy strain on Mexican resources. The metropolitan government transferred three infantry regiments from New Spain for the defence of Louisiana, acquired from France in 1763, Cuba, and Santo Domingo. The Mexican Treasury was at the same time required to pay 3 million pesos annually in government subsidies to these and other outlying Caribbean positions. Branciforte, for his part, conscious of the cost of Spanish participation in the armed struggle against Revolutionary France (1793–95), sent 14 million pesos from the Mexican revenues to Spain in 1794–95.

Imperial costs meant that there was never enough money to maintain a sufficiently strong army within New Spain. Until 1795, the crown gave priority to the defence of the Caribbean, where the British threat seemed the greatest. During the war of 1796–1808, when Spain was in alliance with Revolutionary and Napoleonic France, the possibility of a British attack on New Spain appeared possible. Accordingly, extra funds had to be found to pay for an emergency cantonment of forces in the hinterland of Veracruz in 1797–98. The high cost at 1.5 million pesos led to disbandment within fifteen months. A subsequent cantonment in 1806–8 proved even more expensive and highly controversial in view of the viceroy's decision to abandon the defence of the port itself.

The wars of 1796–1808, however, finally broke the colonial fiscal system, which relied increasingly on extraordinary revenues to cover expenditure. Merchant and mining corporations provided a large measure of this subsidy, whether forced or voluntary. The immediate political consequence meant that the viceregal government would have to reach accommodation with precisely those privileged bodies which had been adversely affected by the Bourbon reforms. This process of financial collapse was a major – and largely overlooked – contributory factor to the disintegration of Spanish rule in Mexico, a process further accelerated by the armed conflicts of the 1810s. The Royal Treasury debt had stood at 13.9 million pesos in 1791, but under the impact of war and civil conflict debt increased to 37.5 million pesos in 1815. The breakdown of a once viable system of government finance well before the impact of the insurrection of 1810 ensured that Independent Mexico would inherit an exhausted treasury and a mountain of internal debt.

Merchants, markets, and industries

Merchants who handled the import trade during peacetime moved into manufacturing during wartime. Always involved in providing investment in the textile sector, as in mining as well, merchant interests in the domestic market expanded with the interruption of European imports. Importers knew the market and could gear production towards demand. In the case of the Puebla cotton-textile industry, they began to extend their investments into the Gulf zone of raw-material supply. By the end of the eighteenth century, a small group of Puebla wholesalers came to monopolise the cotton supply to dealers and weavers in the city and its adjacent producing areas through the provision of credit to the producing communities. As in the parallel (but more extensive) case of Oaxaca, merchant-financiers used the royal district administrators as their intermediaries. Arrangements with Gulf coast muleteers brought the raw cotton up to Puebla.

During the 1790s and early 1800s, the textile crafts of Puebla reached their peak. In the city alone, the textile industries employed more than 20 per cent of the population. Merchants in the city advanced credit to artisans, who delivered the finished product back to them for distribution. Although the small group of investor-distributors benefited greatly from these conditions, the Mexican textile industry as a whole remained technologically retarded at a time of far-reaching transformation in the processes of production in north-west Europe. Although the metropolitan authorities disliked the proliferation of colonial manufacturing, they were in no position to prevent it. Nevertheless, royal legislation in 1767, 1794, and 1802 provided for duty-free cotton export to the peninsula, in the hope of diverting raw material from New Spain's industries into those of Catalonia.

Within New Spain itself, Puebla was overtaken after 1803 by Guadalajara as the principal cotton-textile producer in terms of value. Guadalajara could count on easy access to raw-material supplies in the Colima coastal zone. The textile boom began there after 1765. Before the 1770s, most textiles were imported into the centre-north-west from Europe or from the producing areas in the Bajío. By the 1800s, most were locally produced as a result of a type of regional import-substitution. Commercial capital, rather than technological change, increased artisan production, though the workshops remained in the hands of self-employed producers working with their own equipment. Many artisans operated basic looms in their own homes beyond the surveillance of the declining guilds. The Guadalajara zone was no less vulnerable to European competition than Puebla, as could be seen when British textiles began to enter the region through the Pacific port of San Blas by way of Jamaica and the Isthmus of Panama during the 1810s. This left the city's textile artisans, who formed the largest occupational group, in a precarious position after Independence in 1821.

Up to thirty-nine *obrajes* continued to function in New Spain at the end of the eighteenth century, with an annual production value of

648,000 pesos. The opening of the neutral trade in 1797–99 and again after 1805, as an extemporary government measure designed to circumvent the British naval blockade, adversely affected New Spain's industries by letting in manufactures produced by more technologically advanced societies. After 1805, Puebla's cotton-textile industry ceased to expand. The number of distributors trading in Spanish cloth fell from thirty-four to nine between 1807 and 1820. Several Veracruz merchants, such as Pablo Escandón and Estéban de Antuñano, transferred their business interests to Puebla in an attempt to diversify into the province's textile manufacture during the difficult decades of the 1810s and 1820s. The problem, however, still remained predominantly technological.

The continuing problems of the north and far north

Bourbon measures sought to address the inherited problems of the far north and north. Lack of available resources, continued fiscal stringency, and political division in both Madrid and Mexico City, however, combined to frustrate a new departure in the reorganisation of these exposed territories. Decisions taken – or the lack of them – during the late colonial period ultimately contributed to the final loss of the far north by the Mexican Republic between 1836 and 1853.

Spain established no new political entity there, definitively separated from the viceregal government in Mexico City, which could attempt to end the marginalisation of the north and far north. Like the Intendant system, the introduction of the Commandancy General of the Northern Provinces was an incomplete reform.

The metropolitan government in 1765 appointed the Marqués de Rubí, a senior army officer, to inspect the condition of the twenty *presidios*. He proceeded in the following year from Zacatecas northwards through Durango and Chihuahua to El Paso and thence up the Río Grande to Albuquerque and Santa Fe. Rubí was appalled at the lack of any coordinated defence structure and at the extortion practised on the settler and *presidio* population. He reported low soldier morale. Rubí advocated the concentration of the *presidios* into fifteen positions established on a defence line from the Gulf of California to the Gulf of Mexico, though including Santa Fe. In response, the crown issued a Regulation on Frontier *Presidios* in 1772. Even so, Navajo and Comanche activity in New Mexico and Apache raids deep into Chihuahua and

Coahuila kept the frontier unstable throughout the 1770s. Bucareli, worried at the high cost of frontier defence, advocated concentration on the inner line of Nueva Vizcaya and Coahuila. Even so, the authorities had failed to prevent the Apache–Tarahumara alliance of 1775–76 and had been unable to dislodge their strongholds.

In the meantime, Gálvez led the largest expedition into Sonora since the sixteenth century, with the object of re-establishing full Spanish control in face of renewed Seri and Pima hostilities. His *visita* also sought to establish an effective presence for the first time in Upper California in response to British and Russian advances on the northern Pacific coast.

Gálvez proposed a radical reorganisation of the administration of the northern provinces, which the Crown approved in 1769, through the establishment of a Commandancy General directly responsible to the King. Division within the metropolitan government and the opposition of Bucareli in Mexico City delayed implementation until 1776, when Charles III appointed Gálvez Minister of the Indies. Teodoro de Croix (1730–91), nephew of a former viceroy and a distinguished army officer who had begun his career in the Walloon Guard, became the first Commandant General of the Interior Provinces in that same year. From the outset, the relationship of the new structure to the viceregal government was ambiguous, especially since Bucareli opposed both the expense and the diminution of the viceregal office. The *Comandante General de las Provincias Internas* exercised jurisdiction over Sonora, Sinaloa, Nueva Vizcaya, Coahuila, Texas, New Mexico, the Californias, and later Nuevo León and Nuevo Santander. However, his territory remained subject to the *audiencia* of Guadalajara in judicial matters. Pressure for the establishment of a third *audiencia*, for instance in Chihuahua, seat of the *Comandante General* from 1792, did not have the desired result. At that time, however, the city of Chihuahua could not become the focus of either a reactivated commercial life or a vigorous political life. Croix, in any case, recommended Gálvez in 1778 to divide the *Provincias Internas* into two separate jurisdictions. Nothing, however, was done, and for ten years the *Comandancia General* remained undivided and largely beyond viceregal control.

Croix faced the problem of how to equip an effective defence force in the north at a time of intensified activity by Seris, Pimas, Ópatas, Yaquis, Mayos, and Apaches across the entire frontier zone, with heavy loss of livestock. The colonial authorities, however, broke off offensive action in

July 1779, because of the imminence of Spanish entry into the War of American Independence. Once again, the imperial position of European Spain took precedence over the internal situation within New Spain. At that point, however, an uprising by the Yumas, angered at the Spanish military colony's interference with their agricultural system at the confluence of the Colorado and Gila Rivers, expelled all missionaries, settlers, and soldiers in 1780–81. Since the Yumas were never reconquered, the land route between Sonora and the Californias remained interrupted for the duration of the colonial period. Croix's successor, Jacobo Ugarte y Loyola (1786–90), a veteran of the European wars of 1740–63 and previously Governor of Sonora and Coahuila, struggled with the problem of the Apaches. Ultimately the resolution of New Spain's frontier problem depended upon either defeat of the Apache groups raiding into Chihuahua, Coahuila, and Sonora, or some type of working arrangement with them. Spanish offensives in 1784–85 had also proved unsuccessful. Ugarte first sought alliances with the Comanche and Navajo enemies of the Apaches, made peace with the Chiricahuas and Lipanes in Sonora and Nueva Vizcaya, and then campaigned against the Gileños who, with their Pima and Papago allies, had attacked the Tucson *presidio* in 1784. Between 1790 and 1810, the peace strategy proved relatively successful.

Indian resistance in the north and far north posed a far greater problem to the Spanish colonial administration than interloping by rival European Powers, in spite of the temporary loss of the Floridas to Great Britain between 1763 and 1783. Spain, however, compounded this problem by maintaining only a weak political organisation in the northern provinces and keeping commercial life dependent on Veracruz and Mexico City, in spite of the general policy of trade liberalisation within the Empire. The viceregal authorities in Mexico City, for their part, remained determined to prevent the formation of any separate authority for the entire northern zone. They opposed strengthening the woefully inadequate 3,000-man force which was supposed to defend the entire frontier. Finally, Viceroy Flórez secured royal authorisation in 1787 not only for the creation of two distinct *Comandancias*, one for the eastern and one for the western provinces, but that both should be directly responsible to the viceregal government. In 1793, though, the crown changed its mind and ordered the reunion of the two sections. They remained united until the Cortes in 1813 revived the earlier policy of division. The outbreak of insurrection within central Mexico in

Plate 18 Portrait of Father Miguel Hidalgo (1753–1811) by
Joaquín Ramírez, c. 1865. This painting attempts to portray
Hidalgo less as revolutionary priest and more as potential
statesman and founder of the Republic, though in his lifetime he
was neither. Mural painters of the Revolution of 1910 adopted a
different stance, emphasising Hidalgo's revolutionary leadership,
if not messianic role. Orozco, for instance, covered the stairway
of the Government Palace in Guadalajara during the later 1930s
with scenes of violent revolutionary conflict. Hidalgo, left fist
clenched above his head, spreads a burning brand across the
forces of reaction. Juan O'Gorman (1905–82) portrayed Hidalgo
as nationalist revolutionary in his 'Retablo de la Independencia'
in Chapultepec Castle in 1960–61.

1810, however, forced the authorities to divert manpower and resources away from the north at a crucial stage. As a result, peace disintegrated throughout the northern territories.

Religious crisis and popular perceptions

The religious crisis within New Spain operated on several levels: the perception that the Spanish metropolitan government and its local agents had departed from traditional practices sharpened resentments across the social spectrum. Gruzinski presents the view of a 'Baroque Church' superseded by a 'Church of the Enlightenment', imposed by the largely Spanish episcopate appointed by the Crown.

The religious question polarised opinion and divided loyalties. To some extent, the religious crisis represented a Mexican expression of the general crisis within the Roman Catholic Church during the later eighteenth and early nineteenth centuries under the impact of Enlightenment, Revolution, and early Liberalism. In New Spain, the combination of social and cultural factors enabled a large-scale popular mobilisation to take place for the first time. The insurrection of 1810 was led by Father Miguel Hidalgo (1753–1811), parish priest of Dolores in the dynamic and densely populated province of Guanajuato. Its extent and intensity took the viceregal authorities by surprise.

The change of dynasty in 1700 had led to increased state pressure on the revenues and jurisdiction of the Church. A temporary rupture between the Spanish Crown and the Holy See, followed by the Concordats of 1737 and 1753, reflected state perceptions of superiority over the ecclesiastical power. This 'regalism' rose to a climax in the years 1765 to 1808, when intensified governmental pressure led to the reduction of ecclesiastical immunities and the absorption of Church revenues and properties. Archbishop Francisco Lorenzana (1766–72) and Bishop Francisco Fabián y Fuero of Puebla (1765–73) were the principal exponents of late Bourbon regalism. These policies reflected the strains to which the Spanish state, as an imperial power in a competitive European world, was constantly subjected. At the same time, however, the ideas of the Enlightenment began to enter New Spain. They were not necessarily heterodox, still less anti-Christian, but from mid-century they did lead to criticism of traditional educational methods and curricula. Accordingly, the clergy became divided into 'modernisers' and 'traditionalists'.

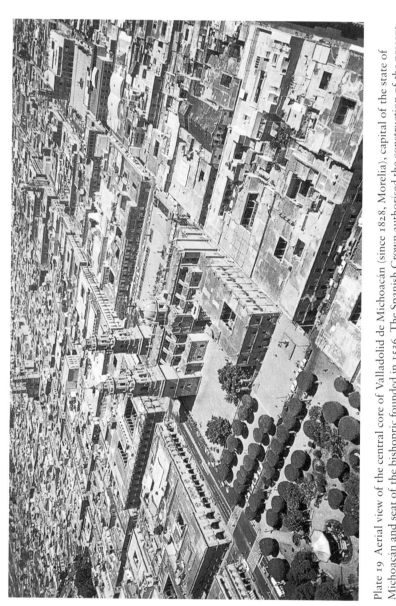

Plate 19 Aerial view of the central core of Valladolid de Michoacán (since 1828, Morelia), capital of the state of Michoacán and seat of the bishopric founded in 1536. The Spanish Crown authorised the construction of the present cathedral (at the centre) in 1655; it was finally consecrated in 1705.

Although not subversive, the new ideas increased state pressures on the institutional Church.

The expulsion of the Jesuits – the majority of the 500 were Mexicans – in 1767 stirred up a widespread opposition in New Spain which cut across social distinctions. Promoters of the cult of Guadalupe, the Jesuits acted at the same time as the principal teachers in colleges attended by sons of the creole elite, confessors in nunneries, and promoters of lay Marian brotherhoods. The expulsion had serious moral consequences, since it was imposed upon creole society in New Spain by the Spanish colonial authorities. A deepening division opened between the peninsular hierarchy and the popular church. The former remained under the Royal Patronage, while the latter had already seen the parting of the ways.

The Caroline bishops campaigned against popular religious manifestations and cults. Their attacks on 'superstition' and 'fanaticism' widened the gap between the colonial government and ordinary people. Although most of this criticism focussed on processions, pilgrimages, cults of the saints and the Virgin, and the centrality of local confraternity practices in Indian villages, a number of millennarian movements revealed the depth of popular unease. Gruzinski has suggested a millennarian dimension to the support focussed on Antonio Pérez in 1760–61 in the highland zone between Mexico City and Cuautla. Similarly, Taylor recently drew attention to the millennarian rebellion of 1769 in the Tulancingo area north-east of Mexico City in which devotion to the Virgin of Guadalupe formed a leading part. The colonial authorities in Guadalajara and the capital took seriously a localised uprising in Tepic in Nayarit in 1801 centred around an Indian 'king' called Mariano, which was to have taken place on the Feast of the Virgin of Guadalupe. The religious dimension, striking deep roots within New Spain's popular culture, extended grievances far beyond the usual disputes over taxation, recruitment, grazing and water rights, land boundaries, or wage levels. Van Young, furthermore, proposes a messianic and millennarian dimension to the Hidalgo rebellion of 1810.

Religious discontent combined with potential clerical leadership to focus popular energies in a struggle against the colonial order. Most of the 4,229 members of the secular clergy in the viceroyalty lived in poverty. A disgruntled lower clergy not only found their prospects of advancement blocked by peninsular dominance of the Church in Mexico but also their material circumstances adversely affected by Bourbon fiscal measures. The diocese of Michoacán proved to be a fertile ground for clerical dissidence. Manuel Abad y Queipo (1751–1825), Bishop-elect at the time of the insurrection of 1810, had warned of the potential for revolution in his opposition to metropolitan reduction of ecclesiastical immunities in 1799. He warned that, even though the clergy enjoyed this special corporate status, 80 per cent of those in his diocese lived in poverty. In Abad y Queipo's view, any removal of corporate status threatened to loosen the ties of loyalty felt by the clergy, who exercised a great influence on the hearts and minds of lower-class people, to the colonial regime. Metropolitan government policy, however, tended to pay little attention to the social role of the lower clergy within the American territories during the late Bourbon period. When rebellion came, it revealed the extent to which large components of the population had implicitly or explicitly broken with the colonial regime and the Spanish episcopate which formed an essential part of it. Those American clerics who took part in the insurrection found themselves caught up in a movement of profound dimensions which they could scarcely control.

Deepening crises at many levels

In New Spain's most dynamic regions a deepening sense of vulnerability characterised lower-class life by the beginning of the nineteenth century. The immediate origins of the insurrection of 1810 lay in the particular conditions of the Bajío and the central zone of Guadalajara. By contrast, the San Luis Potosí countryside did not at that time become a focal point of insurrection. In part, population growth combined with a shift away from maize production undermined lower-class living standards in the Bajío. Structural changes left the rural poor more dependent upon the estate-owning elite. Parallel transformation took place in the textile and mining sectors linked to the Bajío cereal economy. In the central Guadalajara zone, the expansion of commercial agriculture in the wheat-producing haciendas appeared to threaten village maize-cultivators, who competed in the same urban market, with proletarianisation. This perception, often coming in the aftermath of long-standing land and labour disputes between villages and estates, may help to explain the option for insurgent activity in the lakes-basin area of Guadalajara during the 1810s.

Outside the Bajío, village despair at the inability of the colonial authorities to hold back the deterioration of local life explained the widespread discontent. On the haciendas themselves, though, resident workers enjoyed a reasonable security as participants in a patron–client network. They received housing and also a maize ration from the proprietor as part of their wage. If local treatment of estate workers was tolerable, the patron–client relationship stood a chance of survival during the insurgency conditions of the 1810s, providing the landowner did not abandon his property through fear of approaching rebel bands. As a result, proprietors had the possibility, especially if pressed hard by the Royalist authorities, to organise estate defence forces against marauding insurgents.

Between 1795 and 1808, the colonial regime in Mexico City found itself economically weaker and increasingly politically isolated. Tensions within the ruling groups in key cities across the centre-north – Valladolid, San Luis Potosí, Zacatecas, and Guadalajara – during the years 1805–10 aggravated the impact of social dislocation. They threatened loss of political control at a time of imperial-level crisis in 1808 and mounting social tensions in the localities.

The revolutionary attempt and the insurgency of the 1810s

The immediate cause of the insurrection of 1810 was the collapse of the viceregal government's legitimacy in September 1808. For the first time in three hundred years no one authority in New Spain – or even the peninsula itself – could claim unequivocal allegiance. This situation raised to new heights the ongoing question of political representation, which had first emerged during the 1770s in reaction to the Bourbon reforms. French removal of the Spanish Bourbons during the Spring of 1808 presented Viceroy José de Iturrigaray (1803–8) with the problem of which peninsular authority to recognise and which factions to align with in Mexico. Iturrigaray tried to salvage his position by lending support to pressures from within the Mexican elite for a series of juntas which would decide the political future of New Spain without reference to any particular Spanish authority. If successful, this procedure might have ensured a peaceful transition from peninsular absolutism to home rule. Autonomy and an oligarchic form of constitutionalism were brusquely aborted by a swift coup d'état from within the peninsular sector of the elite on the night of 15 September 1808. The coup over-threw Iturrigaray and led to the arrest of the leading autonomists.

The peninsular coup destroyed the legitimacy of the colonial gov-ernment. Furthermore, it prevented the Mexico City elite from taking the lead in the opposition to absolutism and peninsular dominance. The initiative fell to the provinces and their dissident lower clergy, junior militia officers, and members of the civil professions. It resulted not from the breakdown of state institutions but from the colonial regime's loss of legitimacy. For that reason, the process of Independence took a different form in Mexico than in the Spanish territories of South America, where capital-city elites and militia officers took control at an early stage. The impact of the multi-dimensional crisis plunged Mexico deeper into a revolutionary situation in the years 1808–10.

The insurrection of 1810 and the ensuing insurgency were excep-tional phenomena in Mexican history. They were not simply peasant uprisings but from the outset had more general characteristics. Hatred of the Spaniards and a sense of offended religious belief formed a sur-rogate ideology for the risings that took place from September 1810 onwards. Hidalgo, against the advice of his immediate associates, appealed for popular mobilisation and placed the Virgin of Guadalupe at the head of a movement for the removal of Spanish rule in Mexico City. New Spain, thereby, departed from the South American urban strategy of power seizure through subversion of the colonial militias. Creole grievances against peninsular rule, however, proved not to be as potent as fear of social upheaval.

Although not a subversive cult by any means, the Guadalupe tradi-tion symbolised a specific Mexican religious identity, which had devel-oped slowly from the mid-seventeenth century. The religious dimension revealed a millennarian purpose of putting the world right by a sudden act of collective violence directed against those held responsible for the wrongs afflicting society. Van Young, for instance, has argued that the initial impact of the Hidalgo rebellion resulted from 'a fundamental sense that something had gone wrong in the world and that the exter-nal realities no longer conformed to the moral order of country people'.

Within Latin America, the Mexican insurgency was distinguished by the scale of popular mobilisation, its long duration, and deep local entrenchment. It left widespread social and economic dislocation in its wake. Ongoing research continues to examine lower social-group perceptions and the motives for their participation or withholding of support for this first great rural uprising in Mexican history. In central New Spain, for instance, corporate communities remained largely intact, an integral part of the colonial structure. Faced with less competition from the haciendas, they preserved greater control over their lands and labour force. Local communities did not rally to the insurrection of 1810, not even when rebel forces reached the heights above the Valley of Mexico in October. This indifference helped to explain insurgent loss of confidence and the defeats at Monte de las Cruces on 30 October and Aculco on 7 November. Militiamen recruited in San Luis Potosí, an area with a different social structure to the Bajío, formed the core of the victorious Royalist army at Aculco.

Local parish priests, as individuals rather than as a group, contributed substantially towards legitimising rebellion at a time of economic and social dislocation, and providing leadership for it. Royalist army commanders, such as José de la Cruz in Guadalajara, blamed the local clergy, particularly in the diocese of Michoacán, for giving vent to rebellious sentiments. Taylor suggests that perhaps one in twelve of the total parish clergy participated in the insurgency during the 1810s, chiefly from three main areas, the centre-northwest, the Pacific *tierra caliente*, and the highland zones of the present-day State of Mexico.

The viceregal state did not break down in 1810, despite the strategic weaknesses in the inland cities and political weakness at the centre. Most significantly, the colonial authorities did not lose control of their armed forces in spite of defections. These factors made the situation in New Spain different from those of Revolutionary France in 1789 and Mexico itself in 1911. Although metropolitan Spain had been defeated in war and broken financially by 1808 and in spite of civil conflict within the peninsula itself between 1808 and 1814, the viceregal state still did not collapse throughout the ten-year period 1810–20. When, furthermore, Father José María Morelos (1765–1815) replaced the undisciplined bands of the Hidalgo era with a more effective force, reliance on the *tierra caliente* as his base area ultimately frustrated his main attempts to gain control of the central valleys of Puebla and Mexico in 1811–13. Unable to dislodge royalist forces there, the insurgents adopted a political strategy of alternative government in order to challenge the viceregal government's legitimacy. This strategy also failed, in part because of the movement's reliance on local clans and *caciques* for

Plate 20 Portrait of Father José María Morelos (1765–1815) by
Petronilo Monroy (c. 1865).

   As in the case of the parallel portrait of Hidalgo, the stance
preferred is that of the statesman rather than revolutionary,
although the characteristic head-scarf and riding boots are
preserved here.

leadership and support. The insurgents proved ultimately incapable of transforming locally based insurrections into a generalised political revolution. Accordingly, the provincial centres which had first generated insurgency contributed in the long run to its disintegration. Local chieftains' limited horizons and frequent connections with landowners (if they were not so themselves) inhibited the development of a national vision and a social perspective.

Local realities conflicted with the broader social vision of the insurgency leadership. Morelos and his immediate supporters envisaged a dual revolution: independence from Spain combined with the abolition of caste distinctions at home. At the Congress of Chilpancingo, which opened in September 1813, and in the Constitution of Apatzingán (October 1814), they sought to create a republican constitutional system defined by the principle of equality before the law. In one sense this represented an insurgent response to the Spanish Constitution of 1812, which established a constitutional monarchy based on liberal principles. However, the insurgency itself had already fragmented into component local factions and had lost the political initiative in the country. Nevertheless, the Morelos leadership laid down a principle for other leaders to take up in more propitious circumstances. Within the movement itself, Vicente Guerrero (1783–1831), who struggled to assert his primacy after Morelos's execution in 1815, defended these principles until his judicial murder by conservative forces in February 1831. Thereafter, Juan Álvarez (1790–1867), *cacique* of the Pacific hinterland, followed in the tradition of Morelos and Guerrero.

The Spanish constitutional experiment

Above the anger generated at the microcosmic level two other phenomena demand attention: the Mexico City elites' struggle to transform colonial absolutism into an autonomous, constitutional state, and the provincial elites' aim to reduce the power of the centralist viceregal government and enhance the position of regional centres of power. Elite division in Mexico City in 1808 over the distribution of power at the centre and the status of New Spain in relation to the metropolis complemented – and fragmented – this process. The abrupt termination of the first experiment in autonomy in September 1808 deprived the centre of leadership and provided the opening for the provincial elites. They, in

Map 5 The Viceroyalty of New Spain in 1810.

turn, failed to subvert the militia, and appealed, instead, for popular mobilisation. That released the pent-up anger already at boiling point, and, in the aftermath of two harvest failures, unleashed violent insurrection which gave free rein to social and racial animosity. Attention has focussed understandably on this latter process, since efforts to create an independent Mexican sovereign state emerged first during the attempted revolution. Lately, the focus has also been turned to how the Royalist army contained the insurgency – but were themselves worn down in the process. This latter aspect is also important, because it sheds light on how Spain finally lost control in the Northern American part of her empire. Little, however, has actually been written on the behaviour of the elites during these events. Virginia Guedea's study of the *Guadalupes* in Mexico City has thrown the focus squarely on the capital-city elite's wary attitude to the insurgency under Morelos on the one hand and on the other hand its attempts at political advancement through the procedures established by the Spanish Constitution of 1812.

In Timothy Anna's view, 'The primary effect of Spain's first experiment in parliamentary and constitutional reform in the years from 1810 to 1814 under the Cortes and Constitution was that it revealed to Americans the essence of their status as colonial subjects' – 'it became clear that the Cortes and Constitution of Cádiz did nothing to solve the American crisis'. Part of the explanation for this lay in the fact that 'The Constitution's greatest weakness was . . . the way in which it treated the vast empire as a monolith'. The failure of Spanish constitutionalists to deal effectively with the American question was highly significant since many Americans would have preferred autonomy within the empire to outright independence. The breakdown of the Cortes's proposed middle way of unitary constitutionalism (which allowed no concession to American autonomy) pushed Spanish America further along the road to separatism.

From the perspective of the American territories' relationship to the Spanish metropolis, this interpretation is perfectly correct. There is, however, another dimension to the Constitution of 1812 – its *internal* impact. The Constitution made the municipality the basis of social and political organisation. It established juridical equality between Indians and the Hispanic population (though excluded the 'castes' and blacks from representation) and abolished the colonial *repúblicas de indios* in favour of constitutional town-councils. These provisions had a lasting impact in nineteenth-century Mexico. The Cortes extended the number of municipalities in accordance with population, and opened them by free elections with a broad franchise that incorporated a wide range of socio-ethnic groups. The number of local councils increased sharply, particularly in areas of predominantly Indian population such as

Oaxaca, or with a large indigenous representation such as Puebla, Mexico, Tlaxcala, and Michoacán. These councils assumed powers which had been previously exercised by the colonial state. Defence of municipal autonomy became a rallying cry of popular politics right through into the Revolution of the 1910s.

Liberalisation of the municipalities, however, also had other implications. The Constitution established the classic liberal principle of equality before the law. Accordingly, 'Indians' as a category ceased to exist and became indiscriminately part of a generalised body of 'citizens'. They forfeited the protection of Spanish colonial law. The Indian municipalities were opened to all socio-ethnic groups, members of which could henceforth gain control over peasant resources. The struggle for power within the municipalities became a source of much local conflict throughout the century.

The restoration of absolutism by Ferdinand VII (1808–33) between 1814 and 1820 aborted these remarkable new developments. However, the collapse of royal absolutism in 1820 led to the proclamation of the 1812 Constitution by younger army officers in Spain. By September 1820, the constitutional system had been restored in New Spain. Forty-four of the forty-nine elected deputies from New Spain took their seats in the Madrid Cortes of 1820–21. They included Lucas Alamán (1789–1853) and Lorenzo de Zavala (1788–1836). The Cortes, however, delayed taking action on American questions. Peninsular objections subverted American attempts to broaden the structure of the empire and the basis of representation, with the result that any last attempts to salvage Hispanic unity in both hemispheres rapidly floundered. In June 1821, for instance, Mexican deputies called for the territorial division of the Cortes into three sections representing New Spain–Central America, Northern South America, and Peru–Chile–Buenos Aires, with a royal-appointed executive (possibly a member of the royal family) in each of them with its own council of state and supreme court of justice. The Madrid government regarded such a proposal as a violation of the Constitution. By the time the session closed on 30 June 1821, only twenty-three Mexican deputies still remained.

Within New Spain, however, the events set in motion between 1812 and 1814 took even more dramatic effect after 1820. The number of constitutional municipalities proliferated as power devolved on the local tiers of society. At the same time, the number of Provincial Deputations, originally established at six in 1813–14, multiplied in response to provincial demand for these small, elected committees. Eight were functioning in the territory of the Viceroyalty as a whole in 1821, nineteen (including New Mexico) by the end of 1822, and twenty-three by the end of 1823. Although designed by the Cortes to be agencies of metropolitan policy enforcement, they became, in reality, representative of provincial elite opinion. The diffusion of power away from the colonial state into the localities and provinces reflected the far-reaching reaction in the country to the centralism of the Bourbon administration.

The final overthrow of the colonial state (1820–21)

The disintegration of viceregal authority in Mexico City led to a political vacuum which the elite sought to fill in pursuit of its traditional goal of limited representation and autonomy within the empire. The chosen instrument was the disgraced Colonel Agustín de Iturbide (1783–1824), whom Viceroy Juan Ruiz de Apodaca, Conde del Venadito (1816–21), restored to military command in November 1820. Iturbide came from the provincial capital of Michoacán, where he had married into a prosperous family of local businessmen and landowners. He had been Morelos's principal military opponent in the Bajío between 1813 and 1816, but had been removed from command through allegations of corruption and arbitrary conduct. In contrast to 1808, the Mexico City elite now had a military arm. Coordinating his strategy with associated army commanders in the provinces, Iturbide opted for a replay of the strategy of closing in on Mexico City from the peripheral provinces which Morelos had unsuccessfully attempted in 1811–14. Two preconditions of success, however, were the support of a majority of Spanish-born commanders whose careers had been forged in the Royalist counter-insurgency and the cooperation of those remaining insurgent chieftains, such as Guerrero, still in the field. Overtures to these figures made for a broad but contradictory movement guaranteed to fragment once it had achieved success. The support of the largely Spanish-born ecclesiastical hierarchy was gained through their fear of the ecclesiastical policy of the Liberal-dominated Cortes in Madrid.

Iturbide's Plan of Iguala on 24 February 1821 provided a platform for a wide consensus of opinion in New Spain to align tactically for the achievement of a distinct Mexican state within the Hispanic monarchy.

Plate 21 Lithograph of General Antonio López de Santa Anna (1794–1876). President from 1833–35, 1841–44, 1846–47, 1853–55, Santa Anna's reputation remains a matter of dispute. Lauded for the defeat of the Spanish invasion force of 1829, he was subsequently execrated for the loss of Texas in 1836 and the defeat by the US invasion forces in 1847, though praised for his actions against the first French intervention in 1838. His two attempts to establish a dictatorship in 1842–44 and 1853–55 ended in failure. Originating from the state of Veracruz, Santa Anna had a strong clientele there, as well as in Puebla and Mexico City. His strengths lay in an evidently engaging personality, in spite of general unreliability, and in the support of a strong segment of the army. Fluctuating between federalist and centralist factions, he initially fulfilled the function of curbing extremes. His frequent reappearances owed much to his ability as a political fixer.

Iturbide's Army of the Three Guarantees (Independence, Union, Religion) entered Mexico City on 21 September 1821. The new regime sought to preserve as much of the old as possible. It represented essentially an attempt from within the Mexico City elite in alliance with a substantial section of the Royalist army to recreate central power. The object was to halt the rapid devolution of power to the regions and the lower echelons of society since the re-establishment of the 1812 Constitution. Since the thrust of this movement came from within the elite, the autonomist aim (the reality behind the seemingly contradictory objectives of Independence and Union), clearly derived from 1808. A limited form of constitutionalism was envisaged, which could guarantee the perpetuation of the elite in power at the national level.

PART TWO: THE FAILURES AND SUCCESSES OF A NEWLY
SOVEREIGN STATE, 1821–1867

Autonomy, empire, and separatism

The Treaty of Córdoba between the Cortes's appointee, Juan de O'Donojú, and Iturbide in August 1821 guaranteed autonomy for New Spain within the Spanish Empire and under the Bourbon monarchy. The successor state to New Spain, described as the Mexican Empire, would invite Ferdinand VII to rule in Mexico as Emperor, and in his default his younger brother, Don Carlos. In such a way, Mexico City, rather than Madrid, would become the centre of the Hispanic dominions, as Rio de Janeiro had been in the Luso-Brazilian monarchy between 1808 and 1821. Upon refusal, a Mexican Cortes would designate (or, in practice, search for) a monarch from among the various European royal houses. In the meantime, a Regency would exercise the executive power in the absence of the monarch. All existing laws, including the Cádiz Constitution of 1812, would remain in force until that forthcoming Cortes in Mexico City should promulgate a new constitution.

The new regime, in which Iturbide became Emperor Agustín I in May 1822, combined a centralist empire with a constitutional system. The first action of the Supreme Provisional Governing Junta was to convene a constituent congress to determine the structure of the new entity. The principle would be representation according to population, though with indirect election on the Cádiz model. Iturbide and his traditionalist allies within the coalition, however, disliked Cádiz liberal ideas, and sought to establish some form of restricted, corporative representation more favourable to the elites. The Junta, accordingly, declared its intention not to be bound by the 1812 Constitution. When Congress opened in February 1822, it attributed sovereignty to itself. This seemed on the one hand to reduce the role of Iturbide, and on the other to frustrate the desire of the provinces for a stronger constitutional status for themselves through participation in the exercise of sovereignty. Conflict between congress and executive deepened during the spring of 1822. Destabilisation at the political centre would soon provide an opening for the provinces to push for the establishment of a federal system. As Anna observed: 'the source of the problem was that Mexico was trying to transform Spanish colonial structures into ones suitable for an independent state without an indigenous tradition of national representation'.

Mexico's struggle for a viable constitutional solution

The first federal Constitution in October 1824 sought to balance regional institutionalisation in the form of a federal system with central government retention of the coordinating role. Conflict between prominent regional elites (backed by their military champions) in 1823–24 and the residual central government followed from the collapse of the First Mexican Empire in March 1823. Lack of popular backing for these elites enabled the centre to impose a compromise on the distribution of sovereignty with the federal structure that emerged in 1824. The interpretation of nineteenth-century Mexican political history often leads to the tempting hypothesis of a polarisation between region and nation. The argument is that regional loyalties and the defence of states' rights undermined the possibility of national cohesion and consciousness. The first Federal Republic's failure to resolve the states' resistance to an effective and proportionate tax contribution to the national government lends credence to such a view. However, the explanation for this recalcitrance lay in the provincial perception of an overcentralised colonial political system, which Iturbide had sought to continue, and the fear that a fiscally sound centre would lead to the renewed subordination of the regions. The ongoing strength of Mexican federalism lay in the belief that the nation consisted not of an imposition upon the provinces but of the voluntary coming together of the many and varied regional component elements of the Mexican people. Accordingly, excessive centralism was seen as the cause of instability.

By 1827–28, political tensions among the factions sustaining the federal republic broke out in armed conflict. The reversal of the presidential election results of 1828 by the armed intervention of the defeated party produced the first flagrant violation of the Constitution by those who claimed to support its principles. Region–centre suspicion and socio-ethnic tensions combined to undermine the first serious attempt by the new sovereign republic to establish a constitutional system on a lasting basis. Not military intervention but civilian politicians' invitation to military leaders for assistance in pursuit of their particular goals characterised political behaviour in the period between Independence and Reform.

Centralist politicians in the period 1836–46, focussed on the issue of instability. Their aim was to bolster the centralist system through the support of Church and Army. This proved to be over-optimistic, since the ecclesiastical hierarchy was still in the process of reconstitution during the mid-1840s, following the crisis over Independence. The Army, furthermore, consisted of disconnected factions under rival chieftains since the fall of the Empire in 1823. Officers around General Antonio López de Santa Anna (1794–1876) sought to rebuild a coherent national army during the early 1840s and 1850s, but the state of government finances and the varying fortunes of Santa Anna himself both as politician and as general frustrated their objective. Centralists identified two major sources of instability, as they saw it: excessive popular participation in the political processes and an inadequate national tax base. Their measures on direct taxation, however, exacerbated popular discontent.

The centralist regime set about restricting the extent of popular participation in the political processes. Income qualifications and the curtailment of municipal representation formed the two most characteristic aspects of centralism in these years. At the same time, the two centralist constitutions, the Seven Laws of 1836 and the Organic Bases of 1843, sanctioned the abolition of the federal structure created in 1824 and its replacement by departments under governors appointed by the President. A system of prefectures grouped together districts, which were run by sub-prefects in a hierarchy of dependency on the national government. This system also broke down over the fiscal question and the scale of popular resistance during the mid-1840s. Military

division, factional rivalries, and regional polarities broke Santa Anna's first attempt at dictatorship in 1844. The onset of war with the United States during 1846 undermined General Mariano Paredes y Arrillaga's attempt to transcend parties and factions by establishing an authoritarian system, which was rumoured to be a prelude to some form of monarchy.

Finance and the economy

Government expenditure in 1822 exceeded revenue by more than four million pesos. Revenue was half the late colonial figure and expenditure far above the 1810 level. The army had doubled in size to 35,000 men and took up a huge share of the budget. Serious defence considerations accounted for this, since a Spanish force remained off Veracruz until 1823. Spain still controlled Cuba, showed no indication of recognising Mexican Independence, and landed a force of 3,500 men in 1829 in a vain attempt at reconquest. Furthermore, the United States, which in 1819 acquired Spanish Florida, presented a potential threat, particularly due to the expanding cotton economy of the southern states and Anglo-American penetration into eastern Texas. Independent Mexico was ill prepared to cope with such dangers. The Imperial Government, which inherited an outstanding debt of 76 million pesos from the colonial regime, including 10 million pesos of unpaid interest, recognised 45 million pesos of this debt in 1822. Two loans secured in 1824–25 from the London merchant banking houses of Goldschmidt & Co. and

Plate 22 (*opposite*) Entry of United States' forces into Mexico City, 14 September 1847.
Three Mexican defeats, Churubusco (20 August), Molina del Rey (8 September), and Chapultepec (13 September) in the outskirts of the capital, opened the city to General Winfield Scott's army. Internal political conflict, widespread popular rebellions in response to governmental measures from the late 1830s, logistic problems, and tactical failures in the field all contributed to Mexican failure to hold back the US invasion forces. The US occupation of the national capital lasted until 12 June 1848. In the meantime, the federal government reconvened in Querétaro from October 1847 until July 1848.

Barclay, Herring, Richardson & Co. created the new phenomenon of the external debt. Of the projected 32 million pesos, Mexico received only 17.6 million pesos, due to commissions and other administrative costs. These loans, which indicated the precarious position of the republic, failed to alleviate the newly established federal government's financial situation after October 1824. One-third of the customs receipts of Veracruz and Tampico had to be set aside for repayment. The British bondholders, who had welcomed the opportunity to make money in Mexico, saw the country as a richly endowed silver-producer. By 1827, however, the federal government could not pay the interest owing to its London creditors, with the result that the bondholders remained unpaid thereafter. A bondholders' committee was formed in London to press the British government for assistance.

Mexico along with most other Latin American countries forfeited its creditworthiness in the judgement of the international banking community. Accordingly, the government's internal debt rose alarmingly. The practice of mortgaging future customs revenues in return for ready loans from merchants began around 1828. With the focus of revenue-raising clearly on external trade, government avoided the politically controversial issue of systematic, direct taxation. The taxation issue remained at the heart of the fiscal problems of the First Federal Republic and the Central Republic which succeeded it. The phenomenon of the impoverishment of the early independent state remained a major issue in a potentially wealthy country. Attention in political circles focussed, regardless of ideology, on the question of Church wealth, particularly in view of high diocesan revenues in Mexico and Puebla.

During the 1830s, the financial situation worsened considerably. In 1832–35, for instance, the government suspended public employees' salaries and replaced them by bonds. Expenditure reached 16 million pesos by 1833–34, though revenue produced no more than 13 million. The first Liberal government's consideration of the transfer of ecclesiastical revenues to the state contributed to its downfall in April 1834. In 1835–36, the federal system collapsed altogether. The abolition of the states centralised finance in the national government. The centralist regime in 1835 mortgaged the state-controlled half of the Fresnillo silver mines as collateral for a loan of one million pesos from a consortium of businessmen: thirty-six of them, including Manuel Escandón, formed a company to put the mines on a productive basis.

The Texas crisis led to outright hostilities in 1835–36, but the Santa Anna administration initially could find only 3,500 troops ready for combat. The high cost of the army had not produced a sufficiently large force capable of rapid mobilisation. Santa Anna had to raise an improvised, expeditionary army of 6,000 men specifically for the purpose of defeating the Texas rebels. The loss of Texas, which left New Mexico perilously exposed, was followed by a dispute with the French, which led to a naval blockade of Veracruz in 1838 and frustrated efforts at reconquest. This first French intervention brought Santa Anna back to favour after his humiliating capture by Sam Houston's Texan forces at San Jacinto in 1836.

The fiscal measures introduced by the centralist regime between 1836 and 1846 were designed to meet these inherited problems, but in the long run they failed to resolve them. Although the British debt was consolidated in 1837 at 5 per cent interest, unpaid interest continued to accumulate. By 1839, the budget deficit alone approached 16 million pesos. Between 1835 and 1840, there were twenty Finance Ministers. Government continued to be largely at the mercy of importers with sufficient capital to act as creditors. The generalisation of the capitation tax in 1842 provided the spark that ignited a series of local rebellions across the principal areas of peasant and indigenous land retention. By the late 1840s, the most widespread popular mobilisation since the insurgency of the 1810s was taking place.

During the second presidency of José Joaquín de Herrera (June 1848–January 1851), there were sixteen Ministers of Finance, among them Manuel Payno, the most able. In July 1848, in the aftermath of national defeat, Payno estimated the combined internal and external debt to have reached 56.3 million pesos. Since 1821, 26 per cent of customs revenues, the principal government income, had been assigned towards the servicing of debt. Even so, the government already owed civil and military employees 25 million pesos in arrears. Payno attempted a reorganisation of national finances in 1850–51 on the basis of a 5 per cent tax on the value of all urban and rural properties. At the same time, the government sought to renegotiate the London debt incurred since 1824. The obligations of the external debt, not honoured between 1828 and 1851, further restricted government financial manoeuvrability. The Doyle Convention of 1851 initiated a short period of interest repayment of the British debt. Following the final return of Santa Anna to power in

1853, expenditure was estimated at more than 17 million pesos, with the army costing 8.5 million. The rapid decomposition of the regime, following the death of Alamán, its principal figure, further worsened the state of national finances and led to the disillusionment of the entrepreneurs who had initially sustained it.

The adverse state of national finances, combined with the perception of political instability due to frequent changes of government by violent means, gave foreign observers the impression of an abject people incapable of running their own affairs as an independent state. The negative views of foreign diplomats are there to read in the archives. European governments formed their policies on such a basis. Mexico, however, was in many respects wealthier and more stable than it appeared. In the first place, the country's principal export, silver, continued to be in great international demand throughout the first half of the nineteenth century. The Mexican agent of Baring Bros. estimated that the legal export of gold and silver came to an annual average of eight million pesos between 1826 and 1851, but that the illegal export was probably slightly more, making a final total of 18 million pesos. In 1860, the official figure for precious-metal production came to 24 million pesos, comparable with the peak years of the late colonial era.

The war with the United States (1846–48) and the loss of the Mexican far north

The War of 1846–48 formed the most dramatic part of a process which had begun in 1835 with the Texas rebellion and did not fully run its course until the final defeat of the Confederacy in the civil war within the United States in 1865 and the collapse of the Second Mexican Empire in 1867. This process involved the readjustment of the balance of power on the North American continent in favour of the United States and to the disadvantage of Mexico. Although its origins went back to the Louisiana Purchase of 1803 and Spain's loss of the Floridas in 1819, the full implications of the territorial expansion of the USA were not felt by Mexico until the 1830s. The Treaty of Guadalupe Hidalgo in 1848 confirmed the loss of Texas, New Mexico, and Upper California. The significance of these events is obscured by the traditional historical focus on the 1848 Revolutions in Europe. If these events represented, as A. J. P. Taylor argued, a turning point at which Central Europe failed to turn, on the

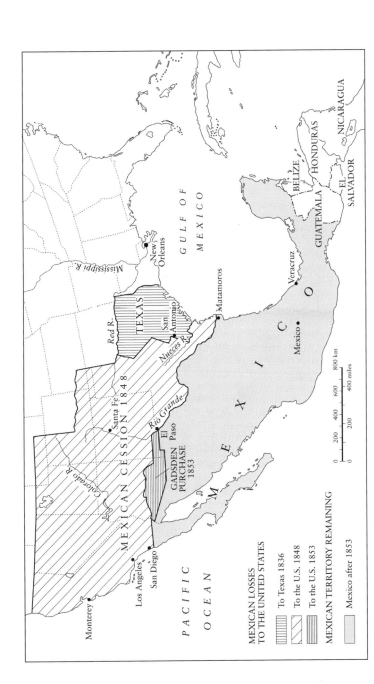

Map 6 Territorial losses, 1836–53.

North American continent history most decidedly turned. Even after the loss of the entire far north between 1846 and 1853, US pressure for further territorial cessions in Lower California, Sonora, and Chihuahua, and for transit rights across Mexican territory to the Pacific Ocean did not cease until at least 1860. In fact, the decade after Guadalupe Hidalgo was a period of intense pressure by the US Government and private interests for concessions from Mexico. This pressure rose to a climax during the Mexican Civil War of the Reform (1858–61) and culminated in the McLane–Ocampo Treaty of 1859.

The war between Mexico and the United States originated from the decree of the US Congress annexing Texas to the USA in June 1845, which the Texas Republic accepted on 4 July. The Herrera administration ordered Paredes y Arrillaga to advance north with 7,000 troops, but the latter ignored the order and remained in San Luis Potosí in order to await the moment to remove the government. Herrera sought ways of avoiding war in view of Mexico's desperate financial situation, military unpreparedness, and divided political situation. The Mexican government was even prepared to recognise Texan Independence, though the moment had passed. The removal of Herrera by Paredes on 31 December 1845 worsened relations, but the new centralist administration's evident preoccupation with internal conflicts delayed responses to growing pressures from the US southern states for an annexationist conflict with Mexico. President James K. Polk's Democratic administration, which took office in March 1845 represented these tendencies. In the meantime, Brigadier General Zachary Taylor's army advanced to the Río Bravo in early March, with the object of threatening Matamoros. This action, which has occasioned too little comment in the literature, constituted a calculated violation of the post-1836 Mexican frontier, which was on the Río Nueces, not further south on the Río Bravo.

Mexican forces initiated action across the Río Bravo (that is, while operating strictly within Mexican territory) on 25 April 1846, in order to remove the danger to the northern river port. Mariano Arista (1802–55) unsuccessfully sought to hold Taylor north of the Río Bravo in the two battles of Palo Alto and Resaca de la Palma on 8 and 9 May, when US artillery took its first heavy toll of Mexican infantry. Failure led to the definitive loss of Department of Tamaulipas territory between the Nueces and Bravo rivers. The US Government maintained that this territory formed part of the Texas Republic annexed in 1845, which historically it did not. Action in that sphere, however, provided the ill-founded pretext for a declaration of war by the United States on 11 May. A disastrous Mexican retreat from Matamoros on 17 May, effectively abandoned by Arista, reduced the original force of 4,000 men to just over 2,600. The Mexican Congress warned the United States on 7 July 1846 that it would repel invasion forces, though it stopped short of a declaration of war.

The war quickly assumed catastrophic proportions. The deteriorating situation within Upper California had already degenerated to the brink of civil war between north and south by 1846. Monterey and San Francisco, the two principal positions in northern Alta California, fell to US forces in the first days. Commodore Robert F. Stockton occupied Los Angeles on 13 August. On 17 August, Governor Manuel Armijo virtually handed over New Mexico to a US force of 850 men from Fort Leavenworth (Kansas) under Colonel Stephen W. Kearny which had marched across the Santa Fe Trail. Kearny took San Diego, the last important Californian position, on 12 December. Fighting resumed in the Los Angeles area but resistance was crushed by 8 January 1847. However, a rising against US forces in Taos, New Mexico, delayed full US control until early February. In such a way, the remainder of the far north, which had been bitterly fought for since the middle of the sixteenth century, was lost in a few months.

The collapse of the north-eastern frontier exposed the country to invasion. Accordingly, Monterrey became the US objective. The seriousness of the situation had brought about the collapse of the Paredes regime, when General Mariano Salas took power in Mexico City on 6 August. The immediate consequence was the termination of the Centralist Republic of 1836–46 and the restoration of the federal system in accordance with the Constitution of 1824. A change of political structure in the middle of a war which Mexico was not winning further destabilised the country. An arrangement between Valentín Gómez Farías and Santa Anna brought the latter back to power as potential saviour of the nation. By the time Santa Anna left for the front on 28 September, Monterrey had already fallen to US forces five days earlier after heavy street fighting. Furthermore, a second US invasion force operated in Chihuahua and Coahuila from October 1846.

Leaving Gómez Farías in control of the administration in Mexico City, Santa Anna made San Luis Potosí his base of operations, but on

16 November Taylor occupied Saltillo. Santa Anna aimed to retake this city at the beginning of 1847. A force of 21,000 men left San Luis Potosí by early February to drive US occupation forces from the Coahuila state capital, but awful marching conditions combined with desertions to reduce this army by 4,000. Taylor held Santa Anna's army, again through the decisive use of artillery, at the Battle of Angostura (or Buenavista) on 22–23 February. Suffering heavy losses in killed, wounded, and missing, Santa Anna fell back towards San Luis Potosí, a retreat which cost him half the remaining force.

In spite of Mexican territorial losses and defeats, the war had continued for ten months since April 1846 without a final Mexican defeat. Fighting would continue for a further seven months until the occupation of Mexico City in September 1847. The territorial outcome of the war has generally obscured the fact of its long duration – long in terms of Mexican weakness. The length of the war took its toll on the three US invasion forces, producing heavier losses than those sustained by the French Army during the War of the Intervention of 1862–67. Again, this is not generally recognised in the historical literature. The USA put 104,556 men in the field as regulars and volunteers, but 13,768 of them died in what came to be known as 'The Mexican War'. This represented the highest death rate in any war fought by the United States in its history up to the present time. The war understandably had considerable impact within the United States, especially since the Republican Party, and one of its rising figures, Abraham Lincoln, strongly opposed it primarily on the grounds that it worked entirely in the southern interest. These factors may well contribute to an explanation of why no further Mexican territory was taken in the 1848 Treaty and why, in spite of US strategic designs and southern material interests, no attempt was made to occupy and annex the Isthmus of Tehuantepec in a manner comparable to the US occupation of the Panama Canal Zone in 1903.

Mexican refusal of US peace proposals led to the opening of a second front at Veracruz, designed to end the war by the occupation of Mexico City. This final process itself took seven months. General Winfield Scott's five-day artillery bombardment of Veracruz led to collapse of morale in the port city, which saw itself financially and militarily abandoned by the national government. The surrender of Veracruz on 28 March 1847 effectively opened the US second front. A hastily formed Mexican Army of the Eastern Front with between 10,000 and 12,000 men failed to hold US forces at the strategic passage of Cerro Gordo between the tropical, yellow-fever country and the uplands on 17–18 April. The breakthrough led to the fall of Jalapa and General Valentín Canalizo's callous abandonment of the fort of Perote. This left Puebla open to US occupation on 15 May. The War with the United States finally reached the Valley of Mexico, when previously it had seemed a remote affair confined to the north, little different to the Texas War which had preceded it in 1835–36. The capital city, unlike Veracruz, immune from foreign attack in 1829 and 1838, faced the prospect of defeat and occupation. For the first time in their national history, Mexico City politicians would have to witness the consequences of their own internecine conflicts and failures.

The first defeats in the perimeter of Mexico City at Padierna and Churubusco on 19 and 20 August, in spite of strong defensive positions and numerically superior forces, opened the prospect of final collapse. A truce on 23 August made way for initial US peace proposals. These, presented on 1 September, envisaged a new northern border at the Río Bravo, with the complete loss of New Mexico and Upper California, and the US right to perpetual free transit across the Isthmus of Tehuantepec. The rejection of these terms led to the renewal of hostilities on 7 September. Two further terrible defeats followed, at Molino del Rey and Chapultepec on 8 and 12 September, the latter involving a thirteen-hour artillery bombardment of the citadel defended in part by cadets of the Military School. On the following day, US forces entered Mexico City. Santa Anna resigned on 16 September, and resistance officially ended on the following day.

In contrast to the subsequent French Intervention, the military struggle against US invasion forces took place virtually entirely between armies and without large-scale popular participation. Much still remains to be said concerning the absence of resistance comparable to that of the Spanish insurrection against the French in the Peninsular War of Independence in 1808–13 or the *juarista* opposition to the French in Mexico after 1862. The War of 1846–47 exposed the failure of the Mexican officer corps, the obsolete weapons of the army, and the inadequacy of its logistical support. US artillery played a key role at all stages.

United States territorial designs on the Mexican far north were assuaged in part by the Treaty of Guadalupe Hidalgo, signed on 2 February 1848. The question of further cessions in Chihuahua,

Sonora, and Lower California and transit rights across Mexican territory to the Pacific ports and also across the Isthmus of Tehuantepec per-
sisted throughout the 1850s. Transit rights and the construction of a
road, railway, or canal across the Isthmus, a major US objective pressed
by New Orleans commercial interests, had been raised in the prelimi-
nary terms proposed by the United States during the brief cease-fire of
24 August to 7 September 1847 but were not included in the clauses of the
final peace treaty. This issue reappeared, however, in the Treaty of La
Mesilla in December 1853, which arranged the Gadsden Purchase of territory including Tucson south of the Gila River. The transit question
provided the basis of the McLane–Ocampo Treaty of December 1859.

The Isthmus of Tehuantepec, since Independence still very much a
frontier zone, remained defenceless during the War with the United
States. Serious rebellions with deep-rooted local grievances ensured that
the state government of Oaxaca effectively lost control of the southern
Isthmus after February 1847. US forces never invaded Oaxaca, however,
despite the advance through the contiguous states of Veracruz and
Puebla. Although the Oaxaca state government remained apprehensive,
US forces never attempted to seize the Isthmus during the war. US desire
to end the war became evident once Mexico City had been taken.

Even so, it took nearly five months to achieve the final peace. The
question remains to be asked: why did Mexico not lose more territory
than she actually did in 1848? The answer may lie in the impact of the
war within the United States, the deepening political divisions there
especially between North and South, the heavy loss of life during the
conflict, and the recognition that the remaining territorial goals could
be pursued by different methods.

The persistence of social unrest

The insurgency of the 1810s resolved none of New Spain's social conflicts. They resurfaced at repeated intervals during the fifty years after
Independence. The close linkage between rural rebellions and major
political upheavals at national level, which had become evident in the
1810s, recurred during the 1840s and 1850s, as it would again during the
Revolution of the 1910s. This interrelation distinguished nineteenth-
century rebellions from those of the colonial era, and suggests a closer
national integration, combined with peasant political awareness, than

has traditionally been supposed. Elite divisions at the centre accompanied rivalries between centre and regions, and between regional capitals and localities. In the 1840s and 1850s, popular rebellions reached their maximum incidence since the time of the insurgency. The War with the United States took place in the midst of a period of internal social conflict, which the war itself made worse.

Conflict over land assumed greater importance in rural protest than it had during the colonial era, when the most common disputes focussed on tax burdens and administrative abuses. The peasantry's resilience could be seen in defence of community traditions and municipal autonomy. Peasants had taken part in cross-class alliances during the insurgency and in the late 1820s, the 1840s, and the 1850s. In certain provinces and contexts, peasants themselves also took initiatives in forging alliances within and beyond their own social group. The experience of the insurgency, in fact, broadened peasant perspectives, with the result that nineteenth-century movements frequently involved wider alliances and a more overtly political intent covering a broad range of issues. Peasant resistance spread across the southern perimeter of the central valleys from Tlapa and Chilapa after 1842 and thence into the Oaxaca Mixteca. In 1847, conflicts over landownership and salt deposits in the southern Isthmus broke into armed conflict after 1847. In the same year, the 'caste war' began in the sugar zone of Yucatán, which would drag on through subsequent decades. Peasant direct action in the Mixteca, again locally described as a 'caste war', continued into the early 1850s; in the Veracruz coastal zone, conflict over land titles and hacienda encroachments inflamed the situation in Tuxpan, Papantla, and Huejutla, between 1847 and 1849; a large-scale uprising took place in Tula, north of the Valley of Mexico, in 1847–48. The Sierra Gorda rebellion from August 1847 spread through Querétaro, Hidalgo, Guanajuato, zones which had experienced strong insurgent activity in the 1810s, and threatened the southern sector of San Luis Potosí. An armed force of over 3,000 men was eventually formed in order to contain the rebellion, a difficult task in the aftermath of national defeat.

The 1840s represented the most extensive popular mobilisation since the 1810s, though with the difference that until the Revolution of Ayutla of 1854–55 no national-level leadership existed. Elite conflict at national and state levels, severe from 1844, provided the openings for such movements to have such impact. National defeat in 1847 explained the general dislocation and military incapacity. Alamán used the opportunity of national defeat combined with internal upheaval to argue for a return to the type of monarchy, which, in his view, had brought Mexico stability during the viceregal period. Alamán founded the Conservative Party in 1849 at this particularly difficult time for Mexico.

The major sources of conflict centred on control of local government and the extent of the franchise, the implications of citizenship and participation in the political processes, and the relationship between centre and regions. The introduction of the capitation tax of 1.5 pesos annually in 1842 compounded these issues, which ultimately fuelled the Revolution of Ayutla. Álvarez, generally uneasy with regard to autonomous peasant activity, used this unrest to construct an alliance of interests determined to bring down Santa Anna's attempt at a centralist dictatorship. Beginning in March 1854, the coalition of forces that eventually composed the revolutionary movement forced out Santa Anna in August 1855.

Essentially a southern and popular movement in origins, the Revolution of Ayutla did not capture power without the intervention of the political barons of the north-centre and north. Many of them, such as Santiago Vidaurri (1808–67) in Nuevo León and Coahuila, acted independently of the original Ayutla rebels and pursued their own specific objectives. The initial leadership provided by Álvarez responded to conditions within the sphere of influence he had been extending northwards from the coast during the 1840s. In effect, he acted as broker between the village communities and the government in Mexico City. The earlier re-establishment of federalism in 1846 recognised Álvarez's power by creating the State of Guerrero in 1849. Álvarez became the first State Governor, an office which later passed to his son between 1862 and 1869.

The reform era (1855–1876) and the rise of Benito Juárez

The Liberal Reform movement presented a direct challenge to the Catholic inheritance of Mexico. The challenge came in several stages, the intensity of each one determined by the strength of resistance. For the ecclesiastical hierarchy, the reform movement came in the aftermath of the reconstitution of the Mexican hierarchy during the 1830s and

BENITO JUAREZ.
PRESIDENTE DE LA REPÚBLICA MEJICANA.

Plate 23 Beníto Juáiez (1806–72).
This picture is taken from *La América Ilustrada*, vol 1, no. 14,
the issue dated 30 June 1872, just before Juárez's death on 9 July.
Virtually all the photos of Juárez are formal and sombre, a
conscious contrast to the splendid depictions of military figures
such as Santa Anna, whom Juárez despised. The chosen image of
Juárez is as the epitome and defender of republican virtue. The
contemporary painter, Francisco Toledo (b. Juchitán 1940) has
explored the Juárez symbolism in two recent series of paintings.

1840s. Catholic alarm at state-level measures adopted since the mid-1820s and the reform measures of Vice-President Gómez Farías (1833–34) had already stimulated a polemical defence of the Catholic identity of Mexico and the close integration of Church and state. Catholic newspapers emerged in the late 1840s and those such as *La Cruz* (1855–58) subjected Liberal ideology to concerted attack. The Conservative Party took up defence of endangered religion as a principal issue.

The antecedents of Liberal Reform legislation lay not just in the earlier polices of Gómez Farías but in the measures taken by the Spanish Cortes of 1810–14 and 1820–23. All had common roots in the European Enlightenment, which sought to reduce the role of the Catholic Church in society. The principal Reform legislation came in two phases, 1855–57 and 1858–60. The promulgation of Mexico's second federal Constitution in February 1857 took place towards the end of the first phase. The two subsequent phases, 1861–63 and the period after 1867, corresponded to Liberal victories in two civil wars with their Conservative opponents, and led to further attempts to impose the Reform programme.

The Revolution of Ayutla represented a broad coalition of forces. Liberals formed part of this but were divided between moderates and radicals. That division went back at least to the 1830s. Moderates were often able to provide the bridge which brought Catholics and Conservatives into the coalition. The key figure on the moderate wing was Ignacio Comonfort (1812–63), retired militia colonel, Puebla hacienda-owner, and former Prefect of Tlapa in the early 1840s. Although closely associated with Álvarez since his time as Customs Administrator in Acapulco, Comonfort brought into the Ayutla coalition moderates such as the Guanajuato politician Manuel Doblado (1818–65) as well as the Conservative General Félix Zuloaga (1813–98), who came from a leading Chihuahua hacienda-owning family. Radical capture of the Álvarez provisional government of October–December 1855, however, broke this alliance apart. The Querétaro-born General Tomás Mejía (1820–67), who had risen to prominence in the War against the United States, went into opposition in the name of defence of the Catholic identity of Mexico, and raised rebellion in the Sierra Gorda. This area provided Mejía with a base of operations from which to launch a series of campaigns against Liberal regimes during the following eight years. Out of these political divisions and military conflicts arose the presidency of Benito Juárez (1806–72).

Although conceived as a moderate measure, the first major Reform decree opened wide the latent divisions in the country. The Juárez Law of November 1855 sought to subordinate ecclesiastical corporate privilege to the civil law, rather than abolish it altogether. Juárez, Governor of Oaxaca from 1847 to 1852 and Secretary for Justice and Ecclesiastical Affairs in the Álvarez administration, was a leading advocate of the supremacy of the civil power. Archbishop Lázaro de la Garza (1785–1862) of Mexico City condemned the Law as an attack on the Church itself. Clerical rebellions in Puebla in 1855–56 undermined the government's conciliatory policies, and led to a full-scale military operation to reduce the province to obedience.

The Law of 25 June 1856, identified with Finance Minister Miguel Lerdo de Tejada (1812–61), proved to be considerably more controversial than its predecessor. The Lerdo Law envisaged the conversion of the corporate properties owned by the Church and by Indian communities into units of private ownership, generally favouring existing tenants. The objectives were initially twofold: to release hitherto inalienable property on to the market, thereby encouraging development, and to raise revenue through government taxation of this process. These highly idealistic goals failed to recognise the unsettled condition of political affairs, the scale of opposition likely to arise, the opportunities provided for speculators, and the generally complicated nature of the procedures involved. Very soon, civil war made fiscal considerations paramount. Accordingly, the Liberal aim to facilitate the emergence of a class of numerous and active small proprietors soon fell by the wayside. The Law, in any case, had made no provision for prior division of properties before sales. Enactment of the Law created many new interests which strongly opposed its reversal.

Adjudication and sales appear to have totalled some 20.5 million pesos by the end of 1856. Lerdo himself believed that less than half the value of eligible ecclesiastical property had been transferred in that period. However, the brunt of the Lerdo Law fell not on the Church, which owned mainly urban property bought up by many Liberal politicians, but on the large number of peasant communities. Their response to Liberal policies depended on the advantages or disadvantages they could expect. This, in turn, depended on the speed with which local

Liberal regimes enacted the Law and the alignment of forces sustaining them. Some communities with a tradition of private or family land usage were able to benefit, especially where they were already well integrated into the market economy. Full implementation of the Law was overtaken by the decade of warfare from 1857 to 1867. Liberal loss of power at the national level between January 1858 and January 1861, and again from June 1863 until July 1867, interrupted the disamortisation procedure.

Comonfort's belief that the 1857 Constitution weakened the central executive and handed effective power to the state governors led to the disintegration of his moderate Liberal administration at the end of 1857, and the imposition of a Conservative regime in the centre-core zone by the army. Juárez, who as President of the Supreme Court had the constitutional right to the succession, was recognised as interim President within Liberal-controlled territories by an alliance of radicals and north-central state governors in January 1858. Repeatedly defeated by Conservative generals, Miguel Miramón (1831–67), Leonardo Márquez (1820–1913), and Mejía, who retained control of the central zones, the Liberals finally established their administration in Veracruz from May 1858 until early January 1861.

The Veracruz administration resumed the Reform measures in July 1859 under Lerdo's pressure. The Law for the Nationalisation of Ecclesiastical Properties on 12 July made explicit the connection between disamortisation and the deplorable condition of national finances. Government estimates of the value of Church properties at between 100 and 150 million pesos at that time were probably too high in view of ecclesiastical property losses since the Bourbon era. Furthermore, Liberal calculations frequently included church buildings and treasures such as sacred vessels. Lerdo hoped in vain to secure a loan in the USA guaranteed against receipts from the sale of expropriated properties. Anti-clerical state governors in Jalisco, Michoacán, Nuevo León, and Tamaulipas had already anticipated the Veracruz decree and implemented measures of their own. Ultimately, government income from the sales proved disappointing. The Mexican state received scarcely more than a million pesos from the disamortisation in 1856 and just over 10 million pesos from the continuing procedure and the nationalisation combined in the years before the Liberals lost control of Mexico City to the French Intervention. By 1910, the total revenue received was still only 23 million pesos.

A further series of laws restricted the role of the Catholic Church in society. On 26 April 1856, civil recognition of religious vows was removed, and on 11 April 1857 the Iglesias Law, responding to local complaints of clerical fiscal pressures, deprived the parish clergy of a range of traditional fees. The Law of 23 July provided for marriage legally to be a civil contract, though it did not go as far as to legislate divorce with the right to remarry during the lifetime of the separated party. A Civil Registry of births, marriages, and deaths came into force under the legislation of 28 July, and Juárez duly registered his newly born son. The number of religious holidays was reduced on 11 August and several secular holidays introduced to commemorate national events. The Liberal administration forbade religious celebrations outside church buildings and made the use of church bells subject to police regulations. Clerical dress was prohibited in public. On 4 December 1860, the Liberal regime legislated religious freedom, in accordance with the Constitution's neutrality on the subject of the exclusive Catholic establishment. This opened the way for Protestant evangelisation in the country, which the Liberals viewed with favour once they had regained power temporarily in 1861 and definitively after 1867.

The Constitution of February 1857, by contrast to its predecessor in 1824, failed to recognise Catholicism as the religion of state. Opposition from the ecclesiastical hierarchy, already incensed by the earlier laws of Juárez and Lerdo, was immediate. The bishops, led by Archbishop Pelagio Labastida (1816–91) and Bishop Clemente de Jesús Munguía (1810–68) of Michoacán, portrayed the Constitution as an assault on Catholicism as such and an attempt to replace what they understood to be a Catholic society with a secularised model based on foreign examples. The hierarchy and clerical polemicists argued for the defence of the Catholic identity of Mexico inherited from the Spanish colonial era. At the same time, they argued against the liberal doctrine of sovereignty of the people and in favour of the Church's right to possess property and to exercise control over education and private morality. Munguía led the attack on the Reform Laws through the Bishops' Manifesto of 30 August 1859.

Lerdo's efforts to secure a US loan accompanied by the negotiation of the McLane–Ocampo Treaty played into Conservative hands. The Juárez administration secured US recognition on 6 April 1859. Although the Liberals regarded this as a political triumph, since they saw it as the closer identification of the two North American Republics, Conservatives regarded it as a sell-out to the national enemy. Since the US Government had withdrawn recognition of the Conservative regime in Mexico City because it refused to entertain further territorial cessions, Conservatives warned that Liberal foreign policy would result in further loss of territory and even the complete subordination of Mexico to the United States. Lerdo, Ocampo, and Juárez were sensitive to this criticism, which threatened serious damage to the nationalist credentials of the Liberal cause. Accordingly, the McLane–Ocampo Treaty of December 1859 avoided territorial cessions to the United States but conceded transit rights both to the Pacific ports and across the Isthmus of Tehuantepec. The Treaty frustrated the expansionist designs of the US administration, but never came into effect because of the deterioration of the political situation within the United States in 1860–61.

After the Conservative military defeat in December 1860, the Liberals recovered control of the capital, although Conservative guerrilla bands operated across the countryside. Miramón, who had won most of the battles but lost the war, went into exile in Havana and thence to Europe. However, Márquez remained active and Mejía operated from his personal stronghold in the Sierra Gorda. A handful of monarchist exiles in Europe, with the support of some Conservatives, intrigued with Napoleon III for the establishment of a monarchy in Mexico by means of foreign military intervention.

Juárez, already three years in office as *de facto* President in the Liberal zone, was elected President of the Republic for the first time in March 1861 with a convincing majority. Nevertheless, his election did not end the factional divisions and personal rivalries within his party. Following the restoration of constitutional government, these hostilities spread through the political processes, pitting congress against the executive, and the state governors against the central power. Internal conflicts weakened national government, already burdened by interest payment on the external debt as a result of the civil war's impact on national finances. The total debt, which had reached 90 million pesos in 1851, stood at 82 million pesos by 1861. The outstanding debt to British bondholders, which formed part of that total, reached over 51 million pesos in this latter year.

At the same time, the fragmentation of the United States with the secession of the southern states and the formation of the Confederacy in February 1861 had serious implications for Mexico. In the first instance, it was unclear whether the Confederacy intended to continue traditional southern expansion at Mexico's expense or bring it to an end. The existence of seceded states on the precarious northern frontier of Mexico affected the relationship of the frontier states themselves to the national government in Mexico City. Considerable discussion ensued concerning the idea of a 'Republic of the Sierra Madre', consisting of the northern tier of states associated perhaps with an independent Texas and drawing New Mexico into its orbit. This idea had gained currency during the Revolution of Ayutla, when the north-east rebelled against the crumbling dictatorship of Santa Anna. Vidaurri, who had annexed Coahuila to Nuevo León in 1856 and had designs on the federal customs revenues of the Río Bravo from Piedras Negras to Matamoros, remained willingly or unwillingly at the centre of regionalist opposition to the Juárez administration.

The Intervention (1862–1867)

On 17 July 1861, the Juárez administration attempted to assert federal-government control over all revenues appropriated by state governors. These included the revenues of the river ports as well as those of the Gulf and Pacific coasts. The government's evident aim was to strengthen its fiscal position at a time when the situation on the northern frontier remained precarious. This decree, however, involved suspension of payments on the external debt for a two-year period – a moratorium on interest disembursements. The European Powers, their financial interests already damaged during the civil war, took this as a pretext for a demonstration of force, designed to oblige Mexico to honour its engagements. Great Britain, France, and Spain signed the Tripartite Convention of London in October 1861, which provided for joint occupation of the customs houses of the main ports, beginning with Veracruz, in order to enforce debt-payment. The threat of a European intervention seriously diverted the Juárez government from its two main objectives: the secure establishment of the constitutional system and the Reform Laws, and the stabilisation of the situation on the northern frontier.

Juárez managed to extract from a reluctant Congress the concession of extraordinary faculties in an attempt to defend national sovereignty in face of the European intervention. Further congressional concessions followed in October 1862 and May 1863. Treason laws would be applied to those who co-operated with the Intervention. The most far-reaching measure was the Law of 25 January 1862, which imposed trial by courts-martial and the penalty of capital punishment for collaboration with the Intervention, without the possibility of government pardon for those condemned under the law. This law provided the basis for the Juárez administration's treatment of the Intervention. Maximilian, Miramón, and Mejía were executed in June 1867 in accordance with its provisions.

French political designs in Mexico were made possible by the civil war which had broken out in the United States in April 1861. Realisation that the French intended to intervene directly in Mexican internal affairs and enforce a change of regime led to the withdrawal of the other two powers by the spring of 1862. The unilateral French intervention after April 1862 presupposed the nullification of Juárez's election in the previous year and the super- imposition of a system in Mexico acceptable to the French government. In such a way, Mexico would fall into the French imperial orbit, though more indirectly than Indo-China or Algeria. The French objective, initially working in concert with Mexican exiles, was to remove the Republic established under the 1857 Constitution in favour of a monarchy under a European prince. The candidate selected was the Archduke Ferdinand Maximilian, younger brother of the Austrian Emperor Francis Joseph. Maximilian had been a liberal-minded Governor of Lombardy in 1858–59, and had travelled to Brazil, where the Empress Leopoldina was also a Habsburg. This scheme, however, involved a prior French conquest of Mexico, and the assumption that Mexican Conservatives would be effective collaborators. French military calculations, nevertheless, failed to learn from the American experience of 1846–47 of long delays and huge loss of life.

The French defeat outside Puebla on 5 May 1862 postponed occupation of the capital for a further year. This military setback delayed Napoleon III's plans for a monarchy. Juan Nepomuceno Almonte (1803–69), illegitimate son of Morelos, returned to Mexico with the Intervention as the principal Conservative figure. Almonte had fought in the Texas campaign of 1835–36 and had been Minister of War in

1839–41 and again early in 1846. His intention was to use the Intervention as the basis for the construction of a Conservative regime. Napoleon III's Secret Instructions to Marshall Forey on 3 July 1862, however, precluded Conservative domination of government in favour of a moderate regime of talents from all factions. The French occupation of Mexico City in June 1863 obliged the Juárez administration to regroup in San Luis Potosí. French and Mexican Imperial forces pushed outwards to control all the principal cities and ports from the summer of 1863 until the autumn of 1866, when their military position began to collapse rapidly. The French government had grossly underestimated the difficulties in conquering Mexico. For political and financial reasons, Napoleon III had sent only an expeditionary force of some 27,000 men, one-tenth the number Napoleon I had put into the Spanish peninsula to subject a country half the size of Mexico. These included soldiers of the French Foreign Legion and auxiliaries from North Africa. The remnants of the Conservative army supplemented them, and subsequently Belgian and Austrian volunteers arrived. Even so, Imperial forces were never able to hold down the countryside for any length of time, and exposed cities changed hands on several occasions.

The Mexican imperial throne had been ominously vacant since the fall of Agustín I in March 1823. Maximilian, with the support of his wife, Carlota, daughter of Leopold I of the Belgians, agreed to be persuaded by Mexican Conservatives and monarchists that he could become the saviour of their country. A Regency Council, initially dominated by Almonte and Labastida, sought to establish its authority until the Imperial couple arrived. The French military commander, Achille Bazaine (1811–88), however, increasingly pushed the Regents to one side, in pursuit of Napoleon III's confidential policy of marginalising the Conservatives and preparing the way for a moderate regime taking support from anyone willing to rally to the Empire. Bazaine had gained his military experience in Algeria, Spain during the first Carlist War of 1833–40, the Crimean War (1854–56), and the Franco-Austrian war in Italy in 1859.

Maximilian and Carlota did not arrive in Mexico until June 1864, when the defeat of the Confederate Army was approaching. Although France had never recognised the Confederacy, Napoleon III's strategy in Mexico had been predicated upon the continuation of the armed struggle in the United States. Once Imperial forces had reached the Texas

Plate 24 (a) The Emperor Maximilian in Imperial robes;

(b) The Empress Carlota in Imperial robes.
Both paintings can be seen in the Museum of History at
Chapultepec Castle. There is an extraordinary quantity of
photos and paintings of the Imperial couple, a desperate attempt
to propagate their image as widely as possible in an increasingly
adverse environment.

border late in 1864, relations with the Confederate authorities were cordial, especially since the Confederacy depended upon Matamoros to circumvent the Union blockade as its point of exit for the cotton crop. In the meantime, however, Juárez's Minister in Washington, Matías Romero (1837–98), worked unceasingly to mobilise US public opinion against the Second Mexican Empire. The US Government, however, even after the defeat of the Confederacy in 1865, continued to attach greater priority to its relations with France than to Republican Mexico. Accordingly, it never gave material support to the *juarista* cause. Arms crossed the border in private transactions, but neither France nor the USA risked a breach in relations over the Mexican issue.

During the War of the Intervention (1862–67), Juárez never abandoned national territory. He regarded himself as the personal embodiment of the Republic – perpetually itinerant but never forced out of the country. Although holding out in El Paso del Norte (later Ciudad Juárez) on the Río Bravo in 1865–66, Juárez and his two accompanying ministers, Sebastián Lerdo de Tejada (1823–89) and José María Iglesias (1823–91), never abandoned the belief that defence of national sovereignty required their continued presence, in spite of the hardships involved, on Mexican soil. In such a way, they prevented the Imperial Government from claiming that it alone represented the legitimate government of Mexico. In spite of notable defections from the republican camp, Juárez could count on the support of a series of northern and western state governors, ranging from Coahuila to Michoacán. The most significant of these was Luis Terrazas in Chihuahua, where Juárez spent the greater part of his internal exile in 1864–66. Terrazas began his rise to local dominance in the political and economic life of Chihuahua in this period. Through such political and military alliances in the north, Juárez was able to break the power of Vidaurri and occupy Monterrey in 1864.

Maximilian's government suffered from the outset from an ambivalence of policy. He had been brought to Mexico by the Conservatives, but tended to liberal views himself. He rapidly alienated the ecclesiastical hierarchy because of his Habsburg belief in the supremacy of state over Church and in his support for religious toleration. He refused to sanction the nullification of the disamortisation laws of 1856 and 1859 with regard to ecclesiastical properties and sought, instead, to rally purchasers of nationalised properties to the Empire. Imperial policy alienated Pope Pius IX (1846–78), who had condemned the Mexican Reform

Laws, led to the prompt withdrawal of the Papal Nuncio, and frustrated the signature of a Concordat between Church and state. Financial disarray provided the basic cause of the Empire's collapse. The Treaty of Miramar between Napoleon III and Maximilian on 23 March 1864 obliged Mexico, its financial situation already the pretext for the initial European intervention, to pay the cost of the French enterprise. As a result, the Imperial government constantly sought financial assistance from European banking houses, including Barings of London.

Maximilian excluded the Conservative Party as such from office. Out of power as a group since the end of December 1860, Conservatives did not predominate in government again until late in 1866, when the Empire was near collapse. Maximilian placed the administration in the hands of known moderates and liberals disposed to cooperate with a reforming Empire. The three principal Conservative figures, Almonte, Miramón, and Márquez, were all sent to Europe. Miramón, an ex-President (1860), clearly had national political ambitions and as such posed a potential threat to the Empire. Márquez had an unsavoury reputation as a result of his murder of Liberal prisoners and medical workers at Tacubaya in 1859. Miramón and Márquez were not recalled until the end of 1866, when French military withdrawal was already in process. From late 1864 until late 1866, Mejía, who had no national-level political ambitions, became, in effect, the principal Mexican Imperial commander in the field.

From the beginning, Maximilian sought to distance his government from the actions of the French military – upon whose success his survival depended. The Emperor's intention was to sponsor the creation of an autonomous Mexican Imperial Army, which he hoped initially to achieve through the efforts of his Austrian and Belgian volunteers. French hostility, followed by complete withdrawal by February 1867, forced him to rely principally on Miramón, Márquez, and Mejía. Increasing costs, political dangers in Europe, domestic opposition, and opposition from the US government contributed to the French decision to abort the Intervention. Although Bazaine's expeditionary force was not actually defeated in Mexico, the withdrawal acknowledged the impossibility of effective occupation beyond the principal cities. Napoleon III, who had hoped for a cheap and rapid victory, was not prepared to pay the political and military costs of an effective campaign of pacification. Bazaine, however, failed to persuade Maximilian to leave

Plate 25 The Execution of Maximilian, 19 June 1867.
There are a number of depictions of this scene, including three
paintings by Edouard Manet, and photographs, a detail of one
of which is shown here, of the original firing squad. A chapel,
paid for by the Austro-Hungarian Government commemorates
the event on the Hill of the Bells. Today a huge statue of Juárez
dominates the Hill.

Mexico with the retreating French armies. Abandoning the original idea
of a liberal monarchy, Maximilian realigned with Conservatives to
prepare for a last stand.

The principal Liberal commanders, Mariano Escobedo (1826–1902)
in the north and Porfirio Díaz (1830–1915) in the south-east, achieved
the final victory over the Empire by the capture of Querétaro and
Mexico City respectively in May and June 1867. Juárez was determined
to bring Maximilian, Miramón, and Mejía, taken prisoner in Querétaro,
to trial by court-martial under the severe provisions of the law of
25 January 1862. Although the defence counsel appealed for a civil trial
in accordance with the Constitution, the three prisoners were executed
by firing squad early on 19 June 1867 on the Hill of the Bells outside
Querétaro. The execution was intended to be a powerful deterrent to
European monarchies which sought to intervene in the affairs of
American republics. The symbolism of an Austrian Habsburg, descen-

dant of the Emperor Charles V, put to death on a hill in central Mexico by a squad of dark *mestizo* soldiers was lost on no one. A less well-known point was that Juárez's code name in the masonic organisation, which he joined in January 1847 in Mexico City while a Oaxaca deputy to the National Congress during the War with the United States, was William Tell. Mexican republicans portrayed the defeat of the Empire as a revindication of the national independence seized from Spain in 1821. It represented the survival of Mexico (in its post-1853 territorial form) as a sovereign state and at the same time sent a powerful signal to the United States to attempt no further dismemberment of national territory.

Juárez, a cunning and ruthless politician who knew how to wait, had survived every intrigue to bring him down and had played the central role in resisting the Intervention and Empire. In shifting alliances with Liberal state governors and political figures who spanned the range of the party from moderate to radical, Juárez had been able to deal with each of the enemies in turn. The consistent support of leading army commanders, most prominent of whom were Escobedo and Díaz, enabled Juárez to deliver the final blow to the Empire during the first half of 1867. Thereafter, the Conservative Party was ruined as a political force in Mexico; however, much in this party's history over the period 1848–67 still remains unexplained. No Catholic-oriented party gained electoral credibility again until the National Catholic Party of 1911–13. This meant that Mexico's future would lie in the hands of the triumphant Liberals, determined after 1867 to give the Reform Laws full effect. The victory of 1867, however, represented more the triumph of nationalism than the secure establishment of a constitutional system. As the administrations of the Restored Republic (1867–76) quickly discovered, the war years exacerbated the tensions between executive and legislative branches, and between centre and regions. Local and sub-regional poles of power, which had emerged during the fighting, challenged central-government Liberalism and sought to defend a provincial and popular-based interpretation of the Reform struggle. Juárez and Lerdo, anxious to strengthen central power by reforming the Constitution in August 1867, found themselves faced with deep suspicion and widespread opposition. Long-lasting divisions within the Liberal camp ultimately undermined attempts to establish solidly the constitutional provisions of 1857.

6

Reconstruction, 1867–1940

Several decades ago, US economist Clark Reynolds argued for three periods of rapid economic growth in modern Mexico: 1770–1795; 1880–1907; 1946–1970. In the first of these, capital was generated within the economy of New Spain and investment was made primarily by Spanish peninsular merchant-financiers resident in Mexico. During the second period, foreign investment played a decisive role in stimulating growth, particularly in the export sector. The final period was, as we shall see in the following chapter, the product of a post-revolutionary political economy, in which the Mexican state fulfilled an enhanced role. From the 1880s, the Mexican economy (and the Latin American economies, in general) became more closely integrated into the international system in which the principal dynamic lay in the industrialised and rapidly industrialising countries of Northern Europe and the United States. The demand for industrial raw materials and tropical produce provided powerful incentives to overseas investment. Accordingly, the recipient countries were faced with the urgent necessity of bringing their inadequate infrastructure up to date by modernising their port, transportation, and banking facilities. These pressures, in turn, pointed to the necessity of political stabilisation at home.

The aftermath of the Reform era shaped the economic structure of late nineteenth- and early twentieth-century Mexico. Although considerable industrial advance took place in the years from 1880 to 1910, Mexico by 1940 still remained predominantly rural. Even so, profound social changes were set in motion, which would ultimately alter the distribution of population between town and country. It can be argued that the cost of certain sectors of the Mexican economy participating in the late nineteenth-century capitalist world was a decline in popular living standards. In areas of particular social dislocation, rural rebellion broke out and banditry was rife. One of the most notorious bandits, Heraclio Bernal, operated across the mining zones of the Sierra Madre Occidental during the 1880s. The social impact of closer integration into the world market became a major issue during the Mexican Revolution after 1910, as it would again with the adoption of 'neo-liberal' economic policies from the mid-1980s.

In the period from 1880 until the wide-ranging impact of the recession of 1907, the Mexican economy expanded particularly in three areas: diversification of the mining sector, development of tropical produce for export, and the capture of the home market by a series of national industries with textiles in the lead. At the same time, however, Mexican population growth from 9.7 to 15.1 million inhabitants between 1877 and 1910 placed fresh burdens on an inadequate agrarian structure. In spite of striking advances in the industrial sectors of the economy, at least 64 per cent of the working population was still engaged in agriculture by 1910. The proportion had, in fact, increased from 60 per cent in 1877. Furthermore, the high illiteracy rate of 77 per cent of the total population impeded the application of technology and the transfer to skilled labour.

Serious political failures at the national level during the 1890s and 1900s ensured that Mexico by 1910–11 found itself in a revolutionary situation. Political division in the national government left the precarious structures of the regime dangerously exposed to popular mobilisation at all levels. The celebrations for the centenary of Independence provided the façade behind which political failure and social dislocation remained at least partially hidden from view. Failure to resolve the succession question throughout the 1900s provided the immediate cause for political disintegration which began within the Díaz regime itself.

Mexico lost a million people during the revolutionary conflicts of the 1910s. The dislocation of supply lines and persistent military requisitioning produced a major food crisis by 1914–15. In June 1915, there were food riots in the capital, which presented a scene of malnutrition and starvation. Maize production fell considerably below 1900–10 levels by 1918, and bean production reached only 60 per cent of the 1910 figure. In 1918–19, only 12 per cent of mines and 21 per cent of processing plants were actually operating. Food prices continued to rise through 1920, while wage levels remained the same as in 1910. Worse still, silver and copper prices continued to fall on the world market. Mexico's booming oil industry, largely untouched by revolutionary fighting due to its remote geographical locations on the Gulf coast and Isthmus, proved to be the country's main export earner during that period of contraction and hardship.

The problem of resolving the question of food supply would be left for the revolutionary governments after 1920. Large-scale peasant mobilisation during the Revolution, however, ensured that the issue of landownership would also have to be dealt with by them. During the 1930s, the Mexican Revolution faced the problem of reconciling the need to maximise food supply with demand for land redistribution to the peasantry. Accordingly, the Revolution generated parallel issues such as labour organisation within the peasant sector and government credit supply to reconstituted communities. This brought to the fore-front the question of the relationship of organised peasant producers to the post-revolutionary political processes.

Reconstruction proved to be a process of long duration. It did not come to fruition until after the mid-1940s, when Mexico experienced three decades of rapid growth. During the course of those decades, the country became predominantly urban for the first time. Economic growth during the Díaz period laid many of the foundations for this subsequent expansion. In many respects, the immediate impact of the Revolution over the period from 1910 to 1940 halted economic growth or even pushed the country backwards into the cycle of violence and turmoil. At the same time, however, the social and political changes imposed by the Revolution released energies hitherto contained and created conditions ultimately more favourable to renewed economic growth. During the 1940s, as we shall see in the following chapter, inter-nal and international conditions combined to enable Mexico to embark on a leap forward that has been described as the 'Mexican miracle'.

PART ONE: THE LIBERAL REPUBLIC: CONSTITUTIONALISM OR PERSONAL RULE, 1867–1911?

The triumph of the Liberal Reform movement in 1867 brought about a flourishing of Mexican nationalism in official circles. Ignacio Altamirano

(1834–93), in particular, appealed for the development of a distinct national literature in reaction to predominant European models. It remained unclear how this would come about, especially since the leading literary innovators continued to be Europeans at least into the last decades of the century. Cultural nationalism remained a series of confused reactions to foreign models among a small group of literary figures struggling with the limitations of their home culture but unable to discover what might define a predominantly 'Mexican' expression. Even so, Altamirano led the way in 1869 with the establishment of the literary newspaper, *El Renacimiento*, which sought to revive national creativity after the war years by bringing together talent from whatever ideological persuasion. A radical Liberal of indigenous origin, born in Tixtla (Guerrero), Altamirano was also a novelist, whose *Clemencia* (1869) has been regarded as one of the first modern Mexican novels. José María Velasco (1840–1912), Mexico's foremost landscape painter, adapted the European tradition to a specifically Mexican environment, vaster and more dramatic. From the 1870s into the 1890s, Velasco painted scenes mainly in the Valley of Mexico, which included depictions of the first railways. Diego Rivera (1886–1957), the revolutionary nationalist at the centre of the muralist movement of the 1920s to 1940s, regarded Velasco as one of his principal influences. The other was José Guadalupe Posada (1852–1913), whose lithographs took up the traditional theme of the Day of the Dead (2 November) and portrayed the mocking omnipresence of death through his satires with skulls and skeletons. Posada became a leading critic of the late Díaz-era plutocracy.

Juárez had always emphasised the necessity of state education, but government finances were inadequate to the task during the 1860s and 1870s. The ten-year struggle between Liberals and Conservatives delayed the projected educational reforms. The National Preparatory School finally opened early in 1868. Rivera in 1921–22 would paint his first murals on its walls. Gabino Barreda (1818–81), for twelve years its first director, introduced a Mexicanised version of French positivism after 1867, which stressed the importance of scientific and practical education over religion and the traditional disciplines to which Liberal thinkers attributed the country's backwardness. In his view, Mexican history consisted of three phases, the religious (the Spanish colonial era), the metaphysical (the Liberal Reform movement), and the positive (the forthcoming era of peace and progress). Although the education share of the national budget doubled to just under 7 per cent of the total between 1877–78 and 1910–11, the allocation for the armed forces and police stood at 22 per cent (though having fallen from 42 per cent).

The expansion of the economy

The attempted reconstruction of the economy began in the aftermath of the collapse of the Second Empire. Although no diplomatic relations existed between Mexico and Great Britain from 1867 to 1884, the Juárez Government in 1870 recognised a total British debt of 66.5 million pesos, which would somehow have to be serviced. At the same time, the country experienced a continual shortage of circulating medium: in 1870 estimates of minted coinage totalled 24 million pesos, but 21–23 million was exported in order to pay for imports. This problem curbed domestic purchasing power and held back national industries. Romero, Secretary of Finance in 1872–73, estimated a budget deficit of 7.2 million pesos for the financial year, with revenues at only 15.9 million pesos.

The Restored Republic (1867–76), beset by internal conflict over the relationship between centre and regions, executive and legislative branches, and civil and military power, largely failed to stabilise the economy. By 1880, Mexico faced a range of economic obstacles: how to reduce traditional reliance on the export of precious metals at a time of falling silver prices and diversify mineral production; how to stimulate home industrial production; how to open up new geographical areas of production; how to reduce annual budget deficits and the adverse balance of trade; how to service the substantial external debt; how to fund a broadly based educational system capable of raising literacy levels and providing a skilled labour force. In 1883–84, the administration of Manuel González (1880–84) attempted unsuccessfully to renegotiate the external debt and restore Mexico's creditworthiness. This was brought to fruition by Finance Minister Manuel Dublán (1830–91), brother-in-law of Juárez, during the period 1884–88. Following the restoration of relations with Great Britain, Mexico was able to negotiate in 1885 the conversion of the debt, which would be serviced by the newly founded Banco Nacional de México with deposits from the Veracruz customs-house. Agreement with the London bondholders followed in 1885, along with a loan of £10.5 million from the German

House of Bleichröder. Finally, in 1888, the issue of new bonds signalled Mexico's return to the international credit market. A second German loan followed in 1890 for £6 million.

Accelerated economic growth after c. 1880 had far-reaching social and political repercussions. Not the least of these was the rapidly increasing importance of the northern states from Sonora across to Nuevo León, where the rise of Monterrey coincided with the governorship of General Bernardo Reyes (1884–1909). The development of a railroad network from the 1880s not only contributed to the integration of a national market for the first time, but also assisted government attempts to control the full span of national territory. The total railroad length grew from only 472 km to 19,205 km between 1873 and 1910, with 1882 as the peak year of expansion. After 1880, the Mexican railroad system was linked to the US network through El Paso. The growth of the railroad system led to concessions to development companies and expanded labour opportunities. At the same time, however, rising land values put pressure on peasant properties located near the proposed lines and provoked considerable rural unrest behind the façade of development. Railroad expansion profoundly affected the economy as a whole and contributed to the growth of Gross National Product in the period between 1895 and 1910. Government recognition of the importance of the infrastructure led to the establishment of a separate Ministry of Communications and Public Works in 1891, located in a magnificent building opposite the colonial Mining College at the edge of the old city centre. The crucial role of the railways raised the question of ownership, which became a major political issue in the late 1900s.

Under General Carlos Pacheco (b. Chihuahua 1839), veteran of the Wars of Reform and Intervention and the 1876 rebellion, railway development was pushed ahead. Pacheco, Secretary for Development from 1881 to 1891, laid the foundations for nearly three decades of economic development. The expansion of the railroad system from the centre core to the US border opened new areas of raw-material supply. This proved to be of decisive importance with regard to cotton production for the struggling national textile industry. Until the 1870s the Veracruz Gulf and Pacific coastal zones still remained the principal areas of supply, just as they had been in the colonial era. The building of the Central Railroad in the 1880s, however, opened the La Laguna zone

across the States of Durango and Coahuila. Irrigated by the Río Nazas, this zone consisted of 6,000 km of cotton lands. Poor share-croppers lost their flood-plain maize lands to the cotton planters. In 1888, a joint-stock company, the Tlahualillo Company, bought up 44,000 hectares and promptly ran into conflict with local landowners over the water supply. La Laguna became the fastest growing agricultural zone in Mexico between 1888 and 1895. The rural population increased tenfold to 200,000 between 1880 and 1910, mostly due to migration from central Mexico. The labour situation in the La Laguna area contributed to mass support for the Revolution in 1910.

Rapidly increasing cotton production reduced Mexico's reliance on imported fibre: raw cotton fell as a proportion of primary imports from 45 per cent in 1888–89 to 22 per cent by 1910–11. A parallel expansion took place in national textile production, particularly during the 1890s, as a result of heavy Mexican and foreign-resident investment. Industrialisation contributed to urbanisation: Mexico City, Puebla, Guadalajara, all traditional textile centres grew considerably, though the most striking growth took place in Orizaba (Veracruz) and Monterrey, which were linked by rail to La Laguna. Torreón, the La Laguna principal town and also a metallurgical centre, rose from 2,000 to 34,200 inhabitants in the twenty years before 1910. The estimated number of textile artisans in Mexico fell from 41,000 in 1895 to 8,000 by 1910, while the number of industrial workers rose from 19,000 to 36,000. In other industrial activities, however, artisan production remained largely unaffected.

Plate 26 José María Velasco (1840–1912): this painting of the volcano, Pico de Orizaba (Citlaltépetl) (1897), corresponds to Velasco's fourth period (1890–1901). Velasco's roots lay in the landscape painting of the seventeenth and eighteenth centuries. From 1855, he studied at the late-colonial Academia de San Carlos in Mexico City (which became the National School of Fine Arts after 1867), and was a pupil of the Italian painter, Eugenio Landesio, resident in Mexico until 1897. From 1865, Velasco studied Natural Science at the Academy of Medicine, Botany, Physics, and Zoology. Diego Rivera became one of his pupils. The train is near Fortín station in the State of Veracruz. The Cañada de Metepec and coffee plantations are in the foreground.

Expansion emphasised all the more the necessity of importing technology from north-west Europe or the USA to respond to domestic demand. This, however, proved to be expensive at a time of declining values of silver exports. Accordingly, the preferred method of increasing textile production tended to be by an increase in manpower rather than through the adoption of new technologies. Although by 1910–11, 9 per cent of Mexican imports consisted of machinery and the proportion of imported cotton fell from 31.5 per cent in 1888–89 to only 2.8 per cent, productivity remained largely static. Skilled labour, furthermore, continued to be at a premium in view of the general lack of educational facilities for the working man and woman.

The rapid growth of the mining sector further underlined the economic importance of the northern states, which according to François-Xavier Guerra accounted for 75 per cent of mine production. Investment rose from 1.75 million pesos in 1892 to 156 million pesos by 1907, when the industry was struck by recession. A large part of that investment was foreign by origin. Mexico's traditional export, silver, was badly affected by declining world values, which halved between 1877 and 1903. International demand for Mexican silver as a medium of exchange fell as the principal countries went over to the gold standard after 1873. Precious metal exports, however, still expanded: from 25 million pesos to 81 million pesos between 1877 and 1910. Even so, industrial and combustible metal production grew from the early 1890s, with the result that by 1910–11 precious metals represented only 54 per cent of the value of mining production. Mining centres moved continually northwards until by the end of the Díaz period Zacatecas, San Luis Potosí, Sonora, and Coahuila were the predominant zones.

The rise of Monterrey as the major commercial and industrial centre of the north-east (1,000 km from Mexico City) was linked to the expansion of the US economy in the post-Civil War era. As in the rest of Mexico, merchant-financiers, many of them foreign-born, supplied the capital. One of the most prominent was Isaac Garza (b. Monterrey 1853), who married into the Sada family and headed the city's most important business connection. The Garza Sada family dominated the beer industry, which forced out foreign competition during the 1890s, and consolidated the three great breweries in the 1920s. Two decades earlier, the glass industry passed from Puebla and Mexico City

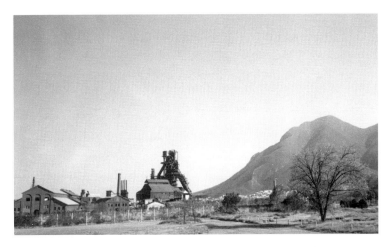

Plate 27 The Monterrey Iron and Steel Plant of 1903 (author's photo).
The Compañía Fundidora de Fierro y Acero de Monterrey began operations in 1903. Established in 1900 with Mexican and foreign-resident capital, the plant contributed significantly to the rapid industrialisation of this north-eastern city from the late 1880s. Founded in 1854, 1872 and 1874, three textile factories already operated in and around the city. The brewery opened in 1890; cement and glassware followed iron and steel in 1905 and 1909, respectively. Coal deposits were located to the north of Monterrey and across the Coahuila border. The Cerro de la Silla (Saddle Mountain) can be seen in the background. The 'Fundidora' now forms the centrepiece of an industrial park.

to Monterrey, where there had been no previous tradition. The family opened the Vidriera Monterrey SA factory in 1909, which had a basic capital of $1.2 million and began production in the following year. The glass factory was situated close to the Cervecería Cuauhtémoc. The first steel mill in Latin America, Fundidora Monterrey, began production in 1903, again under Garza control. However, the blast furnace never ran to more than 50 per cent of its production capacity for any two consecutive years in the decades before 1929. It took until the late 1930s for the Fundidora to produce to 80 per cent capacity for the first time.

Three finance ministers, Romero, Dublán, and José Yves Limantour (1854–1935) contributed to the final stabilisation of Mexican finances.

Limantour succeeded Romero at the Secretariat of Finance in May 1893. In the financial year 1895–96, he managed to produce a budget surplus with revenues at 50.5 million pesos and expenditure at 40 million. This remarkable achievement was sustained right through to 1905–06. Trade figures for 1904–05 also showed a favourable balance, with metals comprising half the exports. In the monetary reform of 1905, however, Limantour put Mexico on the gold standard, reflecting ten years of fiscal stability and with the intention of claiming a place for the Republic among the leading countries of the world. As a result, the terms of trade deteriorated when export prices fell and the price of imports, particularly machinery, rose. In that context, the impact of the New York stock market collapse of 1907 bit deeply into the modernised sectors of the Mexican economy exposed to international price trends. The disastrous harvest of the same year increased social deprivation. Although food production recovered in 1908 and 1909, those two years proved to be disastrous for Mexican industry. Limantour was obliged to ride through the crisis by securing another foreign loan.

During the Díaz period, Mexico's foreign and internal debt rapidly increased, particularly after 1890. Debt rose from 193.2 million pesos in 1896 to 589.7 million pesos by 1911, of which 441 million represented the external debt (including railway credits), even allowing for the 1905 devaluation. The bulk of the external debt was accounted for not by the purchase of military equipment (which was generally neglected), but through the cost of modernising the infrastructure. Limantour, however, was able to reduce the cost of servicing the debt from 38 per cent of ordinary revenue in 1895–96 to 23.7 per cent by 1910–11, by the reduction of interest rates through debt conversions in 1899 and 1910. International confidence in Mexico remained high and the level of debt continued to be manageable. The total of direct investments, furthermore, far exceeded the sum of the loans.

Financial stability, adversely affected by the recession of 1907, significantly deteriorated during the revolutionary conflicts of the 1910s. Although a New York loan was secured in 1911 and three issues of British bonds took place in 1913–14, Mexico in 1914 was unable to service its external debt. Political collapse and civil war during the decade undermined many of the economic advances of the period from the 1880s. By December 1919, the national debt had increased to 722 million pesos. These problems would be left for the regime of Plutarco Elías Calles

(1924–28) to attempt to resolve. In many respects, Limantour's successors were the Finance Ministers of the 1920s.

Territorial power and the rural world

Conditions on the land were by no means uniform. Labour mobility was greater in the rapidly developing north than in the traditionalist south, where (especially in Oaxaca) the Indian peasant community still retained control of much of the land. Population increased at far higher rates across the northern tier of states, Coahuila, Durango, Sonora, Chihuahua, and Nuevo León, than elsewhere in the Republic, largely due to internal migration. In central Mexico, peasant land loss was considerable during the Díaz period but neither generalised nor consistent. Up to 20 per cent of the rural population lived on hacienda lands, generally the best quality land. In states such as Morelos, the rapid expansion of sugar production put heavy pressure on peasant control of land, labour, and water supplies. In northern states like San Luis Potosí, wage labour tended to replace debt servility on the land. In specific areas across the centre-north, in the states of Jalisco, Aguascalientes, Guanajuato, and Querétaro, a vigorous rural middle class emerged as ranch-owners, especially where the hacienda was weak or absent and the peasant community long ago superseded.

The largest concentration of land remained under the control of the Terrazas family in Chihuahua. Luis Terrazas (1829–1923) established the dynasty during the Juárez era, and remained closely linked to national government until Díaz, wary of his regional power, played on local rivalries and brought about his removal between 1884 and 1903. The Terrazas' activities ranged across livestock raising, banking, and commercial interests. By 1910, the family held 15 properties and a total of 2 million hectares, with 500,000 head of cattle and 250,000 head of sheep. The cattle-raising society of Chihuahua and Texas had a great deal in common. The developing middle sectors in the state of Chihuahua, however, found their aspirations blocked by the Terrazas monopoly, and looked to the political democracy and life-styles of the United States as their model. Trans-border contact was a normal facet of daily life. Chihuahua, furthermore, was not a society of sedentary community peasants like the Mexican centre and south, but a diversified and dynamic state with a semi-industrial base. Its Indian traditions remained strong in the form of the resilient Tarahumara presence in the western sierra.

Mexican agriculture, as in the eighteenth century, continued to be exposed to repeated subsistence crises. In 1891–92, for instance, two harvests failed in succession. Worse still, food production diminished in relation to rising population in the decades before 1910. Maize production, for instance, fell from 2.7 million tons in 1877 to 2.1 million tons in 1907. As a result, the country was obliged to import grains at times of shortage, such as 1896–97, 1900–1, and particularly between 1909 and 1911, a period of repeated harvest failures. Food imports in a period of diminishing silver values further jeopardised the financial system, made precariously stable by the efforts of Limantour after 1893. Food prices rose in Mexico – by 20 per cent between 1900 and 1910 – when they were falling in much of the rest of the world. The maize price rose in the same decade from an index of 100 to 190. As in the subsistence crisis of 1809–11, regional disparities were striking. The northern mining states were among the worst affected. Inattention to the food supply fuelled general inflation at a time of relatively stagnant wage-levels. Loss of village lands exacerbated the impact of subsistence crisis in the central zones.

The 'pax porfiriana' did not bring peace to the rural world. Villages in the humid Huasteca zone of San Luis Potosí attempted in 1879–83 to take back lands usurped by haciendas and to assert their right to municipal representation. Communities in Tepic demanded effective suffrage and free municipal elections. Similar instances appeared across the entire central zone of Mexico. Reyes, who believed that the suppression of rural resistance and bandit activity was the precondition for modernisation, put down the San Luis Potosí rebellions. A later series of rebellions spread across Chihuahua and Coahuila between 1889 and 1893, originating in power struggles between rival factions, accompanied by other movements in Guerrero and Veracruz. All such rebellions, in part products of the economic difficulties of those years, remained local in character.

The recovery of the mining economy of the north-west placed renewed pressure on the Yaquis of Sonora. Indian strategies of survival during the nineteenth century had involved tactical alliances with competing political factions in the state. In effect, the Yaquis by the 1870s had managed to maintain a virtually autonomous republic based on the rich agriculture of the Yaqui River system. The advance of development companies, which aimed to seize this land, provoked a determined guerrilla warfare after 1887. State and federal government frustration led to a policy after 1895 of violent repression and the deportation of captured Yaquis to the tropical plantations of the south. Even so, by 1900, there were still some 30,000 Yaquis out of a total state population of 220,000 inhabitants. Yaqui resistance in 1899 and between 1902 and 1905 ensured that up to 5,000 federal troops were in the field. Deportation became general policy after 1904, rising to a peak by 1908, by which time between a quarter and a half of the Yaqui population had been sent out of the state by rail. Many went to supplement local Maya labour on the henequen plantations of Yucatán, which were labour-intensive. Others fled across the border into Arizona. The Díaz regime portrayed the Yaquis as enemies of progress and civilisation, and applied a policy of violent repression. For their part, the Yaquis denied the right of the federal government to alter their way of life and deprive them of their lands. A key role in the government's war against the Yaqui was played by Ramón Corral (1854–1912), the leading political figure in Sonora between 1887 and 1900. The crude solutions of the Díaz era contributed to Yaqui cooperation with Álvaro Obregón's revolutionary forces in Sonora after 1913. The Mexican Revolution in power was left to find a solution to the problems of the Yaquis.

Alan Knight's study of the Mexican Revolution argues strongly that 'rebellions stemming from agrarian grievances were central to the popular revolution of 1910–20'. As in the case of the background to the revolutionary movements of the 1810s, many long-standing, localised grievances filtered into the broader movement with its regional and national leadership groups. Accelerated economic change often exacerbated local problems in the decades prior to the outbreak of generalised revolt. In both cases, a political crisis at the centre opened the way for popular mobilisation. There were, however, substantial qualitative differences. Conflicts over land usage, water rights, and peasant labour on haciendas assumed much greater importance in the 1910s than in the 1810s, though they were not by any means absent then. From the 1890s, land and labour questions predominated as the sources of social conflict. The immediate decades prior to the 1910 Revolution highlighted the widening gap between the modernising sectors of the economy and traditional peasant identity.

Issues and interpretations

Between 1867 and 1884 the Mexican political system functioned in a relatively open manner. Although Conservatives and clericals as a group played no direct part in it, the various factions within the Liberal movement and the conflicting personalities at their head actively competed for influence. The press openly criticised and satirised governments, and journalists were not hounded by the official power. Two issues remained outstanding, however: the peaceful transfer of political power from one president to another, and the marked tendency of the executive at national and state levels to establish control over the electoral process. Failure to resolve these issues brought the Restored Republic to a turning point by the mid-1870s. The issue of re-election thereafter became a central issue in politics, especially when, after 1900, the personalist regime of Porfirio Díaz distinctly failed to resolve the succession question.

During the period 1884 to 1911, it became evident that nineteenth-century Mexican Liberalism had not succeeded in providing the country with a working representative system of government. In spite of the reaffirmation of liberal constitutional principles and the federal structure during the Reform era, the political processes became increasingly authoritarian and centralist. Regime abuse of re-election guaranteed perpetuation in office. Re-election in itself might not have led to crisis, had it not been for the closure of the political system and the regime's undermining of the institutions established in accordance with the Constitution of 1857. By 1909–11, when the crisis over re-election broke, no national institutions were capable of asserting a controlling position or providing a stabilising element when the regime itself broke down.

Between 1910 and 1914, the system put together by Díaz after his capture of power in 1876 collapsed. The disintegration of Mexico's political processes provided the real testament of the Díaz era. The extent of its failures would be felt during the following decades. Economic modernisation and rising statistics disguised in part the subversion of the Constitution and the gradual closure of the political system. Prosperity within the sector of the elite involved in the modernisation process left its members less inclined to challenge the regime on constitutional grounds. As a result, the recession of 1907, at its most severe in the advanced sectors of the economy, exposed to view a society of stunted political development and ineffective institutions.

Latin American historiography frequently lumps together the Mexican regime and those of South America as common expressions of 'oligarchic government'. Such a view, however, misses the point, which is the substantial difference between Mexico and the other principal countries of Latin America. Elsewhere, oligarchic regimes involved transfers of power between elected presidents and, on occasions, between different parties or factions. Such practices, although rarely in any sense democratic, avoided the possibility of both self-perpetuation in power and an ensuing succession crisis. In Argentina, popular organisation forced open the political processes after 1912, which resulted in the election of the principal opposition movement, the Radical Party, in 1916. Even Peru and Bolivia, which had a far weaker constitutional inheritance than Mexico, passed through the period from the mid-1880s to the 1920s without major political and social turmoil. Most of South America, furthermore, experienced a similar economic growth to that in Mexico. The South American experience itself demonstrated that dictatorship (in the form of the Díaz regime) was not a necessary prerequisite for development.

The comparison between Mexico and the rest of Latin America reveals the transcendent consequences of the political measures adopted during the Díaz period. The experiment in representative government begun in 1855 was broken off after 1884. Imperfect and limited as it had been, the intention after 1884 was neither to reform it nor to make it work but to reduce it to nullity. Many commentators have interpreted the Díaz regime (which still remains controversial) in accordance with its own self-justifications. Apologists at the time justified the regime on the grounds that the Constitution of 1857 was unworkable, that the Mexican people were not ready for representative government – or were incapable of it altogether, that dictatorship was necessary for development, and that Juárez and Lerdo, intending to perpetuate themselves in office, laid the basis for the Díaz regime. Their other argument was that only Díaz could hold the country together. Even so, Mexico had produced many men of distinction and ability, such as Mariano Escobedo, Matías Romero, Ignacio Vallarta, Manuel Romero Rubio, Ignacio Mariscal, and Manuel Dublán, for instance, capable of reaching the presidency. The Díaz regime did not result either from the historic conditions of Mexico or from simple accident, but from decisions taken at the highest level. Accordingly, Mexico, which in the Reform era had been at the vanguard of Latin American political development, fell gradually back to the level of less sophisticated societies. Venezuela, for instance, experienced a style of government determined by its national-level caudillos such as Antonio Guzmán Blanco, Cipriano Castro, and Juan Vicente Gómez from the 1870s to the 1930s. The Díaz experience, labelled the 'Porfiriato' by Daniel Cosío Villegas, deprived Mexicans of the few constitutional guarantees they had won since the end of the colonial era. Mexico's constitutional experiments, tentatively begun in 1808, were snuffed out. Political practice depended not on respect for the Constitution but on personal arrangements with General Díaz. Such procedures violated the basic precepts of constitutional impartiality which Juárez had championed.

Lack of definition remained the hallmark of the Díaz regime throughout the period from 1880 to 1900. Divisions within the Liberal party made it impossible to adopt an official ideology: they certainly ruled out the possibility of the party becoming the monopoly party of government. If anything, that in itself explained the personalist course the regime took. With hindsight the regime's interpreters, whether influenced by apologists or detractors, have ideologised it as 'modernising', 'developmentalist', or 'positivist'. Statistics of the period from 1877 until the recession of 1907 show considerable economic expansion, but if the economy – or some sectors of it – 'modernised', the political system did not. Instead, Díaz constructed a personalist, authoritarian system – more style than substance. When this system abruptly collapsed in 1911, no alternative institutions or political tradition existed to replace it and thereby prevent the country from dissolving into chaos.

The Díaz legacy, whether viewed in economic terms or from the perspective of political culture, proved to be a defining experience for Mexico. It left its mark throughout the twentieth century. Decisions taken in the Díaz era influenced the outcome of events during and after the Revolution. What Iturbide and Santa Anna had failed to do, Díaz constructed between 1884 and 1911. In that sense, his regime represented not a continuation of Juárez and Lerdo, but a significant departure from their path. Mexican constitutionalists were too weak and divided to prevent this from happening – or were themselves supporters of Díaz. Nevertheless, they would play a major part in bringing the regime down in 1909–11. During the intervening period, the political system was closed in a way it had not been during the Restored Republic after 1867. Senate and the Chamber of Deputies were paralysed, the state governors brought into line stage by stage, freedom of the press broken down, and opposition politicians and journalists hounded, sometimes even to death.

The modernising tendencies promoted by the Díaz regime have encouraged the interpretation that the origins of contemporary Mexico lie in that particular era. In an economic sense they do. In positive terms, it can be argued that the origins of contemporary Mexico lie in the Reform era with the attempt to define citizens' rights and lay the foundations for representative government. In negative terms, it could be argued that the Díaz regime laid the foundations of twentieth-century Mexican government which has demonstrated strong centralising tendencies (within a federal system), untrammelled executive supremacy, the seemingly perpetual re-election of the monopoly party, the frequent abuse of citizens' rights, the failure to develop a political culture of effective participation, and the prevalence of private deals and personal patronage. The Díaz era wiped out the gains of the Reform era and restored the culture of authoritarianism and extra-legality.

Political practices under Porfirio Díaz

In the rebellion of Tuxtepec, Díaz ousted Lerdo in 1876 on a platform of 'Effective Suffrage: No Re-election', or strict adherence to the principles of the 1857 Constitution. This stance, anticipated in all the rebellions from within the Liberal camp since 1867, endeared him to the radical wing of the movement. These radicals or 'purists', out of power since 1863, had been deeply suspicious of both Juárez and Lerdo. They had formed a ready clientele for the *porfirista* cause. Díaz's first administration (1876–80) reflected the varied base of support within the country and party. Romero became Finance Minister once again, the radical General Pedro Ogazón who had been Governor of Jalisco in 1857–61 became Minister of War, and the atheist Ignacio Ramírez (1818–79) held the Ministry of Justice and Ecclesiastical Affairs. It also revealed the weakness of his support at the top levels of the Liberal movement in the aftermath of the three-way split in the movement during the 1870s. The principal figure behind Díaz was his intimate friend and fellow Oaxacan, Justo Benítez (1839–1900), who had been his secretary during the War of the Intervention and chief adviser during Díaz's two rebellions in 1871 and 1876. Benítez had built up a personal following and could count on a majority of supporters in the Chamber of Deputies. The general expectation – especially in view of the 1876 principle of 'No Re-election' – was that Benítez would succeed Díaz in 1880. Once installed in the presidency, however, Díaz sought to free himself from the tutelage of Benítez.

Díaz needed to elicit support from all available quarters. The roots of his policy of conciliation lay in this first period. Lerdo's conflict with the Mexican Catholics was terminated by a declaration in January 1877 that the new regime would not persecute the Church. Prominent individuals of whatever previous persuasion found they could come to arrangements with the regime, though no faction, group or party was permitted to coalesce. The regime used force to crush *lerdista* movements in states such as Veracruz and Sinaloa in 1877–79. In Veracruz, Díaz's telegram to Governor Luis Mier y Terán in 1877 instructing him to put down rebellion by force resulted in the execution of nine persons without trial. This and the murder of the *caciques* of Tepic by army commanders at a prepared banquet to celebrate their submission proved to be two terrible blots on the first Díaz administration.

The forthcoming trend of the Díaz period could already be discerned in 1880, when, instead of designating Benítez or any of his ministers as successor, Díaz selected an army associate with no political credibility. Díaz, apparently, did not trust Benítez to hand back political power to him on the expiration of the presidential term in 1884. The breach with Benítez was regarded by his supporters, who thereafter called the President 'Perfidious Díaz', as a betrayal. General Manuel González had no base in the Liberal Party, since he had been a Conservative during the Civil War of the Reform. Accordingly, his position depended entirely on Díaz's favour as a *compadre*. González's intervention had saved the Díaz cause during his two rebellions. The presidency of González initially augured well. The distinguished *juarista*, Ignacio Mariscal (1829–1910), was appointed Secretary of Foreign Relations – a post he would hold until his death, and Díaz himself became Minister of Development. A González loyalist, General Gerónimo Treviño (1836–1914), who had risen through the Nuevo León National Guard under Vidaurri, held the Ministry of War, sealing the alliance with the north-east, since González himself came from Matamoros (Tamaulipas).

The political transfer of 1880 was only the second peaceful transfer since Independence. Yet, this ostensibly major development was merely the façade that concealed deeper manoeuvrings: Díaz's intention was that González should hand back power to him in 1884. Accordingly, Díaz left the administration in May 1881, after only six months as a minister, in order not to be too closely associated with it. The intention behind this distancing was to create the conditions to prevent any possibility that González could go beyond one term in office.

It is doubtful whether Díaz himself held a clear ideology of development. He had never been associated with the technocratic wing of Liberalism, the precursor of which had been Miguel Lerdo de Tejada. Its principal expression was during the administration of Sebastián Lerdo, with the rise of such figures as Manuel Romero Rubio (1828–95), Minister of Foreign Relations and principal cabinet figure at that time. The Romero Rubios had made their money during the Reform era in association with the radical Governor of Tamaulipas, Juan José de la Garza (1826–93), through the appropriation of ecclesiastical properties. Romero Rubio had been in the USA in political eclipse since the fall of Lerdo, but had returned to Mexico as a Senator in 1880. Díaz, however, needed sooner or later to base his regime on those most capable of providing him with a solid foundation. The lerdista technocrats began to return to political life as individuals during the 1880s.

Romero Rubio, for his part, had become increasingly conservative and his family Catholic. In December 1883, Díaz, then fifty-three, married Carmen Romero Rubio, aged nineteen. Attracted to her as he evidently was, Díaz's only passion, if we are to follow the view of his later opponent José López-Portillo y Rojas, was for the possession of political power: power, it should be stressed – rather than personal wealth. Carmelita, a practising Catholic, attached herself to an ageing but virile freemason and former radical. The marriage took place in Mexico City, celebrated by the same Archbishop Labastida, who had been a critic of the Reform. This extraordinary coming together of a Liberal General and a formerly exiled prelate was brought about by a half-English priest, Mgr Eulogio Gillow (1847–1922), who had received part of his education at Stonyhurst Jesuit College in Lancashire. Gillow's priestly formation had taken place in the Rome of Pius IX. He used his influence with Archbishop Labastida to secure a *modus vivendi* between Church and

Plate 28 Porfirio Díaz in his prime.
Alone in ceremonial attire in the National Palace in 1905, though
not lost among the splendour, and perhaps reflecting on the
transient nature of power, in spite of seven re-elections to the
presidency – 1884, 1888, 1892, 1896, 1900, 1906, and 1910.

State. Subsequently, Gillow became Bishop and then in 1887 Archbishop of Oaxaca. In 1901, Gillow would become the first American to be nominated Cardinal, although the Mexico government refused to allow the title to be used in Mexico.

Díaz and Carmelita spent their honeymoon in the United States – Carmen was a highly skilled English-speaker – where the couple were fêted as royalty.

In the meantime, the porfiristas began the process of discrediting the González administration, laying against it charges of financial irregularities, particularly regarding railway loans. Díaz was elected unopposed in the presidential elections of 1884. Even so, the campaign against González continued into 1885, when a case was made in the Chamber of Deputies against his alleged misappropriation of public funds. The threat of prosecution, which only Díaz could activate, was designed to paralyse González politically.

The construction of personal rule, 1884–1911

Díaz began the construction of a dictatorship during his second presidency from 1884 to 1888. Mariscal and Pacheco retained their previous offices. Dublán took Finance, but the principal figure clearly became Romero Rubio. As Minister of the Interior, he controlled the police, supervised the state governors, and managed the federal congress. At the same time, Díaz removed González supporters from state governments in favour of loyal *porfiristas*: Teodoro Dehesa (b. Veracruz 1848) ruled his home state from 1892–1911; Mucio Martínez dominated Puebla; Martín González (b. Oaxaca 1839) governed Oaxaca from 1894 until 1902. One loyal *porfirista* who posed no potential threat, Colonel Próspero Cahuantzi, a local Indian, remained Governor of Tlaxcala for the entire duration of the regime, a period consequently known as the 'Prosperato'. In Nuevo León, Reyes governed from December 1885 until November 1909. As Reyes's authority grew with his efficient administration of Nuevo León, Díaz became increasingly suspicious of him.

Guerra argues that by the mid-1880s the political system had become 'a pyramid of old ties and loyalties of different types at the summit of which was the President'. Díaz brought together a multitude of pre-existing networks: personal loyalties at local and regional levels became the foundations of national political cohesion. Most hitherto autonomous *caciques* were replaced and all potential military rivals neutralised. Essential to regime survival was the continued working relationship between all these levels and groupings. In the early phase of the construction of this personal style of government, Díaz remained in direct control. Himself a Mixtecan from Oaxaca who had risen through local and provincial office, both civil and military, Díaz had a profound understanding of how Mexico functioned at its most basic levels. Mexico City-based intellectual and political figures rarely understood this.

Elections continued to be held, but loyal state governors controlled them. In 1885–86, the administration began a campaign to curb journalists. Bribery and government funding were used to silence *El Partido Liberal, El Observador*, and other dissenting newspapers. In June 1886, government action obliged many journalists to flee across the border to the United States, where they were put under surveillance by Mexican consulates. A pliant Congress, on 21 October 1887, authorised a one-term re-election of the President and State Governors. This provision became an amendment to articles 78 and 109 of the 1857 Constitution, but totally contradicted the spirit of the Palo Blanco revisions (21 March 1876) to the Plan of Tuxtepec. As a result, many original supporters of the Tuxtepec Rebellion went into opposition, accusing the regime in the press of violating the principle of no consecutive re-election. The post-Tuxtepec era of 1876–84 had definitively come to an end. Trinidad García de la Cadena, one of the principal opponents of the regime's tendencies, Governor of Zacatecas from 1876 to 1880 and a presidential candidate in the latter year, was assassinated when gravely ill by the subsequent state Governor and the *Jefe Político* of Zacatecas in November 1886. The alleged motive of conspiracy further exposed the criminal potential of leading supporters of Díaz's administration. The moral responsibility was held to lie with Díaz.

Personal rivalries within the cabinet of 1884–88 prevented unity, strengthened the position of the President, and augured ill for an agreed succession in 1888. The national policy of conciliation, then, concealed a cabinet of inveterate hostilities. Díaz encouraged Romero Rubio, Dublán, and Pacheco each to think of themselves as his potential successor. These mutual rivalries cancelled each other out. Furthermore, Romero Rubio could not bid independently for the succession, since he was Díaz's father-in-law. The end result was that in 1888 Díaz stood again for re-election under the terms of the 1887 amendment. Dangerous opponents, such as General Ramón Corona, former Governor of Jalisco, and General Ignacio Martínez, editor of *El Mundo*, were both assassinated, the former in 1889 and the latter over the Texas border in Laredo in 1891. These were exceptions, since the normal practice of the regime was seduction and incorporation. Even so, those who refused to cooperate were hounded implacably.

Romero Rubio's influence remained strong. Through his private secretary, Rosendo Pineda (b. Juchitán 1855), a key figure in the regime, a circle of enterprising young men in their twenties and thirties, several of them pupils of Barreda, grouped around him as his personal clientele until his death in 1895. In general, they favoured the continuation of the dictatorship on the grounds that it guaranteed political stability and economic development. Pineda personally supervised the official newspaper, *El Imparcial*, edited by Rafael Reyes, which conducted a war of polemics against the increasingly marginalised opposition. The paper attracted intellectuals to the government side by offering them space to publish their writings. Renowned poets such as Manuel Gutiérrez Najera (1859–95) and Salvador Díaz Mirón (1853–1928) appeared there. The paper's low price undercut its rivals, which withered away.

After the second re-election in 1888, the opposition journal, *El Diario del Hogar*, founded in 1881 and edited by Filomeno Mata (1845–1911), staunch defender of freedom of the press, was persecuted by the regime. Mata himself was sent to prison thirty times. Daniel Cabrera (1858–1914), founder of the satirical *El Hijo del Ahuizote* in August 1885, was reputedly imprisoned three hundred times before the paper's expiry in 1895. The lithographs of Posada appeared in this paper after his move to Mexico City in 1887.

In 1892, the technocratic circle formed the Liberal Union, an elite faction which campaigned for the third re-election of Díaz. The principal figures were Pineda and Justo Sierra Méndez (1848–1912), former editor of *La Libertad* (1878–84), which argued for strong government and technical advance. Sierra, a critic of the 1857 Constitution, became the leading intellectual figure of the late Díaz era and Minister of Education between 1905 and 1911. The Sunday afternoon *tertulias*, best described as informal chats among like-minded individuals which could lead to both deep friendships and violent arguments, held in his house in Tacubaya, provided a meeting-place for young literary figures and

Plate 29 Diego Rivera's mural, *Sunday Afternoon Dream in the Alameda* (1947). Commissioned in 1946 and set up in 1948 in the Hotel del Prado, Mexico City, this mural was damaged by religious fanatics, who burst into the lobby. The offending segment was the portrayal of the professed atheist, Ignacio Ramírez, Minister of Justice and Ecclesiastical Affairs under Juárez, with placard saying, 'God does not exist'. The earthquake of 1985 struck the hotel, but the mural was saved and relocated in a special museum at the western end of the Alameda. The mural shows the young Rivera, Frida Kahlo, his painter wife, José Martí, the Cuban nationalist, and the 'Skeleton Caterina', one of José Guadalupe Posada's '*calaveras*', in the foreground. Díaz is at the right-hand edge.

job-aspirants. Limantour, son of a French immigrant speculator in nationalised ecclesiastical properties, supported the Liberal Union. Other outstanding figures were Emilio Pimentel, Governor of Oaxaca (1903–10), the banker Joaquín Casasús, Enrique Creel (b. Chihuahua 1854), banker and manufacturer of Chihuahua, son-in-law of Luis Terrazas, and owner of one of the largest fortunes in Mexico, and Pablo Macedo. They also formed part of this group.

The Liberal Union was strongly based in Mexico City, especially among modernising businessmen. In the provinces, however, the group was much weaker. Their aim was to recreate the Liberal Party as a party of state, and use the regime as an agency of reform. They envisaged, however, the reopening of the political processes, restoration of freedom of the press, judicial reform, and a limited form of democracy. The Liberal Union stood in 1892 for the rule of law, rather than the personal supremacy of the perpetual president. Instead, it encountered the obstruction of Díaz, who suspected its real intention to be the provision of a political base for Romero Rubio. Accordingly, aspirations to political reform collapsed and Díaz succeeded himself without any modification of the system. Instead of an 'enlightened dictatorship', trials of journalists and editors continued through the 1890s. The technical circle, known disparagingly as the '*científicos*', became little more than an administrative group owing its position to Díaz's personal favour.

The third re-election opened the way for a further constitutional amendment on 20 December 1892, which removed the specification of 1887 for one re-election, and thereby restored the 1857 position, which made no reference at all to the issue of re-election. In this way, the field lay open for indefinite re-election of the President. Regime measures to stifle the press continued. In 1893–94, it was the turn of *El Demócrata* and *El Monitor Republicano*, the latter a venerable Liberal stalwart since the 1840s. In 1896, Díaz secured his fourth re-election through the assistance of the National *Porfirista* Circle. The façade of continuity, however, was belied by deepening factionalism within the regime. Hostility to the increasingly remote circle of *científicos* led to the emergence of a rival group which formed around Reyes in the late 1890s.

The deepening succession question

The Díaz regime's conspicuous failure to resolve the succession question provided the central cause of the political breakdown in Mexico by 1910. The first rumours of a Reyes candidacy circulated in 1893 and again in 1896, when Reyes briefly became a minister of state at the Secretariat of War. It appears that in 1898, Díaz considered leaving the succession to Limantour, and departed for Monterrey in December in order to secure Reyes's compliance. Limantour's succession, however, was blocked not by Reyes but by Joaquín Baranda (b. Mérida 1840), Minister of Justice and Public Instruction, who argued erroneously that as the son of a foreigner he could not legally stand for the presidency. Díaz, accordingly, dropped the idea as potentially controversial, and stood himself – the fifth re-election. In a vain attempt to reconcile the increasing divide between factions within the regime, Díaz brought Reyes into the government as Secretary for War (1900–2). The latter began a much-needed army reform, since Díaz, through fear of an attempted coup from within the armed forces, had studiously neglected to attend to their deteriorating condition. Reyes's policies, however, aroused the suspicions of the *científicos*, who alleged that he was building a political base in order to take the succession. The removal of Reyes, brought about by the intrigues of the *científicos* and their new ally, Corral, Governor of the Federal District and a personal enemy of Reyes, ensured the termination of the army reform policy. Mexico, consequently, did not follow the other leading Latin American countries in that period in remodelling and professionalising their armed forces generally with the assistance of European military advisers. This left the federal army perilously exposed in the event of external intervention or large-scale internal conflict.

Between 1900 and 1904, Corral moved into the centre of the regime, even though he was not a national political figure and had largely been unknown in the capital. By 1904, when he became Secretary of the Interior, Corral occupied the commanding position previously held by Romero Rubio. Corral was the *bête noire* of the *reyistas*. Reyes himself had conflicted with him, when Military Commander in the north-west in 1880–83, over conduct of the Yaqui wars in Corral's home state of Sonora. Corral, closely involved with banking and development interests, had advocated vigorous campaigns to remove these Indians, always ready to resist effectively, from occupation of the best agricultural lands in the state.

The worsening succession problem encouraged Díaz in 1904 to extend the presidential term (for one time) to six years, ending thereby in 1906. At the same time, he secured congressional amendment of the Constitution to allow for the restoration of the vice-presidential office, previously abolished in 1847. Díaz had always opposed such a measure, which was probably the work of the *científicos*, on the grounds that the traditional function of the Vice-President had been to overthrow the President. Since no one could agree on a successor, Díaz stood for a sixth re-election in 1906, this time with the controversial Corral as candidate for the vice-presidency.

Between the fifth and sixth re-elections, anti-re-election clubs sprang up in the main cities. Most took their stand on strict observation of the precepts of the 1857 Constitution, adding to them the 1876 principles of effective suffrage and no re-election. At the same time, deteriorating labour relations in the most advanced sectors of the economy, copper-mining at Cananea (Sonora) and machine-produced cottons at Río Blanco (Veracruz), resulted in bitter strikes of long duration in 1906–7. These highlighted regime alienation from the interests of a significant sector of the industrial working population. Against such a background, the Flores Magón brothers, who were attempting to organise an opposition Liberal Party, radicalised their programme by 1906 to include working-class grievances.

Failure to resolve the succession question highlighted the issue of the transfer of political power. Long uncertainty destabilised the regime at the centre, leaving provincial nuclei of power as dangerously exposed as in 1810. Immobility at the top delegitimised the regime and made revolutionary action the only means of imposing a transfer of power. It was particularly unfortunate that the removal of the Díaz regime could only take place against the background of generalised crisis, rather than by peaceful means. This meant that the transfer to open politics would take place during a period of economic and social dislocation. The social and economic conditions within the country had already been exposed during the 1900s.

At the height of his popularity in 1908–9, Reyes refused to provoke a confrontation with the regime by standing in the elections of 1910. Even so, his supporters battled in the streets with *porfiristas*. The succession question was further exacerbated by Díaz's announcement in May 1908, at the halfway point between two presidential elections, that he would in fact be standing for a seventh re-election, with Corral as his vice-presidential candidate, in spite of a newspaper declaration in the Creelman Interview three months previously that he would stand down.

The impotence of the Reyes camp led to the opening of a rival anti-re-electionist movement led by Francisco I. Madero (b. Parras, Coahuila, 1873). Madero was the grandson of Evaristo Madero (1828–1911), a major Coahuila landowner, ally of Vidaurri, former Governor of Coahuila (1880–83), and founder of the Banco de Nuevo León. After 1889, Díaz had marginalised the Madero family in the politics of their home state in favour of pro-*científico* appointees. *Científico* predominance at national level also blocked Venustiano Carranza's attempt to secure the state governorship in 1908. Madero, in the following year, published *The Presidential Succession of 1910*, a work in which he called for constitutional democracy in Mexico. In his book, Madero identified militarism as the country's principal enemy. In this respect, he identified with the tradition of Juárez. However, the principal critics of 'militarism' in the 1900s were the *científicos*, anxious to discredit Reyes. Given the Madero family's friendship with Limantour, this stance was not surprising. It meant, however, that a considerable distance existed between *maderismo* and *reyismo*, even though both positions upheld the economic achievements of the Porfirian era and sought to advance from them. Madero took his stand on the peaceful transfer of political power between civil authorities by means of elections. This procedure had eluded Mexico for most of the nineteenth century, and the first decade of the twentieth century was proving to be no different.

The prospect of a seventh re-election of General Díaz, who would thereby complete his eighth term in 1914, flew in the face of these aspirations to resolve the issue of the transfer of power. Madero founded the Anti-Re-electionist Central Club in May 1909. Mata, the frequently imprisoned journalist, became secretary, and José Vasconcelos (1882–1959), a member of the literary circle grouped together in the *Ateneo de la Juventud*, and Luis Cabrera (1876–1954), a journalist writing for *El Diario del Hogar*, nephew of Daniel Cabrera, were founding members. They would subsequently gain national prominence during the Revolution. The regime's decision to eliminate Reyes from the political scene obliged *reyistas* reluctantly to realign behind Madero. Carranza was among them. In November 1909, already stripped of his military authority, Reyes resigned the governorship of Nuevo León and was sent by Díaz on a military mission to Europe. The Díaz regime never took *maderismo* seriously: the *científicos* even favoured it because it was anti-*reyista*. On the eve of the presidential elections, however, the growing anti-re-electionist coalition held a Convention in Mexico City, which alarmed the government sufficiently to ban the movement early in June 1910 and have Madero arrested in Monterrey. While Madero remained in jail in San Luis Potosí for over a month, the re-election of Díaz and Corral took place.

From the perspectives of property-owners and beneficiaries of economic developments since the 1880s, instability at the centre, combined with the imminence of an armed struggle, threatened to give free rein to social grievances hitherto contained by an effective political structure. A sense of alarm pervaded the elite sectors of society, that they would no longer be protected by the Díaz regime's particular combination of manipulation and selective repression. Accordingly, popular mobilisation seemed to threaten the modernisation achieved since the 1880s. Such a fear was shared right through the elite, regardless of *porfirista* or revolutionary allegiance. For that reason, the new power groups, which emerged during the 1910s, first at state levels and finally at national level, were determined to contain or subordinate popular movements, in order to preserve and extend the economic advances inherited from the discredited *porfirista* regime. For that objective, a powerful and newly reconstituted state would be required. Provincial aspirants to wealth, competing violently for power, would seek to impose a monopoly of control over this new state.

PART TWO: THE REVOLUTIONARY SYSTEM: STATE POWER OR DEMOCRATISATION, 1911–1940?

The impact of revolution

In political terms, the Revolution of 1910–11 started as a constitutionalist movement within the Liberal camp. Several crucial issues, arising from the Liberal triumph in 1867, had emerged during the Restored Republic: the expansion of presidential power, the growth of centralism, and re-electionism. Equally fundamental was the issue of 'effective suffrage', raised in 1871 and 1876. This question, with contemporary relevance, formed a central part of Madero's campaign against the dictatorship.

Maderismo, however, represented a tendency very different from that of nineteenth-century Mexican Liberalism. Its founding principle was constitutional democracy as such, no matter which party or faction won power in free elections. For *porfiristas*, who argued that dictatorship kept clericals out of power, and for the heirs of the radical liberalism of the 1850s, such an outcome threatened a capture of power at national level by organised Catholic groups. Liberals in Italy, Spain, and France in the second half of the nineteenth century would have shared that apprehension. Even though he was not himself a Catholic, Madero, 'apostle' of a Mexican democracy that never came into being, was prepared to accept this possibility. The assumption was that once in power Catholics would not then proceed to abolish the democracy which had brought them there. Few other revolutionaries went along

Plate 30 All Mexican towns and many cities have a nineteenth-century bandstand. This is a late-Porfirian era example from the Plaza de la Constitución in Guadalajara, which has exquisitely sculpted women in prominent position. It dates from 1908 (Author's photograph, September 2003).

with such a view. Madero's constitutionalism transcended nineteenth-century anti-clericalism. It marked a significant departure from the political polarisation of the Reform era over the subject of religion. Madero's presidency of 1911–13 reopened the political system, though on a broader basis than the previous experience during the Restored Republic. The electoral successes of the recently formed Partido Católico Nacional (PCN) alone testified to that.

Guerra has argued that the Mexican Revolution broke out not in advanced mining centres of recent origin, such as Cananea, but in zones of contact between smaller units (mines, ranches, or villages) and the great enterprises (mining companies or haciendas). At such points, rapid structural transformation led to intense conflict. The key zone he identified in that respect was the State of Chihuahua, badly affected by the 1907 recession. At the same time, a second source of conflict arose from recently disputed elections, such as those in Morelos and Coahuila. In Morelos, furthermore, local peasant agriculture had already come into conflict with the expanding sugar properties. The leadership of the peasant villages was taken by Emiliano Zapata, whose family had risen to local significance with the Díaz regime in its early stages. The combination of aggressive hacienda expansion and a *científico*-controlled state machine in Morelos provided the explanation for revolutionary alignment.

Merchants and middlemen, such as Abraham González or Pascual Orozco, formed the official *maderista* leadership in the north. At the same time, the Madero administration made overtures to urban labour by creating a National Labour Office in December 1911, and in July 1912 legislating a national minimum wage and a six-day week with fifteen days' annual holiday. In that year the Casa del Obrero Mundial (House of World Workers) came into being. Its principal membership came from printers, tram-drivers, railway-men, stonemasons, tailors and shoemakers rather than from heavy industry, which remained weak in a country like Mexico. With anarcho-syndicalist antecedents, the Casa became a focus of worker unionisation.

The murder of Madero in February 1913 ended the attempt to establish political democracy in Mexico. Venustiano Carranza (1859–1920), who as Governor of Coahuila had generally opposed Madero's objectives, declared against the counter-revolutionary regime of General Victoriano Huerta (1845–1916), central figure in the overthrow and

Plate 31 Francisco I. Madero (1873–1913) with Revolutionary Leaders, 1911.

Madero came from a family of Coahuila landowners with cotton-planting and banking interests. By 1909–10, his anti-election campaign made him the focus of opposition to the Díaz regime (in power since 1876). Madero reluctantly called for armed insurrection on 20 November 1910 after Díaz's seventh re-election. He was President from November 1911 until his murder in February 1913. He is photographed here flanked by Revolutionary Generals Abraham González (right, facing the camera) and Pascual Orozco (left), in early April 1911, before their capture of Ciudad Juárez on 10 May.

murder of Madero, by issuing the Plan of Guadalupe on 26 March 1913. This Plan, supported by the states of Sonora and Chihuahua, made no mention of agrarian and social issues. At first, the Huerta regime (18 February 1913–15 July 1914) was welcomed by all the Great Powers, with the exception of the United States. The counter-revolutionary regime consisted of men of all talents and offered a bright prospect to domestic and foreign businessmen. There were two major problems, however: the nature of the regime's origin and the personality of its leader. The first pushed the revolutionary conflict into a renewed phase of violence.

The second presaged an early dissolution of governmental coherence. Huerta, a calculating politician, could count on the sympathies of

Plate 32 Federal soldiers on campaign against Revolutionaries,
1910–11.
This photograph comes from the Casasola Archive of
revolutionary images. The Federal Army, in contrast to the
armies of other leading (and even lesser) Latin-American
countries, had not been reformed and modernised at the turn of
the century. This left it perilously exposed to large-scale
rebellions in key states such as Chihuahua and Morelos. Díaz's
suspicions of army commanders, including Bernardo Reyes, led
to neglect of the armed forces. When the Madero revolution
broke out, the army had only 14,000 combat-ready troops in a
country the size of France and Spain combined. By contrast, the
Italian army in the late nineteenth century consisted of some
215,000 serving soldiers.

Imperial Germany and Japan. In fact, the German Ambassador, Paul von
Hintze, even proposed military aid on condition that the Mexican government stop oil shipments to Great Britain in the event of a European
war. German disillusionment rapidly surfaced: the ambassador reported
to Chancellor Theobald von Bethmann-Hollweg that Huerta 'holds his
cabinet meetings primarily in taverns and restaurants. Since no one really
knows where he is, this protects him to some extent from assassination'.

The Mexican Revolution produced confused responses within the
United States. Dislike of the late Díaz's regime's tendencies towards

Plate 33 Venustiano Carranza (1859–1920).
Carranza, whose father had supported Juárez, originated like
Madero from Coahuila. Initially a follower of Reyes, Carranza
reluctantly supported Madero. Governor of Coahuila from
1911–13 he became 'First Chief' of the Constitutionalist
Revolution following Madero's murder. Carranza took office as
President on 1 May 1917, in accordance with the Constitution of
the same year. He was assassinated on 21 May 1920, during the
conflict with Álvaro Obregón's forces concerning the presidential
succession. Carranza was more nationalist than revolutionary,
particularly wary of foreign economic interests and US political
pressures. After 1915, he authorised the return of lands taken
from peasants under previous regimes, but, on the whole, labour
relations deteriorated during his presidency.

economic nationalism had led to initial sympathy with Madero.
Ambassador Henry Lane Wilson's scepticism of the Madero administration's capability in face of mounting social conflict, however, led
him to sympathise with the counter-revolutionaries. The extent of his
complicity in the conspiracy to remove Madero has never been sat-
isfactorily cleared up. His ambivalent conduct, nevertheless, aroused
considerable anti-American feeling.

The overthrow of Mexico's constitutionally elected government coincided with the advent to power of Woodrow Wilson. Intending as a Democrat to depart from what he saw as the interventionist policies of his predecessors, Roosevelt and Taft, Wilson condemned the overthrow of Madero and gave his moral support to the opponents of the Huerta regime. The latter's approaches to Germany in the spring of 1914 led to a US blockade of Veracruz to prevent the arrival of German arms. Confusion over the purpose of US ships off Veracruz led to an acrimonious dispute with the *Huertista* authorities there, which culminated in a US landing on 21 April. Wilson thought he was assisting the constitutionalist opposition to Huerta by instructing US marines to occupy the port of Veracruz. However, all contending factions within Mexico united to condemn a US violation of Mexican national sovereignty. Carranza invoked Juárez's decree of 25 January 1862 against the European intervention. The marines were fired on as they landed: 19 were killed and 72 wounded. Accordingly, US ships responded by shelling Veracruz and leaving 126 Mexicans dead and 95 wounded. US forces finally evacuated Veracruz on 23 November, having achieved nothing more than the cleaning of the city's streets.

With the best intentions, President Wilson had sought to help the Mexican constitutionalists but instead found himself in an appalling mess. He strongly disliked what he had heard of Carranza, and mistrusted his German sympathies. Accordingly, Wilson backed the former bandit, Pancho Villa (1878–1923) in the struggle for power within Mexico. The defeat of Villa in 1915 made that policy redundant, especially since the war in Europe opened the prospect of German intrigues in Mexico against US interests. On 19 October, Wilson accorded recognition to Carranza. At that time, the bulk of the US army was stationed along the Mexican border.

The struggle for power within the Revolution

By 1913, the original political leadership of the Revolution, which dated from 1909–10, had disintegrated. When the Huerta regime collapsed in the summer of 1914, a Mexican state at national level ceased to exist. Practical command devolved upon the chieftains operating in the field, usually at the provincial level, in much the way that it had during the insurgency of the 1810s after the capture of Morelos in 1814. In both instances, very little harmony of objective remained. The ideological basis of these varied revolutionary movements tended to be adopted on the spot in response to social demands and political openings.

With the collapse of formal state authority and the defeat of the Federal Army, revolutionary chieftains became decisive political arbiters. At the same time, the inability of any one of them to control the full extent of national territory, at least until after 1920, created space for spontaneous popular mobilisation in pursuit of specific or localised objectives. From the beginning of the Revolution, a central issue had been the relationship between the constitutional leadership and the peasant and popular movements in the country. After 1914, the focus moved to the relationship between revolutionary chieftains and popular movements: how each of them viewed popular mobilisation, sought to use or exploit it, incorporate or neutralise it.

The Carranza movement gained substantial support from middle-class sectors in Chihuahua. They took positions of military and civil leadership behind a chieftain who offered them access to commanding positions at both state and national level. Resentment at foreign companies' domination of the mining sectors of the northern economy fuelled an intense economic nationalism throughout the *carrancista* camp. This nationalism provided a substitute for the absence of social revolutionary objectives in the original Carranza movement. The First Chief (as Carranza was known) and his supporters looked not to the reversal of Porfirian economic advances but to their consolidation and advance, though without the landholding and monopolising elite, most notably the Terrazas–Creel interests. From the outset there was a striking absence of peasants, free villagers, and hacienda peons in the Carranza movement.

Villa, who rose for Madero in 1910–11, was a bandit by the name of Doroteo Arango, who had first emerged in the 1890s. Friedrich Katz has described Villa as 'a complex mixture of social revolutionary and nineteenth century caudillo. His aims (at least in the regions of Chihuahua, Durango, and Coahuila, where his main interest lay) were those of a social revolutionary, though his methods of ruling were similar to those of a classic Mexican caudillo of the nineteenth century'. Villa established no political organisation as the base for his power: he ruled his army through a complex patron–client network. From March 1913, Villa controlled the greater part of Chihuahua. For a time his 'Division del

Plate 34 Pancho Villa (1878–1923) and his wife. Taken in 1920, this photograph also comes from the Casasola Archive. The former bandit, Doroteo Arango, who originated from the state of Durango adopted the name Francisco ('Pancho') Villa and supported the Madero Revolution in the state of Chihuahua at the behest of Abraham González. From September 1913, Villa led his famous Division del Norte in opposition to the Huerta regime in Mexico City. The fall of Zacatecas (masterminded by Felipe Angeles) on 23 June 1914 left, 6,000 federal troops dead and sealed the fate of the Huerta counter-revolution but also confirmed the split with Carranza.

Norte' was the most powerful revolutionary army. At the height of his power in October 1914, Villa commanded some 40,000 men. Hacienda peons rather than proprietors filled the ranks of his adherents.

In many respects, the Villa movement represented a local and popular response to *hacendado* support for the Orozco rebellion of 1912 against the Madero government and the Huerta coup of 1913. As such, the objective was to break *hacendado* power in the state. In fact, Villa's land expropriation decree of 21 December 1913 excluded compensation for landowners. Dispossessed ranchers, pushed out in the 1890s and 1900s and then hit by crop failures in 1907–9, filled *villista* ranks. Chihuahua and other northern states had many cattle estates, which could not be subdivided into small units, although former military colonists – veterans of the Apache wars of the 1880s – continued to press for land. The *villista* army itself often had to undertake food supply to towns faced with unemployment due to the recession in mining and lumber. In any case, expropriated livestock estates provided the basis for Villa's military campaigns and the revolutionary state-government managed two-thirds of them. The land was to be reserved for troops fighting, frequently outside the state, for the revolutionary movement. Villa also gained the support of La Laguna-area villagers who had lost lands to the cotton estates, and from agricultural workers facing insecure conditions of the San Luis Potosí haciendas.

The *villista* movement had a broader social base than the revolution in the centre-south led by Emiliano Zapata (1879–1919), which remained essentially a peasant-based guerrilla movement. *Zapatista* bands of some 200–300 men operated outside the planting and harvest seasons, when they returned to their villages. The movement, however, spread rapidly through the sugar zones of Morelos and southern Puebla, and had strong repercussions among the peasantry of Guerrero and Tlaxcala. By January 1913, the *zapatistas* had destroyed more than half the sugar crop of Morelos.

Planters, who saw no hope of revindication in the survival of the Madero administration, pressed urgently for a military solution in the state. They welcomed the Huerta coup, which, however, only served to escalate further the agrarian movement. By 1914–15, at the height of their power, the *zapatistas* consisted of some 20,000 men and controlled not only Morelos but also Tlaxcala, south and west Puebla, northern Guerrero, and the southern sector of the Federal District. The *Zapatista*

Plate 35 Villa and Zapata in the Presidential Palace, Mexico City. By 1914, Villa, who had received US recognition in the previous year, dominated much of northern Mexico. His forces were tactically aligned with the Zapatistas from Morelos and together they influenced the outcome of the Convention of Aguascalientes (10 October–13 November 1914), which removed Carranza from the revolutionary leadership. They jointly occupied Mexico City in December 1914, but proved unable to establish an alternative leadership. Thereafter, Obregón's army decimated *villista* forces and confined Villa to his local sphere of control. On 20 July 1923, Villa was assassinated in Parral.

Plan of Ayala in 1911 and the Agrarian Law of 1915 attempted a comprehensive agrarian reform in favour of dispossessed peasant communities at the expense of the private estates. Its principal disadvantage, however, was that it addressed problems relating to heavily indigenous areas, such as Morelos, Puebla, Tlaxcala, and the State of Mexico, which were, in any case, the central areas of support. John Tutino has aptly commented that 'backed by the most massive and widespread agrarian mobilisation in Mexican history, Villa and Zapata controlled most of Mexico, occupied Mexico City, and dominated the government known as the Convention during late 1914'. At Aguascalientes, they failed, however, to agree on a lasting political solution. Accordingly, the initiative was taken from them by the coalition forming around Carranza.

Plate 36 *Zapatista* forces at breakfast in Sanborn's 'House of Tiles', Mexico City, 1914. Emiliano Zapata (1879–1919) originated from the Morelos village of Anenecuilco, where his family were early Díaz supporters. Deteriorating labour conditions in his locality led to his rapid politicisation. In 1909, he was elected president of the village council. Supporting the Madero Revolution, Zapata's guerrilla band took Cuautla on 19 May 1911 after bloody fighting, a significant blow to the regime in view of the town's proximity to the national capital. The *Zapatistas'* Plan of Ayala (November 1911) encapsulated fundamental rural objectives: restoration of land usurped by haciendas; redistribution of hacienda lands among the peasants; restoration of municipal autonomy and political liberties. The *zapatistas* were driven from Mexico City by Obregón's forces in August 1915. Zapata was assassinated on 10 April 1919.

Rising Sonora chieftains had already begun to put their stamp on the Carranza movement. In Sonora, the revolutionary leadership came not from peasant or worker backgrounds but from a semi-rural, semi-urban, lower middle class of hacienda-managers, shopkeepers, mill-workers, or schoolteachers, opposed to large-scale landowners and the Porfirian elite. The revolution offered men such as Álvaro Obregón (1880–1928) and Plutarco Elías Calles (1877–1945), and their associates, Adolfo de la Huerta (1881–1955), Benjamín Hill, Pablo González, and Salvador Alvarado the opportunity to move into commanding political positions at national level and reshape economic and social structures in their own interests. Accordingly, they did not reject the economic developments of the Porfirian era, but assumed control of them. Except in the case of oil, they were not particularly opposed to foreign investment as such and were not anxious to reduce Mexico's links to international capital. In the *carrancista* tradition they stood for a secularised society and educational system. They inherited the Jacobin-style anti-clericalism of the radical Liberals of the Reform era. Constitutionalism and agrarian social reform were not their strong points. The climax of their influence would coincide with Calles's long dominance of Mexican politics between 1924 and 1934.

The Convention of Aguascalientes (10 October 1914–10 October 1915) reflected the depth of division among revolutionary forces. The strength of opposition to Carranza led to the momentary alliance of *villista* and *zapatista* forces. The response from within the *carrancista* camp was the Additions to the Plan of Guadalupe, compiled by Cabrera, an advocate of agrarian reform through compulsory purchase in 1912, and issued in Veracruz on 6 January 1915. These Additions modified the original platform in the light of agrarian demands evident throughout the revolutionary movement. This was a belated *carrancista* bid for peasant support. Carranza for the first time referred to the dissolution of the great estate and the restoration of village lands. A promise for the improvement of conditions of urban workers reflected Obregón's tactical alliance with them. Eight worker bands, known as the 'Red Battalions', were organised to cooperate with Obregón's forces by garrisoning towns held by Constitutionalist forces. The Casa del Obrero Mundial sent 7,000 members to fight with these bands in 1914–15. Urban-worker support formed an essential component in the Constitutionalist alliance against the *villistas* and *zapatistas*. For Carranza, Obregón, and Calles, however, agrarian reform was a political instrument for aligning autonomous peasant groups alongside the predominant elements within their revolutionary alliance. It was not their central objective but an instrument of manipulation and subordination.

Obregón was the principal instrument of the defeat of the popular movements. By January 1915, he already controlled Mexico City, Puebla, and Tlaxcala, pushing back the *zapatistas*. By July, he had forced them out of the Federal District altogether. *Villista* forces were routed in the two decisive battles of Celaya on 6–7 and 13 April, when Villa's cavalry charges faced the entrenched machine-gun positions of Obregón's army. The latter's victories enabled Carranza's Constitution-alist Army to secure control of Mexico City and the central political processes.

The Constitution of 1917

Taking into consideration the critique of the 1857 Constitution, the new Constitution strengthened presidential and central-government power in relation to the states. This reinforcement of the authority of the national state has tended to be overlooked in view of the attention given to the social provisions of the Constitution of 1917. Nevertheless, it is important for the explanation of executive predominance – a prac-tice the 1857 Constitution had sought to avoid – throughout the rest of the twentieth century. The defeat of popular forces during 1915 left the way open for Carranza, Obregón, and Calles to reconstruct a powerful national state, focussed on the Presidential authority, which could take the lead in shaping the institutions of the post-revolutionary era.

Four issues preoccupied the constitutional convention of 1916–17 held in Querétaro: agrarian reform, the legal status of subsoil deposits, military–civil relations, Church–state relations. Its deliberations should be seen against the background of the failure of the Convention of Aguascalientes. The Constitution of 1917 reflected the broad spectrum of opinion within the *carrancista* coalition. In contrast to the Russian Revolution of October 1917, an alliance of workers and peasants (led by a vanguard party) did not displace the predominant middle-sector leadership. The 209 deputies at Querétaro ranged from mine and textile workers to teachers, small businessmen and landowners. As such they represented a broad cross-section of the literate male population in their thirties and forties. John Rutherford has described the descent of the revolutionary bands of rough northerners on the central heartlands of Mexico as 'an avalanche of khaki clothing, wide-brimmed felt hats, riding boots, revolvers and cartridge belts' in search of plunder. There is an element of truth in that, since the northern leaders intended not only to alter the colonial-derived Hispanic and Catholic character of central Mexico but also to promote their own material interests through the control of political power.

The revolutionary situation led to a departure from the liberal principles predominating in 1857. Accordingly, the 1917 Constitution sought to respond to rural and urban labour pressures by incorporating measures for redress by positive state action. The influence of radicals, such as Francisco Múgica (b. Michoacán 1884), supported by partisans of Obregón on the constitutional commission, secured the acceptance of the principle that social utility should prevail over private property. The Constitution's two high points, articles 27 and 123, eventually opened the way for far-reaching social policies. The former, the longest in the Constitution, provided for government expropriation of underutilised land in favour of smallholdings or reconstituted community properties. The Constitution gave the federal government the right to determine the maximum size of estates, in order to curb the growth of large-scale properties. At the same time, article 27 declared that all water resources and subsoil deposits (including minerals and petroleum) belonged to the national patrimony and not to the private interests in the process of exploiting them. This clause aroused the suspicions of the oil companies, which soon found themselves subject to federal taxation.

Article 123 laid down principles for improved labour conditions, should labour organisations reach a sufficient position of strength to be able to oblige government or private (often foreign-owned) corporations to put them into effect. Between 1917 and his removal in 1920, Carranza demonstrated little willingness to do so. Nevertheless, the Constitution established a maximum working day of eight hours (or seven at night) in a six-day week, with an obligatory week's holiday, and prohibited female and child night work in industry. The same article laid down a fixed minimum wage, instructed that due attention should be given to workers' safety, and introduced workers' insurance. Even though article 123 recognised labour unions' right to strike, the army broke up oil workers' strikes throughout that year.

After his inauguration as constitutional President on 1 May 1917, Carranza adopted methods of government which strongly resembled those of Díaz. He sought to control congress by means of official candidates and to tame the press through government subsidies to sympathetic newspapers. In effect, constitutional guarantees did not apply to opponents of the government. The clear absence of any form of democracy opened the Carranza regime to the charge that the Madero principle of

ge was being violated. The discord rose to a climax when
ssing Obregón, attempted to impose a pliant successor in
scent labour movement, which made few gains under
ed to Obregón's opposition Plan of Agua Prieta.

Mexico as a major oil producer, 1910–1925

Between 1910 and 1925, Mexico rose to the ranks of a major international oil exporter. Production had begun in 1901, and during the
1910s US and British interests struggled to stake out their share of the
industry. At first the Díaz regime underestimated the importance of oil
and the extent of Mexican resources. The regime's earlier desire to
encourage foreign investment throughout the economy, however, had
left the country exposed to depletion of resources and extraction of
profits by foreign corporations. The issue of the legal status of subsoil deposits went back to the Mining Laws of 1884 and 1892, which
granted the right of exploitation to the owner of the surface land.
This principle extended to the Petroleum Law of 1901. Colonial law,
however, had stipulated that subsoil deposits remained the patrimony
of the Spanish state, a position inherited by the Mexican government
after Independence. Company exploitation after 1884 appeared to
conflict with that legal tradition. When Mexico became a major oil
exporter, this issue came to a head.

Between 1901 and 1912, Mexican production increased from 10,000
barrels a year to over 12 million. Rivalry between the British-owned
Mexican Eagle Company of Weetman Pearson (taken over by Royal
Dutch Shell in 1919) and the US-owned Mexican Petroleum Company
of the Edward Doheny firm (which passed to Standard Oil in 1925)
became bitter during the later 1900s and early 1910s. The Díaz government had brought Pearson's internationally prominent engineering firm
into Mexico as part of its strategy of playing off one foreign interest
against another. After 1901, Pearson invested heavily in the exploration
and exploitation of petroleum deposits in the Huasteca and the
Isthmus, though investors only received dividends from 1910.

The collapse of the regime, however, overtook the rivalries between
the British and American companies. Both Madero and Carranza
sought to uphold foreign investment in the oil industry, while at the
same time defending Mexican sovereign rights to subsoil deposits as a

matter of principle and denying foreign governments any right of intervention on behalf of private oil interests. Revolutionary fighting
scarcely affected the oil industry, which expanded rapidly during the
1910s to reach 55 million barrels by 1917. Article 27 of the Constitution
should be understood against that background. The oil interests, supported by the US government, requested Mexico to clarify its position
with regard to the companies, especially in view of Carranza's imposition of a 10 per cent production tax in April 1917. However, US entry
into the European war in the same year diverted attention from the
Mexican oil question.

The overthrow of Carranza in 1920 provided the US government with
the weapon of non-recognition with which to force the Obregón regime
into concessions. Obregón, however, managed to survive in power for
three years without US recognition due to the strength of his position
within the revolutionary camp. During this period, however, the uncertainty surrounding the status of the oil companies in Mexico increased.
Obregón refused to negotiate recognition as long as the US government
continued in its efforts to impose an unfavourable Treaty of Friendship
and Commerce on Mexico. The leftist and nationalist rhetoric coming
from revolutionary circles in Mexico including the government itself,
most of it hot air, alarmed the US government, dominated by conservatives between 1921 and 1932, which feared the establishment of a
socialist state at its back door.

The essential issue between the two governments continued to be
whether article 27 was to be applied retroactively or not. The US government, in close concert with the oil companies, withheld recognition
until Mexico guaranteed the property rights of US citizens in Mexico.
Although Obregón was more favourably disposed towards the oil companies than Carranza had been, it still took three years to arrive at a
working arrangement. This resulted from four months of informal talks
(May–August 1923), known as the Bucareli Accords. No written declaration appeared, but representatives of the two governments agreed that
while article 27 should not have retrospective effect, the US government
concurred that property titles would be converted into confirmed concessions. In effect, Mexico put the nationalist dimension of the oil question on hold for the time being. As a result, diplomatic relations were
renewed between the two countries on 6 September 1923. This ensured
the Obregón administration US cooperation during the De la Huerta

rebellion of December 1923–February 1924, which unsuccessfully challenged the succession of Calles.

By the time of the Bucareli Accords, Mexican oil production had already passed its peak in 1921 when total annual production came to 193 million barrels. At that time, oil represented 66 per cent of Mexico's external trade and accounted for just over 25 per cent of total world production. In the following year this level fell slightly to 182 million, but thereafter the fall became sharp – to 140 million barrels in 1925 and only 50 million in 1928. Depletion of resources partly explained the fall. However, company dislike of the 1923 Accords, followed by a fresh dispute in 1925–27 over the Calles government's attempt to oblige the companies to exchange titles for fifty-year concessions diminished investor interest in Mexico. Greater incentives appeared in the unrestrained environment of the Venezuela of Juan Vicente Gómez from the mid-1920s.

The decline of the Mexican oil industry adversely affected the Calles's administration's attempts to restore national finances and service outstanding debt obligations. The continuing decline of silver prices on the world market and the concurrent fall in copper prices compounded Mexico's adverse economic position, since along with oil those two commodities represented the country's principal exports. Overall government revenue fell 15 per cent between 1925 and 1928, that is well before the impact of the Great Depression of 1929 was felt in Mexico. In the same period, petroleum exports fell from 50 per cent of the total to 21 per cent. These trends exposed the fiscal vulnerability of the Mexican state. At the same time, the political problems generated by the Revolution did not seem anywhere near to resolution.

The rule of the chieftains 1920–1934

The rising of 1920 overthrew the Carranza regime in twenty-seven days and resulted in Carranza's murder in the mountains of Puebla on 20 May 1920 while in transit to Veracruz with the national treasury and much of the civil service in order to re-establish his government there. The Rebellion of Agua Prieta, led by Obregón, Calles, and De la Huerta, proved to be the last armed insurrection in Mexico which succeeded in capturing power. In that sense, the 1920 Rebellion drew to a close a tradition which had begun with the Plan of Iguala of 1821.

Unlike Madero's rising in 1910, it did not challenge an entire political order. On the contrary, it resembled more Díaz's Rebellion of Tuxtepec in 1876 by forcing a change within the established regime in order to give power to those impatiently waiting in the wings.

The wearing down of the institutions established under the 1857 Constitution during the Díaz era ensured that the Revolutionary Mexico of the 1910s would not witness the successful establishment of representative government and peaceful transfer of power. Instead, localised boss-rule, private networks of power, and armed political factions competed for power within or against the Revolution. Chieftains such as Carranza, Obregón, and Calles emerged at national level not radically different in style from Díaz. The Porfirian system had not displaced *caudillo-* and *cacique*-style politics, but had been constructed precisely on that basis. This explained both its long duration and its collapse in 1911–14. Thereafter, power passed back into the hands of the type of chieftains who had exercised it earlier in the nineteenth century, albeit in the different social and political context of the Revolution. Accordingly, Mexico after 1915 did not face the problem simply of reconstructing the framework of constitutional legality, violated by Díaz after 1884 and then by Huerta in 1913, but also the very distinct problem of how to make government effective throughout the breadth of national territory. Both were deeply serious problems, especially since the solutions were attempted in the 1920s and 1930s at a time of social and economic dislocation. Those attempting to find the solutions, however, were precisely the *caudillos* who had risen through the revolutionary fighting. The problem quickly became less an attempt to establish constitutional democracy than the search for some type of framework which would contain the ambitions and rivalries of the uneasy coalition of chieftains leading the victorious revolutionary movement. In all of this process, the attitude of the US Government remained fundamental, since it wielded the powerful instrument of recognition or non-recognition.

During the ten years 1918–28, the revolutionary chieftains struggled to gain control of the political organs established in accordance with the Constitution of 1917. In this power struggle, the constitutionalising of the political processes fell by the wayside. The Madero principle of Effective Suffrage was lost among the jockeying for position within the new regime. The development of political parties, aborted during the long period of Díaz's personal rule, never matured in the decade after

Plate 37 Álvaro Obregón (1880–1928) with Plutarco Elías Calles 1877–1945) and Adolfo de la Huerta (1881–1955). This photograph was taken in 1921 at the peak of the alliance between these three powerful post-revolutionary figures in the aftermath of Carranza's fall. Calles is at the centre and De la Huerta on the left. The succession question of 1923–24 broke this alliance and led to De la Huerta's unsuccessful rebellion. Obregón (on the right, then President-elect) was assassinated on 17 July 1928, after securing a controversial re-election.

the promulgation of the Constitution. Furthermore, article 130 prohibited religious-based parties, in order to prevent any recurrence of the electorally successful PCN. Carranza's Electoral Law of July 1918 increased the qualifications for parties competing in elections. This, combined with executive control of the electoral process, inhibited political diversification.

The type of party which briefly emerged was usually extemporary, a vehicle for a specific revolutionary group or for an aspiring political figure at election time. As a result, politics generally revolved around the personalities and immediate interests of regional *caudillos* and the presidents. The Partido Liberal Constitucionalista (PLC) had been the vehicle for the election of Carranza in 1917; it quickly passed under the control

Plate 38 Plutarco Elías Calles and his second wife, 1930.
Following Obregón's murder, Calles, who vacated the presidency
on 30 November 1928, began (as 'Jefe Máximo') a period of
control from behind the scenes known as the 'Maximato'
(1928–34). Cárdenas terminated the influence of Calles on
18 June 1935, when the ex-President, who had publicly criticised
the administration, departed for Mazatlán, and definitively when
Calles, in the company of Luis Morones and other associates,
who had been placed in custody, was required to leave Mexico
City for the United States on 10 April 1936.

of *obregonistas*, and became the instrument for Obregón's election in
September 1920. Thereafter, it evaporated. Obregón, Calles, and De la
Huerta all opposed the development of party as a potential restraint to
presidential power. Through the 1920s, the *caudillos* thrown up by the
Revolution consolidated their hold on political life. It seemed, after all,
as though not Madero but Díaz was the true founder of twentieth-
century Mexican political practices.

The failure to construct a viable political party in the early years of revolutionary control of government inhibited the development of a coherent programme. Presidential preoccupation with gaining and holding
power meant that policy would be formulated on the spot and in response

to the pressure groups jockeying for position within the regime. As a result, the revolution could not be consolidated in any consistent fashion and its leaders and factions remained vulnerable to internal division as well as opposition from without. Calles assumed control of the Partido Laborista Mexicano (PLM), founded in 1919, as his instrument for the elections of 1924. This party had developed in association with the Regional Confederation of Mexican Labour (CROM), established in May 1918 under the leadership of the electrician Luis Morones. The initials of the labour confederation soon came to stand for 'Cómo Robó Oro Morones' or 'How Morones Stole the Funds'.

The close collaboration of Calles and Morones characterised the administration of 1924–28. At the newly created Secretariat of Labour, Industry, and Commerce, Morones became the second most powerful man in Mexico. Calles maintained his own independence by playing off Morones and General Joaquín Amaro, Minister of War from 1924 to 1931. Guaranteeing the regime's survival was a tacit alliance between the army and officially organised labour, which foreshadowed other such alliances in Brazil during the 1930s and 1940s and in Argentina during the 1940s and 1950s. At the same time, the regime's priority was financial stabilisation, since Mexico, which had defaulted on payment of its external debt in 1914, could not gain renewed access to international credit until that had been accomplished. In June 1922, Finance Minister De la Huerta had reached agreement in New York with the International Bankers Committee, formed in 1919, concerning renewal of debt payment. In that year, the Mexican debt stood at US$500 million. However, he had been unable to secure either a loan or diplomatic recognition. The reconstruction of the Mexican state depended on three elements: satisfying the bankers, assuaging the oil companies, and reassuring the United States' government. The United States wanted a supervisory role in Mexico similar to the position it held in Cuba, the Dominican Republic, and Nicaragua. The Mexican government, in a much stronger position than smaller Caribbean and Central American states, was determined and was able to resist this.

Calles inherited Obregón's Finance Minister, Alberto Pani, who had taken office in September 1923, as the key person involved in fiscal recuperation. Once the Bucareli Accords had secured US recognition of the Obregón government, only the De la Huerta rebellion delayed resolution of the financial question. For the Calles administration the issue between Mexico and the international bankers was financial sovereignty. The banks were prepared to loan against security of the customs revenues as in the nineteenth century, though with the proviso that the US government act as guarantor of any transaction. Calles's alternative was the creation of a national bank, the Bank of Mexico, under effective government control. Established on 1 September 1925, the Bank of Mexico had the sole right of note issue and gave the government unlimited access to credit. Mexican businesses and banks cooperated with the state in providing the initial funding of 57 million pesos in gold. Pani, at the end of the year, was able to negotiate a 44 per cent reduction of the external debt over the 1922 total. He resigned, however, in 1927 in protest at the overbearing influence of Morones. Although the creation of the national bank did not resolve the problem of budget deficits, the government gained an important instrument in financing its policies and held back the demands of the bankers for priority to be given to debt servicing.

In the early years, Calles continued the agrarian reform policies in accordance with Obregón's Ejido Law of 30 December 1920, but called a halt in 1930. Until 1934, however, the revolutionary chieftains regarded the creation of individual properties as their priority rather than the reconstitution of peasant communal holdings, known after 1920 as *ejidos*. The Laws of April 1922 and April 1923 defined the extent of smallholdings, in accordance with availability of irrigation. Calles's Law of December 1925 established the right of individual ownership of *ejidal* plots. During the first three years of Calles's administration, the Minister of Agriculture, Emilio Portes Gil (b. Ciudad Victoria 1891), Governor of Tamaulipas from 1924–28, redistributed 2.6 million hectares of land. Since problems of irrigation and credit immediately arose, the government established a National Irrigation Commission in 1925 and the Agrarian Bank in 1926. The formation of *ejidos* had made very slow progress between 1915–20, when they accounted for only 0.3 per cent of agricultural land. Measures taken between 1920 and 1934, however, extended this proportion to 13.6 per cent. That, however, was still small: it indicated the low policy priority of the *ejido* before 1934 and the importance attached by government to maximising food production. In this sense, little was done to give effect to one of the high points of the 1917 Constitution.

The religious conflict

The slow pace of agrarian reform combined with opposition to Calles's religious policy to inflame popular discontent across the Catholic heartlands of the centre-north-west. The religious question, however, had many dimensions, which explained why urban middle-class Catholics, rural and small-town Catholics, and the ecclesiastical hierarchy acted in different ways. The hierarchy, profoundly affected still by the shock of the Reform movement, sought to recover lost ground by the most far-reaching process of evangelisation since the sixteenth century. In the years after 1870, the Catholic Church strengthened its position in traditional heartland regions and extended its influence through the countryside. The peak period of revival took place between 1884 and 1910. The broader period from 1867 to 1917 marked the Church's greatest expansion since the missionary days of the sixteenth century, with an increased number of priests, seminaries, Catholic schools, and bishoprics.

The revolutionaries of the 1910s and 1920s encountered a revived Catholicism, which in the mid-nineteenth century Jacobin tradition they viewed as a counter-revolutionary threat. The hierarchy regarded Mexico as an exclusively Catholic country and defined Mexican national identity in that respect. In January 1914, as the Huerta regime was fighting for its survival, the hierarchy dedicated the shrine of Cubilete in the Guanajuato sierra and proclaimed Jesus Christ to be the King of Mexico. Carrancista forces took this to be a provocation, especially since the Catholic hierarchy had made clear its view that the Mexican Revolution was a divine scourge inflicted on the country as punishment for the 1857 Constitution and the Reform Laws of 1858–60. In Monterrey in August 1914, Constitutionalist forces responded to the idea of Christ the King of Mexico by closing all the churches and burning the confessionals in the streets.

Between 1916 and 1937 an intense conflict took place between Mexican Catholics and the revolutionary authorities. The tone of this conflict was set by anti-clerical provisions in the 1917 Constitution. These focussed on education and the presence of the Church in society. Article 3 established the principle of free state education in the Juárez tradition, and banned all religious education in primary schools. Article 5 prohibited religious and monastic orders, and article 24 banned outdoor religious ceremonies. Among its comprehensive provisions article 27 prohibited the ownership of landed property by religious corporations. The Archbishop of Mexico and fourteen exiled bishops protested against the constitutional provisions on 14 February 1917, recalling the earlier hostility of the ecclesiastical hierarchy to the 1857 Constitution. In Jalisco, a stronghold of Catholic traditionalism, repeated conflict broke out in 1917–19.

As Governor of Sonora (1915–20), Calles in 1917 had expelled the Catholic clergy from the state. During his presidency, the crisis between Church and state deepened. Urban middle-class Catholics responded in 1925 by forming the League for the Defence of Religious Freedom, which by the following year had some 800,000 members, half of them women. Calles' Law of 1926 provided for the full application of the precepts of the Constitution, and began by closing all Catholic schools and convents. This had a similar effect to President Sebastián Lerdo's incorporation of the Reform Laws into the 1857 Constitution in 1873, which had led to the outbreak of Catholic rebellions across west-central Mexico.

By August 1926, a full-scale rebellion had broken out in the heartlands of Michoacán, Guanajuato, and Jalisco, extending by the end of the year to Zacatecas, Colima, and Querétaro. The *Cristero* Rebellion of 1926–29, so-called by self-attribution from the government's denunciation of the defenders of Christ the King, reached its peak in 1928. The Federal Army was unable to overcome the type of guerrilla tactics adopted by the *cristeros*. Like the *zapatistas* of the previous decade, the *cristero* fighters returned to their villages for the planting and harvest seasons. They represented a cross-section of rural and small-town society in the participating regions.

Alarmed at the extent of popular mobilisation, the Catholic hierarchy attempted to secure its own position by coming to an arrangement with the government. This was brought about through the mediation of the US special envoy, Dwight Morrow, who was in Mexico from November 1927 to reach an accord with Calles over the oil question. The abandonment of the *cristeros* by the bishops increased existing divisions among Mexican Catholics, since the League had also maintained its distance from the popular movement. The assassination of President-elect Obregón by a Catholic reopened the succession question and threatened to break apart the carefully constructed coalition around the Obregón–Calles axis. *Obregonistas*, for instance, implicated Morones in the murder. The worsening political situation made a termination of the religious conflict imperative.

By the 'arrangements' of 21 June 1929, the hierarchy won a concession of freedom of Catholic worship from the government. Article 130 remained in place, and the government continued to restrict the number of priests in each state to a maximum of fifty and promote secular education. Accordingly, the conflict continued at the regional level for most of the 1930s. After the establishment of the *modus vivendi* at the highest level, the army was then sent into the localities to root out *cristero* activitists and sympathisers. Repression, however, did nothing to resolve the conflict, which passed into a second phase in 1933–37.

The construction of the Revolutionary Party

In spite of the *maderista* principle of 1910 and the provisions of article 83 of the Constitution prohibiting presidential re-election, the Obregón–Calles group in control of the state legislated early in 1927 to allow for one sole presidential re-election at an undefined future date. Accordingly, as Calles's term of office came to an end, the issue of re-election, dormant since 1910, emerged again in the federal elections scheduled for 1 July 1928. The assassination of President-elect Obregón on 17 July threatened to blow apart the precarious revolutionary coalition.

Although Calles put the emphasis on state-building and financial reconstruction, the long-drawn-out Church–state conflicts from 1917 to 1937 weakened the new political order and undermined its legitimacy among large sectors of the population. Neglect of the principle of effective suffrage exposed the faction-ridden reality of the revolutionary coalition. The assassination of Obregón plunged Mexico into a state of permanent crisis between 1928 and 1935, made worse after 1929 by the impact of the Great Depression. The popularity of José Vasconcelos's presidential campaign of 1929 – and the threat it posed to the dominant revolutionary factions – should be understood in that context. For that reason, the government remained determined to subvert to the maximum the potential of Vasconcelos, who had moved into opposition in 1923 through hatred of Calles, to deprive the revolutionary coalition of the gains it had made since 1916.

The revolutionary party did not emerge from the grass-roots. On the contrary, it resulted from hurried *ad hoc* arrangements put together by Calles in response to an emergency. The Partido Nacional Revolucionario (PNR) incorporated existing state machines in return for federal government patronage. This implied the permanent subordination of state-level political leaders to the national executive. The days of autonomous regional *caudillos* were clearly numbered. Party would increasingly predominate over personalities and regions. Calles finally resolved the succession question by applying the Madero principle of no re-election to all elective offices from the Presidency and State Governorships to senators, federal deputies, state deputies, and municipal presidents. While, at the top level, this prevented recurrence of nineteenth-century abuses, the extension of the principle to the legislatures presaged ill for the development of any vibrant political life by denying legislators the benefits of parliamentary experience. In relative terms, this could only mean the further strengthening of the executive branch.

The party, however, would be permanently re-elected. In this way, the Mexican Revolution brought not the constitutional democracy hoped for by Madero but increased authoritarianism, centralism, and one-party rule. The succession question, which had plagued the country since Independence, became depersonalised, but throughout the long remainder of the twentieth century the automatic succession of the official party (in spite of two subsequent changes of name) ensured that the problem of transferring power from one party to another remained unresolved.

In the early stages, the official party resembled a confederation of *caciques*. The electoral defeat of Vasconcelos, achieved by a combination of fraud and violence, ensured that there would be no alternative to the PNR as the ruling entity in Mexico. Calles, who handed over office on an interim basis to Portes Gil at the expiration of his term in December 1928, retained effective power as the 'Jefe Máximo', or Principal Leader, of the PNR. This opened the period known as the 'Maximato', during which Calles governed from behind the scenes from 1928 until 1934 through the medium of three puppet presidents. Portes Gil, for instance, appointed Calles to the crucial office of Minister of War in March 1929.

The PNR became a bureaucratic apparatus. As such it provided a model for subsequent Latin-American state-created parties, such as those associated with the Vargas regime in Brazil, though in very different historical circumstances. The Mexican party eventually became a vast organism, outside of which no access to political power or influence would be possible. At its core stood the *quid pro quo* between the

Plate 39 Lázaro Cárdenas (1895–1970) with Calles, Manuel
Ávila Camacho (1897–1955), and Abelardo Rodríguez
(President, 1930–32).
At this Banquet for National Unity in 1942 both Generals
Cárdenas (second from the right) and Rodríguez (President
1932–34) are in uniform. Calles sits on the far left. Ávila
Camacho was President at that time.

state and organised labour. The patronage of worker organisations by
the state derived from the period of dominance by the Sonora-born
leaders, the 'Sonora dynasty', between 1920 and 1934. As late as the
1970s, the ruling party could still be described, at least in part, as an
alliance between bureaucracy and organised labour.

   Calles's model, developed later by Lázaro Cárdenas (1895–1970), was
the one-party states of Europe, which were emerging against the background of the crisis of political and economic liberalism. For the political reconstruction of Mexico in the aftermath of Revolution, the
United States was clearly not the model applied. On the contrary,
Mexican revolutionaries desperately concerned to retain power in the

face of Cristero rebellion, electoral challenge in 1929, and renewed religious conflict after 1931, adopted a curious hybrid of Fascist Italy and the Soviet Union but without either the fascism or the socialism.

On one very significant matter, the revolutionary regimes after 1920 departed from Díaz's practice – the modernisation of the armed forces. Revolutionary accession to power and retention of it had been made possible by the military collapse of the federal army in 1913–14. As a result, armed power ceased to belong to a central state but became fragmented among the competing revolutionary chieftains. After 1920, maintenance of the Sonora clique's political dominance depended upon the forging of an effective army out of the loyal armed bands. Under Calles, the chief figure in this process became Amaro. During the period of Calles's dominance, the political authorities at state level frequently used the armed forces to curb peasant pressures for agrarian reform and to disband peasant militias, as in the case of Veracruz in 1933. The process of army professionalisation was not completed until the 1940s.

Nationalism, Lázaro Cárdenas, and the Revolution during the 1930s

By the late 1920s, Calles was determined to halt agrarian reform. The impact of the Great Depression, however, made attention to social problems urgent. The effects of the Wall Street Crash of 24 October 1929 were increasingly felt in Mexico from July 1930. As we have seen, serious recession already affected Mexico's three main export commodities, oil, silver, and copper. Since Mexico did not depend on any one commodity and already had a reasonably diversified economy, the impact of the Great Depression was not as severe as in other Latin American countries such as Brazil, Argentina, Peru, or Cuba. Furthermore, the country's institutions were already passing through a process of structural change since the 1910s. Although too much should not be made of this, it did enable a swift adjustment to accelerated change in response to the Depression. Nevertheless, in 1930 nearly 69 per cent of the economically active population still worked in agriculture, despite a hundred years of sporadic attempts to develop national manufacturing industries.

The Mexican economy, however, remained vulnerable. GDP, which had risen 3.3 per cent annually in 1900–10, fell to 2.5 per cent between 1910 and 1925, and then declined further to 1.6 per cent in 1925–40, when it was overtaken by the rate of population growth at 1.8 per cent. Already in 1928, imports were rising while exports were falling. Between 1929 and 1932, government revenues from exports fell 29 per cent, while their purchasing power fell by more than 50 per cent in the same period. The Depression exposed all the more the hazards of reliance on the international market. Within the PNR the debate on the state of the economy and its consequences for society crystallised in an economic nationalist position which stressed the priority of the internal market and the possibilities of state intervention. Some of the foundations had already been laid during the Díaz era, when Mexico became virtually self-sufficient in textiles (manufactured from home-produced cotton) and Latin America's first steel plant had been constructed in Monterrey in 1900–3.

Mexico's domestic problems were compounded by the repercussions of the Depression within the USA. The US government expelled 310,000 Mexican workers between 1930 and 1933, and in May 1930 restricted import commodities from Mexico. Unemployment trebled. Agricultural production, furthermore, still remained below 1910 levels, in spite of an 18 per cent increase in population during the 1930s. Pressure on land and the food supply required renewed attention to irrigation and outstanding issues of land tenure. The 1923–33 maize crop stood at only 60 per cent of the 1910 figure, itself a very poor year. Between 1934 and 1938, food prices rose 54 per cent, a trend aggravated by unfavourable weather conditions for the three years 1936–38.

The worst years of the Depression were 1931–32, but thereafter the economy began to recover, although the 1929 position had still not been regained in 1933–34. The upward trend of oil and silver prices, however, raised the value and volume of exports. The opening of the Poza Rica oil fields after 1930 in the northern Gulf sector enabled a revival of the Mexican petroleum industry, though production still remained comparatively low at 47 million barrels in 1933. The recovery of oil raised once again the questions of its significance for the domestic economy, the status and profits of the foreign companies, and the condition of the Mexican workforce. These issues came to a climax during the oil crisis of 1937–38, which culminated in nationalisation of the petroleum industry by the Cárdenas government in March 1938.

The PNR Convention in Querétaro selected Cárdenas in May 1933 as the official presidential candidate. The party adopted a Six-Year Plan, originally formulated under Calles's influence. This sought to promote the middle-sized farmer as a parallel and alternative to the *ejido*, in order to facilitate an easier adaptation to new techniques. The PNR conference in December pushed this programme leftwards. With the support of the left, Cárdenas committed the PNR to far-reaching reform policies to be put in place by state intervention. Although initially regarded as potentially Calles's fourth puppet president, Cárdenas (1934–40) proceeded to create an independent political base among the peasantry during his celebrated election campaign tour of the country.

A combination of government measures and spontaneous peasant action at the local level had already modified Mexico's structure of landownership before Cárdenas's election on I July 1934. Between 1920 and 1934, the trend towards the consolidation of the hacienda, which characterised the period 1870–1910, was reversed. The hacienda still remained a major unit of production and social organisation, but its primacy was challenged at several levels. This was especially the case on the central plateau and adjacent areas where peasant communities remained numerous. The *ejido* took labour out of the private sector and reduced the power of the landowner in the locality. Where the hacienda survived, it frequently faced the opposition of armed bands of *agraristas* anxious to extend the benefits they had received from government-sponsored agrarian reforms. In many instances, land redistribution on the spot ran well in advance of government measures.

Cárdenas regarded the *ejido* as an alternative to the hacienda, in the same way that he was prepared to experiment with workers' cooperatives as an alternative to capitalism. In June 1937, for instance, the railways (in which the government had held a majority share since 1909) were brought fully under state control, and then on I May 1938 handed over to the Railway Workers' Union to manage them. Until 1938, however, the mining and petroleum sectors remained largely under the control of foreign companies, along with 80 per cent of the railroads and tramways, and the entire electrical industry. State intervention during the Cárdenas era considerably modified this picture and fostered a type of mixed economy associated with one-party government. Key industries such as oil became after 1938 less businesses than adjuncts of the bureaucracy. The acceleration of the *ejido* policy responded less to economic considerations than to social and political calculations. Agrarian reform policies, in fact, forced up food prices at a time of inflation due to deficit financing. At the end of the Cárdenas period, agriculture still accounted for 21.8 per cent of GDP, with manufacturing still well below at 16.9 per cent. The economy remained heavily dependent on the export of minerals.

The agrarian reforms of the 1930s formed less part of a grand overall strategy than a reflection of short-term needs. Although applied with vigour between 1934 and 1938, the *ejido* policy dated from 1917 and 1920, and was by no means an innovation of the Cárdenas era. The significance of those years lay in the different emphasis placed on reconstitution of communal lands in contrast to Calles's preference for private proprietorships. Between 1934 and 1940, the government redistributed 17,906,429 hectares of land, almost all as *ejidos*. The climax came in 1937, when 5,016,321 hectares were handed over to 184,457 titled beneficiaries. By 1940, the *ejido* accounted for over half the arable land in cultivation. The urgency of irrigation and credit in the form of seeds, fertilisers, tools, and livestock led to the creation of new governmental institutions. Until 1940, *Nacional Financiera*, established in 1934, responded to agrarian needs. The Calles era Agrarian Bank was divided in 1935 into two new banks, the Bank of Agricultural Credit for small and middle-sized peasants, and the Bank of Ejidal Credit for the cooperative entities. The Cárdenas administration was aware of the danger of *ejidos* lapsing into subsistence units or unviable and inefficient plots. An overriding aim was to supervise the amalgamation of *ejidos* so that they could contribute to the national need for increased food supply. The harsh realities of peasant agriculture and the inadequacy of inputs into that sector frustrated these ambitions. In spite of the emphasis on the *ejido*, policies of the Calles era were not abandoned under Cárdenas, since the law of May 1938 established an Office of Small Property to protect smallholders from peasant pressure and to issue certificates of exemption from expropriation.

The government, despite the Six-Year Plan, did not have a strategy of industrialisation to work through. Oil nationalisation resulted from a combination of inherited government difficulties with the companies and the contemporaneous deterioration of labour relations in the industry. Relations with the International Bankers Committee broke down in 1934 and were not repaired until 1942. The Six-Year Plan provided for the establishment of a relatively innocuous state company, Petróleos de México, to compete with the foreign corporations. This company, set up in 1935, would resume control of the private leases once they lapsed. At the same time the government sponsored the amalgamation of the twenty-one unions operating in the oil fields into one organisation. In 1936, this union proposed a renewed, nation-wide contract to the companies, which rejected it since it implied a substantial increase in labour costs. As a result, a general strike took place in the oil fields on 28 May 1937.

The Cárdenas administration took the side of the oil workers and denounced excessive company profits. The government's position was upheld by the Supreme Court in December 1937, which warned the companies that if they continued to show no interest in observing the provisions of article 123 of the Constitution, they would be regarded as outside the law. Since the companies did not back down – and instead hoped for intervention from abroad – the Mexican government resolved the dispute on 18 March 1938 by nationalising the petroleum industry. This action should not be regarded as in any sense a lurch in the direction of state socialism. Although the government justified nationalisation in accordance with article 127 rather than article 27 of the Constitution, the calculation behind it was primarily nationalist. For that reason it united all shades of the political spectrum from the far Right to the Marxist Left. Oil nationalisation was immediately seen – and for a long time thereafter – as a major national victory against foreign powers comparable to the great victory of 1867 against the European Intervention. It was not a state attack on private enterprise as such, but an economic nationalist measure directed against foreign corporations that had set themselves above the Mexican state. Yet, domestic political conditions played a large part in Cárdenas's high-risk international politics.

Although a political success, nationalisation took place in an unfavourable economic climate. Falling silver and oil exports had reduced government revenue; agrarian reform and public works schemes had worsened the budget deficit, and the bad harvest of 1937 had pushed up food prices. Mexico managed to ride the nationalisation crisis partly through Cárdenas's skilful attention to internal politics and partly because of the worsening of the international situation. The British government, which regarded the expropriation as illegal, could do nothing either to prevent or to reverse nationalisation, especially since the US administration of Franklin D. Roosevelt (1932–45) was opposed to armed intervention and the European situation continued to degenerate rapidly.

At the time of expropriation, just over half the oil was exported: the 1937 export figure of 24,960,335 barrels fell in the following year to 14,562,250 barrels. The depreciation of the peso from 3.5 (Mexican pesos) to the US dollar to 5 pesos made Mexican exports cheaper. In the short term, the Mexican government sold its nationalised oil to other Latin American countries when it could but more especially to Nazi Germany, Fascist Italy, and Imperial Japan in return for machinery and other capital goods, in order to circumvent the Anglo-American companies' boycott. The US Ambassador, Josephus Daniels, consistently argued in favour of compromise and generally sympathised with the reform policies of the Cárdenas administration, and after the expiration of the latter's term of office ranked him alongside Juárez as a defender of national interests. Neither the State Department nor the US Treasury agreed with Daniels's view of nationalisation.

Oil-company hostility, however, was overtaken by US strategic needs after the outbreak of the Second World War. As a gesture, Mexico in July 1941 allowed US Air Force planes to land at Mexican bases on their way to and from the Panama Canal Zone. The US began to purchase Mexican oil for naval use from June 1942. Agreement was reached over compensation for the oil companies between November 1941 and April 1942. Compensation included only the value of surface-level properties. By 1947, a total of US$280 million had been paid out. Mexico and Great Britain broke off diplomatic relations on 12 and 13 May 1938, and did not reach accord until 1947, when US$130 million was paid to El Águila.

The oil crisis of 1937–38 took place within the context of a complex manoeuvring for power among the leading Mexican political figures. In this process Cárdenas showed himself to be an apt successor to Juárez, not least in his neutralisation of opponents but also in his final destruction of Calles. Cárdenas's initial alliances were with two strong men of different origin and function. The first, and tactically the more important at the time, was Saturnino Cedillo (b. 1891, Villa del Maíz, San Luis Potosí), agrarian boss of the State of San Luis Potosí. Cedillo had risen with the revolution and originally aligned with Villa before adhering to the Obregón–Calles network. Although the forces under his control fought against the *cristero* rebellion, Cedillo did not share the anti-clericalism of Calles. Cedillo controlled San Luis Potosí as his personal fief virtually independent of the federal government. The second ally was Vicente Lombardo Toledano (1894–1968), who came from an upper-class Puebla family but passed from Directorship of the National Preparatory School to become in 1936 leader of the Confederation of Mexican Workers (CTM), which had broken away from CROM. These two alliances guaranteed Cárdenas the crucial support of army and labour.

Cárdenas cultivated enemies of Calles such as Ortiz Rubio and Portes Gil as well, so that when the break with Calles came in May 1935, he was able to destroy the latter's influence in the PNR. After purging *callistas* from Congress and the State Governorships, Cárdenas exiled Calles and Morones to the United States in April 1936. In August, Cárdenas was strong enough to take advantage of a power struggle between Múgica and Portes Gil to remove the latter from the presidency of the PNR, in order to prevent the creation of an alternative power base at the head of the bureaucracy. Cárdenas then proceeded to break the power of autonomous regional chieftains, beginning with Tomás Garrido Canabal in Tabasco in 1936 and finishing with Cedillo in San Luis Potosí in 1938. Garrido Canabal, who controlled his own private army of young, anticlerical radicals known as the Red Shirts, was forced into exile. Cedillo's power was backed by armed *agraristas*, who were the recipients of the third most far-reaching agrarian reform in the country. The chieftain of San Luis Potosí, furthermore, had made the state a haven for Catholics, including priests, since he opposed the religious and educational policies of the Cárdenas administration.

The central government began the process of undermining Cedillo by sending federal troops into the state as a counterbalance to Cedillo's *agraristas*. At the same time, the Left portrayed Cedillo as a sympathiser with international fascism and as Mexico's potential General Franco. Through managed elections, the federal government began in the state capital the creation of an alternative political machine to that of Cedillo which was based in the countryside. The government, furthermore, brought the CTM into state politics at a time of labour unrest there. Added to that, the Cárdenas regime intended to organise all beneficiaries of agrarian reform into one centrally managed union which would then be incorporated into the PNR. This policy struck a mortal blow at Cedillo's independent clientèle. The combination of these objectives forced Cedillo into opposition. The crisis broke in March–May 1938, and ended with Cedillo's abortive rebellion, flight to the hills, and subsequent assassination in January 1939.

The oil crisis accompanied Cedillo's challenge to the Cárdenas regime. That crisis made the position of Cedillo and the growth of a rightist opposition at the same time all the more serious. However, the political triumph of oil nationalisation made it possible for the regime to deal swiftly and effectively with this last major regional *caudillo*. The Defence Secretary, Manuel Ávila Camacho (1897–1955), played the decisive role both in guaranteeing national security during the oil crisis and in the destruction of Cedillo. This would place him in a commanding position in the following two years, when the issue of the succession to Cárdenas came to the forefront.

The reorganisation of the official party and the presidential elections of 1940

In March 1938, Cárdenas broadened the PNR by transforming it into a corporately organised entity with a different name. The Partido de la Revolución Mexicana (PRM) consisted of four 'sectors' – organised labour, the newly formed peasant union, the army, and the so-called popular sector. This corporate structure reflected in part the historic traditions of the Hispanic world and in part contemporary practice in the later 1930s and early 1940s. Cárdenas separated the National Peasant Confederation (CNC) from the CTM, as a distinct sector of the PRM, in order to weaken the position of Lombardo Toledano, who as a Marxist was calling for the Mexican Revolution to move towards the Soviet model. The separate CNC, moreover, put organised rural labour directly under the supervision of the federal government. The *ejidatarios* automatically became members of the CNC, the total membership of which already reached 2 million. This measure was the corollary of the *ejido* policy, which at one and the same time both rectified the earlier revolutionary neglect of the peasantry and absorbed it into the all-embracing sphere of state patronage.

The army remained one of the four sectors until December 1940 after the oil crisis had passed and the presidential elections of 1940 had been won by Ávila Camacho, the PRM candidate. Senior officers welcomed the division of the CTM, since they were apprehensive of its influence within the regime and opposed any suggestion of the formation of worker militias on Spanish Republican lines. The popular sector encompassed not only smallholders but owners of small-scale industries, and government employees. Its strength lay in the Federation of Government Employees Union (FSTSE). In theory, the four sectors of the official party selected the presidential candidate at the nomination convention every six years. In reality, the outgoing incumbent usually indicated unequivocally who was to be his successor. The sectors represented institutionalised pressure groups competing within an increasingly large bureaucratic structure for influence, power, and material rewards. The prime intention was to defuse rural and labour grievances and channel worker aspiration into the party's own institutional channels. In such a way, autonomous or dissident groups would be left out in the cold.

The new party structure effectively strengthened further the power of the central government, especially after the disintegration of Cedillo's position in San Luis Potosí. Cárdenas's labour and agrarian reform policies, including the labour-oriented process of oil nationalisation, revealed a great deal concerning the practical functioning of the Mexican Revolution. This consisted basically of a coming together of popular pressures and government manoeuvrings. The PRM represented a synthesis of government orchestrated popular mobilisation and popular search for channels through which grievances could be redressed. The ultimate achievement of the Cárdenas era was to bind together hitherto disparate – and even opposed – elements within the Revolution since the 1910s. This was imperative for two reasons: the need for national unity during the oil crisis in face of the potential threat of foreign intervention, and the need to bind the peasantry tightly to the government in the aftermath of the *cristero* rebellion and the emergence of a strong Catholic nationalist opposition to the regime in the form of *Sinarquismo* after May 1937.

The conflict over religion had revived after 1931, following military repression of the *cristeros* and the government's effective abandonment of the 1929 accords. It continued throughout the decade. Guanajuato, Michoacán, and Jalisco were the states most affected. Between 1929 and 1936, some 5,000 people died in the conflict. In Michoacán, where Cárdenas had been Governor between 1928 and 1932, only thirty-three priests remained in the state by the end of his term of office. By 1935, the federal government was still unable to put down opposition in the Bajío, where local smallholders opposed the *ejido* policy as inappropriate to their region. The education issue predominated between 1934 and 1938: the Catholic hierarchy protested against government policy and

instructed Catholic organisations and individuals to oppose its application. In May 1937, a Catholic nationalist movement, the Unión
Nacional Sinarquista (UNS), was formed. At its core was the rural
bourgeoisie and professional lower-middle class of the Bajío. Founded
by students of the University of Guanajuato, some of them former
seminarists, in their twenties and thirties and mainly from the middle
class, the UNS was seen as a spiritual movement for national transformation. Its roots lay in the provincial, Catholic heartlands of the centre-
north-west. The UNS followed in the tradition of the Catholic
opposition to Carranza from 1916–17 and the *cristero* rebellion of
1926–29, the rejection of the 'arrangements' of 1929 and the renewal of
conflict after 1931.

The nationalism of the UNS could be seen in its rejection of Marxist
class-struggle theory but support for the nationalisation of petroleum.
The UNS opposed agrarian collectivisation and called for the end to the
state monopoly of education. The movement posed a threat to the *car-
denista* political order not only because it challenged outright monopoly
control by the PNR/PRM but also because it counted among its cross-
class membership smallholders, *ejidatarios*, share-croppers, estate-
workers, day-labourers, artisans, and workers in small industries. There
were some 90,000 militants by 1939, when the UNS denounced the revolutionary system as a new Porfirian era of privilege, poverty, and tyranny.
During 1940, its peak year, the UNS controlled the majority of municipalities in the Bajío. The principal danger for the official party lay in the
UNS capacity for mobilisation, which revived the prospect of a powerful
challenge to the regime from the provincial grass-roots level. Even so, the
UNS lacked a coherent programme and began to lose its thrust as the government modified the anti-clericalism derived from the Calles era after
1938 and especially 1940.

Cárdenas built on the political legacy of the Calles era of which he
was essentially a product in spite of differences of emphasis. The PRM
of 1938–46 arose out of the PNR of 1929–38. The party which faced the
elections of 1940, however, was more tightly organised and centrally
controlled than its more extemporary progenitor. By 1940, virtually all
the local political machines independent of the national executive had
been superseded. In effect, the Mexican Revolution was in the process
of constructing a far more powerful state than had existed either in the
Díaz era or during the Spanish colonial viceroyalty.

Three great turning points determined the construction of the monopoly-party state. The defeat of the De la Huerta Rebellion in 1924 ensured that the inner clique of the revolutionary leadership would decide the presidential succession. The presidential election campaign of 1929 and the overwhelming defeat of Vasconcelos guaranteed that there would henceforth be no effective challenge to the official party by any organised opposition. The election of Ávila Camacho in 1940 demonstrated that no challenge within the party to the presidentially sanctioned official candidate stood any chance of success.

The elections of 1940 also determined that the Mexican Revolution would not move further towards the left. The early withdrawal of Múgica highlighted the move of the Cárdenas administration away from leftist policies after 1938. The arrival of a fugitive Leon Trotsky in Mexico in that year had already divided the left and alienated the pro-Stalinists from Múgica's potential candidature. Accordingly, the principal challenge to official policy from within the regime came not from the Left but from the secular Right. With its focus in the business interests in Monterrey, the Right looked to the candidature of General Juan Andreu Almazán, Military Commander of the Nuevo León District. Ávila Camacho became official PRM candidate principally because his ability to hold the army together in support of the regime had been proved during the Cedillo and oil crises. Franco's victory in the Spanish Civil War in April 1939 and the arrival of Republican exiles in Mexico demonstrated the importance of this. Key state governors, such as Miguel Alemán in Veracruz, came out in support of the official candidate. Half the state governors were, in any case, army officers in 1940. Cárdenas campaigned for Ávila Camacho on a centrist ticket, which cut between the divided Left on the one hand and the divided Right on the other. In this vein, Cárdenas condemned 'state socialism', while at the same time warning that the greatest threat to the Mexican Revolution came from international fascism. Ávila Camacho's victory in elections manipulated by the government ensured that economic nationalism, a mixed economy, corporate political organisation, and a compromise on the religious question would prevail in Mexico during the 1940s.

7

The monopoly party, 1940–2000

The combination of favourable international circumstances and internal conditions enabled the governing party to become a monopoly party of government during the three decades after 1940. Mexican economic advances between 1940 and 1970 created a climate of optimism both at home and abroad. Lack of serious opposition after 1943, whether from right or left, provided the party with the opportunity to expand its control throughout most sectors of society. During the 1940s, business was gradually won over, as the leftist stance of the Cárdenas years was discarded and the old rhetoric dropped except for ceremonial occasions. The country's transformation from predominantly rural to urban, the expansion of national industries, the emergence of a mixed economy with a high state profile, the expansion of educational institutions all fostered the impression that Mexico had finally emerged from the blight of underdevelopment and was on the road to peace and prosperity.

The financial reform of 1954 opened the period known as 'stabilised development', generally associated with the Presidencies of Adolfo Ruiz Cortines (1952–58) and Adolfo López Mateos (1958–64) and Antonio Ortiz Mena's period as Minister of Finance (1958–70). Substantially this lasted until the recession of 1971, although structural problems had already appeared in the economy from the early 1960s. The generation that experienced those decades became accustomed to the combination of political stability, a modicum of social justice, and a growing economy. Middle- and upper-middle-class lifestyles and aspirations were predicated on the continuation of those conditions. Regular visits to the United States and Europe and even study abroad became realisable objectives for the first time beyond the narrow circle of the ostentatiously wealthy and privileged. These expectations, however, ran aground by the end of the 1960s. During the course of the 1970s, the country found itself in completely different political and economic conditions. This transition gave rise to what some Mexican commentators, looking back from the late 1990s with bitterness, regard as the three lost decades. Accordingly, the search has been for who or what to blame.

The decades of economic growth and optimism present a problem of historical interpretation in the light of the stagnation, crisis, and instability which followed after 1970. During the first half of the 1960s, this downturn could not have been anticipated, except perhaps by the most acute observer. However, the three problematic decades after 1970 make it necessary to view the period of expansion in a different light, searching in it for the roots of subsequent difficulties. It is evidently important to identify the limitations of Mexican growth. By the late 1960s, the monopoly party had deepened its control over the political processes and took credit for the economic expansion as a result of the structures it had set in place. However, the connection between economic developments, which were also related to international trends, and the imposition of a monopoly-party system was by no means proved. By comparison, a similar connection had been assumed between dictatorship and development during the Díaz era, as we have seen. In fact, a case could be made for monopoly-party rule as an obstacle to development through the corruption it entailed, the heavy presence of the national state in the economy, and the uneasy relationship which prevailed between Mexican business and government. This case, however, was rarely made at the time. When, however, the economy went off course in the early 1970s, these and related problems rose to the surface. They did so at a time of mounting political criticism in the aftermath of the repression of the protest movements of 1968. From 1970, monopoly-party rule increasingly became a political issue in itself, though three decades later this problem had still not been resolved.

PART ONE: THE 'MEXICAN MIRACLE' AND POLITICAL
CONTROL, 1940–1970

Mexico emerged from the Great Depression by 1934–35. The nationalisation of petroleum in 1938 began the process of redirecting oil resources into the domestic economy. The outbreak of the Second World War in 1939, and particularly the United States' entry in 1941, increased demand for Mexican products while at the same time creating conditions for a renewal of the process of industrialisation which had made headway before the Revolution of 1910. The Mexican economy transformed strikingly from the 1940s. Between 1930 and 1960, the rural to urban relationship in the population structure altered from 66.5 per cent against 33.5 per cent to 49.3 per cent against 50.7 per cent. The contribution of primary activities to the GNP fell from 19.4 per cent in 1940 to 8.9 per cent in 1976. Rapid urbanisation and industrialisation characterised the three decades before 1970. At the same time, life expectancy increased from thirty-three to thirty-eight years in 1925–40 to sixty-two years by 1970, while the rate of illiteracy fell from 42 per cent in 1950 to 16 per cent by 1970. Impressive as these developments were in Mexican and Latin American terms, the inescapable fact remained that the US state of California with 14 million inhabitants in 1970 had a GNP of US$50 billion, more than double that of the Mexican Republic with a population of 54 million. Although Mexico's annual per capita income doubled between 1950 and 1970 to US$600, the figure for the United States stood at US$3,000.

The apogee of the monopoly-party state (1940–1968)

The election campaign of 1940 was characterised by widespread violence and fraud. The outgoing administration was determined at all costs to secure the election of Manuel Ávila Camacho. The division of the Left contributed to this outcome, and the defusion of the religious conflicts of the 1920s and 1930s secured Catholic votes. Large-scale abstentions by the *Sinarquistas* further assisted the official party's victory. Rural schoolmasters working through the CNC played a significant role in securing support for Ávila Camacho. The latter's conciliatory position and ability to defuse opposition enabled the governing party to command the centre-ground of politics at a difficult time of international conflict and internal polarisation. Determined to prevent a repetition of the fraud and violence of 1940, Ávila Camacho altered the 1918 Electoral Law in December 1945. Essentially this involved taking away from local and state authorities control of the electoral process and transferring it to a Federal Commission of Electoral

Plate 40 Library of the National University (UNAM).
Designed by Juan O'Gorman, Gustavo Saavedra, and Juan
Martínez de Velasco, the main buildings of the UNAM were
constructed in 1950–56 during the presidencies of Miguel
Alemán (1946–52) and Adolfo Ruiz Cortines (1950–58). The
university symbolised the cultural dynamism of the post-
revolutionary era, and the designs incorporated motifs from all
previous epochs. The aggressive nationalism would later be
complemented in a different vein by the Museum of
Anthropology in 1964. According to the Rector, speaking at the
end of 1998, only 24,000 of the 33,000 students who entered the
university completed their first degree.

Supervision. The end result proved to be a further strengthening of
central government control and presidential influence.

Political stability encouraged enough foreign capital back into the
country to bolster high rates of growth. Ávila Camacho (1940–46)
began the process of healing the breach between the regime and private
enterprise. This had become a political necessity in view of the formation of opposition parties associated with business such as the PAN
in 1939. Most such groupings vanished during Ávila Camacho's presidency, leaving only the UNS and the PAN as the principal opposition
organisations, though completely distinct from one another and
unlikely to combine. Neither offered more than a token opposition. The

political stance and the social composition of the PRM in the Ávila Camacho era differed markedly from the original PRM conceived as an alliance of workers and soldiers in the highly charged political conditions of 1938.

During Ávila Camacho's presidency, the elements comprising the Popular Sector of the party considerably increased their influence within the regime. These professional and civil service interests, along with smallholders, were grouped together as the National Confederation of Popular Organisations (CNOP) in 1943. Continued divisions on the Left led to the declining influence of Lombardo Toledano after 1941 and the rise of the moderate, Fidel Velázquez, in the direction of the CTM. Under Velázquez's leadership the long-standing three-way relationship between state, labour, and business became institutionalised after 1945.

In 1946, the official party's name became the Revolutionary Institutional Party (PRI), the party of the institutionalised revolution, although the corporate structure inherited from the Cárdenas era was preserved. This change in name recognised the transformation of the PRM and the modification of the earlier predominance of the CTM. Although Lombardo Toledano initially supported the candidature of Miguel Alemán, Secretary of the Interior, the disillusionment came rapidly. The Alemán administration's clear desire to bring business into cooperation with the regime led to Lombardo Toledano's decision to break with the PRI and found an opposition PPS or Popular Socialist Party, which had no chance of electoral success.

The close relationship between government and business, which remained outside the formal structure of the party, had already been foreshadowed during the Calles period between 1924 and 1934. The Alemán administration (1946–52) resumed this pattern after 1946. Businessmen who had made their money during the immediate post-revolutionary decades of the 1920s and 1930s exercised considerable influence in the administration. Although the overwhelming majority of official-party members belonged to the labour and peasant sectors, they were not the prevailing influence in government in this period. Even so, Alemán's agrarian reform law of December 1946 accelerated the break-up of the large estate, though the objective was the encouragement of private smallholdings with defined limits according to type of land. At its upper levels, however, the so-called smallholding was fast becoming a large-scale property.

At the core of the political system was the process of selection of the presidential candidate. Observation of the principle of no re-election defused the explosive succession question. However, the mysteries surrounding the process of selection remained impenetrable. It was widely believed that until 1970 ex-presidents played a role in the process of succession but that the choice of successor lay effectively in the hands of the incumbent President. The criteria for succession were never elaborated publicly: similarly, the number of participants (or their ranking) in the process was never made known. Since 1934, though, each successor had held office in the administration of his predecessor, and, more to the point, earned his selection by the performance of some decisive service to it. Ávila Camacho's role as Secretary of Defence in 1938, for instance, was a case in point. After 1970, the earlier collegiate process lapsed, and the incumbent made the choice of successor. Throughout the era of monopoly-party dominance, the President remained at the summit of the political pyramid. Cosío Villegas, in fact, described the political system as a 'six-yearly absolute monarchy'. One might go even further and describe later twentieth-century Mexico as an elective empire posing as a federal republic.

The strengths and weaknesses of expansion

In many respects, the war years themselves were the decisive platform for later expansion. The combination of external and internal factors as contributors to economic growth could be seen clearly at that time. While external factors would always have to be taken into consideration and, in fact, would continue to determine whether the Mexican economy went into crisis or not, the country had, since the Díaz period, built up a basic infrastructure and already laid the foundations for the future growth of national industries. Problems of technology, investment, entrepreneurial enterprise, and a limited market held back economic growth before 1910. Revolutionary warfare during the 1910s decapitalised the economy and after 1914 terminated Mexico's access to international credit. Internal conflict obscured trends taking place within the economy and delayed recovery. In 1942, Mexico secured its first international loan since the time of Limantour.

Nacional Financiera became the intermediary between the Mexican government and foreign investors during the 1940s. Government itself acted as mediator between the public and private sectors. The latter still accounted for about 70 per cent of domestic investment after 1940. The cotton-textile industry was a notable recipient. From the 1940s, the Mexican economy was able to maintain a rhythm of growth that lasted substantially until the debt crisis of 1982.

During Ávila Camacho's presidency the basis for future political stability and economic expansion was laid. Thereafter, between 1946 and 1954, the country moved fast in the direction of industrialisation, with the key oil industry under state control. The government during the 1940s invested heavily in the basic infrastructure. Manufacturing overtook agriculture for the first time in 1951. During the 1960s, output doubled, when agricultural production increased by only one-third. Economic growth was accompanied by high government expenditure on social policy. These objectives required a stronger tax base than Mexico actually possessed. Even so, the rate of inflation remained virtually stable, particularly after the devaluation of 1948. The Mexican annual rate of inflation stood at 8.4 per cent between 1948 and 1954, in contrast to a 2 per cent rate in the USA.

The uneasy balance – economic nationalism and private enterprise

Economic nationalism remained alive during the 1940s and 1950s, in spite of the clearly different political atmosphere from that of the Cárdenas era. After the end of the Second World War Mexican industrialists pressed the government for higher tariffs designed to protect them from foreign, principally United States, imports. The Alemán government responded with policies establishing import quotas and licences, introduced from 1947 onwards, designed to protect domestic industries. These economic nationalist policies, which followed in the aftermath of oil nationalisation ten years earlier, were designed to isolate the domestic market from external competition. At the same time, the government sought to protect Mexican investors by creating barriers against foreign investment and thereby 'mexicanise' the economy. This was a reaction to the open investment policies of the Díaz era. However, it had the long-term effect of curbing expansion and encouraging the state to finance growth by increased recourse to external credit.

In the short term, the political economy of import substitution decreased Mexican dependence on international suppliers. It revealed the debt of post-revolutionary administrations to the pre-revolutionary development of national industries. The closed economy, however, concealed the inefficiencies and technological limitations of the principal sectors of Mexican industry. These became serious obstacles to further growth when the economy slowed down by the mid-1960s and ran into trouble after 1970. Import substitution showed considerable short-term success by the 1960s, when Mexican manufacturing supplied the bulk of the market for textiles, shoes, foodstuffs, beverages, tobacco, rubber, and glass. Internal demand explained industrial growth during the period from the 1950s to the 1970s.

The state played an active role in the economy and government services expanded considerably. Subsidies and fiscal exemptions, combined with credit from Nacional Financiera, contributed to the establishment of new enterprises. The extent of the public sector in Mexico was greater than in any other Latin American country between 1940 and 1980. By 1975, for instance, public-sector investment accounted for 42 per cent of the total domestic capital invested. New industries emerged in both sectors: in 1947, a synthetic-fibre industry began, designed to import-substitute; an electric-motor industry, begun in 1948, operated through sixteen factories in the Federal District, San Luis Potosí, and Guanajuato by 1966; PEMEX began the development of a petrochemical industry in 1959; by 1965, internal demand absorbed over 98 per cent of the production of electricity-carrying copper, developed after 1943; in 1954, Mexico began the construction of railway carriages for internal use in a railway system already under 85 per cent public ownership.

The Alemán presidency, intensely criticised on the Left both then and afterwards, did not represent the sharp departure from revolutionary principles that has usually been attributed to it. *Alemanismo* attempted to give business, both national and foreign, as free a rein as was compatible within the context of the general principles of economic nationalism. The latter presupposed the continuation, and strengthening, of the high-profile state sector in a mixed economy. Too much has been made of the supposed new directions after 1946. During the presidencies of Luis Echeverría Álvarez (1970–76) and José López Portillo (1976–82), a renewed statism was combined with increasing presidential power and an opportunistic populism. The tension between the Monterrey group of northern business interests and those two administrations seriously compromised the tacit understanding between private enterprise and the monopoly party, which had developed during previous administrations. One has only to consider how much of the Mexican economy there was left to open up by the late 1980s and early 1990s during the Salinas experiment in 'neo-liberalism' to appreciate the degree of state management and patronage inherent in the country's economic life.

'Stabilised Development', (1954–1971)

This nomenclature for the period 1954 to 1971 concealed long-term structural problems, which were not resolved at that time. Essentially, government objectives were to maintain a low rate of inflation and a stable exchange rate, at the same time controlling public expenditure and the money supply. Essentially, this policy derived from the devaluation of 1954. Changed international conditions explained the background to the devaluation. The impact of the Korean War (1950–53) had increased world prices, provided opportunities for Mexican exports, and led to the inflow of foreign capital. At the same time, however, this expansion threatened to fuel inflation and increase imports. When wartime expansion came to an end, Mexico faced a balance-of-payments crisis. The incoming president, Ruiz Cortines, who had been Secretary of the Interior in the Alemán cabinet and also a previous Governor of Veracruz, inherited a widespread sense of discontent from the corruption associated with the outgoing administration.

Rising prices, combined with the deterioration of lower-class living standards, presented major political and economic problems. The administration cut back expenditure and campaigned against corruption. At the same time, however, it sought to hold back food-price rises by state participation in the distribution of maize and bean supplies in 1952–53, in face of private sector objection. The deteriorating position of the currency pointed to an inevitable devaluation of the peso. The 30.8 per cent devaluation of April 1954, from 8.65 pesos to 12.50 pesos in relation to the US dollar, coming in the aftermath of the previous devaluation in 1948, pushed the inflation rate from 6 per cent in 1954 to 15.7 per cent in 1955, though inflation was subsequently brought under control. Mexican inflation rates in the 1950s and 1960s – an annual average of 2.8 per cent – in no way resembled the high figures for Argentina, Brazil, or Chile.

Manufacturing salaries fell by 4.5 per cent in 1955, in contrast to the rise of 10.9 per cent in the previous year. Popular discontent obliged the government to award a wage increase of 10 per cent to all public-sector workers in May 1954, but this could not match the loss of purchasing power since devaluation. The CTM maintained its quiescent policy, Velázquez opposing a threat of higher wage increases or strike. Worker divisions were contained through recourse to the Federal Conciliation and Arbitration Board by the Secretary of Labour, Adolfo López Mateos. The latter enabled the administration to ride relatively smoothly through a period of serious labour discontent. A series of modest wage rises and the increase of the minimum wage managed to defuse the crisis of summer 1954. The decisive position of López Mateos contributed substantially to his selection as successor to Ruiz Cortines in 1958.

The 1954 devaluation laid the basis for the administration's proclaimed policy of 'stabilised development'. Government provided stimuli to the private sector and pushed forward the process of import substitution through tariffs, import quotas, and tax exemptions for new industries. For a time, the internal market continued to be the principal motor of growth. The policy objectives were to combine rapid growth with stable prices and a stable balance of payments, maintaining a fixed exchange rate at the 1954 level. This latter became the orthodoxy of the period, with the result that government failed to use the exchange rate as a mechanism for correcting the trade deficit. The economy, at the same time, was unable to create sufficient jobs. Although the strategic sectors of the economy had expanded since the 1940s, the strain of providing credit in a low-taxation society could already be felt in the financial system.

Between 1950 and 1962, Gross Domestic Product grew at the impressive annual rate of 5.9 per cent, though, as Enrique Cárdenas has shown, there were fluctuations within this period. Between 1954 and 1957, for instance, GDP grew at the annual rate of 8.2 per cent, but relatively stagnated at a 5.2 per cent level from 1958 to 1962, when the signs of what was to come later could be discerned. The electrical industry, which the López Mateos administration nationalised on 27 September 1960, set the pace at a growth rate of 9.1 per cent in the longer period, with the state-owned oil industry at 7.8 per cent in second place, and manufacturing at 7 per cent. Agriculture trailed at 4.4 per cent in real terms. These figures should be understood in terms of the capacity of the economy to meet the demands placed upon it by society at a time of high population growth at the annual rate of 3.5 per cent during the 1950s and 1960s.

At the peak of expansion between 1963 and 1971, the annual average growth rate rose to 7.1 per cent, comparable to the Brazilian rate, and approaching the levels of West Germany (7.5 per cent) and Japan (9 per cent). Mexico, along with Brazil and Venezuela, appeared to share in the post-war economic miracles experienced in Japan, West Germany, and Italy. The latter three countries, however, were recovering from wartime damage. They were not 'Third World' societies attempting to transform their structures from traditional or semi-developed to modern and technologically advanced. Once Japan, West Germany, and Italy had passed through the immediate process of reconstruction, they could build thereafter on stable foundations laid down by previous generations.

High rates of growth, however, put pressure on the balance of payments. Accelerated rates required external credit to finance continued expansion. The problem that lay at the heart of this period of development was that if the government tried to hold back expansion, in order to curb dependence on credit, the labour market would contract. At a time when the economy was already incapable of supplying a sufficient number of jobs, this would result in serious social consequences. Governments sought to maintain high rates of growth, while at the same time keeping to below the 7.5 per cent figure. In 1965, 1969, and 1971, growth rates were reduced with a depressing effect on the labour market. Between 1964 and 1967, real wages in the manufacturing sector actually fell by nearly 25 per cent. Since the agricultural sector stagnated during the 1960s, the labour problem became aggravated. By the late 1960s, the Mexican economy proved increasingly unable to finance itself.

The high rate of Mexican population growth would pose future problems if the economy went into recession, especially in view of weaker performance of the agricultural sector. Mexican industry still suffered from the structural problems inherited from the past, chief of which was its technological backwardness. In many respects, it owed its existence to tariff protection. It proved strikingly incapable of dominating the export trade, a prospect which might have led to an export model of growth which was to carry South-East and East Asia to prosperity before the collapse of 1997–98. Government policy, in any case, sought to curb exportation in favour of the expansion of the domestic market through the policy of import substitution. Exports, in fact, fell as a proportion of GDP from 25.3 per cent in 1960 to 20.3 per cent in 1970. The contraction of exports at a time when Mexico needed to cover its growing balance of payments deficit presented a serious structural problem. In curbing exportation, the Mexican government committed a strategic error. Mexican industry, however, could not match its foreign competitors in terms of cost or quality. The technology and capital necessary to transform the productivity of national industry would have come from abroad. The steel industry, which had originated in Monterrey in 1900, was still producing at relatively low levels in the boom decade of the 1960s.

The geographical focus of manufacturing in Mexico continued to be unbalanced. Nuevo León, with brewing, textiles and shoes, paper, glass, steel, and electrical goods, accounted for 10 per cent of national industrial output during the 1960s. Monterrey's population rose to around 900,000 in 1960, and would reach 1.2 million in the early 1980s.

The border proved to be the weak link in Mexican economic nationalism. In spite of decades of economic nationalism, 50 per cent of Mexico's manufacturing assets were controlled by multinational companies. Expansion of manufacturing in the border cities accounted for much of this investment. In sharp contrast to its earlier history, the border zone became the most urban region of Mexico. By 1970, the proportion of urban inhabitants in the whole Republic had risen to 60 per cent – but to 85 per cent in the border states. Industry there attracted migrants from the rest of the country. Population and industry showed a marked tendency to concentrate in cities such as Tijuana, Mexicali, and Ciudad Juárez along the US border, benefiting from US investment in cheap-labour manufacturing and in the cross-border trade. In 1970, only 35 per cent of Tijuana's 300,000 inhabitants (21,000 in 1940) actually originated from Baja California.

The chief cotton-textile cities continued to be Mexico City, Guadalajara, Monterrey, San Luis Potosí, Puebla, and Orizaba, as in the Díaz period. The greatest concentration of manufacturing production and employment, however, was in the Federal District, the mirror image of the concentration of political power. The metallurgical industry in the Federal District accounted for one-quarter of national production, and chemicals, textiles, and food for one-half by the late 1960s. Other industries grouped around its perimeter, sharing the large pool of unskilled labour and the availability of educational and managerial skills, and tapping the metropolitan consumer market. These factors compounded the dominance of Mexico City and its immediate area in the economic system as well as the political, regardless of the federalism reaffirmed in the Constitution of 1917.

'Stabilised development', in spite of the expansion of the infrastructure, educational and social services, and high growth rates, concealed destabilising elements. These combined to throw into question the development model adopted since the 1940s. Import substitution was already passing beyond merely consumer goods by the late 1960s, but transfer to capital goods required imports that needed to be paid for by increased exports. The export sector remained weak. The lesson was the urgency of transforming the structure of national industry. This was easier said than done. In the first place, the capital market was insufficiently strong to provide the investment required to sustain a more advanced form of import substitution. Foreign investment was not encouraged for political reasons. Economic nationalism, the reaction to later nineteenth-century liberal economics, proved to be a dead hand by the 1970s, but it lived on after death. In 1973, for instance, the Echeverría administration reaffirmed the restrictions on foreign capital, when the economy required the opposite.

Worst of all, successive administrations failed to reform the structure of taxation. Ortiz Mena's attempts in 1958–60, 1961–62, and 1964–65 all failed, in part through obstruction in congress and in part through suspicion in the private sector. As a result, the tax base remained low: by 1970, still only 18 per cent of taxes came from capital and the bulk from salaries. Echeverría's projected fiscal reform also failed in 1972. An inadequate capital market combined with low tax yields obliged the government to borrow abroad in order to maintain high growth rates.

The agricultural sector: growth and problems

Agriculture, which had stagnated since the late Díaz period, began to revive during the 1940s and for a time became a principal motor of growth. From 1946 to 1958, the agricultural sector grew at the rate of 7.7 per cent p.a., higher than the economy as a whole. Investment in infrastructure since the 1920s and the expansion of the area under cultivation as a result of agrarian reforms helped to explain this rapid growth. Between 1940 and 1950, the area of irrigated land in private ownership nearly doubled, in contrast to a 23 per cent increase in the case of the *ejidos*. The unforeseen result of revolutionary pressure on large-scale private estates was to oblige the surviving smaller properties to become more efficient by the adoption of farming technology. The expansion of the national textile industry stimulated demand for cotton, cultivated with government credit on irrigated lands especially in the north. Devaluation in 1954 assisted the export sector, which faced falling prices on the world market in the immediate post-Korean War period. During the rest of the 1950s, however, increased productivity, particularly in vital export sectors where there was high demand, accounted for growth. Cotton production reached its peak in volume in 1955, but a fall in the international price in 1958 reduced the profitability. After 1968, cotton went into a prolonged descent.

By 1950, a total of 1,788,000 hectares remained in private ownership, against 1,221,000 hectares belonging to the *ejidos*. Ten years later, more than 5,000 of the 18,699 *ejidos* in the Republic were still inadequately irrigated. The post-Cárdenas decades exposed the deficiencies of the *ejidos*, with the result that a considerable amount of land became converted into individual plots between 1940 and 1960, assisted with credit supplied by the Ejidal Bank, especially during the Alemán era. The majority of *ejidos* continued to be little more than subsistence plots without credit possibilities. The exceptions were the sugar cooperatives of Morelos. Even so, the *ejido* had been extended in the 1930s not for economic but for political reasons, in order to assuage peasant pressure for land and to prevent opposition movements from securing large-scale rural support. Although the number of *ejidatarios* increased from 1.6 million in 1940 to 2.5 million in 1960, the *ejido* as such had little economic future, especially since the future of agriculture lay in adaptation to advanced machine technology. The principle of restored communal lands remained, nevertheless, an almost sacred revolutionary ideal.

Partly in response to deteriorating conditions on the land, López Mateos, Díaz Ordaz, and Echeverría revived the agrarian reform policies inherited from the 1930s and early 1940s. Between 1958 and 1976, these three administrations distributed (at least on principle) a total of 41,739,800 hectares to 802,000 peasant families. Events in the localities, once the rhetoric of reform had died down, sometimes proved to have a different outcome. In Chiapas, for instance, with a 40 per cent illiteracy level, conditions for the bulk of the rural population significantly worsened between the 1950s and the 1980s, even though this state had become one of Mexico's principal food-producing zones. Cattle-ranching had been spreading in Chiapas across formerly arable land. When Díaz Ordaz awarded a land grant of 50,000 hectares to the town of Venustiano Carranza in 1967, it turned out that 20,000 hectares were already occupied by cattle-ranchers, who refused to budge. In 1976, two years after the federal government had failed to remove the ranchers, local peasants occupied the lands and began planting. The issue then became one of law and order, and the army was sent in to dislodge them. In 1978, peasants seized the municipal hall, and in the following year a second land occupation took place, which was similarly reversed. This case was not exceptional in Chiapas but representative.

By 1959–63, the agricultural sector was growing at less than the rate of population growth. Part of the explanation lay in the diversion of public investment into industry, communications, and urbanisation. The glaring problem became the lag of agricultural production behind national food-consumption requirements. The economic weakness of the *ejidos* combined with growing population pressure on the land and the tendency to minute holdings or *minifundios* incapable of providing subsistence to most peasant families. The question of how to increase productivity fell by the wayside. Government subsidy policies, designed to keep food prices low, proved to be a disincentive to investment. By the late 1960s, Mexico had become a net importer of cereals. In the decade, 1965–75, the agricultural sector grew hardly at all, at an average annual rate of 1 per cent, in contrast to the economy as a whole at the rate of 6.3 per cent annually. The decline of agriculture from the last years of the 1950s had repercussions throughout the economy. It contributed in large measure to the structural problems strongly in evidence during the 1970s.

From the 1960s, the weakness of the agricultural sector, combined with high middle-class living standards, increased the disparities between rich and poor. Furthermore, deteriorating conditions on the land accelerated already rapid urbanisation during the 1960s. Mexico City's population, for instance, grew from 5.2 million in 1960 to 8.9 million by 1970 and 10 million in 1976. Shanty towns proliferated around all the main cities. By 1970, the process of import substitution, begun in Mexico during the later Díaz period and resumed in the 1940s, had largely run its course. When the economy began to deteriorate during the 1970s, the social contrasts partly obscured by expansion were left exposed.

Elections, opposition, and rising discontent

In effect, the President dominated the political processes rather than the party. Monopoly party rule disguised the increasing absolutism of the executive. The absence of competitive politics – except within the administration and within the party structure – enabled the expansion of presidential power. Although each individual president surrendered office definitively after the expiration of his six-year mandate, presidential power as such continued to grow. The issue of accountability, along with other constitutional questions such as the relationship of the powers and the effective participation of civil society in the political processes, fell by the wayside. Economic expansion and a generalised sense of improvement especially during the period from 1954 to 1968 kept these major issues out of the centre of debate.

The official party became an instrument through which social antagonisms could be reconciled without recourse to violence. The actual function of the party has continually been a matter of dispute among analysts. The party throughout its three phases was always a creation of the state rather than of the grass-roots. As such, the state intended it to bolster the position of the incumbent administration. It was not an autonomous vehicle for popular grievances and pressures, although these were expressed through its organs. It did not control the leadership, which functioned on a national basis and through direct appeals to social groups regardless of the party origin of government members. The party as such played no decisive part in the succession issue.

The support of two ex-Presidents and the incumbent ensured López Mateos's succession in 1958 and sustained him in office thereafter. López Mateos, who originated from the State of Mexico, had been educated at the Toluca Institute of Science and Literature. He began his political career as private secretary to the State Governor in 1928 but subsequently opposed Vasconcelos's anti-re-election campaign in the following year. After affiliation in the PNR, however, he became senator for his home state in 1946, secretary-general of the PRI, and leader of the FSTSE, the federal government bureaucracy's union in the early 1950s. He secured the support of Cárdenas as a result of experience in the Treasury and he had earned the long-standing friendship of Alemán. He took office as Ruiz Cortines's Secretary of Labour and Social Welfare in 1952. This experience influenced López Mateos's establishment of the Instituto de Seguridad y Servicios Sociales para los Trabajadores del Estado (ISSSTE) in December 1959, a state social-welfare institute for its own employees, a vast and costly bureaucracy.

During the López Mateos administration, financial policy remained under the control of the highly successful Ortiz Mena. Labour discontent, however, proved to be the bugbear of the López Mateos administration. Accelerated economic development and monetary stability had social consequences which produced tension between the administration and the sectors linked to the official party. Worker opposition to official union leadership threatened state control of labour organisations. The López Mateos administration took the opportunity of the railway workers' movement of 1958–59 to reimpose tight state control. Further disputes led to the arrest of Demetrio Vallejo, the railway workers' leader, in 1962. Labour repression showed the other face of the López Mateos administration.

The administration, under criticism in the early 1960s for alleged machine-politics and electoral gerrymandering, sought to take the heat off by slightly modifying the composition of Congress. In the congressional elections of 1958 the PRI won 153 of the 162 seats; only 6 went to the PAN, perceived as the main party of opposition. The Electoral Law of 1962 guaranteed five congressional seats to any party polling 2.5 per cent of the vote, up to a maximum of twenty seats, even though it may not have actually won in a constituency. In the congressional elections of 1964, the PAN gained eighteen seats as a result of the 2.5 per cent ruling and won two more outright through election. However, the PRI, in reality a government organism, still remained overwhelmingly the dominant party with 175 seats, all elected. Before the Electoral Reform, opposition parties had secured only 9 out of the 162 seats; in 1964, their full total, including the seats of the PPS and PARM, came to 35 out of a total of 210. This modification should not be understood as a gradual evolution of the Mexican political system towards either a multi-party system or participatory democracy.

The road to disillusionment

The full consequences of presidential absolutism were experienced during the administration of Gustavo Díaz Ordaz (1964–70). Originating from Ciudad Serdán (Puebla) and qualified as a lawyer in 1937, Díaz Ordaz had been a congressional deputy in 1943–46 and a senator for Puebla in 1946–52. Between 1958 and 1963, he held the Ministry of the Interior in the López Mateos administration. As President, he retained López Mateos's Finance Minister, Ortiz Mena. During this presidency, two border territories became integrated into the Mexican Republic through agreements with the United States. In December 1968, El Chamizal, the river zone between El Paso and Ciudad Juárez, passed to Mexico, following the rechannelling of the Río Bravo, and in August 1970 Ojinaga, at the confluence of the Ríos Conchos and Bravo, which had been under US control since 1895, was returned to Mexico. The Díaz Ordaz administration revived (with high presidential publicity) land redistribution policies in remote localities, attempted to promote Mexican commercial opportunities in Central America in 1967, and signed the Treaty of Tlatelolco in 1969, which prohibited the extension of nuclear weapons to Latin America.

Domestic politics threw the Díaz Ordaz administration out of gear. The monopoly of the PRI throughout the political system remained largely unchallenged. The growth of presidential power, managed relatively discreetly under Ruiz Cortines and López Mateos, seemed a blatant abuse under Díaz Ordaz, who revealed a confrontational tendency. This led to bloodshed in 1968. The administration faced opposition not so much from organised labour or peasant groups but from within the professional classes, a circumstance it could not have anticipated. Díaz Ordaz viewed criticism as an attack on the presidential office, and regarded public pressures as disturbances which had the object of destabilising the regime and fomenting anarchy. In this spirit, Díaz Ordaz's political miscalculations allowed a dispute over better pay and working conditions with hospital doctors working in the public sector in December 1964 and early 1965 to escalate into a strike movement. The president twice attempted to impose a solution by decree, in February and April 1965, indicating that outside pressure would not be allowed to extract concessions, and finally ordered the doctors back to work on pain of loss of jobs and pay. In the meantime, the government sought to divide and weaken the newly formed doctors' associations. By September, the movement collapsed.

Some individuals within the PRI, conscious of the negative image of the party, attempted reform. The leading proponent was Carlos Madrazo, formerly Governor of Tabasco (1959–64), whom Díaz Ordaz made president of the party. Madrazo sought to open decision-making within the PRI and to end the practice of imposition of official candidates from above and from the outside. The reforms proved unacceptable to Díaz Ordaz, who dismissed Madrazo. Thrust out on a limb, Madrazo, instead of maintaining a timorous silence, went into outright opposition to the administration and drew attention to the unrepresentative nature of the party, a perilous course. Madrazo died in an inadequately explained plane crash in 1969.

Local abuses led to PRI electoral defeats in 1967 and 1968. The PAN won control of the city governments in two state capitals, Mérida (Yucatán) and Hermosillo (Sonora), in 1967. In an unprecedented action, the federal government permitted the opposition to take office. The new municipal governments, however, faced continual obstruction from the PRI-controlled state legislatures and received no support from the centre. The PAN managed to hold on to Mérida for three years. In 1969, the party tried to win control of the state government, but in a violent campaign the PRI claimed a widely contested victory. Federal government permission for an opposition party, which had won an election, to take office should not be regarded as a new trend. When, for instance, the PAN appeared to have won mayoral elections in Tijuana and Mexicali (Baja California Norte) in 1968, the state legislature annulled them rather than permit the opposition party to hold office.

The pliant role of Congress during the Díaz Ordaz era could be seen in the administration's manoeuvres designed to bring about the fall of the Head of the Federal District, Ernesto Uruchurtu, in October 1966. This post was a cabinet office, and Uruchurtu had been initially appointed by Ruiz Cortines in 1952. During the subsequent fourteen years, the capital city's population and aspect transformed. By the middle of the 1960s, it had become a gleaming, modern metropolis, which also boasted the Museum of Anthropology. The population, however, had doubled to 6 million and problems of traffic congestion and pollution were already of pressing importance. Uruchurtu paid scant attention to judicial procedure in his attempts to accelerate urban modernisation by demolishing unhygienic markets and removing squatters. The government was engaged in planning for the Mexico City Olympic Games in October 1968, but Uruchurtu's demolition of squatter shacks on the city's southern perimeter in the autumn of 1966 for the purpose of constructing the Aztec Stadium aroused strong local opposition. Many families maintained they had legal title to the lands involved. Díaz Ordaz used this controversy as a means of bringing down the powerful Uruchurtu, who had been in government employment for forty-six years. The President began by supporting the dispossessed families through the Department of Health. The obvious breach between the president and the Head of the Federal District passed signals through the political system that the latter was marked out for dismissal. Accordingly, Congress opened a campaign designed to discredit him, followed by a parallel campaign in the press. After that, Uruchurtu's fall was simply a matter of course.

Just as in Europe and the United States, the protest movements of 1968 had a profound impact in Mexico, where the memory of them would prove to be long-lasting. The Díaz Ordaz era has remained permanently overshadowed by the brutal repression of the student movement of August–October 1968 on the eve of the Olympic Games. The choice of Mexico City for the Games represented the first major international event organised in the country since the Centennial of Independence in 1910. Accordingly, the administration remained hypersensitive during the preceding months. Always unpopular and repeatedly given to overreaction, Díaz Ordaz's reputation never recovered from the massacre of 1968.

The student protests were part of a broader opposition to repressive actions by the Díaz Ordaz government. The moral credibility and political competence of the administration were already significantly undermined before the student movement in the capital city gained momentum. After a demonstration at the university in Morelia, Díaz Ordaz on 6 October 1966 ordered federal troops to occupy the buildings under the pretext of searching for arms. At the same time, he used the opportunity to dismiss the Governor of Michoacán. The movement in Mexico City began innocently enough with a conflict between rival groups of students on 22 July 1968. The intervention of the city's special force, the *granaderos*, transformed this into a conflict with the police and then into a full-scale protest movement against government violence. Before 1968, students had not been a significant political force in Mexico. By 26 July, demonstrators were attempting to reach the *zócalo*, the central square reserved for organised demonstrations of support for the president. Díaz Ordaz appears to have regarded the movement as an affront to the dignity of Mexico.

Army occupation of the National Preparatory School, a violation of constitutional immunities, led to a march of 50,000, at the head of which was the Rector of the National University (UNAM). Such a protest had never been seen before. Furthermore, the demonstrations were outside the control of the PRI. The original protests escalated into demands for respect for constitutional rights. By 13 August, 100,000 people, not simply students, were protesting in the *zócalo* against the regime's disrespect for public liberties and the presence of tanks in the city streets. The government saw this growing movement as a revolutionary conspiracy, fomented principally by Cuba, designed to bring down the existing political order. Naive appeals by student protesters to far-left heroes of the late 1960s, such as Che Guevara, inadvertently gave credence to such a view. Given the Mexican context, and above all the social composition of the movement, demand for civil liberties rather than attempted revolution provided the explanation for the scale of protest. The administration made no attempt to establish dialogue. Instead, a silent protest along the Paseo de la Reforma on 13 September was followed five days later by army occupation of the National University until the end of the month, again in violation of its immunities.

Large numbers of arrests and the blatant use of armed force seriously weakened the protest movement. The Tlatelolco demonstration, accordingly, should be seen as a late attempt to rally support after the main thrust of the movement had already passed. The total number of persons killed on the evening of 2 October, when troops and police opened fire on this meeting in the Plaza de las Tres Culturas, remains disputed right up to the present day. The massacre took place in front of the Ministry of Foreign Affairs building and many who worked there witnessed it. The horror of this incident was compounded by the large number of persons arrested or who disappeared thereafter. The unanticipated bloodshed in Mexico City, in full view of the international media, provoked a lengthy crisis between the intellectual middle classes and the PRI regime – until that time a significant supporter and beneficiary. More than thirty years after the event, the question of who gave

Plate 41 Gustavo Díaz Ordaz with his Generals on Army Day, March 1969. Taken after the massacre of Tlatelolco (October 1968), which brought an end to the student movement during the summer of that year. President Díaz Ordaz (1964–70) claimed to have saved the country from an international conspiracy and civil war. His presidency remains the most controversial of the second half of the twentieth century.

the order to open fire or how the firing started continues to be disputed. To date, no one has been held judicially responsible.

The massacre, which effectively terminated the protest movement, ultimately gave rise to new forms of opposition which eroded the governing party's support. Although not uniform, these opposition movements provided a challenge to the PRI from outside the established processes and from within civil society. The events of 1968 became the dividing line in the modern history of the PRI and of Mexican political life in general. Much of what happened since has been interpreted in relation to them.

Renewed examination of the events of 1968 during 1998 failed to unearth new evidence, largely because of government retention of control of information. Statements by Díaz Ordaz's Secretary of the Interior, Echeverría, who became his successor in 1970, did little to clarify the situation. Echeverría claimed to have no knowledge of the massacre at Tlatelolco, and only learned about it by telephone. As Interior Secretary, he maintained that he had exercised no control over the armed forces. Díaz Ordaz himself claimed to have saved the country from civil war and an international conspiracy to undermine its institutions, though it remained unclear which foreign country sought to destabilise them and why. In a television examination of those events, shown in April 1998, Díaz Ordaz, in a recording made at the end of his presidency, took full responsibility for the decisions made in September 1968, thereby clearing the way for Echeverría's accession to the presidency. Significantly, no one resigned from the government in protest at the massacre. Furthermore, tight PRI control of urban labour ensured that the Paris scenario of May 1968, in which radical workers had joined with student protesters, did not happen in Mexico.

PART TWO: ECONOMIC CRISES AND POLITICAL DIVISIONS, 1970–2000

The moral and political catastrophe of 1968 began the long and painful decline of the PRI. This political descent was accompanied by the downturn of the economy. Already in August 1969 Ortiz Mena had warned the annual meeting of the IMF and World Bank that Mexican development was still not irreversible and that 'what had been gained can be lost with relative ease'. After 1970, the negative elements, present beneath the surface during the years of expansion which had enabled middle- and upper-class prosperity, became first evident, then pervading, and finally predominant. Even so, the oil boom of 1977–81 appeared to revive Mexican economic fortunes after the severe financial crisis of 1976 and the first devaluation of the peso since 1954. Political reform, promised in the aftermath of 1968 but delayed until April 1977, appeared to point to a developing pluralism in Mexican political culture. Neither of these promises fulfilled their expectation. Accordingly, the disastrous financial collapse of 1982, which exposed Mexico as the world's second largest debtor state after Brazil, undermined large sectors of support for political structures built up since the 1940s.

The road to disaster: the economy, 1970–1982

The new administration abandoned 'stabilised development', which it saw as socially divisive, in favour of 'shared development'. The proclaimed objective was to promote through state action a fairer distribution of wealth. The growth of the public sector led to an ongoing debate concerning the relationship of the state and private sector during the Echeverría period. Antagonism between the two led to a loss of business confidence. Between 1973 and 1976, the administration was in open conflict with the Monterrey group, at the centre of which since 1974 stood the Grupo Industrial Alfa presided over by Bernardo Garza Sada. The Garza Sada family, brewery owners from the 1890s, controlled a vast network of industrial and banking enterprises, principally in Monterrey. After 1978, Alfa moved into cooperation with multinational companies. By 1981, the Alfa group employed around a quarter of a million people. The state-controlled sector of the economy, however, expanded, in spite of the failure to introduce fiscal reforms in 1972 designed to increase revenue and introduce a fairer distribution of wealth. Accordingly, the Mexican state resorted to foreign loans, in order to finance increased public expenditure. The external debt grew to alarming proportions, and the cost of servicing it drained potential investment funds from the internal economy. Although the López Portillo administration made overtures to the Monterrey business interests, the discovery of large petroleum and natural-gas deposits renewed the importance of PEMEX and deepened the regime's dependency on public-sector support.

In a completely mistaken analysis, the Left portrayed the crises of 1976 and 1982 as the crisis of the 'capitalist order', when, in fact, the overheavy state sector was part of the problem. Certainly, the administrations of Miguel de la Madrid (1982–88) and Carlos Salinas de Gortari (1988–94) concluded that there was not enough capitalism in Mexico. The latter, in particular, set about ensuring that there would be much dismantling of the public sector, although it stopped short at the denationalisation of the petroleum industry. The gravity of the crisis of 1982 ensured that the strangling of the first sacred cows passed with scarcely a whimper. The PRI-dominated state, however, made sure that the holiest, PEMEX, the creation of its predecessor party, would continue to graze in lush pastures.

Deepening difficulties after 1982 marked the crisis of the economic nationalism and mixed economy championed during the Cárdenas era. Yet the economic crisis of the 1980s did not produce a parallel political crisis, still less one which threatened to topple the regime held responsible for the mess altogether. Instead, Mexicans demonstrated remarkable resilience in living in a condition of permanent economic uncertainty. This enabled the PRI regime to buy time in order to attempt to clean up its image and thereby continue in power.

The political descent

When he took office in December 1970 at the age of forty-eight, Echeverría promised to reform Mexico's political system. Much else was promised. Echeverría portrayed himself as a radical social reformer dedicated to income redistribution in favour of greater equity 'until the very poorest have attained an adequate standard of living'. He stated that 'over-concentration of income and the marginal position of large groups threaten the harmonious continuity of our development'. He expressed faith in Mexican business and asserted that 'foreign investment should not displace Mexican capital'. The Echeverría cabinet was the youngest since the Alemán era. Its members, however, had the least experience of direct election to office as part of their political careers, since most had passed from university to administrative and technical positions in the federal bureaucracy. This gave the cabinet a 'technocratic' appearance.

Throughout his presidency the condition of the PRI, a result of the erosion of legitimacy since the events of 1968, remained Echeverría's central preoccupation. The urgency of the matter could be seen from the congressional election results of July 1973, when voting for opposition candidates replaced at least for a time the usual practice of large-scale abstention. In spite of the fact that voting is compulsory in Mexico, the abstention rate grew over the period from 1961 to 1979 from 31.5 per cent to 50.8 per cent of registered voters, despite the lowering of the voting age from twenty-one to eighteen years in 1969. In July 1973, the PRI still won 51.7 per cent of the votes cast, but the PAN showed strongly in leading cities such as Puebla, Guanajuato, Cuernavaca, Toluca, León, and Ciudad Juárez, in spite of the party's lack of a national organisation capable of building on such gains. Echeverría, following his predecessor's policies, accelerated agrarian reform, in order to bind the peasant sector more closely to the official party in the aftermath of the widespread erosion of support in urban centres after 1968.

The Organic Law for the Federal District (1970), which reconstituted the capital city administration, did not have real effect until López

Portillo's reform of 1977. Although the Regente (Mayor) of the Federal District continued to be a presidential nominee, as he had been since 1928 (and would so remain until July 1997), the political reform introduced a greater elective element into the tiers of municipal administration. The problem for the PRI became how to prevent opposition parties from gaining access to elective office on the ward residents' committees (*juntas de vecinos*), the sixteen presidents of which would provide the mayor's consultative committee.

Under political reform, the government set aside 100 of the 400 seats in the Chamber of Deputies for opposition parties. The PRI still retained control of the entire state apparatus, but the executive sought in official terms to integrate opposition parties more fully into the political processes. The government legalised an array of parties, so that the multiplicity would be mutually contradictory. Initial popular indifference led to a higher than ever rate of abstention in the mid-term elections of 1979. By the time of the presidential elections of July 1982, which took place in different economic circumstances, the number of votes cast increased to 74.9 per cent, with 50.1 per cent of the total electorate voting for the PRI.

The scale of repression during 1968 generated a new wave of opposition movements, prepared for outright confrontation with the state. In certain rural areas, political relations broke down completely during the late 1960s. A full-scale guerrilla movement developed in the state of Guerrero by 1971, involving 5 army battalions and 10,000 police with air support. The focus lay in some thirty-two communities largely in the Sierra de Atoyac. The central figure was Lucio Cabañas, in hiding since May 1967, and leader of a 'Party of the Poor', who was killed at the end of 1974. Army counter-insurgency tactics broke the movement, though the politics of Guerrero remained turbulent throughout the following decades. The Cabañas rebellion, seen in retrospect, provided a prototype for the Chiapas insurrection of 1994. The survivors of the leftist groups which had participated in the Guerrero events eventually regrouped at the end of the 1980s. The Chiapas rising led to recrudescence of activity and preventive assassinations in Guerrero. By June 1996, twelve such organisations merged to form the EPR (Popular Revolutionary Army).

After 1968, an alliance of students, peasants, and urban workers in Oaxaca succeeded in forming a political movement independent of the

PRI by 1972. This was the forerunner of the Worker–Peasant Coalition of the Isthmus (COCEI) two years later. Opposition confrontation with the state government in 1975–77 led to federal intervention in the Benito Juárez University and the occupation of the state capital and main towns by the armed forces. PRI organisation of rival factions led to violent clashes in Juchitán in 1977. Three years later, the COCEI won the municipal elections in Juchitán, only to be subjected to harassment from the PRI-controlled state legislature. In December 1982, the COCEI council was removed and 300 individuals arrested in a government attempt to undermine opposition organisation. The movement recovered by 1987 and won control of the municipal council for the second time in September 1989, though in changed national political circumstances.

The oil boom of 1977–1981

López Portillo's administration failed to set the economy on a strong basis in the aftermath of the financial crisis of 1976. Instead, it found itself the beneficiary of renewed expansion in the oil industry. New discoveries in Chiapas and Tabasco in 1972 substantially raised Mexico's productive capacity and reduced bills for imports, especially since Mexico from the late 1960s had no longer been able to supply the country's petroleum needs. The impact of the new developments came too late to save the high-spending Echeverría administration from a 59 per cent currency devaluation in September 1976, when inflation already stood at 22 per cent.

The oil boom of 1977–81 initiated the last period of high growth rates until the late 1990s. It provided the administration's solution to the collapse of the import-substitution strategy pursued by its predecessors. In one sense this marked a return to the pre-1938 strategy of export-oriented expansion. However, the government still faced the problem of how to finance expansion in a low-taxation economy. Accordingly, it took recourse to foreign credit. Capital requirements for the development of oil and natural gas rose to more than five times the amount invested between 1971 and 1976. Off-shore drilling along the Campeche coast frequently involved private drilling concessions and the sale of rights, about which few questions were asked. The foreign debt had already increased under Echeverría from US$4.5 billion to

US$19.6 billion between 1970 and 1976. Debt-servicing rose to 32.3 per cent of the value of exports by 1976. Oil expansion, however, led to the overvaluation of the peso. This and other factors fuelled inflation, which stood at 30 per cent when López Portillo took office but reached 60 per cent by 1982, and 100 per cent by the autumn of that year. For a time, the oil boom took rates of growth to 1960s levels at 8.5 per cent p.a. in 1978–81. Beneath the euphoria, however, the gap between rich and poor was widening.

By 1981, Mexico became the fourth largest oil exporter in the world. Oil discoveries took Mexico out of the 1976 crisis and renewed international confidence particularly within the banking community, which pressed loan packages on the country. López Portillo managed the oil sector in conjunction with the Director-General of PEMEX, Jorge Díaz Serrano, a Sonoran mechanical engineer who had represented General Motors in Mexico between 1969 and 1983. Together they decided oil policy largely without reference to the rest of the cabinet. Díaz Serrano, who had presidential ambition, was forced out of office in June 1981 over the issue of oil production ceilings.

External demand for Mexican oil and natural gas raised political problems. Economic nationalists expressed fears of renewed dependence on the US economy. In 1978, oil production at 485.3 million barrels more than doubled that of the peak year, 1921, during the previous boom period. Even so, oil and petrochemicals still accounted for only 49 per cent of exports in 1979, a clear indication that Mexico was not exclusively an oil-exporting country. Furthermore, nationalisation in 1938 had ensured that Mexican oil was not subject to the multinational corporations' pricing policies. Oil production rose from 202,100 barrels per day in 1977 to 1,098,000 barrels in 1981. The administration, however, believed world oil prices would continue to rise and consequently ignored signs of a downfall after May 1981. Accordingly, public expenditure and external debt commitments continued to rise. Capital flight, mainly to the USA, encouraged the López Portillo government to take large amounts of short-term credit, which it would have difficulty paying back.

The collapse of world oil prices during the course of 1981 thrust the newly oil-dependent Mexican economy into turmoil. A series of devaluations followed, beginning in February 1982, when the rate of exchange fell to 47 pesos per US$1; by the end of the year, the US dollar cost 144 pesos. Panic set in throughout the international financial community, which gave notice to Mexico in July that it could expect no more credit. As a result, Finance Minister Jesús Silva Herzog found himself obliged in the following month to admit that Mexico would be unable to pay its short-term debts, reaching around US$10,000 million. The total estimated debt came to US$84,100 million. López Portillo sought a political road out of the financial collapse by nationalising the private banks in September 1982, during the lame-duck period between the presidential elections and the transfer of power. The regime portrayed this as a patriotic action, a culminating process in the stages of economic nationalism beginning with the nationalisation of petroleum in 1938 and continuing through the nationalisation of electricity in 1960. In reality, it was an act of unscrupulous opportunism designed to disguise the frantic political manoeuvrings of a discredited administration.

The task of recovery

The scale of the 1982 crisis raised the question of whether this represented the terminal crisis of the post-1940s model of development and the political practices that went with it. The broader perspective of the 1980s indicated that this was the case. Accordingly, the administration of De la Madrid faced two major tasks: how to stabilise the economy and survive the immediate crisis, and to find some alternative model of development for the country. This latter course might conceivably imply a change of political direction as well. Although the economic tasks appeared almost insuperable in the 1980s, the political problems of the regime presented even more complex problems. During the period from 1940 to 1982, the presidency had grown more powerful in relation not only to the legislative branch and the states but also to the rest of the cabinet, the bureaucracy, and the party. Both Echeverría and López Portillo had sought to combine renovated populism with executive absolutism. As in the previous presidencies, the economic model had been rapid development through industrialisation in a relatively closed economy with heavy state participation. As in the Díaz period, political liberalisation and the application of constitutional precepts had been kept in abeyance. Equally, the justification for this had been the government's apparent success on the economic front. The collapse of the model in 1981–82 raised the problem of what should be done on the political front once the principal justification for holding back reform had been undermined.

The De la Madrid administration ultimately adopted the policy of liberalising the economy in order to bring down inflation. Since inflation presented grave social problems, this policy had profound political implications as well. The administration faced the problem of how to avoid strikes and social conflict at a time of generalised hardship. Fidel Velázquez played a central role in sustaining the government at this time by exacting concessions for the official labour unions, price controls, and amendments in the Federal Labour Law. Even so, the purchasing power of wages fell 8.3 per cent between 1983 and 1988, while the cost of living rose 90 per cent. Mexican per capita income, which had been estimated at US$2,405 in 1982, fell to US$1,320 by the end of 1987. Continued problems in the agricultural sector meant that 6 million tonnes of food would be imported from the USA under an agreement of March 1983.

In the period 1982–85, the De la Madrid administration began a series of long-awaited structural changes in the economy. The high-profile state sector and large state subsidies had reached the end of the road. The economic structures put in place since the 1930s and already in crisis after 1970 could no longer be sustained. Much of the monopoly-party system, however, remained intricately related to these now-antiquated structures in the form of state-approved unions, patronage, and corruption. Economic reform would inevitably require substantial modification of the prevailing political culture. The authoritarian style of the presidency ensured that these reforms would be imposed on a recalcitrant party and bureaucracy from above. Even so, the administration had no intention of jeopardising the PRI's monopoly of power.

Economic reforms liberalised the market in order to achieve a measure of sustainable growth. Business, alienated under Echeverría and definitively so in 1981–82, returned to tacit cooperation with the regime during these years. De la Madrid himself was a fiscal conservative, who instinctively rejected the neo-populism predominant since 1970. The entry of the technocrats symbolised the definitive exclusion of Echeverría from influence over the administration. Within a year of nationalisation, 34 per cent of the banking system had returned to private ownership. Public-sector deficit was halved during 1983, through economies, an increase in VAT, and personal income-tax rises.

Inflation was reduced to 53.8 per cent during the first eight months of the year. Nevertheless, manufacturing output contracted by 40 per cent and an estimated two-fifths of Mexicans remained without a proper job. The external debt stood at US$89 billion at the end of 1983. The international banking community took substantial measures to assist Mexico in the struggle to survive the financial crisis. Since IMF criteria were met in the reduction of the budget deficit, the administration gained a favourable reputation abroad. On 30 December, the banks granted a loan of US$3.8 billion for ten years designed to meet requirements during 1984. Between 1976 and 1995, Mexico would sign seven letters of intent with the IMF.

The economic relationship with the United States remained as crucial as ever. By the end of 1982, Mexico was supplying 15 per cent of US oil imports, slightly above the figure for Saudi Arabia. In an attempt to alleviate the dependence on the US market and to raise its price, Mexico decided to coordinate marketing strategy with OPEC, the organisation of world oil producers. When it became clear that OPEC intended to hold back production in order to force up prices, Mexico ceased to attend meetings as an informal observer after December 1985 and reverted to its own independent pricing policy. At that time, 50 per cent of Mexican crude went to the USA, 25 per cent to Europe, and 10 per cent to Japan. Again apprehensive of over-reliance on the USA, the Mexican government limited oil export there to 50 per cent of the total. Even so, Mexico's main import from the USA continued to be refined oil products.

Tension between Mexico and the United States developed over the impact of rising US interest rates on the debt-burdened countries. The huge US-government deficit (around US$200 billion annually) forced up interest rates, especially since the US itself was competing in the international capital market in order to finance its deficit, caused in part by heavy defence expenditure. To this was added the high cost of US financing of counter-insurgency movements in Central America, principally designed to destabilise Nicaragua controlled by the Sandinistas since the Revolution of 1979. The Mexican Government, along with others in Latin America, strongly disapproved of this policy. Since a rise in US interest rates meant an increase in Latin American debt, debtor states found themselves, in effect, financing US policies they opposed. At the same time, IMF requirements that debtor states reduce their public expenditure contrasted strongly with the current US policies. High interest rates pushed up the value of the dollar and therefore the cost of Mexican imports at a time when two-thirds of Mexican trade was with the USA. Disadvantaged in its import sector, Mexico also faced US protectionist measures directed against its exports. Since US policies in the mid-1980s impeded debt repayment, the international banking community also expressed its concern.

The Mexico City earthquake of September 1985, which resulted in an incalculable number of deaths and missing persons, and strained hospital resources to the limit, severely dented not only government economic strategy but also its political reputation through failure to react promptly. In the longer term, however, the economic recovery continued, since the overall debt level stood at US$95 billion and appeared to be under control, and a trade surplus of US$541 million was registered for that year. In many respects, 1985 proved to be a major turning point, since the government took the decision to join GATT. Membership of the General Agreement on Tariffs and Trade, finalised in 1986, had significant implications for Mexico, since it involved the opening of the economy and the elimination of state subsidies throughout the economy. These were regarded as unfair obstacles to free commercial intercourse between participating members. Such a requirement, however, went against traditional Mexican political economy established since the 1930s. Accordingly, the World Bank, which had already contributed US$300 million towards recovery from the earthquake, provided a further US$500 million as a trade adjustment loan designed to ease passage into GATT. The immediate consequence of trade liberalisation was a deficit of US$1,930 million by the end of 1986.

Indebted countries sought to coordinate a response to their creditors at the Cartagena summit of April 1985, especially in view of the international bankers' preference for specific dealings with individual governments. The Baker Plan, which originated within the US government and was presented to the IMF in October, responded to the impasse. Resources assigned by the Plan, however, covered only 25 per cent of the interest payments due from the fifteen nominated countries for 1986–88. It recognised, nevertheless, the urgency of reducing not only the interest but part of the principal as well, in order to enable indebted countries' economies to resume growth. Their governments would be expected to introduce policies designed to facilitate growth, specifically the abandonment of economic nationalism in favour of open economies. The subsequent Brady Plan of March 1988 developed these principles further. The central theme was reduction of debt. Renewed growth provided the means of resuming payments. Mexico, Venezuela, and Costa Rica became the leading beneficiaries.

As a result of the collapse of world oil prices, Mexico had to diversify its pattern of exports. By 1990, the 1982 pattern had been reversed: over two-thirds of the total value of US$27 billion was mainly in non-petroleum products, mainly new manufactures. However, an increasing proportion of exports – from 52 per cent of the total in 1982 to 70 per cent by 1989 – went to the USA. Since the Japanese share was also falling, this further highlighted Mexican vulnerability to US economic trends. From 1980, furthermore, natural gas had also gone to the US market. Japan, which was the fourth largest investor in Mexico, doubled its investments between 1983 and 1988 and thereby re-entered the Mexican market in a significant way. Although Japanese enterprises disliked the strong union presence in the petrochemical industry and fisheries, their increased investment sought to facilitate oil exports from the zones of production to the Pacific coast. With both Mexican-government and Japanese-investor eyes on Mexico's position in the Pacific Basin, Japanese capital entered the oil infrastructure, export promotion, and the post-1972 Pacific coast steel complex of Sicartsa II. Honda, Nissan, and other Japanese firms were in production in Mexico by 1987, often as a result of debt-for-equity exchanges. At the same time, investment-rule relaxation enabled Japanese capital to enter the border-located *maquiladora* plants.

Declining oil prices adversely affected the balance of payments and cut the spending capacity of the treasury. Between October 1987 and October 1988, the price of Istmo crude fell from US$17.83 per barrel to US$10 per barrel, when in 1982 the price had been US$30.90 for light crude and US$25.50 for heavy. This decline was very serious in view of the escalation of prices during 1987. By the summer, the rate of inflation had risen to a disastrous 110 per cent and by the end of the year to 461.4 per cent, far above the IMF targets of 80–85 per cent. With additional loans and outstanding debt obligations, the external debt rose to US$ 101.8 billion in 1988. This figure in isolation gives the erroneous impression of a collapsing economy. Nevertheless, general recovery throughout the manufacturing sector took place at the same time. The government successfully managed to contain the crisis and thereby maintain international confidence in the country's overall performance. The inflation rate fell to 46.6 per cent for consumer prices and 33.4 per cent for producer prices (compared to Brazilian and Argentinian inflation rates of 816 per cent and 372 per cent, respectively, in the same year). It is vital to realise that the debt question was caused not by backwardness or stagnation, but by over-zealous expansion, a period of buoyancy, and over-eagerness within the lending community. The bankers put Mexico, Brazil, Venezuela, and other countries into the indebted position in which they found themselves so inexorably in 1982. Accordingly, the indebted countries found it difficult to benefit from the general economic recovery in the 'First World' in the latter part of the 1980s. Worse still, they found themselves after 1989 competing with the former socialist economies of the 'Second World' for credit and investment in the aftermath of the collapse of the Soviet bloc.

'Neo-Liberalism' and post-crisis responses

The presidential elections of July 1988 proved to be the most contested since 1929, since they involved a direct challenge to the governing system. This challenge, however, came from two opposition parties, the PAN and FDN. According to the disputed official results, the PRI won 50.7 per cent of the votes cast, the FDN 31.06 per cent, and the PAN 16.81 per cent. Even the official figures showed that only 25.3 per cent of the total electorate had voted for the PRI. Many critics of the regime argued strongly that the FDN had in fact won the elections and alleged fraud, especially since the PRI-managed electoral computers broke down as the results were being calculated. After the elections, Salinas sought to defuse opposition by proclaiming the end of the single-party system, in spite of opposition within the PRI. Between 1988 and 1993, political reform was in the air, but little resulted from it. Nevertheless, the fraud issue of 1988 ensured that the government remained virtually obliged to acknowledge opposition victories. Between 1988 and 1991, for instance, opposition parties secured 240 of the 500 seats in the Chamber of Deputies.

The economic reforms introduced by the Salinas administration provoked further debate and controversy. With the ostensible exception of the Chiapas rebellion of January 1994, they did not lead to outright confrontation. On the contrary, few opponents could find a cogent alternative, beyond appeals for a return to a more corporative and state-dominated past. Many commentators, and certainly those gravitating around the regime, seemed mesmerised by the reforms, which appeared to be such radical departures from traditional economic nationalist policies. The ensuing adoration of Salinas resembled the flattery at the court of Porfirio Díaz. The proclaimed administration policy of taking Mexico into the 'First World' resembled the euphoria accompanying the oil boom of 1977–81 during the López Portillo era.

The motives for Salinas's economic reforms remained the least discussed aspect. The reforms were initiated by the executive. They did not result from national consensus or far-reaching debate. Accordingly, they were imposed from above without discussion, and thereby served to strengthen presidential power all the more. Typical of this procedure was the reform of article 27, a high point of the 1917 Constitution. The administration, while making appeals to the tradition of Zapata, appeared to be reversing one of the most fundamental tenets of the Revolution and the hallowed principles of the Cárdenas era. The reform terminated government responsibility for land redistribution to peasants claiming land from private estates above established norms with the intention of forming *ejidos*. At the same time, it authorised individual members of *ejidos* to become private proprietors in their own right, once the *ejido* itself had voted to participate in the new procedures.

Central-government intervention in the states increased to proportions which nearly reached that of the Cárdenas period, though in completely different circumstances. During his struggle with Calles, Cárdenas replaced nineteen state governors; Salinas removed seventeen of the total of thirty-two, nine of them as a result of electoral issues. Local circumstances resulted in the election of four state governors representing the PAN during the mid-1990s – in Baja California Norte, Jalisco, Chihuahua, and Guanajuato. The PAN also held important positions in the cities of Aguascalientes and Jalapa.

Privatisation in the early 1990s was a response to the problem of budget deficit, which had reached $150,000 million pesos in 1986. Accordingly, the government saw it as a principal means of bringing down inflation, the priority in its strategy. The 1989 figure of 19.7 per cent demonstrated the measure of success achieved. In May 1990, the Salinas administration reprivatised the banks nationalised in 1982. Subsequent privatisations marked a reversal of deeply rooted tendencies in Mexican political economy since the 1930s. Between 1920 and 1982, the number of publicly owned enterprises had risen to 1,155, the majority of them brought into the state sector during the 1970s and early 1980s. The Salinas administration used the opportunity of the bankruptcy of a number of prominent state-sector industries to accelerate a programme of privatisation. For the first time since 1982, a net transfer of funds to Mexico took place.

In view of the ever-closer economic links, Salinas pressed the US administration in 1990–91 for the formation of a North American free trade area, which would also include Canada. The aim was to link the Mexican economy, in its reformed state, more closely to the US economy, in order to involve the United States in the process of maintaining the monopoly-party in power. The argument was sold to the Bush administration in terms of fortifying North American competition with the established free-trade area of Europe and the growing economies of East and South-East Asia, at a time of US recession. The agreement was signed in December 1992 and went into effect in January 1994. NAFTA reflected the Salinas government's perception of the future economic course for Mexico, which would be integrated into the international market, the nearest and most powerful representative of which was the United States. The Mexican government intended at the same time to negotiate bilateral trade agreements with Costa Rica, Chile, Venezuela, and Colombia, and to establish a commercial relationship with the European Economic Community. NAFTA, however, differed radically from the EEC (or European Union as it subsequently became known) in that it did not have a political dimension designed to promote sub-continental integration. Similarly, no project existed at the time for movement towards a common currency.

'Salinisation' represented the second, and major, phase of the restructuring of the Mexican economy begun under De la Madrid. The reforms were designed to remove the barriers preventing the economy from becoming more efficient and competitive. At the same time, the government opened the Mexican market to foreign capital: a new law in December 1993 replaced the restrictions of 1973, themselves dating from the 1940s, on the investment of foreign private capital in the country.

Privatisation aimed to reduce government expenditure permanently and at the same time reduce the dead weight of bureaucracy throughout the economy. The government rapidly found, however, that it would have to deal urgently with a deteriorating balance of payments, due to the increase of imports between 1988 and 1993.

The return of the Catholic Church as a political counter

The Salinas government introduced a new factor into the country's domestic politics in February 1993 when it authorised the re-establishment of diplomatic relations with the Holy See, broken since the Juárez era in 1867. Mgr Girolamo Prigione, who as Apostolic Delegate had already gained substantial knowledge of Mexican conditions, held the post of Papal Nuncio until October 1997. Although an initially controversial measure, Prigione was careful not to provoke latent anticlerical feeling within political circles. A papally approved conservative, Prigione became the focus of opposition among progressive elements within the Church and among opponents of the administration. At the same time, he had earned the enmity of the Cardinal-Archbishop, Ernesto Corripio Ahumada, who resented his involvement in the internal affairs of the Mexican Church and had been pressing the Vatican for his removal. Even so, the diplomatic recognition of the Vatican's role in what still remained a largely Catholic country provided the Mexican bishops with an opportunity to criticise government policy and the deepening corruption and everyday violence in the country.

A symptom of this was the unexplained death of the Archbishop of Guadalajara, Cardinal Juan Jesús Posadas, in May 1993, allegedly 'caught in crossfire between rival drug gangs' in the car park outside Guadalajara Airport, where he had gone to await the arrival of the Nuncio. Posadas had been a strong critic of drug trafficking and alleged monopoly-party links. Few were willing to explain how a Cardinal-Archbishop of the Roman Catholic Church could be caught in a gunfight between drug barons. The mystery surrounding the event raised suspicions that Posadas had been specifically targeted: no one could say by whom. Some commentators suggested machinations by the Tijuana drug cartel, widely believed to have PRI connections in Baja California: the gunmen appeared to have flown to Tijuana on a waiting scheduled flight after the killing. The two principal members, it subsequently transpired, had, in fact, visited the Nuncio's office a few months earlier and been let out of the back door to avoid the scrutiny of security guards.

The re-establishment of relations with the Holy See implied close contact between the Mexican hierarchy and the papacy of John Paul II. Free expression of religious practices in public has meant a profound modification of the inheritance of the Reform movement of 1855–76. At the same time, it has drawn the governing party further away from its earlier roots in the church–state conflicts of the 1920s and 1930s. Catholicism always was a powerful undercurrent, even during the Reform and Revolutionary eras. This current, although still not dominant, grew stronger during the 1990s. Certain fundamentalist tendencies have begun to appear at a number of levels: such as attempts by PAN city councils to remove the name of Juárez from streets, or the statement by the Primate, Cardinal Norberto Rivera Carrera, that packets of condoms should carry a health warning like cigarette packets. Cardinal Rivera's condemnation of Mexicans who 'let themselves be seduced by liberal education', which he regarded as sustained by the Mexican state, implied criticism of an entire tradition of secular education established since the Reform era. Again, the emphasis was on lack of observation of Catholic moral precepts as taught by the clergy. Blaming homosexuals, feminists, and other 'minorities' for the ills of contemporary Mexico similarly exposed Cardinal Rivera to charges of intolerance. Episcopal criticism of the neo-liberal model, on the grounds that it exacerbated social deprivation, combined with attacks on liberal sexual conduct to give the impression that the official Church was engaged in a concerted critique of liberalism from both the left and right at the same time.

In the post-1993 situation, the Catholic Church sought to exercise significant political pressure on government and society at a crucial turning-point in recent Mexican development and before the proper establishment of democratic practice in the country as a whole. Even so, the general Mexican custom of ignoring fixed rules and working out solutions suitable to particular circumstances will probably act as an effective brake on clerical aspirations to tighter control of public behaviour.

Political challenge and the issue of regime durability

Political reform in the sense of making way for pluralism, guaranteeing effective suffrage, and respecting constitutional rights did not accompany economic reform. The Salinas administration, it is true, departed from general practice by 'allowing' victorious opposition candidates in several cases to take office. To outsiders, this policy appeared to presage political reform and the final emergence of a working constitutional system in Mexico. Such an interpretation, however, proved in the long run to be mistaken. A slight redistribution of political power resulted, though without in any way compromising monopoly-party dominance. In 1989, PAN won the elections for the governorship of Baja California Norte, the first time an opposition party had won a state governorship. In an attempt to restore credibility, Salinas, through the medium of Luis Donaldo Colosio, President of the PRI, ordered the local PRI to accept the PAN victory. This, in effect, meant the removal of a long-established and highly corrupt local party structure, senior members of which seethed with resentment at the Salinas administration thereafter.

The assassination of Colosio, official PRI candidate for the presidency, in Tijuana in March 1994 further plunged the Salinas administration into crisis. The regime's credibility rapidly became further dented as it became clear that no one could be convincingly proved responsible for the murder. The murder took place just as Colosio had begun his campaign for the presidency. Although not president-elect, as Obregón had been at the time of his assassination in 1928, the murder threw the Salinas government into extreme consternation and the country into a state of alarm. Conspiracy theories abounded, especially in view of the Salinas administration's loss of credibility over the Chiapas rebellion. The murder of Colosio meant that the PRI candidate for the presidency would be Ernesto Zedillo Ponce de León, who had not been groomed by Salinas for the succession. Zedillo was obliged to pick up what he could of the legacy of his predecessor. The situation worsened still more with the assassination of José Francisco Ruiz Massieu, party secretary of the PRI, in September 1994. The complicity of the President's brother, Raúl Salinas de Gortari, was alleged.

The disintegration of the Salinas administration, accordingly, led to a far-reaching crisis for the monopoly party, which appeared at times to be terminal. To the contrary, the administration deliberately avoided

Plate 42 Cuauhtémoc Cárdenas (b. 1934) takes oath as Mayor of
Mexico City in 1997. Son of President Lázaro Cárdenas
(1934–40) and himself a former PRI Governor of Michoacán
(1980–86), Cárdenas took office as first elected *Regente* of the
Federal District on 5 December 1997. He thereby presented a
serious political threat to the ruling party. Cárdenas had broken
with the PRI leadership in the 1980s in defence of traditional
leftist policies and helped form the 'Democratic Tendency' in
1986 and led the Frente Democrático Nacional (FRD), formed in
January 1988 to challenge Carlos Salinas de Gortari (PRI) in the
presidential elections that year. Cárdenas appeared to have gained
31 per cent of the vote, though the FDN maintained that the PRI
had won only by fraud. The dispute concerning that election
continues. In the aftermath of the 1988 election, Cárdenas
founded the opposition, Partido Revolucionario Democrático
(PRD), which in the 1994 elections won only 17 per cent of the
vote. Cárdenas was presidential candidate for a third time in 2000.

political reform, since it believed that economic reform would renew the basis of PRI domination, and, more especially, tie the country closer to the US economy. The NAFTA formed the basis of this strategy, and the fruits were reaped when the Clinton administration, in spite of Democratic Party scepticism of the Treaty, decided to bale out the Mexican administration after the financial collapse of December 1994. The economic reforms, however, formed the culmination of a longer process which had begun in the aftermath of the debt crisis of 1982. The dismantling of much of the state sector of the economy and the threat to the interests associated with it had weakened the PRI's position without at the same time opening the political system to effective electoral competition. Once more, the Madero principle of Effective Suffrage remained unobserved.

The financial crisis of December 1994, the most severe since 1982, took the administration by surprise, and the precipitate devaluation which followed deepened the already widespread disillusion throughout the country. Just as De la Madrid inherited the catastrophes of the López Portillo era, so Zedillo (1994–2000) inherited the consequences of the Salinas presidency. As a result of the December 1994 crisis, GDP fell 6.9 per cent in 1995, in contrast to the previous collapses of 1983 by 4.15 per cent and 1986 by 3.82 per cent. One of the overriding causes of the crisis was the Salinas administration's attempt to avoid the devaluation of the peso from a fixed exchange rate in relation to the US dollar. The explanation for this lay in the administration's attempt to guarantee the continued inflow of investment, attracted by a strong peso and high interest rates. The government went so far as to transfer returns on investments into dollars rather than pesos. The incoming Zedillo administration, however, was not tied to a fixed exchange-rate policy. Furthermore, the PRI election victory in August meant that, in the short term, there would be no adverse political consequences of devaluation.

The question of devaluation had been in the air since March 1994. The background was the worsening trade deficit, since an appreciating peso between 1989 and 1993 had eroded the country's export capacity and led to a boom in imports. The high interest-rate policy of the late Salinas period contributed to the stultification of growth in the internal economy. Deepening uncertainty over devaluation impeded capital inflows, in spite of government policy, and obliged the government to cover the deficit on the current account out of its reserves. The floating of the peso in December ultimately meant that the cost of meeting debt obligations of the dollar-indexed *Tesobonos*, which increased from US$3,100 million in March to US$29,200 million by December, would be doubled. This huge indebtedness at short term exceeded even that of 1982.

The Clinton administration's rescue package in February 1995 and further loans from the IMF and an array of banks, totalling US$50,000 million, and the stabilisation policies introduced in March contributed greatly to the rapid recovery of the Mexican economy. The international financial community's confidence in the country thereafter marked a surprising volte-face. During 1996, there was much talk of Mexico 'back in the ring'. The recovery of industry, exportation, and employment, and the fall of inflation lent credence to such a perspective. Even so, two points need to be made concerning the crisis of December 1994. In the first place, it revealed once again the vulnerability of the Mexican economy to external shocks. This in itself reflected the degree of integration of the economy into the international market, a situation which had considerably deepened as a result of the trade liberalisation policies implemented after 1985. It further exposed the perennial problem of the shortage of domestic capital and the low level of domestic savings. By contrast, precisely this degree of integration also represented the Mexican economy's source of strength. The linkages involved, particularly to the US economy (and through NAFTA) meant that a subsequent economic upturn would be the likely consequence of an internal upset due to miscalculations in fiscal and monetary policy. By the late 1990s, the strength of the US economy could be seen in the buoyancy of the 2,624 *maquiladoras*, which employed 861,143 persons, many of them women. They accounted for 40 per cent of Mexican exports, though they imported nearly all their input due to the advanced technology employed. *Maquiladoras* specialised in automobiles, electronics, and computers, and showed a high level of efficiency, quality, and adaptability, though combined with low wage levels. They had been seriously hit by the collapse of the peso in December 1994, but recovered remarkably thereafter. The general resilience of the Mexican economy, however, in spite of repeated shocks, stood in marked contrast to the social disintegration and political disenchantment which continued to characterise the country at large.

Despite continued gerrymandering combined with promises of political reform, PRI electoral support continued to erode throughout the
broader period from 1976. The increasing divergence between PRI-
controlled electoral processes was revealed again in the mid-term elections of 5 July 1997, when both opposition parties made significant
gains. The July congressional elections gave the combined opposition
parties a total of 261 seats (PRD 125; PAN 122) in the Chamber of
Deputies, against the PRI's 239. For the first time, the governing party
lost its majority in the lower house, though it still retained a majority in
the Senate. Electoral reverses were compounded in the municipal elections of 20 October 1997, when the PRD gained control of Jalapa. PAN
retained control of Orizaba, Córdoba, and Veracruz. In Veracruz, the
State Governor issued a declaration which stated his readiness to 'accept
and see installed' the new municipal authorities irrespective of party.
Before too much is read into these gains, however, the striking total of
50–60 per cent abstentionism should be taken into account.

The government's demonstrable inability to uphold basic law and
order in the main cities was apparent to all inhabitants. Cuauhtémoc
Cárdenas's electoral victory in Mexico City could conceivably have
explained government lack of enthusiasm for such measures. Cárdenas
won the first elections for Mayor of the Federal District, and a new PRD
capital-city administration took office on 5 December. This is a position
generally regarded as the second most powerful in the country. In view
of the seemingly insurmountable problems of popular housing, education, urban transit and infrastructure, law and order, and pollution in
the metropolitan area, the achievements or failures of the new administration would provide the test of the PRD's credibility. PRI interests
combined to impede the smooth functioning of the PRD municipal
administration.

In the meantime, the country began to acquire a bad reputation in the
international community for corruption, narco-trafficking, and violations of human rights. Complaints from Amnesty International and
Non-Government Organisations were heeded by government representatives, though the causes were not reversed. By the last months of 1997,
the country's profile had become so negative that it threatened to jeop-
ardise the establishment of a working commercial relationship with the
European Union. This arrangement was finally signed in Brussels on 8
December 1997, and provided Mexico with a potential opening that

Plate 43 Tension in Agua Tinta, Chiapas, in 1998.
The EZLN or *zapatista* uprising in central Chiapas on 1 January 1994, designed to coincide with Mexico's entry into the North American Free Trade Area (NAFTA), unnerved the Salinas administration, then beset by deepening economic problems. Long-standing peasant grievances in the San Cristóbal area and its Lacandonian hinterland were taken up by a small leftist guerrilla band led by 'Sub-comandante Marcos'. Always shown in a balaclava and smoking a pipe, 'Marcos' became a clever propagandist, making full use of the Internet. Government inability to discover a solution to the Chiapas problem threw the focus on indigenous issues throughout the Republic. Media coverage in Mexico combined with international attention limited the national government's options. In Amparo Agua Tinta, some 800 *zapatistas* are photographed during a march in May 1998 in support of the rebel authorities in the district (*municipio*) of Tierra y Libertad (named after the original *zapatista* rallying cry of the 1910s), dislodged on 1 May, and in protest at the military presence in the area.

could counterbalance, although in a small way, heavy dependence on the NAFTA. Nevertheless, it would still require an uphill climb, since the European Union share of Mexico's trade had fallen from 11.4 per cent in 1990 to 6.1 per cent in 1996.

The overall impact of the implementation of European monetary union from 1 January 1999, a scheme originally projected on 9 December 1991, for the NAFTA, and for Mexico in particular, cannot yet be foreseen. The adoption of the Euro by eleven of the participating members (out of fifteen) may simplify Mexico's commercial relations with the European Union, since the US dollar will no longer remain the principal medium of exchange. Mexico's ability to exploit commercial openings in Europe, however, depended on the overall performance of the economy during 1999–2000.

The Chiapas question and the indigenous problem

1994, the year of calamities, terminated the credibility of the Salinas government, beginning with the Chiapas uprising on 1 January. Highly media conscious, the rebels timed their occupation of San Cristóbal de Las Casas and Ocosingo to coincide with the coming into force of the NAFTA. The leading figure, 'Sub-comandante Marcos' (Rafael Sebastián Guillén, b. June 1957), originated from a family of small businessmen in the port of Tampico. A product of UNAM, where he studied philosophy, he taught at UAM, then affiliated with leftist guerrilla organisations and passed through a period of training in Sandinista-controlled Nicaragua in 1981 and in Cuba in 1982 before appearing in Chiapas in May 1984. The Zapatista National Liberation Army (EZLN), a name designed to recall the Morelos agrarian leader of the 1910s, sought to take advantage of long-standing and varied indigenous grievances. This enabled it to establish a military zone in the Las Cañadas area of the Lacandonian Forest under its exclusive control on the Cuban revolutionary model, claiming this as 'liberated territory'. In such a way, the EZLN presented the Mexican government, taken completely by surprise, with an insurgency situation which required a political as well as a military solution. Since January 1994, no government managed to find a solution to this problem, with the result that it festered indefinitely.

The EZLN portrayed itself as an armed opposition to the prevailing ideology of neo-liberalism. Declarations in January 1994 and 1995 called for the overthrow of the regime, the formation of a government of transition, the convocation of fresh elections, and the formulation of a new constitution. In spite of the guerrillas' response to contemporary issues, the antecedents of the indigenous question went back into Chiapas history. Significant peasant uprisings had taken place in 1711–12 (when the province still formed part of the Kingdom of Guatemala) and 1868–69 in the same Tzotzil and Tzeltal highland areas, where the diocese of San Cristóbal had promoted peasant mobilisation from the 1970s.

Recession in the dynamic coffee sector in the lowlands during the 1980s cut off the feasibility of peasant migration from the highland Indian communities for profitable seasonal labour. In order to defuse peasant land pressure, the government authorised colonisation of the Lacandonian Forest, where some 100,000 people set up home from the 1970s onwards. Recently formed *ejidos* seemed under threat from Salinas's reform of article 27 of the Constitution in 1992.

Although possibly consisting of no more than 300 armed guerrillas, the rebellion paralysed government and army, neither of which could afford the political risks of direct confrontation. A section of the capital-city opposition press, such as the ostensibly leftist *La Jornada*, supporter of the PRD, took up the rebellion as an issue with which to castigate the government. Even so, no national movement followed, in spite of the invocation of the name of Zapata and thereby an appeal to the revolutionary tradition of the 1910s. The uprising divided the countryside between the EZLN and their opponents, and widened the breach between the *zapatistas* and the Catholic Church.

The Bishop of Chiapas, Samuel Ruiz, assumed the role of mediator between local rebels and the authorities, and earned considerable enmity within the PRI for that reason. The ambiguity of the relationship between Ruiz and 'Marcos' remained a constant feature of news coverage. Few opportunities were lost in official circles to discredit Ruiz. Since his arrival in Chiapas in 1960, the bishop had attempted an ecclesiastical reconquest of the indigenous population of the Altos de Chiapas, the highland zone around San Cristóbal, and in the settlements of the Lacandonian Forest. In 1974, an Indigenous Congress was held in San Cristóbal to stimulate peasant politicisation and mobilisation. The objectives were removal of government appointees and invasion of large-size properties. Ruiz sponsored indigenous self-defence groups during the 1970s. An intense struggle for control of land followed from 1976 onwards. In the second half of the following decade, however, the *zapatistas* penetrated these organisations and thereby threatened diocesan control.

The Zedillo administration's repeated attempts to compromise over the Chiapas question, in order to defuse potential for armed conflict, opened the way for increased pressures for a new constitutional settlement on the basis of a concession of autonomy for areas with an indigenous majority. The practical political implications remain unclear. Such issues were not unique to Mexico, still less to Chiapas, but the idea of separate constitutional status for indigenous zones appeared to threaten a reversion to corporativism and the break-up of territorial integrity. Protagonists of such a solution argued that demands for indigenous autonomy at the end of the twentieth century revealed the full extent of nineteenth-century liberal failure in Latin America. The debate on that particular issue will continue during the forthcoming decades.

The Zedillo administration's last years

The Zedillo administration in December 1997 and January 1998 looked to be in a shambles with ministerial changes in the key offices of Finance, Interior, and Foreign Relations. The departure of the Secretary of the Interior was announced before a new Minister of Finance had been found, after the transfer of Guillermo Ortiz to the governorship of the National Bank. The incoming Interior Secretary, Francisco Labastida, a former Governor of Sinaloa, whose election in 1986 had taken place amid charges of electoral fraud by his PAN-ista opponents, was a UNAM economist who had first held government office under Echeverría. Zedillo transferred the Secretary of Foreign Relations, José Ángel Gurría, to the Finance Ministry on 5 January, a move which then left the Foreign Ministry vacant. Before the news of the replacement could be announced, the Governor of Chiapas resigned on 7 January. Taking into account his replacement, there had been five Governors of Chiapas since Zedillo took office in December 1994 and eleven since 1976. In total, ten State Governors had during two decades failed to complete their constitutional terms. Zedillo's choice for the new Secretary of Foreign Relations was the PRI Senator, Rosario Green, a UNAM political-science graduate and Under-Secretary under Francisco Solana in 1992.

During 1998, Mexico appeared to be approaching a further period of recession, the depths of which could not be predicted. Two principal influences were the ending of the Asiatic economies' boom phase and the collapse of world oil prices. The first factor, which involved Asiatic currency depreciation by over 200 per cent, had indirect influences throughout the Latin American economies, and led, as the earlier collapse of the Soviet bloc had done, to the diversion of international

Plate 44 The Mexico City Exchange.
Prime example of the late-modernist architecture of the 1980s,
this is the symbol of the rebirth of capitalism in the open
economy of that decade and its successor. The *Bosla mercantil*
represented a showpiece of the Salinas era, which culminated in
the ratification of the NAFTA Treaty in 1993. The crash of
December 1994, the collapse of the Asiatic 'tigers' in 1997, and
world financial instability in the latter part of 1998 took a heavy
toll on the Mexican stock market and the exchange rate.

financial support. The US government set about preparing a rescue package for the former 'tigers' of eastern Asia. The second factor directly affected Mexico, even though government sources had frequently maintained that, since the collapse of 1982, Mexico was no longer oil-dependent. Gurría's response was three rounds of budget cuts, which purportedly affected no major programmes, though the widely believed consequences envisaged quite the contrary, especially with regard to education. The National Bank adjusted the growth rate of GDP downwards from 5.7 per cent to a still optimistic 5 per cent late in January 1998.

The oil crisis threw into relief the long-standing belief in financial circles that the Mexican peso (at a rate of $8.5) was overvalued in relation to the US dollar. The government, fearing the political impact of devaluation, sought to hold back the monetary consequences of the fall in petroleum prices through the National Bank. Although the economy (in terms of GDP) grew at the impressive rate of 7 per cent in 1997, macroeconomic movements in the course of the following year threatened to slowdown growth. Monterrey industrialists in late January 1998 called for a reasonable devaluation, in order to avoid a subsequent catastrophe, but that went unheeded. The object was to boost exports and to encourage investment, and to prevent a full-scale recession during 1999. At the beginning of 1999, the dollar exchange rate oscillated around 10 pesos.

Mexican crude-oil export grew steadily during the mid-1990s, from 1,307,000 barrels per day in 1994 to 1,721,000 barrels in 1997. The collapse of world prices took place at the peak export level of 1,844,000 barrels between January and March 1998. Accordingly, an agreement was signed on 22 March between Mexico, Venezuela, and Saudi Arabia to reduce export by 100,000 barrels per day. This reduced the April to December estimate to 1,744,000 barrels, though with the possibility of a second round of cutbacks later in the year. Zedillo's visit to Venezuela resulted in an Energy Co-operation Agreement on 16 April, though details of implementation remained to be ascertained. At the beginning of the year, the Mexican government had estimated an oil price of US$15 per barrel, which was reduced at the time of the first budget cuts to US$13. However, the market price for Mexican mixed crude by mid-1998 still reached only US$11 per barrel. Prices fell sharply during the rest of the year.

Plate 45 Demonstrators leave their calling cards (in English and Spanish) outside the Governor's Palace overlooking the *zócalo*, the central square, in the city of Oaxaca in November 1998 (author's photograph).

Jockeying for position among presidential hopefuls began during the rest of the year. During the Spring of 1998, the Zedillo government appeared to have abandoned the practice of presidential selection of the official PRI candidate for forthcoming presidential elections. This would leave the candidacy open to all contenders, and several controversial personalities such as Manuel Bartlett Diáz, Governor of Puebla (1992–98), a hard-line PRI traditionalist, put their names forward, in the hope of taking the limelight away from Cárdenas, a prospective candidate for the PRD, and the PAN's self-proclaimed candidate, Vicente Fox Quesada, Governor of Guanajuato. Defections from the PRI in many states and challenges to local hegemonies in Chiapas, Oaxaca, Guerrero, and elsewhere appeared to suggest the imminence of defeat, whether in the elections themselves or through a prior internal disintegration. However, the resilience and even unpredictability of the PRI remained an unknown quantity. Few were willing to predict the outcome of the presidential election.

The PRI recovered considerable electoral ground during the second half of the year, retaining the governorship of Oaxaca and winning back Chihuahua from the PAN in August. The PRI held the governorships of Puebla and Sinaloa in November, but lost Tlaxcala to a local opposition coalition which included the PRD. The PRD also took control of the Federal District and the governorship of Zacatecas. By the beginning of 1999, the PAN held governorships of the two border states, Baja California Norte (where Tijuana is located) and Nuevo León, as well as those of Querétaro, Guanajuato, and Jalisco, and the city governments of Puebla, Oaxaca, Mérida, and Ciudad Juárez, although Culiacán was lost in November 1998 to the PRI. Those elections, however, demonstrated the incapacity of the PAN to take advantage of popular discontent.

Manuel Bartlett (b. Puebla 1936), who announced his candidacy in April 1998, was the son of a former Governor of Tabasco manoeuvred out of office by his bitter rival, the same Carlos Madrazo who died in mysterious circumstances in 1969. Bartlett was generally regarded as the principal PRI dinosaur of three potential challengers for the succession; the other two were Robert Madrazo Pintado, Governor of Tabasco from 1994 and son of Carlos Madrazo, and Labastida, incumbent Secretary of the Interior, who had been De la Madrid's Secretary of Commerce. Both Bartlett and Madrazo had criticised the Zedillo administration. Although Labastida remained controversial within Mexico, it appeared that Washington was not ill disposed towards him. Bartlett and Madrazo, however, had reputations and alleged connections which might have flawed their rival bids for the succession. Bartlett had been Secretary of the Interior under De la Madrid, and had presided over the election campaign of 1988, when the computer calculating the final results broke down at the crucial moment. Madrazo, who had put himself under Echeverría's wing, despite his father's unexplained death, ran into controversy over his election expenses of 1994, which greatly exceeded prescribed limits. In primaries, a new procedure representing the 10 million PRI members, the party in November 1999 selected Labastida as its presidential candidate. The leader of the PRD, Porfirio Muñoz Ledo, an ex-PRI-ista like Cárdenas himself, challenged from left of centre.

Many commentators argued at the time that the presidential election of 2000 would be a decisive moment in Mexican history. At least, the result would decide the fate of the PRI. It was true that Mexico was a constitutional state, but no opposition party had ever taken office as a result of victory in a national election. The presidential succession of 2000 was a remarkable transition, which took many Mexicans by surprise. The victory of Fox on 2 May meant that for the first time in living memory a political party other than the PRI (or its predecessors) would be governing the country. The defeated party, stunned and divided, subsequently began to regroup around Madrazo, who seemed to be its strongest figure. Fox, however, represented an unknown quantity, only loosely attached to his party, which in any case had other leaders. Mexico's prevailing social and economic problems remained for the new administration to deal with as best it could. Its business orientation ensured that the policies of the Salinas and Zedillo era would continue. Good personal relations between Fox and President George W. Bush, formerly Governor of Texas, appeared to presage better relations between the two neighbours.

8

The Fox Administration, 2000–2006

THE ECONOMY

The Fox administration benefited from a largely stable and expanding economy. The peso gained a new stability after a period of weakness between 1997 and 2000 and grew stronger by late 2005. Prices remained relatively stable, and oil revenues acquired fresh buoyancy. The picture, however, was not entirely rosy, especially in view of the far-reaching implications of continued government dependence on oil revenues. Although higher oil prices benefited Mexico considerably, since it removed the need for budget cuts in education or health, US interests considered themselves to be adversely affected. Since 88 per cent of Mexico's exports in 2005 continued to be to the USA, the economy remained vulnerable to weaknesses and fluctuations there. Even so, by September 2005, Mexico had a trade surplus of US$52.2 billion with the USA. The business orientation of the Fox administration did not lead to radical changes in policy direction, since policies favouring the private sector had already been set in motion under Salinas. In many respects, the Fox administration, despite the change of party in power, represented in practice little change with respect to economic policy.

In 2000, the Mexican government still took 37 per cent of its total revenue from the oil industry, dominated by the state-owned PEMEX. Each fall of US$1 per barrel in the export price of Mexican oil could cause the Mexican Treasury to lose US$600 or more in revenue. The government found itself caught between PEMEX's desire for more investment and greater freedom of management, on the one hand, and

US pressure for Mexico to open its oil industry to foreign investment and to increase supply to the US market, on the other hand. The bulk of Mexican oil went to the US market. In 2004, for instance, Mexico exported 1.87 million barrels per day, of which 1.65 million went to the US. Since 1998, Mexico has cooperated with Venezuela and Saudi Arabia to ensure higher oil prices. The export price of Mexican crude rose from a low of US$6 per barrel in 1998 to US$12.45 per barrel in 1999. The average export price for 2001 reached US$19.3 per barrel and in March 2002 US$20 per barrel, when the Mexican government had budgeted for a price of US$17 per barrel. This rise generated unease in the US, especially in view of the deteriorating situation in Iraq. While keeping its foreign policy distinct from that of the United States on the Iraq question, the Mexican government watched the country's average oil export price rise to US$24.6 per barrel during the first half of 2003. It rose to US$38.13 per barrel in March 2004, when the administration had budgeted for a price of US$20. This upward trend continued through 2005, and by August the price of Mexican crude reached US$48 per barrel, with a production level of 3.4 million barrels per day.

A high proportion of Mexican oil output remained in the country to fuel development. This had been the original objective of the Cárdenas administration's nationalisation of the industry in 1938. Total production was expected to rise to 3.8 million barrels per day by the end of 2006. Although no Mexican administration has so far dared to dismantle PEMEX, the need to develop further off-shore fields has raised the question of where the investment would come from. Since PEMEX paid a tax rate of 62 per cent to the Mexico state, it did not possess sufficient available capital for significant investment projects. That, in turn, has focussed discussion around energy reform, which by 2005–06 had already become a major – and controversial – issue. Given the buoyancy of oil export prices, the Fox administration was prepared to lower the tax rate to 55 per cent, a policy which would need congressional approval. The Mexican Senate opposed on principle any government measure designed to relax PEMEX's monopoly over off-shore oil development. The need for investment to maintain and increase production levels, however, led to PEMEX's authorisation of foreign companies to operate during the second half of 2005 in the northern Veracruz off-shore fields, particularly Chicontepec, where geological conditions presented serious difficulties. In 2006, this would extend to other fields as

Plate 46 Rally organised by 'Los Amigos de Fox', a group organised to promote Fox's candidacy, at the Calderón Theatre in Zacatecas, 31 July 1999. Well-heeled and well-fed rancheros from the centre-north predominate here (Author's photograph).

well. PEMEX's director argued that production could double to 7 million barrels per day, if the investment were available. If it were not, the Energy Minister darkly warned early in 2005, then production would fall in the near future to the extent that after twelve years or so, Mexico might find itself in the dire position of having to import crude oil. To date, these energy issues have not been resolved. Furthermore, the precarious condition of the US economy – with a trade deficit running at $60 billion a month in the first half of 2005 – threatened to destabilise not just the Mexican economy but the global financial order as well.

Mexico's loss of its former position as the second source of US imports (after Canada) in 2003 gave rise to further concern. In relative terms, Mexican exports to the US had been steadily falling, despite overall growth. The growth, however, was too slow, and was largely accounted for by oil exports at high prices. As a result China overtook Mexico and became second supplier to the USA. In 2004, China supplied 14 per cent of US imports and surpassed Japan as the country with the largest trade surplus with the US. In many respects, the US has depended on continued Chinese and other Asian buying of its bonds and equities to shore up its trade deficit. The continued strength of the peso further inhibited Mexican exportation. China was able to under-cut Mexico in the US market, because of state subsidies to its export industries and manipulation of the exchange rate. The Chinese lead over Mexico in the US market seems likely to increase. Mexico, at the same time, was facing Chinese competition in textiles in its domestic market.

During the second half of Fox's term, job-creation became an over-riding political issue. Although the administration attributed job losses in Mexico to the US economic slowdown after 2000–01, it was also clear that the Mexican economy was unable to absorb the increasing numbers coming on to the labour market each year. From the middle of 2003, industrial output – and with it consumer spending – declined. In September 2005, the central bank revised its forecast of the growth rate down to 3 per cent. As a result, unemployment remained a persistent problem in the capital and Monterrey and the other main industrial cities. The figures remain disputed, but the possibility exists that more than 12 per cent of the urban labour force remains unemployed, and that just under 30 per cent operates within the informal economy.

MEXICO'S PLACE IN THE WORLD

President Fox and his first Foreign Minister, Jorge Castañeda, hoped to give Mexico a more prominent role in world affairs. Fox made large numbers of foreign trips in his first years of office, partly in order to promote this aim, and partly to restore Mexico's image in the world as a democracy which respected human rights. By mid-term, however, it had become clear that the Mexican government had very little inter-national impact. Fox received criticism for lack of diplomatic skills. Inevitably, relations with the USA continued to dominate Mexican foreign relations. Fox favoured the transformation of NATFA, a free trade area, into a customs union with free movement of labour within ten years, a position which continued to find little support in the US. Issues such as reciprocal prohibitions of imports – Mexican tuna, mangoes and sugar or US meats and apricots – ruffled relations without radically disturbing them. Mexican suspicion of US protectionist intent remained strong. Outstanding matters such as control and distribution of the waters of the Río Bravo (Grande), established under the 1994 treaty, were resolved.

However, conflict continued over Mexican immigration into the United States. US commentators drew attention to the fact that in 1990 the so-called 'Hispanic' element of the population had amounted to only 9 per cent of the total. By 2000, this figure had risen to 12.5 per cent, largely as a result of the high birth rate at 4.3 per cent, in contrast to the rest of the population at 0.8 per cent. The number of Mexicans within the USA rose from 13.5 million in 1990 to 20.6 million in 2000. Some 3 to 3.5 million of them had no legal status. To date, no solution satisfactory to both sides has been worked out. During the first five months of 2000, US border patrols expelled 200,000 undocumented immigrants from Arizona. Mexican authorities repeatedly raised the question of the killing of illegal immigrants by Arizona ranchers or Texas border patrol officers – 340 in the first eight months of 2000. According to US calculations, 300,000 illegal immigrants enter the USA annually. Mexican critics of the Fox administration pointed to its failure to ensure that the human rights of migrant workers were respected in the United States.

Despite the initially good personal relations between Fox and the newly elected President George W. Bush, both ranchers with a business background and impatience with entrenched bureaucracies, US foreign policy priorities soon left Mexico high and dry during 2001. This situation became all the more obvious in the aftermath of the New York and Washington terrorist attacks of 11 September. Worsening relations between the US administration and the European Union, deepening involvement in the Middle East, and mounting concern with China and the Far East reduced Latin America – and Mexico – to matters of minor consideration. This did not signify that events there were of no consequence, even for the United States. It meant that the US administration chose not to look at them. During 2005, immigration still remained an issue between the two countries, despite further meetings between the two presidents. In August 2005, the State Governors of New Mexico and Arizona declared a state of emergency along the Mexican border, arguing that illegal immigration was out of control.

Mexico held one of the two Latin American seats on the United Nations Security Council for the two-year period, 2002–04. This coincided with the worsening of the international crisis over Iraq. The Mexican government opposed unilateral intervention against Iraq by the United States and associates, and adopted the position of France, Russia and China, three permanent members of the Security Council. At the same time, the government laid itself open to the possibility of US retaliation by a refusal to make concessions over immigration.

The tenth anniversary of NAFTA on 9 December 2002 fell in the middle of this crisis. The three founding leaders, George Bush Senior, Brian Mulroney of Canada, and Carlos Salinas of Mexico arrived in Washington, along with current incumbents, for the celebration. The appearance of the disgraced Salinas, in self-imposed exile since his departure from office in 1994, raised eyebrows in Mexico. At the meeting, Fox once more expressed his desire to see NAFTA evolve into a customs union. Over-optimistic, he proposed 2005 as the transformation date. This was very unlikely to occur. Nevertheless, Fox drew attention to the extent of Mexico's trade with the US, and to the fact that Mexico had now become the world's ninth largest economy. Nevertheless, the benefits drawn from NAFTA had been uneven. Car-component plants had moved forwards, whereas ranching had suffered after the loss of tariff protection at the beginning of 2003. Furthermore, Mexican peasant producers were likely to suffer in the near future. The 1992 treaty had exempted Mexican maize from the NAFTA provisions, a position which, Fox explained, could not last – and with it continued state funding of low-yield food producers.

Mexico hosted two international conferences in 2002. The first of these was the United Nations Conference on the Financing of Development held in Monterrey in March. Bush, Fidel Castro, Jacques Chirac and some fifty heads of state or government attended what turned out to be a rather inconsequential meeting. At the end of October, Mexico hosted the Asia Pacific Economic Cooperation summit in Los Cabos (Baja California Sur). The APEC had been established in 1994 to promote free trade and increased investment among member states in two stages by 2010 and 2020, and to harmonise financial and banking systems. Issues such as Mexico's commercial relations with Japan and immigration to the US reappeared during the discussions. The Mexican government viewed the newly industrialising countries within APEC as potential associates in relation to the developed economies, especially with regard to the latter's observation of World Trade Organization agreements on tariffs. The final communiqué warned against agricultural export subsidies by developed countries, such as

Japan, the EU and the US. The fifth ministerial summit of the WTO, held
at Cancún in mid-September 2003, disintegrated over this issue after a
conflict between Brazil and the United States. Cancún, however, saw the
emergence of the Grupo 23, with Brazil, China, India and South Africa
in the forefront, in spite of US efforts to disperse it. Mexico also joined
this group of developing countries, along with Pakistan, Turkey,
Indonesia, Thailand, the Philippines, Nigeria, and a range of other Latin
American countries. The thrust continued to be directed against industrialised states, which argued for free trade but refused to liberalise their
own agricultural sectors.

At the 21-member APEC summit in Santiago (Chile) in November
2004, Fox again raised with Bush the issues of cross-border migration
and the status of undocumented Mexican residents in the USA. Bush
assured Fox that the US government regarded the matter as a priority,
but saw it in terms of security of frontiers and the 'war on terrorism'.
After Bush's re-election earlier that month, the Republican Party for the
first time in seventy years controlled both Houses of the US Congress,
but conservative opposition continued to delay any agreement on legal-
isation of status. Furthermore, most Latin American countries, including Mexico, had opposed the invasion of Iraq, with the result that
relations with the US had soured considerably since March 2003. Bush
used the summit to expound further his doctrine on the 'war on terrorism', in which few Latin Americans had much interest.

The key figure in this summit turned out to be not Bush but the
Chinese President, Hu Jintao, who upstaged his US counterpart by
proposing large Chinese investment in Latin American businesses and
infrastructure and pointing to a closer commercial relationship between
the two geographical areas. Hu Jintao, moreover, attended the summit
in the aftermath of a visit to Brazil and Argentina, where present agreements had been finalised and future ones discussed. China, with 1,300
million inhabitants, currently had the fastest growing economy in the
world at the rate of 9 per cent p.a., fuelled by high levels of production
technology and a low-wage labour market. Latin America had already
become in 2003 the second largest destination of Chinese foreign investment (at 36.5 per cent) after Asia (at 52.6 per cent). Chile, Brazil and
Argentina, in particular, welcome Chinese overtures, which would stimulate exports of soya, meat, wool, gas, steel, cement, rubber, and a range
of minerals, beginning with Chilean copper. Mexico, however, tended

to view the increasing Chinese presence in the Americas as a threat both to its domestic textile industry and its position in the US market. This pointed to the need for greater productivity in Mexico and an increased understanding of the Chinese market by Mexican businessmen. A two-day state visit by Hu Jintao in September 2005 underlined these necessities. Mexico, in the meantime, sought to negotiate greater Chinese import of Mexican fruits and hoped to secure increased involvement of its companies in the Chinese domestic market. Business pressure inside Mexico urged the liberalisation of the electricity and petroleum industries, the latter still a political taboo. Rival demand for Mexican oil in the US might dent any potential petroleum export to China.

Neither the visit to Mexico by Condoleeza Rice, the new US Secretary of State, nor the Tripartite Meeting of the three North American Presidents at Bush's Crawford ranch, both in March 2005, had any significant result, least of all with regard to the status of Mexican migrants in the US. These two meetings, furthermore, took place against the background of disparaging remarks about Mexico made by officials in the CIA and the US State Department and the US Ambassador's statement that Mexico presented an unstable security situation. In the first half of 2005, relations between the two countries continued in the doldrums. Senior US government personnel seemed to have lost interest in Mexico altogether. The Mexican government faced another significant humiliation, when the Organization of American States selected the Chilean rival to the Mexican Secretary of Foreign Relations to be its Secretary-General late in April 2005. Brazil, increasingly putting itself at the centre of South American policy initiatives, supported the Chilean candidate, whom the United States claimed to have supported as well.

NARCOTICS

Mexico, in common with Colombia and other Latin American countries, continued to object to the United States policy of 'certification' as demeaning. By this policy the United States, the principal consumer of narcotics, attributed to itself the right to pass moral judgements on other countries, which consumed them to a far lesser degree. They happened to be the producers or the transit channels of the narcotics traffic. In March 2000, the US 'certified' that both Mexico and Colombia (among a total of twenty-six countries) were cooperating in the struggle against drug trafficking. 'Certification' meant that they would not be liable to sanctions by the US. Even so, the US government still regarded Mexico as the main channel of cocaine destined for clients in western and central USA.

The Salinas administration had brought the Mexican Army into the centre of operations against drug-traffickers. The complicity of a number of senior officers had weakened this policy in its early stages. President Zedillo's principal anti-narcotics officer, General J.J.Gutiérres Rebollo, had in fact been convicted for being in the pay of a drugs baron. The Fox administration, accordingly, tended to play down the role of the Army and make greater use of the police and special units. However, its policy of arresting key gang leaders often led to power struggles within the cartels and increased violence. This became out of control by late 2005, with an increased drug-related murder rate in the border states and Sinaloa.

Tijuana, Ciudad Juárez, and Nuevo Laredo became the most violent places in Mexico as a result of the drugs trade. The Cartel de Tijuana, originating in the early 1980s and run by the Arellano Félix brothers, who were well-educated and fluent in English, dominated the trade in the border city, had contacts among Mexico's wealthy, and maintained a hideaway in San Diego. Originally contrabandists, the group had graduated into narcotics. This Cartel continued in the early 2000s to struggle for supremacy with the Cartel de Sinaloa and other rival gangs in Ciudad Juárez and Guadalajara.

During the first months of 2002, the US and Mexico governments made parallel moves against the Tijuana Cartel in both countries. FBI arrests in San Diego curbed money-laundering and hit the financial base of the Cartel's cross-border operations. A shoot-out with police in Mazatlán in February probably resulted in the death of Ramón Arellano Félix. On 9 March, units of the Army arrested Benjamín Arellano Félix in Puebla. Leadership of the cartel, which still continued in existence, more than likely passed to Javier, another of the brothers.

In the first part of 2005, the US State Department International Narcotics Control Strategy stated that 90% of the cocaine consumed in the USA came from Mexico, and that Mexico remained the second largest supplier of heroin. The DEA identified the main source of the transit problem as the Mexican border states, particularly through the city of Nuevo Laredo, the focus of large-scale border commerce and smuggling, and proposed to increase its total number of agents operating inside Mexico from 32 to possibly over 40. Frequent gun battles in Nuevo Laredo led to the closure of the US consulate there in July 2005. In the meantime, the Gulf Cartel battled with the Sinaloa Cartel for control of the drug trade. The Gulf Cartel was led by Osiel Cárdenas, in jail in the La Palma high security prison from March 2003. Cárdenas had recruited a private army, known as the 'Zetas', from former government paramilitary forces.

THE CATHOLIC CHURCH

After Fox's election victory in 2000, it quickly became clear that the business wing of the PAN would take precedence over any attempted religious revindication, desired as it might have been by the Catholic Right. The new administration made no attempt to undo the Reform Laws, despite attempts to denigrate the character and legacy of Benito Juárez among the wilder elements of the PAN. The Mexican Church, for its part, continued to press for religious education in state primary schools, criticised secular education, denounced liberal sexual practices, and inveighed against controversial films – such as *El crimen de Padre Amaro* (2002) – or TV programmes. At the same time, it pressed strongly for the canonisation of Juan Diego, the Indian declared to have had visions of the Virgin of Guadalupe in 1531. An out-going prior of the Guadalupe religious community, however, had incurred Vatican criticism for expressing doubt late in 1999 about even the existence of Juan Diego, let alone the visions. In August 2002, Pope John Paul II paid his fifth visit to Mexico. On arrival, President Fox made the unprecedented and controversial gesture of kissing the Pope's ring, an action which went against the entire *juarista* tradition. During the course of this visit, the Pope canonised Juan Diego and beatified two Zapotec Indians, who had been killed by other villagers for denouncing the celebration of clandestine rites to the Spanish colonial authorities. Even though large crowds welcomed the canonisation, both of these actions by the Pope received considerable criticism.

John Paul's attention to Mexican issues and attempts to bolster the Mexican Church never wavered since his first visit shortly after his elevation. In 1992, he beatified the Martyrs of the Cristiada in a Solemn

Plate 47 The new shrine at Santa Ana de Guadalupe, family
home of newly canonised Santo Toribio Romo, in the Altos de
Jalisco, dedicated to the Martyrs killed by federal forces at the
time of the Cristero Rebellion (1926–29) (author's photograph,
September 2003).

Mass of Christ the King in Rome. These were some twenty priests and
lay people who had been murdered by sections of the Federal Army
during its repression of the Jalisco countryside at the time of the
Cristero Rebellion of 1926–29. None of the martyrs had actually taken
part in the armed rebellion. John Paul canonised them in 2000. He saw

them as victims of the modern revolutionary state. The Mexican hierarchy sponsored the creation of a new shrine in the village of Santa Ana Guadalupe, not far from the great pilgrimage centre of San Juan de los Lagos in the Altos de Jalisco. Santa Ana had been the home of Padre (now Santo) Toribio Romo. This priest had been dragged out of hiding and shot dead at the age of 28, in front of his sister, by a Federal cavalry patrol on the lookout for priests and those working closely with them in defiance of government prohibitions.

Inevitably, the Catholic hierarchy gained a higher profile as a result of the restoration of diplomatic relations between the Mexican state and the Holy See in 1993. This ensured continued public interest in the still unresolved case of Cardinal Posadas of Guadalajara and in that of the alleged money-laundering of his successor, Juan Sandoval Iñiguez, on behalf of drugs cartels. The Church had always rejected the government's explanation, as expressed by Jorge Carpizo, Attorney-General in the Salinas administration, for the death of Posadas – that he had been accidentally caught in a gunfight at the airport between the Tijuana and Sinaloa drug cartels. The view of the hierarchy was that Posadas, previously Bishop of Tijuana, had been targeted by the Salinas government, because he had information linking the administration to drug-traffickers. A deputy Attorney-General in the Fox administration officially reopened the Posadas case in June 2002. After his arrest earlier in that year, Benjamín Arellano Félix maintained that the Salinas government has given the two brothers immunity for the occasions when they had spoken to the then Nuncio, Girolamo Prigione. This Carpizo denied. Nevertheless, it transpired that 1,000 pages were missing from the file on the Posadas case.

Carpizo was the central figure in the allegations against Sandoval, first made in 1996. Relations between the two public figures had never been cordial. The Procuraduría General de la República was obliged to investigate the case. Sandoval had been suffragan Bishop of Ciudad Juárez from 1988, and before that he had been Deputy Rector of the Guadalajara Diocesan Seminary from 1971. The allegations were that he had taken contributions from drug-traffickers, while holding that office. Since Sandoval was one of the four Cardinals composing the Vatican Finance Commission, these allegations had serious implications. As Archbishop of Guadalajara, it seemed probable that Sandoval had sought connections with the city's wealthy, and it might have been the case that several of them had connections with or were themselves *narcotraficantes*. Sandoval maintained that Carpizo's intention had been to stifle his attempts to keep the Posadas case on the national agenda.

While the Attorney-General's office investigated the case after May 2003, the Mexican hierarchy made clear its support for Sandoval's innocence by means of the media and through mobilisation of support at parish level. Sandoval attempted to involve President Fox in September by stating publicly that the President had said that the case would be over in two weeks. Fox, already embarrassed by the Cardinal-Archbishop's presence at his mother's birthday celebrations in Guanajuato, strongly denied any executive interference in judicial procedures. The Attorney-General sought to limit the damage to the judiciary by affirming the independence of the PGR and denying any government intention to discredit the Church or stir up a conflict between Church and State. In the meantime, the Nuncio went to Rome to consult the Vatican Secretariat of State concerning the case. On 26 December 2003, the PGR finally dropped all charges against Sandoval, who in the previous month had become Chairman of the Committee of Mexican Bishops and was regarded in some circles as a potential candidate for the papal succession. This occasioned a statement on 1 February 2004 by the Mexican Primate, Cardinal Rivera, that abortion and emergency contraception (the 'morning-after pill') constituted worse crimes than drug-trafficking. Rivera then attributed the ensuing outcry to the surviving current of anti-clericalism in Mexican society.

Between 1950 and 2000, the proportion of self-declared Catholics in Mexico fell in relation to the overall growth of population. Similarly, the number of vocations also declined in relative terms, although it remained higher in Mexico than in Europe and the rest of Latin America. Out of an estimated 15,000 priests in a country of around 100 million inhabitants, some 2,500 were at the retiring age of 75 years in September 2003.

POLITICAL DEVELOPMENTS AND ISSUES

Fox won 42.5 per cent of the vote in the presidential election of 2 July 2000. Since opinion polls had underestimated his level of support, this victory took many observers by surprise. Clearly, many voters had switched allegiance at the last minute, as the prospect of removing the PRI from power for the first time since its formation in 1946 became a possibility. The PRI took 36 per cent of the vote and the PRD 16.6 per cent. Congressional elections reduced the PRI to 211 of the 500 seats in the Lower Chamber, against 225 for pro-Fox deputies (not all of them belonging to the PAN), and 60 for the PRD. The PRI remained the largest party in the Senate, with 47 seats to the PAN's 40. The PRI, then, still remained a force both in congress and the country. The party controlled two (the Estado de México and Veracruz) of the five states (including the Federal District) with the largest number of congressional seats and 42 per cent of the electorate. It controlled 19 of the 32 state governorships, and began to make fresh electoral gains, particularly in Oaxaca, from October 2001. The party, however, lost Michoacan, the Cárdenas home state, to Cuauhtémoc Cárdenas's son, Lázaro Cárdenas Batel of the PRD, in November. The PRD continued to hold the office of Mayor of the Federal District, the second most important political position in Mexico after the Presidency, and in December 2000, Andrés Manuel López Obrador began a six-year term. López Obrador, left of centre, became a possible presidential candidate for the presidential elections of 2006. He had been the defeated candidate in the controversial gubernatorial elections of Tabasco in 1994, when the victory went to Roberto Madrazo, who, after the elections of 2000, began to manoeuvre for the leadership of the PRI.

After 2000, the electoral position of the PAN began to erode. Fox himself was a controversial figure within his own parry and did not command the support of congressional leaders and former presidential candidates. The cabinet sought to balance an array of forces opposed to the PRI, not all of them PAN-istas and few of them associated with the Catholic Right. Fox's spokesperson, Marta Sahagún, who was also his companion, acquired a high profile in the administration. This continued to be a matter of controversy, particularly during the mid-term period, when discussion focussed around the possibility of her standing as a presidential candidate in 2006. On the first anniversary of the presidential victory, Fox and Sahagún married in a civil ceremony in Los Pinos, the presidential residence. They were both divorced, though Catholics. Cardinal-Archbishop Rivera explained that, although they were barred from the sacraments, they were allowed to attend Mass and had not been excommunicated.

Fox sought to reshape the image of the presidency from the Moctezuma-style of inscrutable, absolute ruler, to a more accessible – and fallible – figure. The contrast between Fox's general abstention from interference in state governments and Salinas's constant interventions could not be greater. He preferred to make grand gestures and fine statements, while paying little attention to policy detail. His high popularity rating continued into 2002, when disillusionment set in across the social spectrum. Lack of delivery became the central issue. Results rarely followed rhetoric. The rising crime rate in Mexico City was testimony to this. Major political failures dented the administration's image. The Supreme Court halted electricity liberalisation (nationalised in 1960) on the grounds that it required new legislation. Fiscal reform floundered, and the Indian Rights Bill faced vigorous opposition from state congresses and governors.

The objective of fiscal reform was to diminish dependence on oil revenues by increasing tax revenue from other sources. The administration wanted to extend Value Added Tax (IVA) to food and medicine at the rate of 15 per cent, but faced strong opposition in congress, particularly from PRI deputies, throughout 2001. Congress only allowed the package to go through in January 2002 after considerable dilution. The IVA extension was dropped, although the income tax rate was made uniform at 35 per cent and designed to settle at 32 per cent in 2005. This meant a considerable reduction of personal income tax (from 40 per cent) but was balanced by an increase in corporate and capital gains tax, a 10 per cent tax on cellular telephone calls, and a 20 per cent tax on luxury items.

The Indian Rights Bill responded to increasing consciousness of this issue during the previous decade. According to the Census of 2000, a total of 8.65 million individuals described themselves as 'indigenous'. Of these, 2 million lived in Oaxaca and 1.3 million in Chiapas. The Bill floundered on the two issues of the definition of Indian autonomy and the right to constitute new municipalities. The electoral system also became an issue. In states such as Oaxaca, Indian municipal authorities had already secured widespread exemption from the electoral processes established in accordance with the 1917 Constitution, in favour of their own 'usages and customs'. Although these had been intended to prevent outside party dominance, they could result in local cliques dominating elections. The Federal Congress took a long time to approve the Bill, which still faced the opposition of fourteen state congresses, including Oaxaca, where the Governor, closely allied to Madrazo, was hoping to 'play the indigenous card'. When a majority of states supported the bill by August 2001, the Supreme Court then challenged its legality. Indigenous communities with the 'usages and customs' electoral system continue to oppose the measure. This means that, in effect, the legislation stays in suspense.

Fox's aim in the congressional elections of July 2003 was to secure a clear majority. However, the PAN lost 20 per cent of its seats and was reduced to 153, while the PRI gained 10 per cent and finished with 224 seats. The PRD doubled its number of seats to 95, but its vote had dropped 30 per cent in the three years since the elections of 2000. Although the PAN won the governorship of San Luis Potosí, traditionally PRI but with a long tradition of opposition since the 1970s led by Dr Nava, and held Querétaro, which it had won in 1997, it lost its former stronghold of Nuevo León to the PRI.

During the second half of Fox's term, however, the PRI showed increasing signs of internal division. This threatened to compromise its attempt to regain the Presidency in 2006. Madrazo's rise in the party, furthermore, provoked opposition. This led to the formation of a group popularly known as the 'TUCOM' ('All United Against Madrazo'), led by several state governors and prominent senators, who threatened to nominate a rival candidate for the PRI primary late in 2005.

Party structures had been reformed in November 2002 and Madrazo elected as the PRI's new leader for a four-year term by a narrow majority in the following February. After the congressional elections of 2003, Esther Elba Gordillo, Madrazo's principal rival, became PRI leader in the lower chamber. She had been leader of the powerful National Teachers' Union (SNTE), and had a strong political base there. Gordillo could count on support from the Governors of the Estado de México, Veracruz and Tamaulipas, and had contacts and friendly relations with Fox, Sahagún and Jorge Castañeda, who had resigned as Foreign Minister in January 2003. It was also said that she had contacts with ex-President Salinas, back in Mexico from December 2001. Late in 2005, Gordillo seemed even more resolutely opposed to Madrazo and to be moving in the direction of the 'TUCOM' group. Her position seemed to represent a potential challenge to Madrazo from within the PRI for the presidential elections of 2006. The PRI suffered a major blow with the loss of Guerrero to the PRD in February 2005. This had been a PRI-ista governorship since the party's inception. Guerrero, however, was one of the poorest states in Mexico and had the highest illiteracy rate. At the same time, the PRD retained control of Baja California Sur. Nevertheless, the PRI retained control of the governorship of the Eastado de México in July 2005, which pointed to key support in the most politically important state in the Republic.

The PRD continued to be divided and riven by debt. Cuauthémoc Cárdenas resigned all his party offices in March 2004 after an internal dispute. The party's potential presidential candidate, López Obrador, initially faced a charge of contempt of court for having ignored an injunction, as mayor, to halt work on a construction project, which he had deemed to be socially justified. This case had opened in August 2002. On 7 April 2005, the congressional committee investigating the issue of the mayor's immunity from prosecuting decided to strip him of this protection. As a result, López Obrador, facing criminal charges, could technically no longer offer himself as a presidential candidate, even though the opinion polls showed him to be the front-runner. Fingers pointed to the Fox administration as promoter of the elimina-tion of López Obrador, while the latter saw the hand of ex-President Salinas in the machinations to discredit his administration in the capital and to bar him from the candidature in 2006. Fox vigorously denied political involvement in the case, maintaining that the matter was judi-cial and not political. When more than a million people demonstrated silently through the streets of Mexico City on 24 April, the administra-tion, already perturbed by international criticism on the issue, was shocked into an embarrassing about-turn. The Attorney-General resigned on 27 April, and on 4 May, his successor announced that López Obrador, to the consternation of the PRI, would be free to campaign, when on 31 July he would resign his post as Mayor and seek the PRD nomination. If elected in July 2006, his left-of-centre position would bring Mexico into line with the presidents of the other principal Latin American countries. Whether this would signify a stronger and more coherent stance with regard to the current US administration or in world affairs in general would remain to be seen.

Attention focussed in early 2004 on the supposed presidential ambi-tions of Marta Sahagún, who stood at the head of a personal charity organisation which critics described as an election fund. The polls had put her second to López Obrador. Madrazo supporters in the PRI were determined to prevent her standing, especially since they feared the possibility of some arrangement with Elba Esther Gordillo. On 14 March, Sahagún declared that she would not be standing in 2006, a statement which still occasioned doubts. Accordingly, she had to rule herself out a second time in July. During the spring of 2005, the possibility emerged of her standing as candidate for the mayoralty of Mexico City.

All of this left open the question of who would actually be the PAN's presidential candidate, since no incumbent could run for a second term. The Interior Minister, Santiago Creel, who represented the centre of the party and was not identified with the Catholic Right, emerged as one of the three PAN hopefuls, along with Alberto Cárdenas, a former Governor of Jalisco, and Felipe Calderón, technically the party leader. Creel, however, had not been successful in his dealings with congress. This could well be crucial after 2006, if the elections resulted in another presidency, which did not have a majority there. Fox's measures had been largely hindered by congress. During the second half of his term, he seemed to have lost authority and direction altogether. Such a situation could well be repeated with a new president after 2006, unless the incumbent showed great skill in winning congressional support from opposition parties and building a working consensus.

Already obvious by mid-term, the Fox administration's lack of direction and poverty of achievement became glaring during its last two years in office. The context and extent of the reforms, which Fox wanted congress to approve, remained ill-defined. By November 2005, the PAN had chosen Calderón, who came from the business wing of the party and was a moderate Catholic. Calderón had deep family roots in the PAN, a party eager to move beyond what might be called 'Foxismo'. The Catholic hierarchy's determination to extend its role in education and other aspects of society could well deter Gordillo's Teachers' Union and other PRI dissidents from association with the Calderón camp. López Obrador, still the favourite early in 2006, will be the PRD's presidential candidate.

9

Cultural developments since Independence

A rich Mexican historiographical tradition with roots in the colonial period preceded the development of a distinct fictional tradition. In spite of discrepancies in timing and quality, both grew in relation to the dawning of a national consciousness during the course of the nineteenth century. At the same time, each drew on external influences as well as native roots. Mexican historiography really came into its own with the attempt to ascertain the origins, nature and implications of the struggle for independence from Spain. Carlos María Bustamante (1774–1848), *Cuadro histórico de la revolución de la América mexicana* (1821–27; second edition 1843–46), saw the overthrow of Spanish rule as the reversal of the Conquest. Bustamante had participated in the War of Independence with Morelos and played an active role in politics after 1821. Lucas Alamán, *Historia de México* (5 vols., 1846–52), adopted a different perspective. Alamán posed the problem of the relationship between the new sovereign state, beset by internal division and external threat, and the Spanish colonial tradition. In his view, Mexico's character derived from its Hispanic and Catholic identity. Alamán's political and historical ideas fused in his lesser known, *Disertaciones sobre la historia mexicana* (1844–46). Commentators in the Liberal tradition, such as José María Luis Mora (1794–1850), looked to the European constitutional liberalism as the model for a nineteenth-century state. Later Liberals drew their inspiration from the American and French Revolutions. Most of the writers of the post-Independence era raised the questions of Mexican identity and character, which would preoccupy essayists and novelists of later generations. From these fertile sources Mexico's later historiographical and literary traditions sprang.

The Reform era became the subject of an intense polemic and accompanying historical investigation in 1905–06 at the time of the centenary of Juárez's birth. Much of this discussion soon merged into the controversy surrounding the damage to the political processes by Díaz's extensive personal rule. The career and ideas of Justo Sierra (1848–1912) epitomised the ambiguities of support and opposition to Díaz's rule at the same time. The radical liberal, Altamirano, had been an early influence on Sierra, who had later moved in the direction of a strong, centralised state which could exercise constructive influence on society, particularly through universal, public, secular, elementary education. Sierra championed this position from the 1880s onwards in the Juárez tradition. Minister of Education from 1905, Sierra oversaw the foundation of the National University in 1910. Under the influence of European Positivism and Social Darwinism, he saw Mexican history in terms of evolution through progressing stages of development. He saw the Reform era as the decisive point in laying the foundations for stability and material progress in a secular state. Works such as *México: su evolución social* (1900–02) and *La evolución del pueblo mexicano* (1902) gave historical expression to this position. Sierra believed that Mexico's identity lay in racial and cultural mixture. As protagonist of the predominant role of the *mestizo* in society, Sierra concurred with Andrés Molina Enríquez (1868–1940), a strong advocate of agrarian reform in the revolutionary years, and anticipated the ideas of José Vasconcelos concerning the new, cosmic race at the heart of Mexican culture.

THEMES AND METHODS IN MEXICAN LITERATURE

The long colonial hegemony was followed by non-Spanish cultural influences, particularly French, for much of the nineteenth century. Yet, Mexican realities, such as ethnic diversity, the predominance of the rural world, and the struggles between lawlessness and a stabilised form of living, penetrated both historiography and fiction. Elements of clandestinity and illegality, always below the colonial surface, rose after Independence to become major literary themes, as the preoccupation with contrabandists and bandits demonstrated. In the late colonial and early Independence era, José Fernández de Lizardi's *El Periquillo*

Sarniento (1816) ('The Mangy Parakeet'), a loosely structured novel of
set-pieces and vignettes of social life, became a best-seller in its day.
Disguise was a major theme in the book, in the tradition of the
picaresque novels of the Spanish Golden Age. Lizardi, founder of the
newspaper El Pensador Mexicano in Mexico City in 1812, sympathised
with the ideas of the European Enlightenment and the Cadiz constitutional system, and criticised the colonial authorities, for which he was
jailed in 1814. Distinct 'national' types began to emerge in the literature, for instance the Mexican *ranchero* in Luis Gonzaga Inclán's novel
*Astucia, el jefe de los Hermanos de la Hoja, o los charros contraban-
distas de la rama* (1843) ('The Smart One – Chief of the Brothers of the
Leaf, or the Cowboy Contrabandists of Tobacco') about a bandit leader
and his followers. In this Inclán transposed the type of novel popu-
larised by Alexandre Dumas to Mexico. The context was essentially
rural and explored the extra-legal activities in which *El Periquillo* also
luxuriated. The book was written without literary pretentions.

Altamirano's call after 1867 for a 'national literature' not derived from
European models 1867 did not fall on responsive ground. Few Mexican
artists chose to write novels, even though this was a period when the
realist novel flourished in Europe and the United States. Equally,
Mexicans in the latter part of the nineteenth century continued to be

Plate 48 The lithograph of 'Roldán Street and its Landing Stage'
('La calle de Roldán y su desembarcadero') by J. Decaen formed
part of a larger work compiled by Casimiro Castro in 1864,
which included a large number of images of well-known
buildings in Mexico City, such as 'The House of the Emperor
Iturbide', 'The Mining College', and 'The National Palace'.
A lithograph of Mexico City Cathedral during the time of the
French occupation showed the French North-African soldiers,
the *zouaves*, in their bright red pantaloons. There is also a
splendid image of the Basilica of Guadalupe with pilgrims on
12 December, the feast day of the Virgin of Guadalupe. Castro,
evidently as fascinated by the introduction of the railways as the
painter, José María Velasco, went on to produce an *Album del
ferrocarril mexicano* in 1877. (I am grateful to Dr Roderick
McCrorie (University of Essex) for permission to use this
lithograph from his private collection.)

fascinated by intellectual developments in Europe. Low literacy levels in the country ensured that writers would remain an elite within an elite. Writers such as Altamirano continued to use romance and allegory to promote national identity. *Clemencia* (1869) and *El Zarco* (written in 1888 but published in 1901), were primarily designed for the education of the ordinary people. They portrayed love across socio-ethnic lines didactically as an implied contribution to national integration in the Mexican Liberal tradition. *El Zarco* also dealt with a bandit group, *Los plateados*. Another important political figure of the Restored Republic, Vicente Riva Palacio (1832–96), demonstrated greater powers of imagination in his reconstruction of the colonial era, *México a través de los siglos* (1884–89), than in his novels. His historical novel, *Los piratas del Golfo* (1869), was set in the colonial era. A second edition did not appear until 1974. Riva Palacio drew on the archive of the Inquisition as source material for his historical novels.

Manuel Payno (1810–94), Finance Minister in the early 1850s, published *Los Bandidos de Río Frío* in serial form in 1889–91. Its significance lies more in the description of life, customs, and countryside during the time of Santa Anna than in psychological depth or power of imagination. It is more Romantic than realist, despite the author's profession of admiration for the European realist models of his time, and is hardly a novel at all but a vast series of sketches. Payno, writing in exile in Spain, based his narrative on the case of Col. Juan Yáñez, who had been a cabinet member under Santa Anna, and used his position to set up a network of criminals. He was garrotted in 1839 along with several companions. Payno was influenced by the popular tradition of sheet literature, purchased on the streets at low prices from blind vendors. This tradition often specialised in violent deeds.

Rafael Delgado (1853–1914), author of *La calandria* ('The Lark') (1890), the first of four novels, was considered by Mariano Azuela (1873–1952), leading novelist of the Revolution, to be the first modern novelist in nineteenth-century Mexico in terms of form, style and psychological depth, especially in relation to his predecessors. Fernando de Fuentes (1894–1958), one of the most celebrated film directors of the early sound days, filmed this novel in 1933. Like many Latin American novels of the late nineteenth and early twentieth centuries, Delgado based his writing in his native area of Orizaba in Veracruz, and traced social and generational conflict. The novels have been described by later

critics as 'creole-type' novels because of their search for national identity through regional and ethnic divergence, and their frequent use of
descriptive narrative and local dialect. This *criollista* mode reached its
climax in the years, 1915–45.

The social conflicts of the later Porfirian era generated one of its outstanding novels. Heriberto Frías (1870–1925), in *Tomóchic* (1894), deals
with a millenarian rebellion in the mountains of western Chihuahua in
the early 1890s. The conflict focussed around the cult of Teresa Urrea,
known as 'la santa de Cabora'. The author was a second lieutenant in the
Federal Army sent to put down the rebellion. After several failures, reflecting of the lack of preparedness of the late Porfirian army, the soldiers
finally annihilate the rebels. The novel reflected the author's revulsion at
the acts in which he had participated. It was first published in the opposition newspaper, *El Demócrata*, which was suppressed by the regime and
its editors jailed. Frías was a soldier rather than a writer, and his work
reads more like a reporting of experiences than a literary creation.
However, its strength lay in his knowledge of the subject matter. This
book greatly influenced the later novelists of the Mexican Revolution, in
particular Azuela's *Los de abajo* ('The Underdogs') (1915), in approach
and direct style. The events provide the context for Paul Vanderwood's
*The Power of God against the Guns of Government. Religious Upheaval
in Mexico at the turn of the Nineteenth Century* (1998).

In Federico Gamboa's (1864–1939) *Santa* (1903), brutish male sexuality, out of control, leads to seduction, which drives the female character,
having succumbed to her own sexual desires, from her home in the then
village of Chimalistac (now a suburb of Mexico City) into a life of prostitution and degradation. This became the most popular novel since
Lizardi's *Periquillo* and had already passed into eight editions by 1927.
Gamboa was heavily influenced by Emile Zola and the French naturalist novel and its subsequent Spanish counterpart, although the didactic
Christian element in the book, which allowed for Santa's final redemp-
tion through selfless love, significantly departed from naturalist deter-
minism. After a youth spent enjoying the low life of several capital cities,
Gamboa had returned to the Catholic Church in 1902. Awareness of
European literary trends, such as naturalism, modernism and surrealism, demonstrated the readiness of Mexican writers and artists to
respond and adapt to broader movements during the period from the
1890s to the 1930s.

Gamboa's background and professional life revealed a great deal about not only Mexican political alignments but also the role of the writer within the wider political context. His father's career, for instance, had been in the Army. He had fought US invasion forces at the Battle of Angostura in 1847 but had adhered to Maximilian's Second Empire in 1864–67. After a period of eclipse, General Manuel Gamboa worked as an engineer on the construction of the Mexican Railway after 1874, a post which took him to New York in 1880, where his son learned English and became a lifelong critic of the US way of life and culture. From his later position as First Secretary at the Mexican Embassy in Washington DC, Gamboa published articles in Mexico denouncing the violence and corruption in US society. He saw the US humiliation of Spain in the Spanish American War of 1898–9, the occupation of Cuba, and the fomenting of Panamanian independence from Colombia as evidence of the USA's hostile designs towards Spanish America. Díaz's rehabilitation of his father made Federico Gamboa an ardent defender of the dictator, even after his fall from power in 1911. Gamboa, like Payno and Riva Palacio before him, spent a considerable part of his life in diplomatic positions outside Mexico. In fact, his first literary publication came a year after his appointment in 1888 to the Mexican Legation in Guatemala, where he would eventually return in 1899–1903 and 1905. After a first visit to Europe in 1890, he was sent to Buenos Aires, where he made the acquaintance of the Nicaraguan poet, Rubén Darío, then Consul General of Colombia. On a second visit to Paris in 1893, he had brief and disillusioning meetings with Zola and the Goncourt Brothers. Gamboa began work on *Santa* during his second period in Guatemala, influenced strongly by his reading of Leo Tolstoy's *Resurrection*, which appeared in 1899. Through contact with Sierra, Gamboa was able to publish his novel in Barcelona.

In the twenty-five years between 1890 and 1915, the literary style known as Modernism took the advance guard of Mexican poetry. Originating with the French symbolist poets of the later nineteenth century, Modernism arrived in Spain with Darío in 1892, and spread from there to Hispanic America. Modernism reacted against the rhetorical flourishes of Romanticism and sought a sharper precision of language, while at the same time displaying a vivid appreciation of colour. Although not strictly a Modernist himself, the presiding influence over the movement was Justo Sierra. In Mexico, Manuel Gutiérrez Nájera

(1859–95), founder of the *Revista Azul*, which continued until 1897, became the Mexican precursor in the short story, essay and poetry, as well as in literary reviews and journalism. The *Revista* became the Modernists' organ in this early phase. From the turn of the century, Mexico City replaced Buenos Aires as the Latin American capital of Modernism. The *Revista Moderna* (1898–1911), principally associated with the poet Amado Nervo (1870–1919), provided outlets for the poetry of Manuel José Othón (1858–1906), rooted in the rural world of his native state of San Luis Potosí, and Salvador Díaz Mirón (1853–1928), who originated from Veracruz. Ramón López Velarde (1888–1921), who came from the town of Jerez in the state of Zacatecas, had provincial roots as deep as those of Othón. One of his most striking poems, passionate and evocative, describes the well inside the entrance to his family house in Jerez. A plaque above it carries a tribute to him by the Chilean poet, Pablo Neruda. Much of López Velarde's poetry portrays the tension between eroticism and religious belief. An opponent of the Díaz régime, he affiliated first to Madero's Anti-Re-election Movement and then to Constitutionalism. During Carranza's administration, López Velarde worked in Mexico City at the Interior Ministry. This was the native poetic tradition from which Octavio Paz (1914–98) arose.

Critics of the prevailing emphasis on Positivism in the late Porfirian era founded also under Sierra's patronage, *El Ateneo de la Juventud* (1906–12, renamed *El Ateneo de México*, 1912–14). The precedents were the *Ateneo Mexicano*, founded in 1840, refounded by Riva Palacio in 1882, and renamed *Ateneo Mexicano, Literario y Artístico* in 1902. The new *Ateneo* of 1906 went in conscious opposition to the established organisation and championed a humanism founded in Classical Greece combined with a vision of the future of Mexico rooted in cultural and racial mixture. The arrival of Pedro Henríquez Ureña from the Dominican Republic provided leadership for the new younger generation of anti-Porfiristas. He became the mentor of many future representatives of the Mexican cultural vanguard, such as Alfonso Reyes (1889–1959), Vasconcelos, Azuela, Martín Luis Guzmán (1887–1976) and Salvador Novo (1904–74). The group promoted the essay, *Ariel* (1900), by the Uruguayan José Enrique Rodó, which symbolically employed the leading characters in William Shakespeare's *The Tempest* to make a negative contrast between 'Anglo-Saxon' culture, represented by Caliban, and the aesthetic and spiritual values of 'Latin' culture.

Rodó's position resembled that of Gamboa at the same time. Reyes, son of Governor Reyes of Nuevo León, secured the patronage needed for the first Mexican publication of *Ariel* in Monterrey in 1908. Reyes, who became the champion of both Classical Greek theatre and the literature of the Spanish Golden Age, would spend much of his life in exile in Spain and France. His first major work, *Visión de Anáhuac*, an impression of pre-Columbian Mexico, was published in Europe in 1917. Like Gamboa, Reyes held a series of diplomatic positions – Ambassador to both Argentina and Brazil, for instance – between 1920 and 1939.

The Revolution resumed the earlier nineteenth-century exploration of national identity. Henríquez Ureña augmented the movement in Mexico, which sought a specific Latin American identity for the country through the experience of the Revolution itself. He became one of the first to apply the imagery of the labyrinth to this problem and portray it as a rite of passage. Vasconcelos became Minister of Education under Obregón between 1920 and 1923. His ideas derived more from the *Ateneo* than from the Revolution itself, although he saw the Revolution as the means of elevating the cultural level of the mass of the population by means of a state-sponsored literacy campaign. He used his position to offer the walls of many public buildings, such as the auditorium of the National Preparatory School in 1922–23, to muralists such as Rivera. Sierra had first mooted such an idea on the eve of the Revolution. In *La raza cósmica* (1925) Vasconcelos idealised the process of racial mixture, which the author saw as the basis of Mexican identity. It continued in the tradition of Rodó's juxtaposition of Anglo-Saxon and Hispanic cultures, and argued that the future of humanity lay in racial fusion, of which Mexico was a prime example.

The novel of the Mexican Revolution sought to break the relationship to European literary movements and draw, instead, from Mexican experience. The Revolution, however, brought back *caudillismo* and *caciquismo* to the forefront of political and social life. The failure of the Díaz system to provide durable institutions prevented a peaceful transition to constitutional forms of government. The precipitate collapse of central government threw power back into the regions and localities and on to whoever could grab hold of it with his loyal bands of men. Much of the Porfirian style revived during the 1920s under Calles until the extemporary construction of a monopoly party in 1929. For writers and artists, nevertheless, the Revolution had moral significance, which they often sought to portray through the means of symbolism. Although they pushed the *mestizo* and lower-class workers in town and country into the forefront of their creations, the Revolution also brought out the brutal and coarse 'México bronco', which lay not far beneath the surface of civilised life. The nineteenth-century Latin American theme of civilisation versus barbarism assumed renewed form in Revolutionary Mexico. Much of twentieth-century fiction in Mexico focussed on the unbridled struggle for power and the theme of betrayal which accompanied this.

Azuela, in *Los de Abajo*, reflected the disintegration of central rule during the heavy fighting of the 1910s. The focus is on a small band of peasant fighters led by the young and illiterate, Demetrio Macías, operating in the locality at a moment when revolutionaries were fighting both Federal troops and each other. The book cuts straight into this disillusioning conflict without much attention to either background or description. Its principal innovation was to set ordinary people, personalised in characters often faintly drawn, at the centre of the action. The author, who came from Lagos de Moreno in the Altos de Jalisco, based the novel on his own experience as medical officer with the Villa forces during their retreat from Guadalajara northwards in 1915. Written while the fighting continued, Azuela's work was first published in weekly instalments in a newspaper across the US border in El Paso in October and November that year. The novel did not appear again until 1925, when the newspaper *El Universal* published it in serial form. Thereafter, it went into many editions and established the author's reputation. Azuela portrays bourgeois intellectuals as exploiting peasant rebellion for their own distinct political objectives. He was an early critic of the changing nature of the Revolution, once Carranza and his allies had taken power.

This criticism became devastating with Guzmán's *La sombra del Caudillo* (1929). The novel portrayed a hierarchy of masculine power, within which individuals entered into ruthless competition with one another for position and wealth. Army officers, such as the central protagonist Ignacio Aguirre, the youthful and athletic Minister of War, labour leaders and aspiring politicians jockey for influence in the new system throughout the novel. Heavy group drinking bouts attest to the assumed masculinity of the protagonists. Not friendships but only self-interest dictate these tactical alignments. Revolutionary intellectuals

Plate 49 (a) and (b) These two woodcuts were made at the celebrated *Taller de Gráfica Popular*, the engravers' workshop, which flourished from 1937 until disbanded in 1959. They form part of a series of 'Prints of the Mexican Revolution' and are in the University of Essex Collection of Latin American Art, to which I am grateful for permission to reproduce them.
(a) This woodcut, 'The Revolution will Triumph', first appeared in 1947 and was republished in 1974.

(b) Ignacio Aguirre's (1900–90) scene of the capture of Zapata during the peasant struggle first appeared in 1947 and was reprinted in 1974. Leopoldo Méndez (1902–69) was one of the founders of the *Taller*, along with Pablo O'Higgins (mentioned in Elena Poniatowska's *Tinísima* as being in Moscow in 1930–33). They broke away from the *Liga de escritores y artistas revolucionarios* (1934–37) which had originally aimed to educate the working class through images as well as words. Méndez and O'Higgins aligned more with Communism than with the Cárdenas administration. The *Liga*, however, became subsumed into *cardenismo* through the offer of government subsidies in 1937. Posada's influence on the *Taller* could be seen in the reappearance of skeleton motifs. The workshop printed posters and pamphlets warning of the dangers of fascism and upholding the Republican cause during the Spanish Civil War. Méndez was a striking illustrator, who printed woodcuts of 'Porfirio Díaz the Dictator', 'Madero and Pino Suárez, Popular Candidates', and 'Villa on Horseback', as well as executions and revolutionary trains.

were portrayed as unprincipled and unreliable hangers-on. Guzmán wrote this novel during the *maximato* of Calles (1928–34). The dark, devious figure of the supreme political boss, the *caudillo*, – 'with tiger eyes' – lurks in the background. Violence, betrayal and murder are the normal means of political ascent. Guzmán went into exile in Spain in 1925 and remained there until returning to Mexico on the outbreak of the Spanish Civil War in 1936.

Revolutionary nationalism, with its reassertion of violence and masculine prowess, brought a strong reaction from within the literary world. *Los contemporáneos*, who criticised the new orthodoxies of Revolution and nationalism during the 1920s, sprang from the tradition of the *Ateneo*. They drew on the cosmopolitanism of the later nineteenth century, which the *Modernistas* had represented. They went further than their progenitors, however, in criticising gender stereotypes. Active in literary journals and vanguard theatre, they took the Enlightenment, Walt Whitman, Oscar Wilde, Marcel Proust and André Gide as their models. The poets Xavier Villaurrutia, translator of William Blake, and Carlos Pellicer were among their most notable members, who also included Jaime Torres Bodet, the painter Roberto Montenegro, Jorge Cuesta and Samuel Ramos (1893–1959).

These contradictory currents generated a more intensified exploration of 'Mexicanness'. This, it could be argued, was the least productive or interesting of the literary modes generated by the Revolution and the renewed upsurge of cultural nationalism. This latter, in fact, might be described as a search for exclusivism, though influenced by foreign methods. At worst, it represented a descent into introspection and xenophobia, while at the same time catering to a foreign as well as a national audience. Ramos, with *Perfil del hombre y la cultura en México* (1934), opened the modern exploration of this theme, which reached its climax in the much-commented-upon Paz study, *El laberinto de la soledad* (1950). Both writers took as their defining point a supposed Mexican inferiority complex derived from the psychological impact of Spanish Conquest and subordination to European values. Over-compensation led to *machismo* as a type of camouflage, extreme competitiveness among men, looking for fights, exaltation of virility and animal nature, and the belittling of the feminine and 'civilised'. Paz developed the view that Mexicans sought to keep themselves closed, solitary and unwilling to communicate. Accordingly, the argument continued, they regarded proximity to another person and self-revelation as a form of cowardice and breaking-down. The 'sons of La Malinche', however, were, he posited, fatherless, relating more to maternal figures. The Mexican preference was for the Virgin of Guadalupe and God the Son as victim at the Passion. These tendentious propositions, which preferred psychology to history, have fascinated both Mexicans and foreign observers, perhaps without justification.

Paz came from a distinguished family in the Liberal tradition. His grandfather, Ireneo Paz, had been director of the satirical newspaper, *El Padre Cobos* (1869–75), which had criticised Juárez's persistence in power. The early influence of the Spanish literary Generation of 1927, particularly the investigation of identity and desire in Luis Cernuda's poetry, had a defining impact on Paz, whose first book of poems appeared in 1933. European development of surrealism – with antedecents in Blake, Rimbaud and Mallarmé – encountered opposition from cultural nationalists in Mexico during the 1920s and 1930s, despite support from Villaurrutia. Paz deepened his exposure to surrealism while in Europe. André Breton, one of its leading figures, became a particular model for Paz, in spite of his rejection of Breton's dependence on Marx and Freud. Surrealism went beyond reason and explored irrationality and the subconscious through hallucinations, dreams and sexuality. While in Spain, during the Civil War, Paz met the film director, Luis Buñuel (1900–83), who, in collaboration with Salvador Dalí, had brought surrealism to the cinema with *Un chien andalou* (1928). Buñuel would subsequently go into exile in first the USA and then Mexico. Paz also encountered Neruda, a Communist Party member, in Madrid.

Breton, in Mexico for the first time in 1938, organized the Third International Surrealist Exhibition in Mexico City in 1940. In the spirit of *Los Contemporáneos*, Paz rejected nationalist xenophobia in Mexico and sought, as the novelist Carlos Fuentes has done, to set Mexican culture into the context of international developments. From 1945 to 1952, he was Mexican Cultural Attaché in Paris. During this time, his collection, *Libertad bajo palabra* (1949), appeared for the first time. It would go into several editions through the 1960s and onwards, the content slightly modified with time, as the removal of any influences of Neruda would show.

Diplomatic service culminated in appointment in 1962 as Ambassador to India, whence he would draw considerably on eastern as well as western poetic sources. Paz's rupture with the Mexican regime over the repression of the protest movements of 1968 terminated his diplomatic career. *Posdata* (1970), a type of appendix to the republication of *El laberinto de la soledad*, related the massacre at Tlatelolco in 1968 to the blood sacrifices of the Aztecs and presidential dominance through the monopoly party to the traditional prevalence of hierarchical structures in Mexican political life. Critic and commentator on Mexican literature and politics, Paz collaborated with many journals and took the lead in the foundation of *Vuelta* in 1976, which still continues in print. Paz, who broke with Neruda and also criticised the Cuban Revolution, opposed official ideologies whether in the Soviet Union or Cuba or in the form of Mexico's PRI. This stance formed the ideological framework for his study of the life and art of Sor Juana Inés de la Cruz, *Las trampas de la fe* (1982), without doubt his most important work in prose and a major contribution to literary history. The framework, however, detracts somewhat from the principal thrust of the book, which was the attempt to reassess Sor Juana's approach, style and themes in both poetry and drama.

Looking back on the Mexican novel from the perspective of 1947, Azuela concluded that to date the country had no fictional tradition comparable to that of Europe. He preferred Inclán and Delgado to any others, but pointed out that Mexico's best writers had, in any case, been neglected by the public. Azuela modified his view somewhat after the publication of Agustín Yáñez's (1904–80) *Al filo del agua* (1947). In spite of his admiration for the boldness of the novel's application of European fictional techniques, he, nevertheless, disliked its episodic or cinematic character. Yáñez, like Azuela, came from the Altos de Jalisco, and his early work was rooted in that environment of traditional Catholicism (which he criticised), *ranchero* predominance and provincial-city liberalism. Six novels, in two cycles of three, written between the 1940s and 1970s, explored the rural and urban impact of the Revolution and the relationship between society and the new revolutionary elites.

Al filo del agua (*On the Brink of the Storm* in the English version), the first of the rural cycle, focussed on a small town in the Altos, which might have been the author's home town of Yahualica. The *ranchero* environment was uppermost, and the town's sexual repression would be accompanied by outbursts of violence. Yáñez adopted the stream-of-consciousness technique and the internal monologues derived from

Virginia Woolf and James Joyce. The group around Yáñez in Guadalajara ran a magazine, *Bandera de Provincia*, which introduced Joyce to its Spanish-speaking readers. The influence of Paul Claudel, the French Catholic writer, was also apparent. The narrative displayed the inner reactions of his characters, particularly their pent-up emotions in a suffocating small town, set against the background of the disintegration of the Díaz regime. This innovative work, which opened the way for a later generation of writers, also marked the ending of the phase of novels of the Revolution.

The imagery of women in mourning and the ringing of church bells pervades the novel. The Revolution is seen as a breath of clean air, refreshing rain, cleansing and liberating. In reality, however, it was in historical terms far from that. *La creación* (1951), the first or the urban cycle, took several of these themes and characters into the artistic world of the 1920s, where Gabriel Martínez, the mysterious bell-ringer of the 1947 novel, becomes, after ten years in Europe, a successful composer in Mexico. A panoply of intellectuals appears in the book, from Rivera and the composer Silvestre Revueltas (1899–1940), to Villaurrutia and the photographer Tina Modotti (1897–1942). One of Gabriel's main endeavours is to write music, which captures the mood of López Velarde's poetry. In many respects, Gabriel's fictional dilemma of integrating Mexican popular music into contemporary European experimentalism, ran parallel to that of Revueltas in real life. Yáñez himself taught in Guadalajara, rose to become State Governor of Jalisco in 1952–58 and Secretary of Public Education from 1964 to 1970 under Díaz Ordaz. After the publication of Sierra's *Obras completas* (1948), a testimony to the regime's estimation of this earlier figure dedicated to stabilised development, Yáñez published in 1950 his own study of Sierra's achievements and ideas.

The provincial grounding, which had provided the inspirational starting-point for Yáñez, became the mainspring for Juan Rulfo (1918–86), who came from the small town of Sayula, south of Lake Chapala, also in the State of Jalisco. He began his career in the Instituto Nacional Indigenista, founded in 1949, where he would have been familiar with peasant and Indian perspectives. *Pedro Páramo* (1955) and the collection of stories *El llano en llamas* (1953) portrayed a dissolution of external reality, a world of hallucination, in which the spiritual and material worlds were imperceptibly but irrevocably connected. Rulfo removed the barrier between the dead and the living. Again in the locality, the mythical Comala, which hardly seemed to exist in time and space, Rulfo portrayed village folk, downtrodden, forgotten and often disoriented, and dominant figures like Pedro Páramo, who ruled with no respect for law or life. Here again is the lost father-figure, for whom the son is searching. Rulfo's work remained ignored for some years, although he is now regarded as one of Mexico's foremost writers, in spite of his small output.

By the 1960s, the earlier regional and rural focus, which had characterised the novel of the Revolution and the 'creole-type' novel, gave way to the urban milieu, a reflection of the rapid changes over the previous two decades. Carlos Fuentes (b. 1928) in his early novel *La región más transparente* (1958), with its location in Mexico City, illustrated this new urban focus. It provided a critique of contemporary society – materialist and selfish – in the aftermath of the Revolution from a mildly leftist perspective. Experiments in form and technique showed external influences, notably that of the US writer, John Dos Passos. Fuentes, who grew up in several American countries, where his father was in the diplomatic service, studied law at UNAM from 1944, and worked in the foreign service himself from 1950 to 1962, becoming Ambassador to France in 1975–77. Fluent in several languages, particularly English and French, the young Fuentes made many acquaintances on the political and literary scene, including the Latin American writers, such as Miguel Angel Asturias, Julio Cortázar and Alejo Carpentier, exiled in Paris because of dictatorships at home.

In *La muerte de Artemio Cruz* (1962), Fuentes offered a retrospective and critical assessment of the Revolution through the eyes of the central figure, looking back from his death bed. Chronology became dissolved in disjoined flashbacks. In the tradition of Guzmán, this novel pointed to the pursuit of wealth and power by the post-Revolutionary elite. Both novels had considerable resonance. Angeles Mastretta (b. 1949), in *Arráncame la vida* (1985: tr. as 'Mexican Bolero', 1989), subsequently dealt, in less experimental form than *Artemio Cruz*, with the subject of abuse of power within the monopoly party. The perspective is that of the young wife of a brutal boss-figure, who rises from the small-town lower classes – in this case Zacatlán in the Puebla sierra – to become state Governor and then presidential adviser in the late 1930s and early 1940s. The novel traces her growing awareness of the unscrupulous political practices around her and of her own marital circumstances.

The character of Andrés Ascencio looks back to the illiterate and uncouth General Encarnación Reyes, Chief of Military Operations in the State of Puebla, another military politician on the make, in the earlier Guzmán novel, during the previous decade. Fuentes brought his ongoing critique of the post-Revolutionary order into the centre of presidential politics with his *La silla del águila* (2002).

Fuentes's literary influences ranged broadly. Reyes, whose elegant style had been praised by Jorge Luis Borges, remained a powerful early influence. He had consistently argued, as Fuentes himself would later do, for Mexico's integration into the European literary tradition. The young Fuentes, while resident in Buenos Aires, first became familiar with the work of Borges, who questioned the nature of history, reality and language, and argued for the primacy of imagination and symbol. Cervantes, however, proved to be the profoundest influence of all, especially because of the early seventeenth-century Spanish author's use of character and language to juxtapose reality and imagination in *Don Quijote* (1605).

After his first successes, Fuentes soon become a well-known speaker on the international circuit, while at the same time maintaining a large, varied and often experimental literary output from the 1960s to the present. A prime concern of his was to set Mexican literature within a Pan-American and European context. Fuentes went beyond Azuela's earlier examination of the development of the specifically Mexican novel. In 1969, he published an essay, *La nueva novela hispanoamericana*, which by 1980 had already gone into six editions. Fuentes's standpoint was not simply Mexico but Spanish America as a whole. He discussed the changes in the nature and techniques of the novel under the impact of Cortázar, Gabriel García Márquez, Mario Vargas Llosa, José Donoso and other writers of the so-called literary 'Boom' of the 1960s, many of whom were published by the enterprising Barcelona house of Seix Barral.

As the Spanish Civil War had in the later 1930s, the Cuban Revolution of 1959 galvanised a generation of Latin American writers and intellectuals, who saw it initially as a brave challenge to subordination by the United States. Disillusionment took some time to follow but increased authoritarianism in Cuba and repeated curtailment of freedom of expression eventually brought it about. Thereafter, the Cuban Revolution became a source of division among Latin American writers. The 1968 upheavals in Mexico City further heightened consciousness. Elena

Plate 50 Mariana Yampolsky's (1925–2002) photographic print 'Since You Went Away' (1980) also forms part of the University of Essex Collection of Latin American Art. Yampolsky, although born in Chicago, went to Mexico in 1944, joined the *Taller de Gráfica Popular*, and remained in the country for the rest of her life. Sharply defined black-and-white (then subsequently colour) photography became her speciality from the 1960s, with preference, in the tradition of the *Taller*, for popular and *mestizo*-Indian subjects. During the 1980s and 1990s, Yampolsky resumed these earlier themes and included country buildings and rural landscape. This photo was taken in Chilpancingo (Guerrero). The message on the scroll suggests the absent father image to which Paz drew attention in the *Labyrinth of Solitude* and which forms the central theme of Rulfo's *Pedro Páramo*. The austere contrast between the white dress and the shade around the young woman's figure contrasts with the baroque costume and pose, and verges almost on surrealism. Yampolsky took a series of pictures of Mazahua women from the Metepec area of the State of Mexico at the end of the 1980s. Some of the women's poses resemble those of the young men taken in 1931 by Eisenstein for his film on Mexico (see pp. 333, 336).

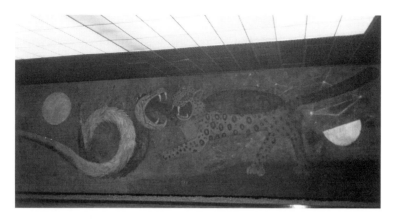

Plate 51 Detail from the mural 'Duality' by Rufino Tamayo. The mural, located in the entrance lobby of the National Museum of Anthropology in Mexico City and painted in 1964, shows the struggle between the serpent and the jaguar, mythological figures from Mexico's Pre Columbian era. Tamayo rejected the earlier muralists' mingling of politics and art. At the same time, he sought to reassert a specific Mexican identity through vibrant forms and colours (author's photograph, October 1998).

Poniatowska (b. 1933), who began as a journalist on the quality newspaper, *Excelsior*, delivered an impassioned critique of PRI hegemony after the 1968 massacre in *La noche de Tlatelolco* (1971). Her characteristic autobiographical or documentary narrative has frequently focussed on forgotten female voices. Documentary technique also produced striking results in *Nada, nadie* (1988), which drew on the horrors experienced by ordinary people during the earthquake of 1985 as a result of decades of government corruption and negligence. In a later work, Poniatowska re-examined one of the figures of the immediate post-Revolutionary period, the photographer Modotti, in a 663-page biographical novel *Tinísima* (1992) which set her in the artistic and political context of her time. Modotti, a pioneering photographer in the 1920s, became a member of the Communist Party and was expelled from Mexico in 1930 as an undesirable alien, after the rupture of diplomatic relations with the Soviet Union. She trained as a Soviet agent in Moscow, and later took part in the defence of Madrid during the Spanish Civil War. At the Valencia International Writers' Conference of 1937, she encountered both Pellicer and Paz with his first wife, the novelist Elena

Garro. Revueltas, conducting in Madrid, Barcelona and Valencia, was also there, along with André Malraux, Max Aub, Stephen Spender, Neruda and other Spanish American poets. The presence of the Mexican contingent reflected not only individual support for the Spanish Republic but also the Cárdenas administration's commitment to the Republican cause. In fact, the climactic point of Fuentes's *Death of Artemio Cruz* comes as the jaded revolutionary recalls the death of his son, one of the Mexican volunteers who fought on the Republican side.

The search for Mexican identity, which had been such a major concern of Paz, deeply preoccupied Fuentes, who at first was heavily influenced by him. However, Fuentes by the late 1960s and early 1970s moved away from the earlier Mexican search for the roots of modern culture in the Aztec and Conquest periods, and began to explore more fully its Spanish origins. The result was *Terra Nostra* (1975). This huge novel of varying modes and techniques explored not only history and the problem of time but also the nature of language and fiction. Philip II's monastery-palace, El Escorial, provided the point of departure, from which hypothetical, alternative histories of Spain and its uneasy relationship with Spanish America might be imagined. The heart of the matter lay in the closure of Spain to mainstream European influences during the latter part of the sixteenth century, which in the writer's view had deleterious consequences for the American dominions thereafter. The range of fictional influences, from Cervantes to Joyce and Borges, deepened this ambitious novel's thematic and structural complexity. The multiple and often contradictory nature of the Hispanic culture, which Spain gave to the Americas, inevitably becomes a central theme of the novel. In a later historical novel, *La campaña* (1990: Eng. '*The Campaign*', 1991), Fuentes contrasted the values of the European Enlightenment, entering through Buenos Aires, with the Spanish American realities of family, patriarchy, chieftains with armed bands, and the traditional Church during the Wars of Independence.

In many respects, the 1960s became the defining decade in which Mexican (and Latin American) Literature joined the international mainstream. It sought at the same time to relate developments in literary technique to the changed urban society from the 1940s onwards. Yet, the emphasis fell more on psychology than sociology, and more on the subconscious than the rational. The long-term influence of Joyce was distinctly apparent in literature of the 1960s and early 1970s. Many

Latin American writers knew English, American and French literature in the original language and were not strictly dependent on delayed Spanish translations. Latin American writers explored the nature of language and reality, and saw more truth in symbolism than in a literal understanding of their past. The novel began to focus on the nature of historical change, with themes often set in the past rather than in the contemporary world. Given the falsehoods disseminated by dictatorships or monopoly parties, and the abuses committed by them, the nature of reality became a major literary theme. Nevertheless, Latin American literature, and Mexican in particular, not only continued to respond to European and North American themes and techniques, but also took a leading part in the new developments.

Fernando del Paso's novel, *Noticias del Imperio* (1987), applied the techniques of late twentieth-century fiction to the historical novel, which received a treatment far removed from its early nineteenth-century antecedents. As a writer of fiction, the author's overriding concern here is the nature of the novel. This concern explained the approach Del Paso took to the subject of the French Intervention, the Mexican Second Empire, and the implacable opposition of Juárez to them. Nevertheless, his intention was to draw on both historical sources and literary forms, and thereby bind together the intrinsic qualities of these different processes of discovering what the reality, always elusive, might be. Borges's ambivalence towards historical accuracy, truth and reality appears here as it also does in the Fuentes novel of 1990. Fiction in the period 1915–47 had taken the Revolution as a source of inquiry. Del Paso went back further to examine the meaning of the Reform, the Empire and the legacy of Juárez. Finally Fuentes returned to the era of Independence. In this way, Mexican fiction dealt retrospectively with the three pillars of traditional historiography – Revolution, Reform and Independence. However, the departure from the realism of the novel of the Revolution could not be more striking. With Yáñez's *Al filo del agua* as the starting-point, surrealism first made its appearance in the historical novel. Fuentes transformed Independence into an *opera bouffe*, bizarre and impossible to take seriously at any level, except in terms of the disastrous attempt to eliminate Spain from Spanish America. For this self-mutilation, Spanish America still pays the penalty. Del Paso viewed Reform and Intervention through the confused memory and hallucinations of a deranged Carlota. Madness became transposed on to history, which thereby was transformed by it in ceaselessly shifting perspectives.

MEXICAN CINEMA

The development of a Mexican cinema industry should be seen from two perspectives, in part artistic and in part economic. The film industry, with its structure and techniques of production and complex labour organisation, should be seen as part of Mexico's process of industrialisation. Urban themes began in the course of the 1940s to supersede the predominantly rural-focussed films, which dealt with aspects of the Revolution. Like most nascent industries in Latin America, the Mexican film industry encountered repeated competition from the more highly organised and capitalised US industry. Yet, it still managed to survive. At the same time, it provided actors for Hollywood films and a place of refuge for European political exiles and fugitives from US blacklisting after the Second World War. Mexican actors, cinematographers like Gabriel Figueroa and directors, such as Roberto Gavaldón (1910–86), also gained experience in Hollywood and returned to Mexico to enrich the home industry. Some worked in both industries. Figueroa, for instance, won an Oscar for his camera work in John Huston's *Night of the Iguana* (1964), filmed in an as yet undiscovered Puerto Vallarta.

The formation of Churubusco Studios in southern Mexico City after the end of the war marked the attempt to coordinate production in response to increased foreign competition. Legislation in 1949 sought to coordinate the structure and performance of the industry, but contributed little to its revival. The Mexican industry could not compete with Hollywood in the post-war years, and faced US trade retaliation against any serious attempt to protect the home industry. Labour problems and an unwillingness to innovate also beset the Mexican film industry. The state assumed control over the Churubusco complex from the late 1950s, as a response to the closure of many studios earlier in the decade, but this did not have much impact on the quality of the output. In the year of financial collapse, 1982, a catastrophic fire destroyed the Cineteca Nacional, opened in 1974, in the southern zone of Mexico City, with the loss of thousands of reels which had been carefully accumulated over the years and were irreplaceable. Negligence appeared to be the cause. In response to the ailing condition of the industry, the government established the IMCINE (the Mexican Cinema Institute) in the following year. The revival of the Spanish film industry, after the end of the Franco dictatorship in 1975, gradually became a pole of attraction for Mexican actors, frustrated by inadequate opportunities at home. From the 1990s, Mexican directors, such as Guillermo del Toro and Alfonso Cuarón, have taken leading places in US cinema and competed successfully in the international film industry. Similarly, Mexican actors, such as Salma Hayek, have worked in both Mexican and US films, and Daniel Giménez Cacho and Gael García Bernal have also acted in the Spanish film industry, with Pedro Almodóvar as director, and in other foreign films. Beset by repeated problems of shortage of capital and excessive bureaucracy, the industry faced the closure of popular cinemas during the 1990s and the building of expensive, multi-cinema complexes by US companies in all the main Mexican cities.

From filming notable events in the Díaz era and then actions of the Revolution, the first Mexican film was really *El automovil gris* (1919), directed by Enrique Rosas. The film introduced the urban gangster syndrome to Mexico, but had little impact outside the country. Silent film naturally presented no problem of language. Little incentive existed to develop a national, Spanish-language cinema until the adoption of sound at the end of the 1920s. Since dubbing and sub-titling both presented serious problems in Mexico, it became urgent to develop a cinema industry at home. *Santa* (1931), based on the Gamboa novel, was the first Mexican film with sound. Although actors also gained experience in Hollywood during the 1930s and 1940s, Mexico developed its own industry from its own rich cultural but scant financial resources. Other foreign influences, however, were also present, particularly since the ongoing Mexican Revolution attracted not only a variety of European sympathisers but also interest from the Soviet Union, engaged in a parallel, though different revolutionary process. Mexican–Soviet relations had started off well, with the renowned poet, Alexandra Kollontai, Soviet Ambassador to Mexico in 1926–27.

One such influence was Sergei Eisenstein, born in Riga in 1898 and an engineer with the Red Army in 1918. Eisenstein, disillusioned with Hollywood, stayed in Mexico for fourteen months in 1931–32 and kept in contact with the muralists, particularly Rivera, who had resided in Moscow for nine months in 1927–28. Other muralists, such as Orozco

Plate 52 (a) and (b) Mexican Films of the Classic era. The
Classic era of Mexican cinema corresponded to the later 1930s
and 1940s, and lasted into the 1950s. Film-production was one of
Mexico's principal industries at a time of transition from a rural
to a predominantly urban society. Urbanisation provided large
audiences for these films.
(a) *María Candelaria* (1943) won a prize at the first Cannes Film
Festival in 1946, a sign of international recognition for the
Mexican cinema. This film, set in Xochimilco (then outside
Mexico City) in 1909, on the eve of the Revolution, featured the
very popular combination of two of the country's most striking
talents, Dolores del Río and Pedro Armendáriz, directed by
Emilio 'El Indio' Fernández and with cinematography by Gabriel
Figueroa. This winning team made four films together in 1943
and 1944. Dolores del Río had already built a career in

Hollywood but had never been given the leading parts. She returned to Mexico already a star but with a completely new role in her home country. A humble and saintly peasant woman in this film, she was still remarkably glamorous. Armendáriz, powerfully handsome with his shining eyes, black moustache and sensuous lips, rose to fame in the late 1930s and continued to dominate Mexican cinema through the 1940s. He took roles in Hollywood films in the 1950s, though was never given the lead. His son became a leading film actor in Mexico in the 1970s.

(b) *La Bandida* (1948) formed part of the popular genre of *ranchero* films about bandits, a favourite theme of nineteenth-century literature, this time with a major female star in the lead. (These posters, Spanish reproductions, were found by the author among others in the Sant Antoni Sunday Book Market, Barcelona, in June 2005.)

and Siqueiros, had a profound influence on his cinematic representation in *Que Viva México!*, begun in 1931. Eisenstein wanted a realistic view of post-revolutionary Mexico, seen in the context of its history, but using contemporary visual techniques. He already had a rich cinematography – such as *Battleship Potemkim* (1925) – and theatre work behind him in the Soviet Russia of the 1920s, and viewed the Mexican Revolution from the perspective of the social transformation he had witnessed in Russia. He found Mexico more congenial than Hollywood. His scenes of town and country used no professional actors. The aim was to present to the world a Mexico more authentic than the largely unfavourable image mediated through US cinema. He received considerable support from the Mexican government at the time of filming, despite the rupture of diplomatic relations with the Soviet Union in January 1930.

Eisenstein returned to the Soviet Union in May 1932, but was never able to edit his film, in view of commitments in the Soviet film industry – *Alexander Nevsky* (1938) and the first two parts of a trilogy of *Ivan the Terrible* (1943–45) – and subsequent difficulties with Stalin. He died in February 1948.

The 'Classic Age' of the 1930s and 1940s saw the rise of stars, such as Pedro Armendáriz, Dolores del Río (1904–83) and María Félix (1914–2002). Del Río, the astonishingly beautiful actress from Durango, went to Hollywood in 1925, where she signed a contract with United Artists. However, she would be given secondary and 'foreign' roles, as in the celebrated Fred Astaire and Ginger Rogers film, *Flying Down to Rio* (1933). After an affair with Orson Welles, she returned to Mexico in 1942 and worked closely with the director, Emilio 'El Indio' Fernández, with whom she also had a romance. Her reappearance in Mexico came at the right time. She could apply her experience in Hollywood to the burgeoning film industry in Mexico and also draw on home roots. She played against her star reputation in such films as *María Candelaria*, portraying a humble Indian woman, and acting with Armendáriz. Del Río worked primarily in the theatre during the 1960s, but returned to star as the doyenne of a brothel in *Casa de mujeres* (1966). Armendáriz also worked in US cinema and similarly received secondary or inconsequential roles.

Félix reputedly had lovers such as the muralists, Rivera and Orozco, and was married to the composer-singer, Agustín Lara (1897–1970), and later the celebrated *ranchero* singer, Jorge Negrete (1911–53), himself a major cinematic attraction. Moving from her birthplace in Sonora to education and first marriage in Guadalajara and thence to the greater opportunities of Mexico City, María Félix made her first film in 1942 alongside Negrete. She achieved fame in Fernando de Fuentes, *Doña Bárbara* (1943), based on the novel by Rómulo Gallegos. Félix became notable for her portrayals of strong women who refused to be the victims of men but often sought to destroy them in a culture in which men placed themselves at the centres of authority. *Enamorada* (1947), with Armendáriz, set during the Revolution, showed this conflict at its most characteristic She never filmed in the US, but between 1948 and 1955 acted in Spain, Italy, France and Argentina. She continued to be active in films into the 1960s.

During the Classic period, Mexican films occupied prime place in Spanish-language cinema output. Mexico City also became the film capital of Latin America in the mid-1940s, although studios operated in an uncoordinated fashion and the outstanding problem of distribution remained. Output increased during the war years, partly through the dearth of European films and partly though US sponsorship as an aspect of foreign policy designed to win Latin American support. Furthermore, Mexicans themselves had been attempting to coordinate production at home through a tighter studio system with both government and private participation. Alberto Pani's sponsorship of Cinematografía Latinoamericana SA (CLASA) in 1935 formed a major part of this process. This continued to be the most important studio into the 1940s. Its first feature was the retrospectively classic film, *Vámonos con Pancho Villa*! (1935), directed by Fuentes. This film, however, lost money, perhaps because of its depressing theme. Made in the Cárdenas era, when Villa still remained out of favour, the film portrayed the sad experience of six peasants who adhered to *villismo* only to discover betrayal, cruelty and disillusionment. Juárez, however, continued to be very much in favour in the period of oil nationalisation, and the Mexican Government cooperated in supporting the US film, *Juárez*, in which ironically an Austrian actor played the title role and the Hollywood star, Bette Davis, portrayed the Empress Carlota in 1939. Figueroa did the camerawork in the film of Azuela's *Los de Abajo* in 1940, for which Revueltas composed the music.

The comic actor, Mario Moreno (1911–93) known as Cantínflas, first appeared in film in 1940, the beginning of a huge success story, which encompassed the whole of Latin American and Europe as well. Seeing the potential, the US film company, Columbia, distributed the 'Cantínflas' films worldwide. The humour transcended the problem of language and sub-titling. In Mexico, in particular, new catchphrases and word contortions became daily expressions as a result of these films. This genre accompanied the development of the popular, *ranchero* musical drama, often starring Negrete or his rival, Pedro Infante (1917–57). In many respects, this was the Mexican home brand answer to the US Western, which could have no direct equivalent in Mexico in view of the differing history of the two societies. Fuentes made *Ay, Jalisco, no te rajes!* with Negrete in the lead in 1941, which achieved great popularity, especially after worldwide distribution by United Artists, but, nevertheless, represented a descent in quality for the director in response to the popular market.

Mexican cinema hit the doldrums in the 1960s and 1970s, despite a number of highly controversial films by Buñuel, including *Nazarín* (1958) and *Viridiana* (1961), the latter banned in Spain and condemned by the Vatican. Although in *Los olvidados* (1950), Buñuel had explored in stark terms life in the impoverished quarters of Mexico City, few Mexican films of this period actually dealt directly with Mexican social problems in any way comparable to the Italian neo-realism of the post-war decade. Even so, a number of important films were still being made. One of them was Julio Bracho (1909–78)'s *La sombra del caudillo* (1960) from the Guzmán novel discussed earlier. Bracho, who also came from Durango, was a relative of Dolores del Río and the Mexican Hollywood star, Ramón Navarro. This film, however, proved too controversial in its portrayal of the post-Revolutionary political establishment, and was suppressed on government authority until finally shown in 1990, as the PRI regime began to open. Similarly, Roberto Gavaldón's *Rosa Blanca* (1961) was banned, since it dealt with the machinations of a US oil company to deprive a peasant proprietor of his land. Gavaldón, one of Mexico's most capable directors, began filming in Mexico in 1944, and made two celebrated films during the 1950s, *La Escondida* (1955), which again paired the inflammatory Félix and Armendáriz, and was set during the early Madero phase of the Revolution, and *Macario* (1959). Gavaldón became one of the founders of the STPC, the Union of Workers in the Cinema Industry. He usually worked in close cooperation with the novelist and scriptwriter, José Revueltas, and the cinematographer, Figueroa, although, in a new departure, he collaborated with García Márquez, already resident in Mexico City, to film one of Rulfo's stories, 'El gallo de oro' (1964). Gavaldón continued filming into the 1970s. The repression of the 1968 protest movements had a curious repercussion in Felipe Cazals', *Canoa* (1975), which focussed on an event that had taken place in September. This was the murder and mutilation by deluded villagers of four University of Puebla employees on a trip to the Puebla highlands, after the local priest had incited the villages to believe that the employees were agents of city Communism.

Revival in the 1980s really began with two films released in 1985. *Frida*, a popular film in Mexico, focussed on the life of Frida Kahlo, the painter wife of Rivera. Jaime Humberto Jaramillo's *Doña Herlinda y su hijo* at the time had scant distribution in Mexico but found great international success. This film's explicitly homosexual theme marked a dramatic departure for Mexican cinema and opened a new period of more open exploration of sexual themes. It also provided a witty critique of family values and presented a subtle female predominance over the home, regardless of who were the components of the family. Thereafter, several Mexican films gained a wide international audience, and a range of new directors and actors took the industry to new heights. One of these films was María Novaro's *Danzón* (1991), in which María Rojo took the part of a single-mother telephonist in Mexico City, whose main form of entertainment is a regular visit to the dancehall, which specialises in the slow dance of Cuban origin, the 'danzón'. When her usual partner unexpectedly vanishes, she goes to Veracruz in search of him. At that point a penetrating and very poetic exploration of the emotional life and identity of a middle-aged woman from the urban lower middle class begins. The dance theme linked this film to those of an earlier generation but also stamped the modern industry with a distinct style and originality. Salma Hayek became a star in Mexico with *El callejón de los milagros* (1993), a transposition of Naguib Mafouz's Cairo Trilogy to the back streets of Mexico City. Innovative and popular though such films were, perennial problems of production, quality and distribution, and the swamping of the country with US films of varying type, continued to hamper the home industry. An under-utilised actress like the expressive Gabriela Roel, found, nevertheless, a magnificent role in the long-lasting TV serial, *Callejón de sombras* (1997–98), with Giménez Cacho and Demián Bichir, which explored the inner workings of the drug trade and its penetration of the army and judicial processes.

In Del Toro's first major film, *Cronos* (1993), an old man, played by Federico Lippi, discovers an alchemist's box, dating from the colonial era, which bestows eternal life if fed with blood. The director applied several techniques of popular cinema to this curious vampire film. Del Toro later directed the Hollywood film *Mimic* (1997) and then the Spanish film *El espinazo del diablo* ('The Devil's Backbone') (2002), set in the Republican zone in the Civil War. Cuarón has worked equally in Mexico and the United States, directing Gwyneth Paltrow and Robert De Niro in *Great Expectations* (1997) and Gael García Bernal in *Y tu Mamá también* (2001), as well as one of the films from the Harry Potter cycle. Mexican films also tapped into the popular international market with Alfonso Arau's *Cómo agua para chocolate* (1991), based on the popular novel by Laura Esquivel, which, although focussing to a limited extent on the Revolution, had none of the depth of treatment of the older films on that subject.

Gael García Bernal has continued to rise through the Mexican film industry, from *Amores Perros* (2000) (loosely translated as 'Love's a Bitch'), onwards and upwards. BAFTA gave this film, directed by Alejandro González Iñárritu, its Best Foreign Film award in 2002. García Bernal has shown his metal in a series of widely differing roles in films from *Y tu Mamá también*, to *El crimen de Padre Amaro* (2002), a Mexican version of Eça de Queiroz's Portuguese novel of 1875, in which he was the young priest, to Pedro Almodóvar's *La Mala Educación* (2004). In this film, which focussed on priestly abuse of minors and also starred Giménez Cacho, García Bernal played three roles, one of which was a transvestite. Then came Walter Salles, *The Motorcycle Diaries* (2004), in which he portrayed the 23-year-old Ernesto 'Che' Guevara, a Buenos Aires medical student, whose journey of discovery through the poverty and suffering in South America transformed him into a revolutionary.

Vibrant though the Mexican industry can be – and capable of producing a striking range of talent from actors to cinematographers and directors, composers and writers – its foundations still remain precarious in the home country.

Final comments

Two periods in the nineteenth century explained much of twentieth-century Mexico's characteristics. In the first place, the period 1836–67 altered the balance of power on the North American sub-continent in favour of the United States and against Mexico. The shock of military defeat, invasion and territorial loss in the war of 1846–48 ensured that relations with the United States would be the predominant issue in foreign relations thereafter. However, this preoccupation with the powerful, imperial neighbour has tended to obscure the supremely important Mexican success in repelling the French Intervention of 1862–67 and preventing the imposition of a European neo-colonial tutelage. The republican victory of 1867 enabled the continuation of the Liberal Reform programme, the essence of which was the solidification of a constitutional system and the secularisation of society.

The second defining period is 1884–1911, when Díaz consolidated his personal rule. Controversy over how to interpret this period still continues. The constitutional experiment of 1855–76 – with all its imperfections – was, in effect, abandoned after 1884. A regime, which originated in a military rebellion in 1876, proceeded to weaken rather than reform or strengthen the institutions established in accordance with the Federal Constitution of 1857. Personal arrangements, which Juárez had deplored, once again became the political norm. The practice of self-succession in the presidential office, maintained by trickery and manipulation, and when many other capable candidates existed, explained the seriousness of the succession question after 1900. As Madero reluctantly foresaw, only violence could rid the country of the

Díaz regime. When that violence came during the 1910s, the personal nature of the regime was exposed. No effective institutions could either address the widespread grievances or contain the revolutionary upheaval. The collapse of the Federal Army in 1914 opened the way for a struggle for power and wealth between rival chieftains and their armed following. Nevertheless, these chieftains had to take into consideration the social and economic demands resulting from large-scale popular mobilisation. Economic and social changes from the latter part of the nineteenth century had altered the nature of political pressures on government and the elites. The different social and regional movements of the Mexican Revolution aligned behind one chieftain or another, in such a way that the naked power struggle also acquired an ideological and social-reformist hue. A new, post-Revolutionary order arose out of these rivalries between 1917 and 1940.

The first revolutionary presidents – Carranza, Obregón and Calles – owed more to Díaz's style of government than they did to the principles of Juárez or Madero. Despite the far-ranging debates at the Querétaro Convention, which shaped the Constitution of 1917, exercise of power at national or state levels often owed less to revolutionary ideologies and popular aspirations than to the political culture before 1911. An often ignored characteristic of the post-1917 system was the reconstruction of presidential power. The creation of a national party of government in 1929 ultimately resolved the succession question by preventing the re-election of the President and allowing the perennial re-election of the party. None of this followed automatically. Like the Reform before it, the Revolution was uniform in neither its policies nor their application. Much depended on local conditions and the capacity for reception within the states, districts and municipalities. The structure of power, as well as ethnicity and culture, varied widely in many of these. National policy depended in reality on the response of local chieftains, authorities and organised groups. Ultimately, presidential power and party monopoly gradually reduced the autonomy of the states of the federation but even then not without compromises and arrangements at state and local levels.

A considerable degree of grass-roots mobilisation, for instance in San Luis Potosí and Guanajuato, modified PRI dominance in the states and municipalities during the two decades before 2000, once it became clear that opposition parties could win elections. Local and centrifugal forces began to flourish outside the context of the monopoly party and the official political system. In some states, such as Oaxaca, indigenous community demands for an alternative political process led to recognition of what were called electoral 'practices and customs' functioning beyond the constitutional system established in 1917. Indigenous autonomy became an issue in the Chiapas insurrection of 1994. Centralism and the prospect of continued monopoly-party rule did contribute to the opposition victory in the presidential election of 2000.

The three interrelated issues of the latter part of the twentieth century – the state of the economy, the distribution of wealth, and the mechanics of the political system – continued to prevail early in the twenty-first century. The presidential election of 2000 confirmed the opening of the political system. An opposition candidate took office in an orderly transfer of power. This victory over the PRI, made possible by the coming together of many contradictory forces, aroused widespread popular expectations, which proved difficult to fulfil. Social and political mobilisation in response to a broad range of issues, from standards of living in the cities to indigenous autonomy in the provinces, point to the kind of problems which the administration (of whatever complexion) taking office after the presidential elections of 2006 will have to face.

The restoration of relations with the Holy See in 1993, ruptured since 1867, gave the Catholic hierarchy a much stronger profile in the country and reopened the issues of relations between Church and State and between Church and society. Five papal visits during the pontificate of John Paul II were intended to reinvigorate the Mexican Church and bind it more closely to Rome. The canonisation of a range of Mexican saints from the sixteenth to the twentieth century was designed to bring Mexican spirituality deeper into the mainstream of Catholicism. The official Church saw itself as a misunderstood institution, persecuted during the Liberal Reform and victimised during the Revolution. By the end of the twentieth century, it saw its mission as the re-Catholicising of Mexican society and culture in opposition to secularism and liberal social mores. In those respects, the Catholic Church shared a common view with the Protestant evangelical groups, which had been moving into the empty spaces of religious recruitment during previous decades, both in Mexico and elsewhere in Latin America. The apparent conflict between a clerical view of Mexican society and how ordinary people conduct their daily lives may well reveal a subtle blending of what on the surface might seem to be contradictory attitudes. Flexibility and pragmatism may be the way in which both religious belief and acceptance of secular values coexist in Mexico within individual lives.

The secularisation of society from the Reform onwards raised the question of the continued survival and flourishing of religious belief in its many forms. To anyone who travels across Mexico, the number of shrines, devotions and pilgrimages reveals the depth of these undercurrents of belief. Beyond the Basilica of Guadalupe, there is a proliferation of other shrines dedicated to differing aspects of Christ or the Virgin, or to particular saints, whether sanctioned or not by the official Church. The walls in some of these shrines – at, for instance, San Juan de los Lagos in Jalisco, or the church of the Holy Child of Atocha in Zacatecas – covered with drawings, paintings or photographs giving thanks for some life-saving miracle reveal the nature and extent of this faith. Similarly, regular pilgrimages by large numbers of people to such remote places as the church of St Francis in Catorce (San Luis Potosí) or to the former Mission of St Francis Xavier in Baja California Sur show a remarkable capacity for voluntary mobilisation. In other contexts, religious practices incorporate, consciously or not, elements of other religions, which existed before the introduction of Christianity and continued alongside it.

BIBLIOGRAPHY

PRE-COLUMBIAN ERA

Richard E.N. Adams and Murdo J. MacLeod, *The Cambridge History of the Native Peoples of the Americas: Mesoamerica*, vols. I and II (Cambridge: Cambridge University Press 2000)

Frances F. Berdan, *The Aztecs of Central Mexico. An Imperial Society* (New York: Holt, Rinehart and Winston 1982)

Michael D. Coe, Richard E. Diehl, *et al. The Olmec World. Ritual and Rulership* (Princeton: The Art Museum 1995)

Inga Clendinnen, *The Aztecs. An Interpretation* (Cambridge: Cambridge University Press 1991)

Kent V. Flannery and Joyce Marcus, *The Cloud People. Divergent Evolution of the Zapotec and Mixtec Civilisations* (New York: Academic Press 1983)

Enrique Florescano, *El mito de Quetzalcóatl* (Mexico: Fondo de Cultura Económica, second edition 1995)

Susan D. Gillespie, *The Aztec Kings. The Construction of Rulership in Mexica History* (Tucson: University of Arizona Press 1989)

Ross Hassig, *Trade, Tribute, and Transportation. The Sixteenth Century Political Economy of the Valley of Mexico* (Norman and London: University of Oklahoma Press 1985)

—, *Aztec Warfare. Imperial Expansion and Political Control* (Norman and London: University of Oklahoma Press 1988)

Joyce Marcus and Kent V. Flannery, *Zapotec Civilization. How Urban Society Evolved in Mexico's Oaxaca Valley* (London: Thames & Hudson 1996)

Esther Pasztory, *Teotihuacan. An Experiment in Living* (Norman and London: University of Oklahoma Press 1997)

Linda Schele and David Freidel, *A Forest of Kings. The Untold Story of the Ancient Maya* (New York: William Morrow and Company Inc. 1990)

Ronald Spores, *The Mixtec Kings and Their People* (Norman: University of Oklahoma Press 1967)

—, *The Mixtecs in Ancient and Colonial Times* (Norman: University of Oklahoma Press 1984)

Joseph Whitecotton, *The Zapotecs. Princes, Priests, and Peasants* (Norman: University of Oklahoma Press 1977)

SPANISH COLONIAL ERA

Peter J. Bakewell, *Silver Mining and Society in Colonial Mexico, Zacatecas 1546–1700* (Cambridge: Cambridge University Press 1971)

Marcus Burke, *Pintura y escultura en Nueva España. El Barroco* (Mexico: Azabeche 1992)

Nancy M. Farriss, *Maya Society under Colonial Rule. The Collective Enterprise of Survival* (Princeton: Princeton University Press 1984)

Charles Gibson, *Tlaxcala in the Sixteenth Century* (New Haven: Yale University Press 1952)

—, *The Aztecs under Spanish Rule. A History of the Indians of the Valley of Mexico, 1519–1810* (Stanford: Stanford University Press 1964)

Serge Gruzinski, *La colonisation de l'imaginaire. Sociétés indigènes et occidentalisation dans le Mexique espagnole, XVIe–XVIIIe siècle* (Paris: Editions Gallimard 1988)

Louisa Schell Hoberman, *Mexico's Merchant Elite, 1590–1660. Silver, State, and Society* (Durham, NC, and London: Duke University Press 1991)

Jonathan I. Israel, *Race, Class and Politics in Colonial Mexico, 1610–1670* (Oxford: Oxford University Press 1975)

James Lockhart, *The Nahuas after the Conquest. A Social and Cultural History of the Indians of Central Mexico, Sixteenth through Eighteenth Centuries* (Stanford: Stanford University Press 1992)

Cheryl English Martin, *Governance and Society in Colonial Mexico. Chihuahua in the Eighteenth Century* (Stanford: Stanford University Press 1996)

A. R. Pagden (ed.), *Hernán Cortés. Letters from Mexico* (Oxford: Oxford University Press 1972)

Octavio Paz, *Sor Juana Inés de la Cruz. Las trampas de la fe* (Mexico: Fondo de Cultura Económica 1982); English version: *Sor Juana Inés de la Cruz, or The Traps of Faith* (trans. Margaret Sayers Peden; Cambridge, Mass. and London: Harvard University Press 1988)

William B. Taylor, *Magistrates of the Sacred: Parish Priests and Indian Parishioners in Eighteenth Century New Spain* (Stanford: Stanford University Press 1996)

Guillermo Tovar de Teresa, *Miguel Cabrera: pintor de cámara de la reina celestial* (Mexico: InterMéxico, Grupo Financiero 1995)

Elías Trabulse, *Ciencia y tecnología en el nuevo mundo* (Mexico: El Colegio de México 1994)

Eric Van Young, *Hacienda and Market in Eighteenth-Century Mexico. The Rural Economy of the Guadalajara Region, 1675–1820* (Berkeley, Los Angeles, London: University of California Press 1981)

LATE COLONIAL AND INDEPENDENCE PERIOD

Timothy E. Anna, *The Fall of the Royal Government in Mexico City* (Lincoln and London: University of Nebraska Press 1978)
—, *The Mexican Empire of Iturbide* (Lincoln and London: University of Nebraska Press 1990)
—, *Forging Mexico, 1821–1835* (Lincoln and London: University of Nebraska Press 1998)
Christon I. Archer (ed.), *The Birth of Modern Mexico, 1780–1824* (Wilmington: Scholarly Resources 2003)
Nettie Lee Benson (ed.), *Mexico and the Spanish Cortes, (1810–1822). Eight Essays* (Austin: University of Texas Press 1966)
Edith Boorstein Couturier, *The Silver King. The Remarkable Life of the Count of Regla in Colonial Mexico* (Albuquerque: University of New Mexico Press, 2003)
Virginia Guedea, *En busca de un gobierno alterno: los Guadalupes de México* (Mexico: UNAM 1992)
Hugh M. Hamill, *The Hidalgo Revolt. Prelude to Mexican Independence* (Gainesville: University of Florida Press 1966)
Brian R. Hamnett, *Roots of Insurgency. Mexican Regions, 1750–1824* (Cambridge: Cambridge University Press 1986)
Jaime E. Rodríguez (ed.), *Mexico in the Age of Democratic Revolutions, 1750–1850* (Boulder and London: Lynne Rienner Publishers 1994)
John Tutino, *From Insurrection to Revolution in Mexico. Social Bases of Agrarian Violence, 1750–1940* (Princeton: Princeton University Press 1986)
Eric Van Young, *The Other Rebellion. Popular Violence, Ideology and the Mexican Struggle for Independence, 1810–1821* (Stanford: Stanford University Press 2001)

NINETEENTH-CENTURY ISSUES

Robert Griswold del Castillo, *The Treaty of Guadalupe Hidalgo. A Legacy of Conflicts* (Norman and London: Oklahoma University Press 1990)
Francie R. Chassen-López, *From Liberal to Revolutionary Oaxaca. The View from the South, 1867–1911* (Pennsylvania: Pennsylvania State University Press 2004)
Daniel Cosío Villegas, *La constitución de 1857 y sus críticos* (Mexico: Editorial Hérmes 1957)
—, *Historia moderna de México*, 7 vols. (Mexico: Editorial Hérmes 1955–72)

William A. DePalo, Jr, *The Mexican National Army, 1822–1852* (College Station: Texas A. & M. University Press 1997)

John D. Eisenhower, *So Far From God. The U.S. War with Mexico, 1846–1848* (New York: Random House 1989)

Paul Garner, *Porfirio Díaz* (London and New York: Longman 2001)

Charles A. Hale, *Mexican Liberalism in the Age of Mora, 1821–1853* (New Haven: Yale University Press 1968)

—, *The Transformation of Liberalism in Late Nineteenth-Century Mexico* (Princeton: Princeton University Press 1989)

Brian R. Hamnett, *Juárez* (London and New York: Longman 1994)

Alfred Jackson Hanna and Kathryn Abbey Hanna, *Napoleon III and Mexico. American Triumph over Monarchy* (Chapel Hill: University of North Carolina Press 1971)

Jean-François Lecaillon, *Napoléon III et le Mexique. Les illusions d'un grand dessein* (Paris: Editions L'Harmattan 1994)

Juan Mora-Torres, *The Making of the Mexican Border. The State, Capitalism and Society in Nuevo León, 1848–1910* (Austin: University of Texas 2001)

Donathan C. Olliff, *Reforma Mexico and the United States: A Search for Alternatives to Annexation, 1854–1861* (Tuscaloosa: University of Alabama Press 1981)

Laurens Ballard Perry, *Juárez and Díaz. Machine Politics in Mexico* (DeKalb: Northern Illinois University Press 1978)

Martin Quirarte, *Historiografía sobre el imperio de Maximiliano* (Mexico: UNAM 1993)

Paul J. Vanderwood, *The Power of God against the Guns of Government. Religious Upheaval in Mexico at the Turn of the Nineteenth Century* (Stanford: Stanford University Press 1998)

Josefina Zoraída Vázquez (coord.), *México al tiempo de su guerra con Estados Unidos (1846–1848)* (Mexico: Fondo de Cultura Económica 1997)

Silvestre Villegas Revueltas, *Deudo y Diplomacia. La relación México–Gran Bretaña, 1824–1884* (Mexico: UNAM 2005)

EARLY TWENTIETH CENTURY

Joe C. Ashby, *Organized Labor and the Mexican Revolution under Lázaro Cárdenas* (Chapel Hill: University of North Carolina Press 1963)

Jonathan C. Brown, *Oil and Revolution in Mexico* (Berkeley and Los Angeles: University of California Press 1993)

Matthew Butler, *Popular Piety and Political Identity in Mexico's Cristero Rebellion: Michoacan, 1927–29* (Oxford: Oxford University Press 2004)

John W. F. Dulles, *Yesterday in Mexico. A Chronicle of the Revolution, 1919–1936* (Austin: University of Texas Press 1961)

François-Xavier Guerra, *Le Mexique. De l'Ancien Régime à la Révolution*, 2 vols. (Paris: Editions L'Harmattan 1985)

Stephen H. Haber, *Industry and Underdevelopment. The Industrialization of Mexico, 1890–1940* (Stanford: Stanford University Press 1989)

Friedrich Katz, *The Secret War in Mexico. Europe, the United States, and the Mexican Revolution* (Chicago: University of Chicago Press 1981)

—, *The Life and Times of Pancho Villa* (Stanford: Stanford University Press 1998)

Rosa E. King, *Tempest over Mexico* (New York: Howes Publishing Company 1944)

Alan Knight, *The Mexican Revolution*, 2 vols. (Cambridge: Cambridge University Press 1986)

José Antonio Matesanz, *Las raíces del exilio. México ante la guerra civil española (1936–1939)* (Mexico City: El Colegio de México 1999)

Jean Meyer, *The Cristero Rebellion. The Mexican People between Church and State, 1926–1929* (Cambridge: Cambridge University Press 1976)

El sinarquismo: ¿un fascismo mexicano? (Mexico: Editorial Joaquín Mortiz 1979)

Pablo Piccato, *City of Suspects: Crime in Mexico City, 1900–1931* (Durham, NC: Duke University Press 2001)

Pablo Serrano Alvarez, *El movimiento sinarquista en el Bajío (1932–1951)* 2 vols. (México: Consejo Nacional para la Cultura y las Artes 1992)

Michael Snodgrass, *Deference and Defiance in Monterrey. Workers, Paternalism, and Revolution in Mexico, 1890–1950* (Cambridge: Cambridge University Press 2003)

Paul J. Vanderwood, *Juan Soldado. Rapist, Murderer, Martyr*, Saint (Durham, NC: Duke University Press 2004)

LATE TWENTIETH CENTURY

Enrique Cárdenas, *La hacienda pública y la política económica, 1929–1958* (Mexico: Fondo de Cultura Económica, El Colegio de México 1994)

—, *La política económica en México, 1950–1994* (Mexico: Fondo de Cultura Económica, El Colegio de México 1996)

Colin Clarke, *Ethnicity and Community in Southern Mexico. Oaxaca's Peasantries* (Oxford: Oxford University Press 2000)

Rafael Izquierdo, *Política hacendaria del desarrollo estabilizador, 1958–1970* (Mexico: Fondo de Cultura Económica, El Colegio de México 1995)

Enrique Krauze, *La presidencia imperial. Ascenso y caída del sistema político mexicano (1940–1996)* (Mexico: Tusquets Editores 1997)

Leopoldo Solís, *Crisis económico-financiera, 1994–95* (Mexico: Fondo de Cultura Económica, El Colegio Nacional 1996)

MEXICAN CULTURE

Donald William Foster (ed.), *Mexican Literature. A History* (Austin: University of Texas 1994)

Gustavo García and José Felipe Coria, *Nuevo cine mexicano* (Mexico City: Clío 1997)

Robert McKee Irwin, *Mexican Masculinities* (Minneapolis and London: University of Minnesota 2003)

Linda King, *Roots of Identity, Language and Literacy in Mexico* (Stanford: Stanford University Press 1995)

Hugo G. Nutini, *Todos Santos in Rural Tlaxcala. A Syncretic, Expressive, and Symbolic Analysis of the Cult of the Dead* (Princeton: Princeton University Press 1988)

José Ortiz Monasterio, *Historia y ficción: los dramas y novelas de Vicente Riva Palacio* (Mexico: Instituto Mora and Universidad Iberoamericana 1993)

Paulo Antonio Paranaguá (ed.), *Mexican Cinema* (London: British Film Institute 1995)

Manuel Payno, *Los bandidos de Río Frío* (Mexico: Editorial Porrúa, sixteenth edition 1996) (First edition, Barcelona and Mexico 1889–91)

Octavio Paz, *El laberinto de la soledad* (Madrid: Ediciones Cátedra 1995)

Aurelio de los Reyes, *Medio siglo de cine mexicano (1896–1947)* (Mexico City: Trillas 1987)

Elizabeth Wilder Weismann, *Art and Time in Mexico. From Conquest to the Revolution* (New York: Harper & Row, Publishers 1985)

US–MEXICAN RELATIONS, IMMIGRATION, AND THE BORDER

James D. Cockcroft, *Outlaws in the Promised Land: Mexican Immigrant Workers and America's Future* (New York: Grove Press 1986)

Carlos Fuentes, *La frontera cristalina: una novela en nueve cuentos* (Madrid: Alfaguara 1996) (English version, London: Bloomsbury 1998)

Oscar J. Martinez, *Troublesome Border* (Tucson: University of Arizona Press 1988)

Lorenzo Meyer, *México y los Estados Unidos en el conflicto petrolero (1917–1942)* (Mexico: El Colegio de México 1972)

Jaime E. Rodríguez and Kathryn Vincent (eds.), *Myths, Misdeeds, and Misunderstandings. The Roots of Conflict in US–Mexican Relations* (Wilmington, Delaware: Scholarly Resources Inc. 1997)

Josefina Z. Vázquez and Lorenzo Meyer, *México frente a Estados Unidos: Orígenes de una relación, 1776–1980* (Mexico: El Colegio de México 1982)

THE NORTH, FAR NORTH, AND THE 'AMERICAN SOUTH WEST'

Albert Camarillo, *Chicanos in a Changing Society. From Mexican Pueblos to American Barrios in Santa Barbara and Southern California, 1848–1930* (Cambridge, Mass.: Harvard University Press 1979)

David G. Gutiérrez, *Walls and Mirrors. Mexican Americans, Mexican*

Immigrants, and the Politics of Ethnicity (Berkeley: University of California Press 1995)

Ramón A. Gutiérrez, *When Jesus Came, the Corn Mothers Went Away. Marriage, Sexuality, and Power in New Mexico, 1500–1846* (Stanford: Stanford University Press 1991)

David Montejano, *Anglos and Mexicans in the Making of Texas, 1836–1986* (Austin: University of Texas Press 1994)

Leonard Pitt, *The Decline of the Californios. A Social History of the Spanish-Speaking Californians, 1846–1890* (Berkeley: University of California 1966)

Andrés Reséndez, *Changing National Identities at the Frontier. Texas and New Mexico, 1800–1850* (Cambridge: Cambridge University Press 2005)

Roberto Mario Salmón, *Indian Revolts in Northern New Spain. A Synthesis of Resistance (1680–1786)* (Lanham: University Press of America 1991)

Marc Simmons, *Spanish Government in New Mexico* (Albuquerque: University of New Mexico Press 1990)

David J. Weber, *The Mexican Frontier, 1821–1846: The American South-west under Mexico* (Albuquerque· University of New Mexico Press 1982)

INDEX

CAMBRIDGE CONCISE HISTORIES